Pro Internet Explorer 8 & 9 Development

Developing Powerful Applications for the Next Generation of IE

Matthew Crowley

Apress®

Pro Internet Explorer 8 & 9 Development: Developing Powerful Applications for the Next Generation of IE

ISBN-13 (pbk): 978-1-4302-2853-0

ISBN-13 (electronic): 978-1-4302-2854-7

Printed and bound in the United States of America 9 8 7 6 5 4 3 2 1

President and Publisher: Paul Manning
Lead Editor: Jonathan Hassell
Development Editor: Jonathan Hassell
Technical Reviewer: Eric Lawrence

Coordinating Editor: Adam Heath
Copy Editor: Damon Larson
Compositor: MacPS, LLC
Indexer: BIM Indexing & Proofreading Services
Artist: April Milne
Cover Designer: Anna Ishchenko

Distributed to the book trade worldwide by Springer Science+Business Media, LLC., 233 Spring Street, 6th Floor, New York, NY 10013. Phone 1-800-SPRINGER, fax (201) 348-4505, e-mail `orders-ny@springer-sbm.com`, or visit `www.springeronline.com`.

For information on translations, please e-mail `rights@apress.com`, or visit `www.apress.com`.

Apress and friends of ED books may be purchased in bulk for academic, corporate, or promotional use. eBook versions and licenses are also available for most titles. For more information, reference our Special Bulk Sales–eBook Licensing web page at `www.apress.com/info/bulksales`.

The source code for this book is available to readers at `www.proiedev.org`.

For my Mom, Dad, and Grandma.

Thanks for your love, support, and endless patience.

Contents at a Glance

Contents

About the Author

Matthew David Crowley is Chief Technology Officer of Browsium, a company that provides solutions to enterprises experiencing browser-related compatibility and operational issues. Prior to this role, Matthew was the Program Manager for Developer Community and Tools on the Microsoft Internet Explorer team. During that time he focused on planning, development, and implementation of features such as the IE Developer Tools, ActiveX, Protected Mode, and the IE 9 Platform Preview.

Matthew currently works and resides in his hometown of Cleveland, Ohio. It was there he earned a BSE in computer engineering from Case Western Reserve University.

His blog can be found at `http://var.iabl.es`.

About the Technical Reviewer

■ **Eric Lawrence** is a program manager on the Internet Explorer team at Microsoft, responsible for performance and networking features. Eric is best known as the developer of the Fiddler web debugging platform, used by security and web professionals worldwide. A frequent speaker at web technology conferences, his Internet Explorer Internals blog can be found at `http://blogs.msdn.com/ IEInternals`. Eric's other IE-related tools and utilities can be found at `http://www.enhanceie.com/ie`.

Acknowledgments

Thanks to everyone who contributed to this book, either directly or indirectly. This certainly includes Eric Lawrence, my friend, colleague, and technical editor of this text, as well as the wonderful folks at Apress (Jonathan Hassell, Anne Collett, Adam Heath, and Damon Larson) for their guidance, support, and (seemingly unending) patience. Thanks to my parents, David Crowley and Susan Crowley, and my grandma, Betty Thompson, for their amazing support and encouragement; and to Nick Tierno, Carmen Cerino, and Mary Margaret (Meg) Mowery for putting up with me through the process. Thank you to my mentors, past and present: Dan Moderick, Jason Weaver, Marc Buchner, Beth Fuller-Murray, and Matt Heller. Finally, a big thank you to the Internet Explorer team for the experiences, the good times, and the idea to write this book.

Preface

This book was written to provide solid technical guidance to developers who wish to build web sites, browser extensions, and desktop applications using Internet Explorer 8 and 9. During my time on the IE engineering team at Microsoft (and as a web developer before that), I noticed a lack of easy-to-understand and up-to-date information regarding the IE development process.

The release of IE 9 has allowed Microsoft to regain legitimacy in the online space after almost a decade of slipping market share and sour relations with the web development community. This renewed relevancy means IE can no longer be an afterthought or a set of bug fixes for web developers, but rather part of the primary web and browser extension development cycle. Developers need to renew their understanding of this browser, especially IE 9, as it re-emerges as a modern and mainstream development platform.

I hope that this text enables you to grasp key concepts of IE 8 and IE 9 programming quickly and effectively. Using the concepts and examples provided within, you will learn how to create and maintain powerful browser, application and web service software that both uses and extends the functionality of Microsoft's next-generation Internet platform.

What Will You Learn?

This book aids developers in the process of creating browser, application, and web service software that extends the functionality of IE. It will allow you to:

- Understand the architecture and design of IE
- Build browser-based extensions such as ActiveX controls, toolbars, Explorer bars, Browser Helper objects, and pluggable protocols
- Extend existing web services with Accelerators, Web Slices, and search providers
- Enhance applications using IE APIs, COM objects, and controls
- Design extensions that integrate with Windows security features
- Debug applications designed for IE
- Address compatibility and upgrade scenarios for applications
- Utilize powerful tools for enhancing extension development
- Master best practices in constructing world-class applications

Who Should Read This Book?

Intermediate to advanced developers make up most of this book's intended audience. This book assumes you are familiar with HTML, JavaScript, and CSS. Later sections require some understanding of

C++ and/or C#. COM/COM+ programming experience is useful in some areas; however, the examples are clear enough that it is not necessary.

This text, while geared toward code-minded individuals, is also meant for a larger segment of the web community. Potential readers include:

- Entrepreneurs seeking new ideas for development and deployment
- Product planners looking to create new features based on IE's development framework
- Marketers pitching add-ons to consumers or enterprise administrators
- Hobbyists interested in web browsers and Internet programming

How Is the Book Structured?

IE is a rich application platform covering the cloud, the desktop, and everything in between. While I cannot cover every nuance and area that IE's API touches, I've organized this book in a way that teaches a breadth of topics without sacrificing the needed depth in each one.

Apart from the first chapter, this book covers topics using a top-down approach from the Web to the desktop. The general areas of this book (reflected by the chapter ordering) are as follows:

- **Browser architecture (Chapter 1)**: This part gives an introduction to the history, intent, and architecture of the IE platform. It provides a full architectural overview of the browser and its interactions with web services and the operating system. This chapter makes it easy to understand topics covered in subsequent chapters.
- **Web applications (Chapters 2, 3, 5, and 7)**: These chapters include an overview of web improvements in the IE platform. Topics include HTML and CSS standards support, DOM additions, Ajax and JSON features, and accessibility improvements. You will learn how web applications can be enhanced by using the new (and cross-browser) features added in the latest version of the browser.
- **Web service extensions (Chapter 4, 8, and 9)**: This part introduces web service interactions. Chapters within this section reveal many ways you can design applications that bridge the gap between the browser UI and web services. Accelerators, Web Slices, search providers, and many more applications are discussed in detail. Advanced topics and best practices are also presented, providing a convenient reference guide.
- **Browser extensions (Chapters 10, 12, 13, and 14)**: These chapters include lessons on constructing and deploying browser extensions. I teach you how to build and interact with a number of extensibility services, including Browser Helper objects, ActiveX controls, toolbars, and Explorer bars. Each chapter includes advanced topics and best practices that can be referred to on a regular basis.
- **Desktop applications and scripts (Chapters 11 and 15)**: The chapters in this part focus on desktop applications and scripts interacting with the browser platform. Sections include an introduction to the WebBrowser control and a how-to guide for scripting the browser.

Additional Resources

This book covers a wide range of topics relevant to building applications for IE 8 and IE 9, but it may not provide all the answers you seek. I encourage you to use the following resources in your development projects if you have questions, notice missing information, or find an error in the text:

- **The Microsoft Developer Network** (`http://msdn.microsoft.com`): MSDN is a big online help file used by many developers when creating applications for the Windows operating system. IE has a fair amount of documentation, articles, and videos online, especially with the release of IE 9.
- **The Code Project** (`www.thecodeproject.com`): The Code Project is a well-known resource for aspiring developers of IE extensions and applications. There are a large number of tutorials, open source examples, and completed projects that guide users through creating the most common extensions for the browser in a variety of languages.

Microsoft CodePlex (`www.codeplex.com`): CodePlex is Microsoft's open source project site. It provides developers with storage, versioning, promotion, and communication resources for open source development projects. If you are looking for a place to post your IE projects, this is a great option.

CHAPTER 1

Internet Explorer Architecture

Internet Explorer (IE) isn't just a web browser—it's a broad platform that provides Windows with the components necessary to integrate web services with desktop applications. Its complex architecture and extensibility points reflect this, as well as the number of applications that tie into it.

In this chapter, I present a general overview of the internal and external makeup of IE, describe the architecture of the browser and its libraries, and lay the informational groundwork for detailed discussion of major feature areas and development using exposed interfaces.

Application Architecture and Dependencies

IE is composed of a browser application and a series of libraries tied together through a COM-based architecture. These binaries are available for Windows platforms only and, as of IE 8, are available on x86, x64, and IA-64 architectures for supported systems. IE 8 is available for Windows XP SP2 and higher, and Windows Server 2003 and higher.

The IE browser is a loosely connected set of executables, libraries, and resources that provide a user interface (UI) and security infrastructure on top of a number of libraries that control networking, document hosting, extensibility, and markup handling. For example, the Trident library (mshtml.dll) controls parsing, layout, rendering, and display of web pages. The URL Moniker library (urlmon.dll) wraps Windows networking APIs to provide IE with a base communication, security, and download infrastructure. The Shell Document View (shdocvw.dll) provides the WebBrowser control, a widely used library that integrates IE functionality with stand-alone applications.

IE is dependent on a number of interfaces and APIs provided by Windows and other Microsoft products. Windows dependencies include cache and cookie handling using WinINET, feed organization and management through the Windows RSS Platform, and security and account integrity protections through Mandatory Integrity Controls (MICs) and Credential UI. Along with Windows APIs, IE uses other Microsoft libraries such as scripting engines (JScript and VBScript).

In Windows Vista and above, IE implements a special set of security APIs that create clear separations between processes in terms of permissions and data access. IE features such as Protected Mode and Loosely Coupled Internet Explorer implement this infrastructure to improve the overall security, reliability, and performance of the browser.

The general architecture of IE (shown in Figure 1–1) consists of some executables and DLLs:

- **Frame/broker process (iexplore.exe, ieframe.dll)**: Process used to control IE's UI (the browser "frame"), control object communication, and manage sessions.
- **Tab process (iexplore.exe)**: IE's tab manager and container, used to display web pages and extensions. This process is controlled by the IE frame/broker process.
- **Shell Document View/ShDocVw (shdocvw.dll)**: The Active Document Container for MSHTML and other OLE Active Documents (document objects). This library also exposes the WebBrowser control.

- **Trident/MSHTML (mshtml.dll)**: An OLE Active Document object that represents IE's layout, rendering, and editing engines. This is what IE uses to display web pages.
- **URLMon (urlmon.dll)**: The URL Moniker library; used to wrap Windows networking APIs and provide a base security and download manager for IE.
- **WinINET (wininet.dll)**: Windows library responsible for web protocol communication, response cache, and cookies.
- **Feeds Store (msfeeds.dll)**: The Windows RSS Platform API; used by IE's RSS and ATOM feed reader to open, display, and manage feeds through the Windows Common Feed List.
- **High Integrity Broker (ieinstal.exe), ActiveX Installer Service (axinstsv.exe)**: Applications used to perform "high-integrity" actions such as installing ActiveX controls.
- **Internet Settings Control Panel (inetcpl.cpl):** The Windows control panel interface for IE settings and configurations.
- **HTML Application Host (mshta.exe)**: An implementation of the WebBrowser control that runs trusted HTML and scripts with a minimal UI.
- **JScript and VBScript (jscript.dll, vbscript.dll)**: Major scripting engines for JavaScript and VBScript, respectively.

This is not an all-encompassing list of IE's dependencies and libraries, but merely the most important components. In the following sections, I'll take a deeper dive into the interactions between IE, its dependencies, and the Windows system.

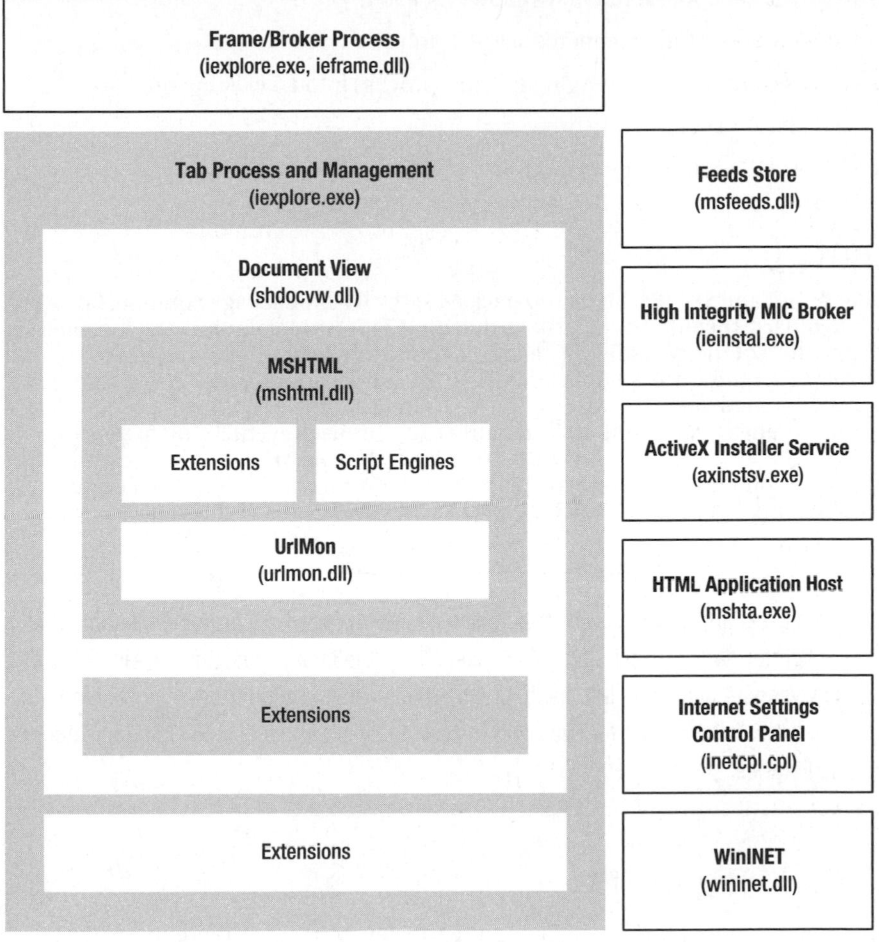

Figure 1–1. *General IE architecture and applications*

Command-Line Parameters

The IE executable (iexplore.exe) can be run from the command line or otherwise executed through a system call with custom parameters. IE's command-line options allow for basic customization of a new process; IE's settings and feature controls, discussed later, offer finer-grained regulation of browser configurations.

The following command-line parameters represent those that are officially supported by IE 8:

```
iexplore.exe [-embedding] [-extoff] [-framemerging] [-k] [-noframemerging] [-private][<URL>]
```

- `-embedding`: Creates IE without a UI for OLE embedding
- `-extoff`: Runs IE in No Add-Ons mode; turns extensions off for this IE instance

- `-framemerging`: Allows IE to opportunistically merge new frame processes into preexisting ones (while keeping separate windows for each)
- `-k`: Runs IE in kiosk mode, a full-screen, reduced-UI frame
- `-noframemerging`: Prevents IE from merging the new process into an existing one
- `-private`: Runs IE in InPrivate (private browsing) mode
- `<URL>`: Target URL used for initial navigation

Processor Support

IE 8 is offered in both x86 (32-bit) and x64 (64-bit) setup packages; the 64-bit package contains both 32- and 64-bit copies of each IE binary. Included as a part of a default Windows installation, the installed IE package matches the architecture of the Windows installation; the 32-bit-only setup package will refuse to install on 64-bit platforms. As of this book's publication date, 64-bit IE cannot be set at the system's default browser for reasons described later.

In addition to setup and settings restrictions, architectural restrictions prevent 32-bit extensions from being loaded in 64-bit instances of IE. This means that toolbars, Browser Helper objects, and ActiveX controls compiled as 32-bit libraries cannot be placed into a 64-bit container. For example, Adobe Flash currently does not load in 64-bit IE since Adobe has only released a 32-bit version.

■ **Note** While 64-bit IE has some great advantages over 32-bit (such as DEP/NX memory protection enabled by default and, in theory, increased performance from native 64-bit execution), the lack of available 64-bit ActiveX controls and other extensions by vendors (including Microsoft) prevents this configuration from being viable for general purpose browsing. However, it is important for Microsoft to provide 64-bit IE because 64-bit applications depend on 64-bit versions of IE libraries.

Protected Mode (Low-Rights IE)

Windows Vista introduced the concept of MICs, which use integrity levels (ILs) to differentiate filesystem objects, registry locations, and APIs by trust and privilege levels and User Account Control (UAC) to funnel elevation requests to users. This architecture helps to protect system and user files against malicious access by untrusted applications.

The integrity levels present on Windows Vista and higher fall into four major categories:

- **System**: Core operating system (NTAUTHORITY); system components, files, and data
- **High**: Machine-level access (administrators); program files and local machine registry hive
- **Medium**: User-level access (users); user files and settings and current user registry hive
- **Low**: Untrusted content, temporary files, and data

Windows lays out some basic rules for process communication and data access. First, processes can only "command down, not up"; for example, applications running in Low cannot directly run an API or access a file that requires medium-level access. Next, processes at differing levels can only communicate through the least-privileged IL present in that group; for example, if a Medium and a Low process want to talk, they have to do so over a channel with a Low IL, such as low-integrity named pipes. Finally, running processes cannot launch new processes at a higher level without user content; for instance, if an app running in Medium needs to launch an application in High, a user is given a UAC prompt to allow or deny the request. There are clearly more nuances and rules to this data flow, but the basic premise is clear: applications are allowed a clearance level they must operate within, and they must request more access if needed.

Protected Mode is a feature in IE that separates IE components among Windows' integrity levels. IE touches many different parts of the system; for example, temporary Internet files for cache and cookies, user folders and registry keys for per-user settings, and machine-level files and registry keys for persisted data and machine-wide ActiveX controls. The IE development team compared this broad access to the new MIC architecture in Windows and determined that a wide variety of malicious attacks could be mitigated by taking advantage of these controls. As a result, IE is now broken up into separate processes, threads, and communication controllers that allow the overall application to conform to Windows' new architecture separation.

Protected Mode uses two key components of the Windows architecture: MICs and User Interface Privilege Isolation (UIPI). MICs, as I described before, restrict access from lower-level processes to higher-level locations and APIs. Protected Mode relies upon MICs to protect against unprivileged access to user profiles, the registry, and APIs such as `OpenProcess()`, `OpenThread()`, and `CreateRemoteThread()`. UIPI is an enforcement mechanism that blocks certain window event messages from being sent to higher-level processes. Protected Mode relies upon UIPI to prevent Low process from sending potentially malicious messages to higher-privilege processes (so-called shatter attacks).

IE separates its processes and features in a way that conforms to MIC architecture (Figure 1–2). Protected Mode web pages are loaded in an iexplore.exe process instantiated in Low IL. By default, pages and extensions operating in this process can access temporary Internet files, use APIs and messages marked with Low IL, and call a set of secured APIs provided by the higher-IL IE "broker" process.

Low IL is generally a good place for untrusted page content, but such restrictions prevent some pretty basic communication between the page and its parent frame. For example, a page might need to send its title to the parent for display in the IE title bar, or a page might need to start an ActiveX control installation. The IE frame process allows Low IL pages to perform higher-level tasks through UIPI; lower-integrity pages can ask their broker frame processes to perform tasks for them that they are not permitted to do.

■ **Note** In IE 7, the Medium IL broker was implemented in the ieuser.exe process. In IE 8, functionality present in ieuser.exe was refactored back into iexplore.exe as a part of the implementation of Loosely Coupled Internet Explorer.

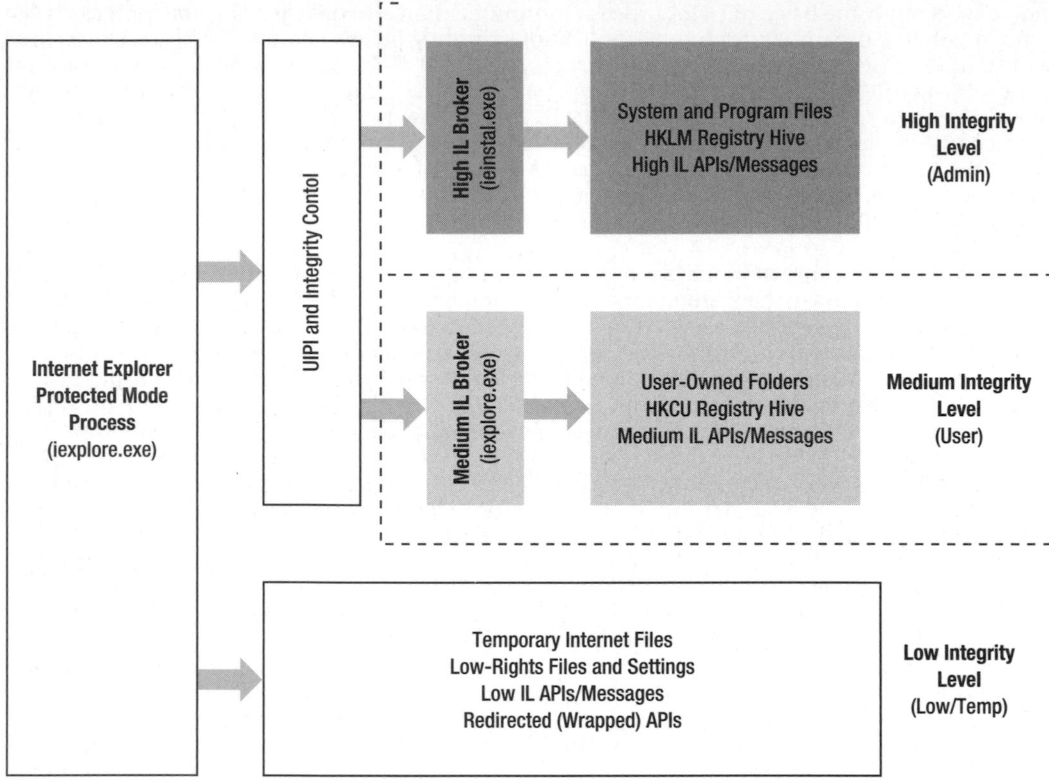

Figure 1–2. Protected Mode architecture diagram

ActiveX controls, behaviors, and other extensions running in the content of a web page (also called "content extensions") are required to run in the IL of their parent process. Also, extensions that visually appear in the frame (such as toolbar and menu items, Explorer bars, and toolbars) must also conform to these new policies. This change presented a problem when IE 7 was introduced—a number of add-ons relied upon APIs that are not available to processes running in Low IL. To mitigate the compatibility impact, IE 7 and IE 8 provide read/write virtualization and wrapper APIs. These changes do not resolve all compatibility problems, and some can only be mitigated by creating broker applications. I discuss these APIs and how to create broker applications in later chapters of this book.

This feature is controlled by the security zone settings (discussed later on in this chapter). In IE 7, Protected Mode runs on all pages in the Restricted, Internet, and Intranet security zones, and in IE 8 it only runs in the first two. In the cases where Protected Mode is not used, the IE process runs at the same privilege level as the current user account (as is always the case in Windows XP).

Protected Mode is not used for every page or on every Windows version. On Windows XP and Windows 2003, this feature is not present because the MIC feature is not present on those platforms. It is not available for hosts of the WebBrowser control or MSHTML.

Loosely Coupled Internet Explorer

Loosely Coupled Internet Explorer (LCIE), introduced in IE 8, uses process separation to improve browser reliability and performance. As with changes made for Protected Mode, LCIE reorganized and redefined components and their communication model. Figure 1–3 shows this model.

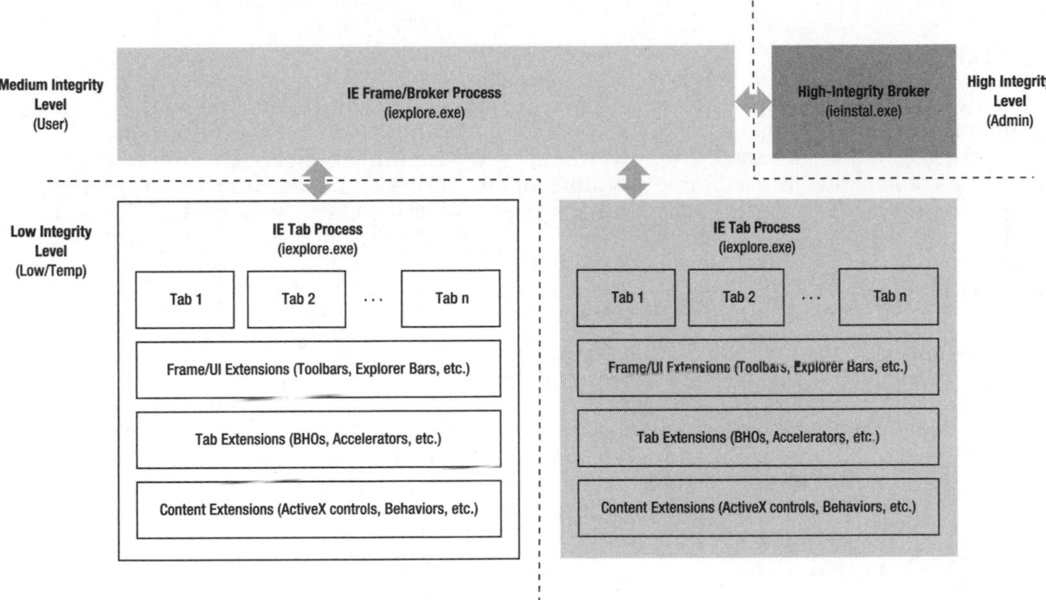

Figure 1–3. *LCIE architecture diagram*

LCIE rearchitects the browser such that the frame and tabs run in separate processes rather than separate threads in a common process. The frame process, running at Medium integrity, replaces IE 7's ieuser.exe as the general broker object. The broker object handles integrity and elevation requests using an asynchronous communication model. Prior to IE 8 and in cases where LCIE is disabled, the browser frame, tabs, and extensions run as separate threads in a common browser process.

Shared UI and Virtual Tabs

While tab processes and their components are isolated from the frame process, they are still displayed in the UI context of the frame. The IE frame process places all tab processes running in either Medium or Low IL into the IE frame UI in the proper tab locations. IE also ensures that toolbars, Explorer bars, and any other extensibility points are properly overlaid onto the frame—even though those extensions run in the tab process.

Virtual Tabs is a LCIE subfeature that allows a single frame process to visually host different tab processes at different ILs. During navigation, the broker process determines whether a new page should be loaded in Protected Mode. If necessary, the broker will spawn a process at a new IL and integrate that process's UI with the frame. This allows for low- and medium-integrity processes to be hosted in the same frame UI.

■ **Note** In IE 7, if a navigation occurred that crossed between zones of different ILs (such as navigating from Internet to intranet), IE spawned a new frame window to load the page. This was necessary because in IE 7, the frame and tab ran in the same process, and a single process runs at only one IL.

Crash Recovery

Process separation not only allows the browser frame to monitor and control what tabs can do, but also react to problems or crashes with those tabs. In versions of IE prior to IE 8, any exception (e.g., a divide-by-zero, an access violation, or a stack overflow) would crash the entire browser—the frame, all tabs, and all extensions. As of IE 8, the browser frame monitors for tab crashes and, if one does occur, attempts to create a new tab process and recover state into that process. If crash recovery fails, the user is notified.

Browser Frame, Tabs, and UI

IE's UI represents a significant portion of its features, not to mention that a browser's UI is what users end up having to deal with. In the next few sections I'll detail the UI architecture of IE's frame and areas that can be extended from a platform perspective.

Most features presented in this section are not available in hostable versions of IE (the WebBrowser control and MSHTML). For the sake of simplicity, I note those few features available in both IE proper and hosted versions in the "Hosting and Reuse" section of this chapter.

Search and Navigation

Search and navigation features provide a way for users to use the IE UI for traversing web sites and files. Most features, such as navigation buttons and the address bar, are located in the upper portion of the IE frame. Navigation is controlled through the Travel Log, a set of methods and data structures that handle page and subpage navigations.

Address Bar and Navigation UI

The IE frame provides an address bar for keyboard navigation and UI buttons for invoking back, forward, refresh, stop, and go actions. History of navigations within the current tab is available via the down arrow adjacent to the forward button. The back and forward buttons cannot be moved; the refresh and stop buttons can either be placed between the forward and back buttons and the address bar or positioned to the right of the address bar (Figure 1–4).

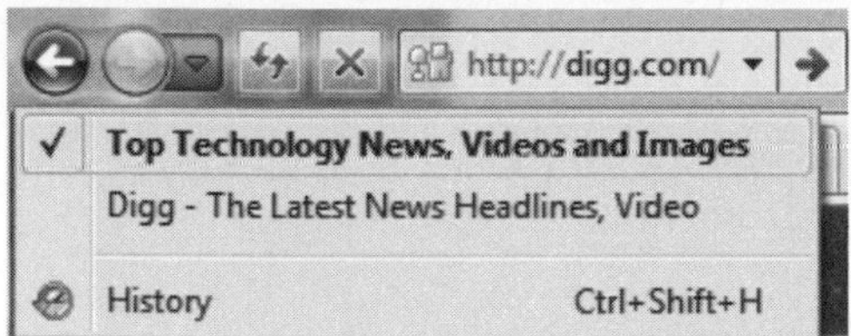

***Figure 1–4.** The IE address bar and navigation UI*

Navigation is controlled through IE's Travel Log, discussed later. As of IE 8, the navigation UI supports HTML 5 Ajax page navigations.

The Smart Address Bar

In IE 8, the Smart Address Bar was added to aggregate URL information from across the browser into the address bar. As an address is typed, a drop-down control is displayed that displays search results for the current string present in the address bar. Search results are derived from previously typed URLs, history, favorites, and feeds. Figure 1–5 shows results from Digg being shown in the Smart Address Bar's drop-down control.

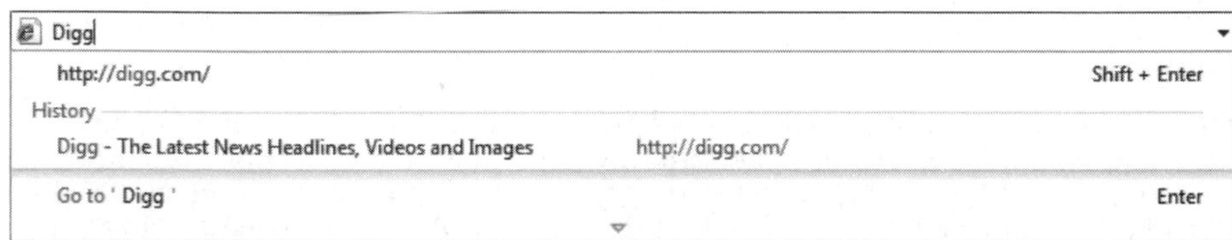

***Figure 1–5.** The IE 8 Smart Address Bar*

The best match, or AutoComplete suggestion, represents what the browser believes to be the best contextual match for the current search term. This feature requires Windows Search to be installed. Windows Search is installed by default in Windows Vista and later; it is an optional component for Windows XP.

Search Providers, Visual Search Providers, and the OpenSearch Specification

At the time of this book's publication, every major browser includes a search pane somewhere in the browser UI. IE is no different; a search box on the right-hand side of the browser frame gives users the ability to query search engines and other web services without navigating to them (Figure 1–6). Search providers were introduced in IE 7, followed by visual search providers in IE 8.

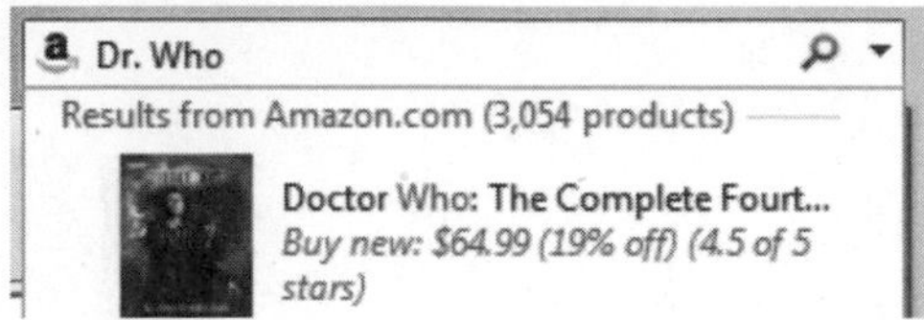

Figure 1–6. *Amazon.com visual search provider*

Both search and visual search providers consume the OpenSearch specification, a Creative Commons–licensed XML format that defines a communication model between browsers and the web services exposed by search engines.

Printing

IE provides basic capabilities for print web pages, print preparation, and review through print preview. IE 5.5 and above provide options for default header and footer, page size and shrinking, and font settings, and IE 7 introduced the widely popular Shrink to Fit feature. IE 8 adds support for a number of printing features; CSS 2.1 properties are supported for printing, including the `@page` rule for margins, orphans, widows, and page breaks.

Tab Management

Tabs have been a part of the browser frame since IE 7, and tab controls consist of four major features. Quick Tabs, accessed through the leftmost icon, creates a single page view of all open tabs. Tab grouping places tabs into color groups based on user or web page activity. A new tab button displayed at the end of the tab list creates a new tab when clicked. Tab drag-and-drop allows tabs to be moved within the tab pane. There are a number of minor features that exist as well, including a number of tab management options through the context menu.

Tab grouping (Figure 1–7) is a colorization algorithm that groups related tabs together; relatedness is based on the source of the tab creation. For example, a page that opens a new tab or a user-initated tab creation through the Open Link in New Tab menu item will result in tabs that share a common color.

Figure 1–7. *IE 8 tabs with tab grouping*

IE does not expose APIs for tab management. While developers have gone to great lengths to walk the window tree to obtain tab information, the lack of a supported API means that such attempts may break in future updates.

Favorites Center, Feeds, and History UI

IE provides a number of UI entry points for favorites, RSS feeds, and navigation history. The Favorites Center consolidates lists of these data points through a tab interface accessed via the Favorites button or menus. Favorites and history data are located in user profile folders; feeds can be accessed outside of IE through the Windows RSS Platform APIs.

Favorites UI and Favorites Bar

The Favorites UI can be found on the Favorites tab within the Favorites Center. This UI displays the folder structure present in a user profile's Favorites folder. Favorites can be added through IE menus, keyboard shortcuts, and the Add to Favorites button to the left of the tab bar.

The Favorites bar is a toolbar that can hold Favorites from the Favorites Bar folder (a subfolder in a user's Favorites folder). The Favorites bar also holds selected RSS feeds and Web Slices, offering a drop-down menu for their respective subscription content. URLs in web pages, excluding bookmarklets and URLs whose protocols are not explicitly permitted, are exposed as draggable OLE page objects (allowing them to be moved from a page location to the Favorites bar).

Feeds

As of IE 7, the browser frame supports RSS and ATOM content syndication through the Windows RSS Platform (msfeeds.dll). IE supports its own internal feeds viewer, and syndication changes made through IE are applied to the Windows Common Feed List. Feeds can be managed programmatically by loading msfeeds.dll and using appropriately exposed Windows RSS Platform APIs.

History UI

The current user's navigation history is displayed on the History tab of the Favorites Center. This data can be accessed through a few different filters, such as date and search history. Web pages loaded in InPrivate mode are not included in this list. History can be cleared using IE's Delete Browsing History feature, or programmatically using the `ClearMyTracksByProcessW()` API exposed from inetcpl.cpl.

Status and Notifications

The IE frame provides a number of ways to notify users of events during browsing sessions. These notifications vary in purpose and type and are displayed in various locations in the IE browser frame.

Address Bar Notifications

The address bar (Figure 1–8) is used for notifications pertaining to the current web page being accessed. Flyout notifications (buttons with an information pane), balloon tips, color changes, and icons signal changes in state or events related to a specific web page.

Figure 1–8. *The IE 8 address bar*

Address bar notifications are used to convey security information to users. I go into more detail on address bar notifications in the "Security, Trust, and Privacy Architecture" section later in the chapter.

Status Bar

The IE status bar (Figure 1–9) displays information about the current state of a tab and allows access to commonly used features such as Zoom, InPrivate, and the Pop-Up Blocker.

Figure 1–9. IE status bar

On the left is Display Text, followed by space for icons used by features like the Privacy Manager, the Pop-Up Blocker, and Manage Add-Ons. Security zone information is displayed next, followed by the progress bar. Last, interactive buttons for InPrivate and Zoom are in the rightmost corner. Balloon tips, described later, are sometimes launched from the status bar by Manage Add-Ons and the Protected Mode subsystem.

Since the status bar stores custom state information for each tab, every instantiated tab is given its own subclassed window and status bar instance.

■ **Note** The status bar, interestingly enough, has functionality that can be accessed even when no icon is showing. In Figure 1–9, you may notice a number of blank spaces between the Display Text block and the security zone information. These icons only display when there is a notification associated with the features in question. Play around by right- and double-clicking to find some hidden treasures.

Information Bar

The information bar is used to convey important information about a web page to a user without requiring immediate action. Its UI is placed between the tab bar and the web page frame, within the context of a tab.

Information bar notifications are used mostly for security-related messages. I expand on the information bar and its uses in the "Security, Trust, and Privacy Architecture" section of this chapter. Also, while lumped in with the frame from a UI perspective, the information bar is also loaded within the WebBrowser control (as is the case with the Travel Log).

Balloon Tips (Notifications)

According to the Windows User Interface Guidelines, balloon tips (or notifications) are used to "[inform] users of events . . . by briefly displaying a balloon from an icon in the notification area." These events are noncritical, optional information that do not require user intervention.

A number of IE features use balloon tips to convey information. Compatibility View, as shown in Figure 1–10, indicates when a domain is placed into compatibility mode. Other features, such as Manage Add-Ons, will use balloons sparingly to convey information that does not require any or immediate action from the user.

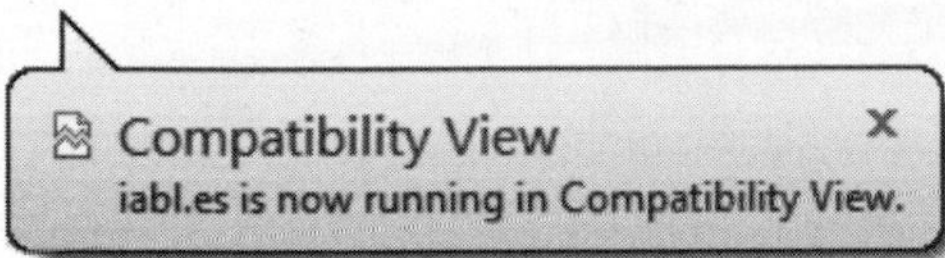

Figure 1–10. The IE Compatibility View balloon tip

Modal Dialogs

Modal dialogs are used when an imminent trust or functionality decision is required from the user. These dialogs display on top of the IE window and disable its functionality until a decision is made.

Modal dialogs are used by a number of IE features, including Auto Complete (Figure 1–11), the Trident engine (script dialogs), and the browser's security infrastructure (e.g., mixed-content warnings).

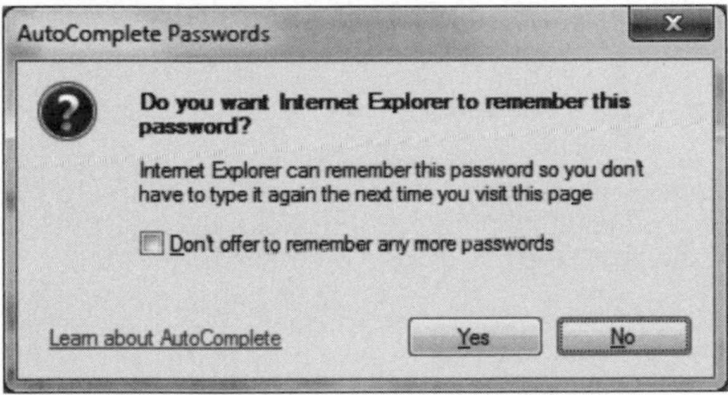

Figure 1–11. AutoComplete modal dialog

Full-Page Notifications

Full-page notifications are used as a replacement for a page after a request occurs. These pages attempt to inform users why a page was not displayed and offer possible solutions.

A number of scenarios exist for full-page notifications; failed requests (Figure 1–12) and cancellations, page expirations, and attempts to access noncached pages in offline mode will trigger such notifications. IE's security framework also uses full-page notifications to inform a user when access to a resource was blocked.

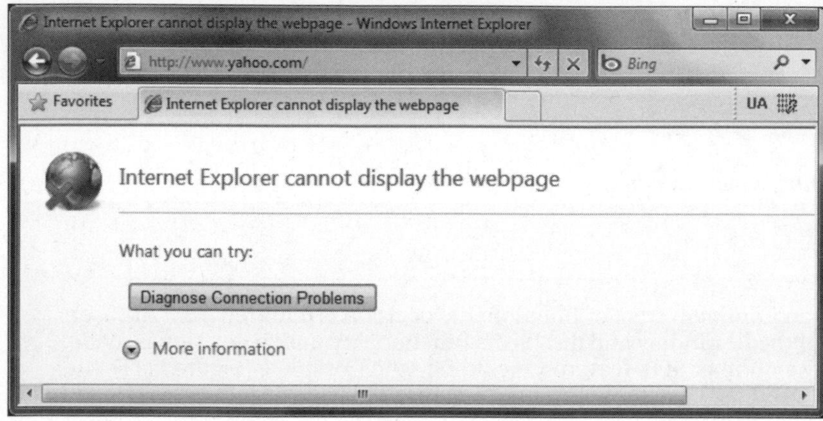

***Figure 1–12.** Page display failure notification*

Frame and Tab Extensibility

The IE Frame and Tab extensions offer a number of interfaces that allow developers to extend the functionality of IE. This section doesn't cover all major extensibility points; extensions such as ActiveX controls and behaviors are considered "content extensions"; these live in the Trident engine.

Toolbars

Toolbars are COM-based extensions built off of `IUnknown`, `IObjectWithSite`, `IPersistStream`, and `IDeskBand` that reside as children of IE's `ReBar` container. These extensions are placed in between the tab strip and the top of IE's client area (Figure 1–13). Out of the box, IE comes with two toolbars: the menu bar and the Favorites bar.

***Figure 1–13.** TwitterBar toolbar running in IE 8*

While visually part of the frame UI, toolbars are owned by tab processes; a new instance of each toolbar is created for each tab in each tab process. Their presence in the frame UI is for consistency with prior releases. As they are loaded by the tab process, toolbars run at either low or medium integrity, based on the MIC level of the owning tab.

Installed toolbars can be managed through the Manage Add-Ons interface. In addition, each toolbar is given a close button; a red "x" is placed on the left side of each toolbar, allowing users to disable individual toolbars. Toolbars can also be enabled, disabled, or locked from the View menu.

Explorer Bars

Explorer bars are UI constructs that render within the client area of an IE window. These extensions can be displayed vertically on the left-hand side of the client area, or horizontally at the bottom (Figure 1–14).

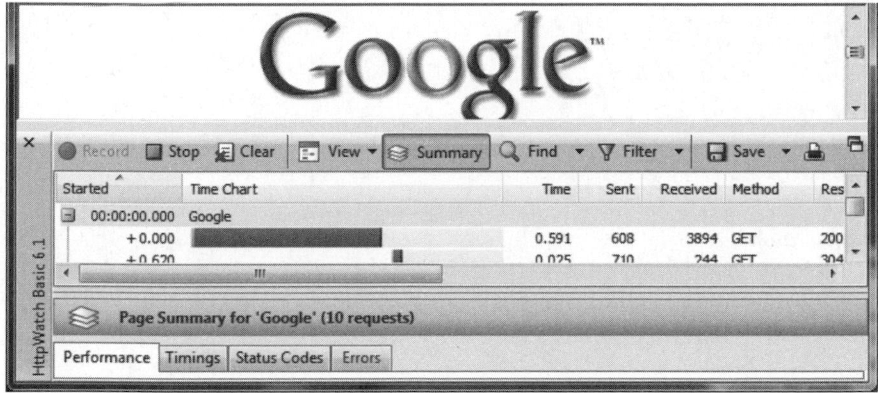

Figure 1–14. HTTPWatch Explorer bar running in IE 8

Like toolbars, Explorer bars must implement `IUnknown`, `IObjectWithSite`, `IPersistStream`, and `IDeskBand`. Explorer bars are provided with a child window in the IE frame and, like toolbars, Explorer bars are instantiated for each tab even though their UI is visually a part of the browser frame. Location of the toolbar (vertical at the left or horizontal on the bottom) is determined by a category ID set during library registration.

Explorer bars can be created without building a COM-based library. Instead of the appropriate registration pointing to a specialized DLL, the ShDocVw library can be loaded and navigate to a specific URL; as a result, a commonly used web site could be turned into an extension for persistent access. More information on how to build both types of Explorer bars can be found later in this book.

Some restrictions are placed on Explorer bars for performance, security, and integrity purposes. Only one instance of each Explorer bar type is shown at a time. These extensions run at the IL of the owner tab process, which could be either Low or Medium depending on the zone or security settings applied to a web page. Finally, Explorer bars that point to a page rather than a COM library cannot communicate with the currently loaded page.

Accelerators and the OpenService Specification

Accelerators are markup-based menu extensions that can be installed through IE and accessed via the browser's context menu. These XML-based extensions, derived from the OpenService XML specification, are installed to a user's profile and have the ability to send contextual information to a web service.

Each accelerator definition includes metainformation, including an icon, a title, a category URL target, and a URL preview target, which displays a contextual preview prior to execution (Figure 1–15). IE exposes an `AddService()` function on the `window.external` object, allowing installation of accelerators from a web page, and the `IsServiceInstalled()` method to check if an accelerator is already installed.

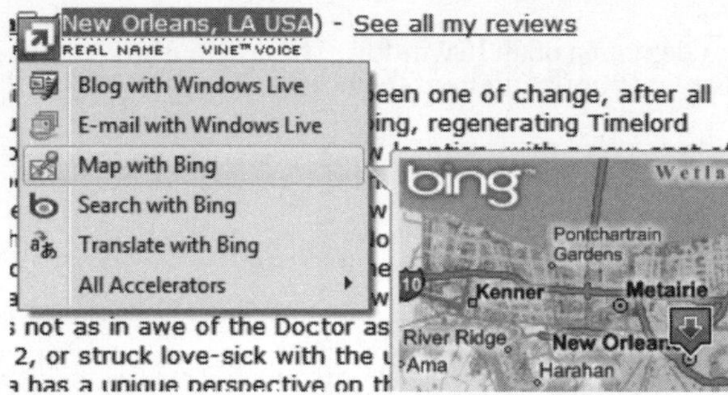

Figure 1–15. Bing Maps accelerator

All Accelerators are installed to a user profile rather than system-wide. They can be managed or removed through the Manage Add-Ons UI.

Web Slices

Web Slices (Figure 1–16) are extensions modeled after the hAtom microformat, which allows users to "subscribe" to predefined portions of markup. Any portion of HTML can become a Web Slice by encapsulating it in appropriately styled `<div>` elements based on the Web Slice format definition.

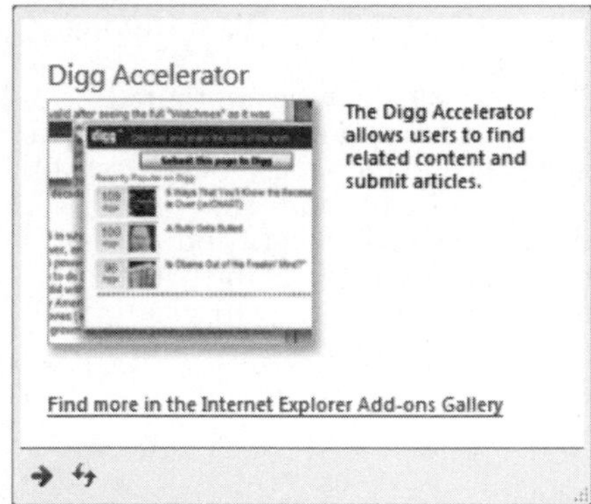

Figure 1–16. The Get More Add-Ons Web Slice reccomending Digg.com

Web Slices can specify the title for the Favorites bar through `<div>`s with an id of `entry-title`; content is denoted in a similar manner with `entry-content`. Properties can be set by wrapping their value in an element using a class name of the property. For instance, time-to-live (TTL) can be set by wrapping a desired value in `<span>` tags whose class value is `ttl`.

Bookmarklets

Bookmarklets are a form of favorites that are defined using JavaScript. They differ from traditional favorites in that they do not (unless directed to through script) launch a new tab or page; instead, markup and script present in the bookmarklet are run in the context of the active web page.

Bookmarklets, considered simple in terms of technical difficulty, host a number of powerful tools for all the major browsers; for example, a web developer could run a CSS analysis tool to provide optimization information, as in Figure 1–17.

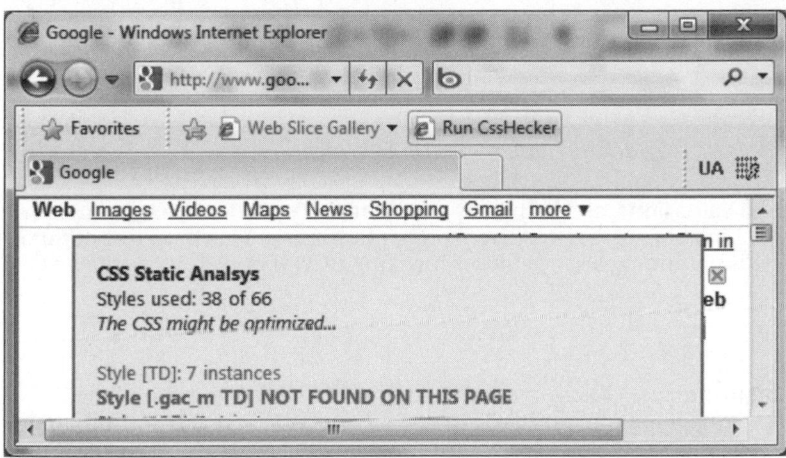

Figure 1–17. *A bookmarklet that checks for CSS optimization*

Bookmarklets are generally interoperable between modern web browsers; however, IE places a number of restrictions on the content and size of these extensions.

Menu Extensions

IE provides three menus where items can be added: the in-page context menu, the Tools menu, and the Help menu. While IE's fixed menu items cannot be removed, developers can append new items to the menu that perform custom actions (Figure 1–18).

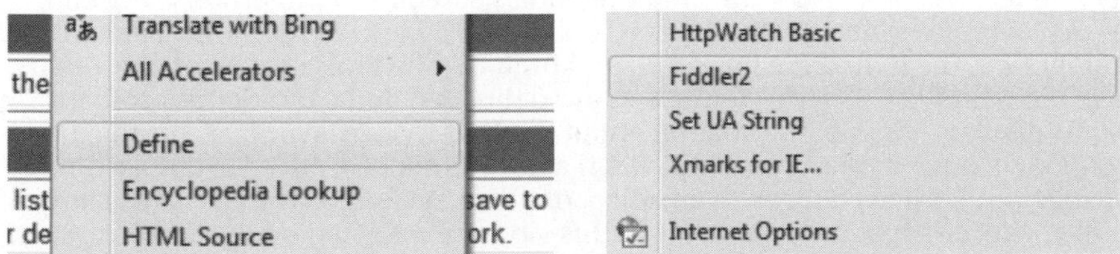

Figure 1–18. *Eric Lawrence's Define context menu item and the Fiddler Tools menu item*

Menu entries are fairly simple to construct. Each menu entry is defined in either the `HKEY_LOCAL_MACHINE` or the `HKEY_CURRENT_USER` hive of the registry and is given its own GUID. Actions associated with menu items can be written in three forms: a call to an external application, a script file to execute, or the Class ID (CLSID) of a COM object to execute.

Toolbar Buttons

Toolbar buttons are 16×16-pixel icons (or 24×24 in cases where large icons are enabled) that reside on IE's command bar (Figure 1–19). IE displays them in the main UI next to the tab row, allowing users to access commonly used IE features and extensions with one click. Users can modify the order of toolbar buttons through a settings dialog.

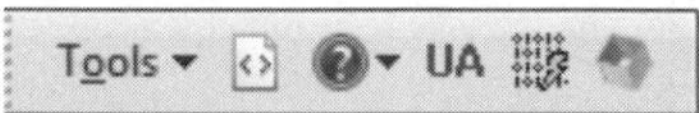

Figure 1–19. *Toolbar extensions for UAStringPicker, Fiddler, and HTTPWatch*

Toolbar buttons, just like menu extensions, are defined by simple registry entries. Each has its own GUID and can be placed in the machine or user registry hive. Toolbar buttons can perform one of three actions: calling an external application, running a script file, or invoking a COM object.

Browser Helper Objects

Browser Helper objects (BHOs) are in-process COM servers instantiated by IE for extension of the browser's base functionality. BHOs, which implement `IUnknown` and `IObjectWithSite`, are instantiated through `CoCreateInstance()` and placed in the IE main execution thread with `SetSite()`. Unlike other common extensions, IE does not give BHOs drawing surfaces; they are intended to simply run in the background.

IE only passes back general, multipurpose interface pointers (such as IWebBrowser2) to BHOs; since IE does not know what a BHO is going to be used for, it waits for BHOs to query for interface pointers in order to prevent a negative effect on system resources. If an extension wishes, for instance, to access interfaces like `IWebBrowser2`, it must use `QueryInterface()` and request any interface pointers from IE. This rationale also applies to events; in order to receive events from eventing interfaces such as `DWebBrowserEvents2`, a BHO must sink events using `IDispEventImpl` or an equivalent interface.

Developer Tools

Developer tools are a set of built-in HTML, JavaScript, and CSS tools geared for rapid prototyping and web page debugging. These tools were called the Developer Toolbar in IE 7 and were available downlevel as an add-on Explorer bar; for IE 8, the tools were improved and built in. The tools consist of four main tabs: an HTML and Style inline editor, a CSS style viewer, a script debugger, and a JavaScript profiler.

The HTML and CSS tabs display editable information about the DOM, page layout, and applied styles. The DOM can be edited through a treeview object; when a node is clicked, style, layout, attribute information, and CSS tracings can be viewed through an adjacent panel. As long as the elements shown in this editor still exist in the page, changes made to items in this view are reflected on the current page.

The Script Debugger and Profiler offer live script debugging, console editing, breakpoint insertion, and script timing information for the current page. On the Debugger tab, developers can turn debugging on and off; step in, over, and out; and view breakpoints, locals, watch, and call stacks. The profiler displays timing calls for JavaScript functions loaded on the current page, as well as call count and overall call trees.

Script Errors and View Source

The Script Error dialog informs users of script errors on a web page; the script engine loaded to handle a script block on the page returns errors for IE to display. In prior versions of IE, some script errors were sent to the default system debugger if one was registered.

As of IE 8, IE includes a built-in source viewer. View Source displays and colorizes markup, and also includes line numbers for reference. The default source viewer can be changed by accessing the "Customize Internet Explorer View Source" menu option under the Developer Tools' File menu.

Shell Document View

The Shell Document View (ShDocVw) is an Active Document Container (also referred to as a Document Host). This container hosts OLE Active Documents (or document objects) within the Shell namespace. Typically, IE hosts MSHTML, a document object designed to render HTML. To host OLE Active Documents, the Shell Document View implements `IOleClientSite` and `IOleDocumentSite`.

The WebBrowser control discussed later is a wrapper around this same `IShellBrowser` interface. Instead of being hosted in the IE frame, the WebBrowser control is an ActiveX control that can be hosted by other applications. It is through ShDocVw and a private (yet visible in export headers) class called `CBaseBrowser2` that the IE frame and the WebBrowser control share common features like the Travel Log and context menu extensions.

The Travel Log and Shared Features

A number of features are shared by both the IE frame and the WebBrowser control, and this sharing is done through ShDocVw and the internal `CBaseBrowser2` class.

The Travel Log is IE's functional storage and access mechanism for navigation information. Simply, it is a data structure and corresponding interface that stores a "stack" of navigation changes for an instance of ShDocVw. There exist a few exposed interfaces, such as `ITravelLog`, but those interfaces (while most likely still accessible) are listed as deprecated by SDK documentation.

Many other functions and properties shared between the IE frame and the WebBrowser control can be found in ShDocVw's `IWebBrowser2` interface, through the `ExecWB()` function, and through ambient events.

Trident (MSHTML)

Trident (MSHTML) is an OLE Active Document that is hosted by ShDocVw. It's most commonly seen by end users as the box in IE that displays web pages. Underneath the display lie a number of subsystems that handle the parsing, rendering, and layout of web pages, as well as expose a number of APIs. I go into more detail on how Trident works to download, parse, and display web pages in the next section.

Third-Party and Custom Document Objects

A COM object can expose a custom OLE Active Document, and that implementation can be hosted within ShDocVw. Some common document objects include Microsoft Office viewers (PowerPoint, Word, and Visio) and PDF readers (Adobe Acrobat and FoxIt Reader). These applications simply point a MIME type and file association to their Active Document handler, and IE will load associated implementations when a document that matches an association is loaded.

Trident Layout and Rendering Engine

MSHTML, known to many and sometimes referred to here as "Trident," is the layout and rendering engine used by IE to handle HTML, CSS, and other markup parsing. Trident itself is an OLE Active Document, built as a fully asynchronous library using apartment threading.

While Trident is hosted by an Active Document Container, it has its own very deep and broad extensibility model. Exported components, for the most part, implement `IDispatch` or `IDispatchEx`, and thus can be accessed using OLE automation and scripting. Many of its subsystems also support binary extensibility through COM; objects such as ActiveX controls, script engines, and behaviors can be loaded at runtime and executed during engine operations.

Trident is also responsible for determining and handling compatibility scenarios for IE, both in terms of binary interfaces and web standards. Given the length of time between releases and the number of major IE versions in the wild, web and system applications that rely on Trident vary in the versions they were designed against. Consequently, portions of Trident remain in place from version to version, giving IE the ability to handle downlevel web standards support as well as legacy implementations of COM interfaces.

The IE frame and the WebBrowser control are not the only applications and objects that host MSHTML. Since all functionality is wrapped in an Active Document object, any valid Document Host can load, display, and control Trident.

Trident itself can be thought of as a container of tightly connected subsystems, each with its own role, function, and, in most cases, set of exposed public interfaces (Figure 1–20).

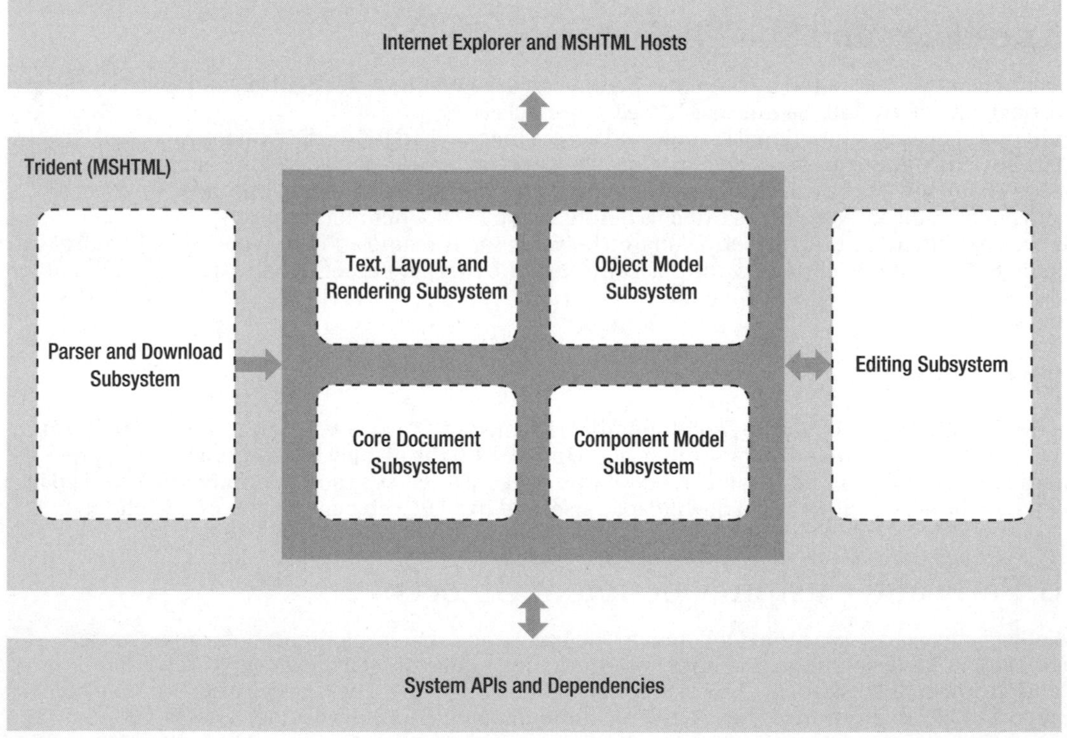

Figure 1–20. *General Trident architecture diagram*

Trident consumes markup and extensions and executes commands involving them in a number of core subsystems. While this diagram does indicate the major areas of MSHTML, there are many private components that are unique to IE and its design that are not covered here.

Parser Subsystem

The parser is responsible for reading, tokenizing, and parsing markup for consumption by the remaining engine components. The first stage in the parser is known as the preparser. As a document is fed in, internal classes handle text decoding. Decoded text is then translated into a token stream using an internal tokenizer.

As the preparser reads in the text stream, IE passes that information through a look-ahead downloader. This feature scans for URLs of resources (such as CSS and JavaScript files) that might be required later during the parsing process. Because waiting for dependent files to download can significantly slow rendering, it is important to identify and request such resources as quickly as possible. When a candidate URL is found, the URL is added to the network request queue. This predownloading—sometimes referred to as "speculative downloading"—helps minimize the time Trident spends waiting for dependencies to download.

After decoding and tokenization, the main parser reads in elements from the stream and performs repairs on the overall HTML document. Tree nodes and markup are created, and the token stream is passed off to the Core Document subsystem.

Document Modes and Compatibility View

Compatibility View is a mode of IE's layout engine that allows web pages to be rendered and displayed as they would be in downlevel versions of IE; these versions are referred to as Document Modes. Compatibility View can be triggered through an HTTP header, by a web page, through the UI, or through the Compatibility List.

Core Document Subsystem

As markup passes through the parser, it is handed off to the Core Document subsystem, also referred to as Markup Services. This part of Trident takes parsed markup, builds the markup stream, and prepares it for use and conversion into the object model. The public implementation of this subsystem can be seen through the Markup Services APIs, and is exposed through the `IMarkupServices` interface. Once the markup stream is built, it is passed to the remaining Trident subsystems.

■ **Note** While markup is eventually placed into a tree-like structure by the object model subsystem, it's a common misconception that IE's parser creates a document "tree." Markup Services creates a specialized text stream that is optimized for use by the rest of Trident. For more information, check out the IMarkupServices documentation and articles on MSDN.

Text, Layout, and Rendering Subsystem

The Text, Layout, and Rendering subsystem represents a broad set of internal interfaces whose responsibility is to position and display content on the screen and printed pages.

The text engine is responsible for storage and display information, including passing text blocks to other dependent subsystems such as editing and layout.

The layout engine is a set of algorithms responsible for gathering information, building data structures, and outputting size and positioning information to the rendering engine. While there are no public interfaces associated with this block, it is known internally and is sometimes referenced in blogs as Page, Table, and Line Services (PTLS).

The rendering engine handles onscreen display of web pages. It receives content size and positioning information from the layout engine and custom elements or element effect definitions from scripted and binary behaviors, and renders an interpretation of that content to the screen.

Object Model Subsystem

The object model, at a high level, controls postparse communication with document elements. It binds document elements discovered in the parser to the script engine in order to enable dynamic HTML content.

IE Dynamic HTML Object Model and W3C Document Object Model

The IE Dynamic HTML Object Model (DHTML OM) exposes internal element constructs to external interfaces, allowing developers to programmatically access elements' properties, methods, and events from scripts and binary applications.

The W3C Document Object Model (DOM) is an interoperable and platform-neutral object model implementation that was created to standardize object model implementations across major browsers. The W3C DOM can be accessed through JavaScript and is implemented on top of many preexisting IE DHTML DOM interfaces.

The IE DHTML OM and the W3C DOM, while both accurate representations of the document object, are not inherently the same. The W3C DOM gives developers easier access to manipulate documents, change properties, and build applications that work across multiple browsers and platforms. Some aspects of the DHTML OM, such as eventing, are not exposed through the W3C DOM.

Script Engine Interfacing (JScript.dll, VBScript.dll)

Trident acts as a scripting host (implementing `IActiveScriptSite` and `IActiveScriptSiteWindow`) for any script engines that implement `IActiveScript` and `IActiveScriptParse`. Developers most commonly use JavaScript (JScript.dll) and VBScript (VBScript.dll) through Trident; however, it has the ability to load any scripting engine implementing these active scripting interfaces.

Script engines can be instantiated as early as the first parsing run through a page; they are often required to compute changes in a document right after the first response. When Trident locates a script, it queries the language used and references the appropriate registered engine associated with that language for initialization.

Cross-Domain Request Objects (XMLHTTP, XMLHTTPRequest)

XMLHTTP, widely known as `XMLHTTPRequest`, is an object that enables client-side script to issue HTTP requests. This interface allows developers to issue requests and receive their responses without having to reload or load a new web page.

In IE 7 and above, XMLHTTP is wrapped by IE and exposed as a native object. Developers can write JavaScript that directly requests server-side content without directly invoking an ActiveX control. Prior to IE 7, developers wishing to use `XMLHTTPRequest` were required to load the MSXML XMLHTTP ActiveX control through script, or instantiate `IXMLHTTPRequest` through a COM-based add-on.

Accessibility

In order to enable access to the DOM by assistive technology applications, the Trident OM exposes most HTML elements through the `IAccessible` interface. This interface allows screen readers and other assistive applications to read elements in the DOM and convey them to users.

As of IE 8, the object model supports the cross-browser W3C Accessible Rich Internet Applications (ARIA) specification. This specification creates customizable element definitions using "roles," "states," and "properties." ARIA complements the functionality used by assistive technology vendors through the Microsoft Active Accessibility API (MSAA).

Component Model Subsystem

The Component Model subsystem handles *content extensibility*: COM- and script-based applications that can both extend the base functionality of Trident and add new features to it. Unlike the Frame and Tab extensions, content extensions can typically run outside of IE without any extra work; any application that hosts MSHTML or implements the WebBrowser control can "automatically" load content extensions through Trident.

Scripted and Binary Behaviors

Behaviors are mechanisms in MSHTML that allow developers to create element effects and even create new elements. They were added as of IE 5.5 to both extend CSS and allow for customization of traditional DOM elements. For example, a developer could add a default onClick event to all `<div>` tags, or automatically have all `<br>` tags act like `<p>` tags.

Scripted behaviors, commonly called HTML components (HTCs), extend element functionality and behavior through markup, JavaScript, and CSS. Binary behaviors act in a similar fashion, but use COM objects that implement the `IElementBehavior` interface and react to events by passing in element and script constructs. HTCs differ from binary behaviors in the fact that they can be downloaded and run during page load, whereas binary behaviors must be installed locally.

ActiveX Controls

ActiveX controls are COM servers loaded into a web page. They provide functionality that extends traditional markup and script. For instance, ActiveX controls may implement `IOleClientSite` to draw to a Trident rendering surface, for instance, or use `IPersistPropertyBag` to pass parameters between a binary and in-page script.

MSHTML can expose a control's public methods to a script. In order to call an ActiveX object's methods from, for example, JavaScript, a developer must implement `IDispatch` or `IDispatchEx`. Events can also be surfaced to script; controls can use `IProvideTypeInfo` to expose events for use in declarative languages. In virtually all supported versions of IE, controls must implement `IObjectSaftey` in order to perform either of these actions; as of IE 7, this interface (or an equivalent registry key) must be implemented for IE to even load a specific control.

Instantiated ActiveX controls have a significant number of restrictions, a number that has increased with every release of IE. For example, as of IE 8, controls in the Internet zone in Windows Vista and above will run in a low integrity context by default.

Editing Subsystem

The Editing subsystem handles text editing and web authoring features for MSHTML. This includes features such as text and form editing, selection, caret browsing, keyboard navigation, clipboard management, and `contentEditable` handling.

Each element in the DOM (meaning every control, image, table, etc.) has a layout created by the Text, Layout, and Rendering subsystem. When any region or element is marked as editable, it is passed off to this subsystem to handle user and programming editing commands.

Networking and Zones

IE uses a number of libraries and Windows APIs to handle networking, object download, and security infrastructure. Windows itself provides numerous interfaces and services that IE does not have to duplicate; for example, Windows provides cache and cookie services to many different applications, and APIs such as the Credential UI and elevation manifests provide mechanisms for interacting with the system's security infrastructure.

URLMon

URLMon (short for URL Moniker) is a COM library that wraps the WinINET library in a way that aligns closely with IE's operation as a web browser. URLMon also provides an extensibility layer for pluggable protocols, allowing IE to request content using protocols beyond the HTTP, HTTPS, and FTP protocols supported by WinINET. URLMon also controls "zones" and general content security, code download, and download management.

Zones and Security Managers

IE uses security zones to group data sources and to apply differing restrictions on those groups. By default, IE includes five different zones:

- **Local Machine**: Pages originating from the local computer
- **Intranet**: Pages originating from local network servers
- **Trusted**: Domains that have explicitly been listed to be trusted
- **Internet**: Pages originating from remote servers
- **Restricted**: Domains that have specifically been listed to be restricted

Objects loaded from each zone context are given different permissions with respect to IE's feature set; for example, scripts can run from the Internet zone, but are blocked in the Restricted zone. Microsoft has defined templates, from Low to High, that represent default settings.

URLMon exposes granular security management functions through `IInternetSecurityManager`. This interface allows IE and other installed applications to play a part in the trust decision chain for content loaded in the browser. Applications registered as security managers are allowed to review and potentially modify the default URL actions applied to a page from that page's appropriate zone.

Pluggable Protocol Handlers

URLMon provides a number of ways for applications to handle protocol requests through the registration of protocol handlers. When an URL is requested, IE checks to see if there are any associations registered for that URL's protocol; this association can be in the form of an application or a library that implements the Asynchronous Pluggable Protocol (APP) APIs.

WinINET

WinINET is the Windows API for networking and common web protocol handling. It is widely used for HTTP(S) and FTP downloading, caching interfaces, and cookie management. WinINET also controls the (infamous) index.dat files—the storage containers for cached content, cookies, links, and so on.

Security, Trust, and Privacy Architecture

IE has been a target of attacks against its platform on many fronts, and opinions as to why are varied and much debated. Taking a step back from IE, end users can be affected by broader attacks against web sites and even attacks against users themselves through social engineering and privacy exploitation. Either way, modern browsers typically include a number of security features to prevent such attacks. IE is no different, providing built-in security architecture to mitigate potential vulnerabilities.

Security UI and Feedback Mechanisms

Security features are great: they help protect users, data, and systems. This is especially important when loading potentially dangerous content or content from untrusted sources. At the same time, browsers exist so users can open potentially dangerous content and content from untrusted sources. Surprisingly enough, users expect to be able to browse the Web!

Considering both of these conflicting yet necessary goals, security UI and feedback mechanisms exist to convey information to users about the security implications of browsing. The methods and mediums vary, but their goals are to describe the current state of a web page, download, or communication channel and let users know why content may be dangerous, why it was restricted, or why it was blocked.

Information Bar

The information bar (referred to by the IE team as the Goldbar) is a UI element that exists within `IDocHostUIHandler` that attempts to inform a user of a significant browser event and, in some cases, ask a user to make a trust decision (Figure 1–21).

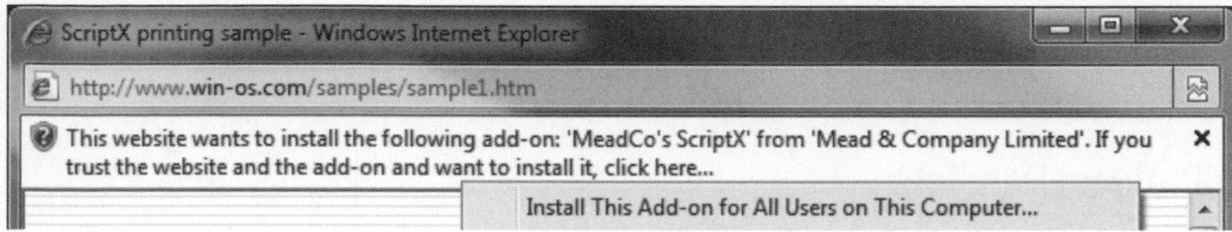

Figure 1–21. ActiveX installation information bar

The information bar's text informs the user of any necessary action regarding the event, and, if action is required, provides a context menu with decision flows. Many IE features use the information bar, including the Pop-Up Blocker, XSS filter, and ActiveX Installer.

Badges

A badge is a button located between the address bar combo box and the address bar navigation controls. It is used to inform the user of a URL's security state (Figure 1–22).

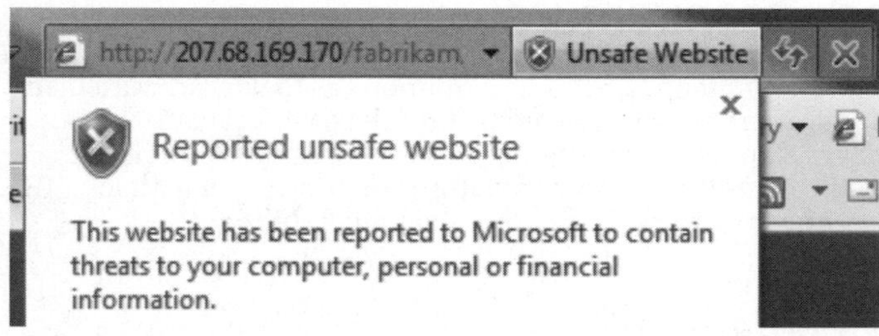

Figure 1–22. Unsafe web site badge

When clicked, a flyout window appears providing more information and context. The icon, title, and flyout contents change in both color and content depending on the type and severity of the message being relayed. IE's SSL, Extended Validation SSL, Internationalized Domain Name (IDN) spoofing protection, and anti-phishing features share this information construct. IE does not expose an API to create or interact with the badges.

Full-Page Notifications

IE's security architecture displays full-page notifications for certain security warnings. For instance, IE will prevent a web page from displaying if there is a certificate problem or the page is known to be a source of malicious content. Figure 1–23 shows a full-page notification that is displayed when IE encounters a page with an expired or invalid SSL certificate.

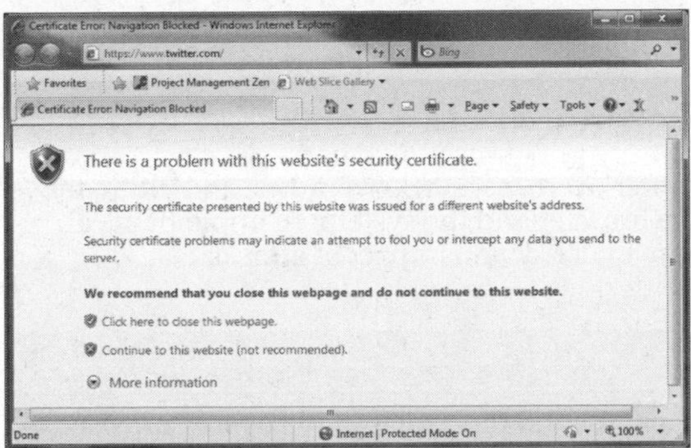

Figure 1–23. Full-page notification for a problematic security certificate

Protected Mode and UAC Dialogs

Applications and extensions running within IE are subject to Protected Mode and UAC restrictions through integrity controls and UIPI. If objects attempt to elevate a process outside of Protected Mode, attempt drag-and-drop outside of Protected Mode, or attempt to perform any other action that compromises the integrity of the sandbox, IE will ask for user consent through a Protected Mode dialog. Applications attempting to elevate to high integrity (including IE's High IL Broker) will trigger a UAC prompt. Figure 1–24 shows both the Protected Mode and UAC dialogs in action.

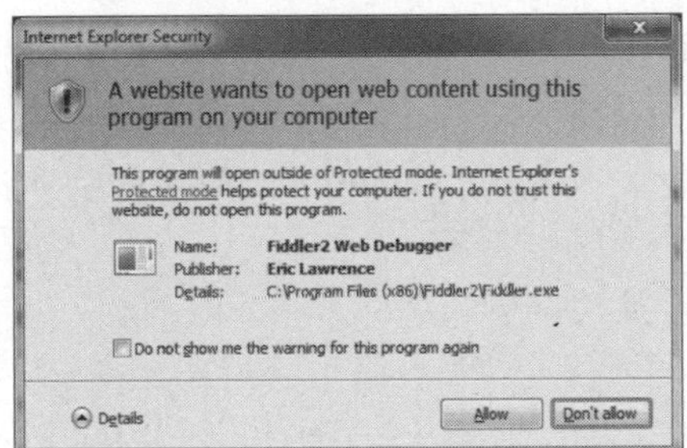

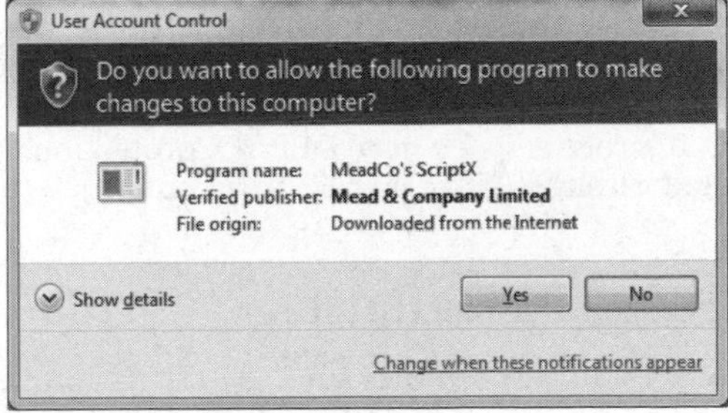

Figure 1–24. Protected Mode dialog for Fiddler and UAC prompt for ScriptX

While the UAC prompt is mandatory for all applications unless turned off for the system, Protected Mode dialogs can be avoided through process name registration in the Silent Elevation list. An application installer can add the process name to IE's elevation list (since a trust decision was made by the user to install the application in the first place).

Status Bar Entry Points

IE uses portions of the status bar to relay security information to users that doesn't block their browser session or require immediate action. The security zone is always displayed, as well as the status of

Protected Mode. Aside from this, features such as the Pop-Up Blocker, InPrivate, and P3P cookie implementation use the status bar to notify users of their operation.

Application Integrity and Browser Defenses

The browser itself is at risk against attacks that exploit buffer overruns, stack overflows, and ultimately, code injection that compromises the integrity of both the browser and the system. IE implements a number of mitigations for these scenarios, lessening the overall risk and impact of attacks.

Protected Mode and Zones

I talked about Protected Mode and zones earlier in this chapter and their roles in the overall browser model. Stepping away from an architectural view, these features were mainly put in place for application security and data integrity. Protected Mode sandboxes untrusted content, placing a clear separation between Internet data and user profile data. Zones, in conjunction with Protected Mode, create well-defined security setting differences between content sources.

DEP/NX and ASLR

DEP/NX (Data Execution Prevention and No-Execute) is a compiler option for applications that blocks execution of data placed in portions of memory marked nonexecutable. ASLR (Address Space Layout Randomization) forces the contents of the address space of a process to be randomized. Randomization helps prevent attackers from guessing the location of specific commands or structures in the address space, thus blocking execution or injection attempts. Together, common vulnerabilities such as buffer overruns and heap corruption become harder to exploit.

All IE binaries are compiled with ASLR enabled by default; add-ons should set the /DYNAMICBASE linker option to enable this protection for their binaries. On XP SP3, Vista SP1+, Win2K8, Windows 7, and Win2K8R2, IE opts into DEP/NX by default. Because DEP/NX is a process-wide setting, all extensions loaded within the IE process space have DEP/NX protection enabled by default. Stand-alone executables should be compiled with the /NXCOMPAT linker option.

Extension Integrity Defenses

Browser extensions, especially binaries such as ActiveX controls and behaviors, have traditionally been a target for exploits. As a result, IE has added additional mitigations in every new version of the browser. Such mitigations attempt to block common scenarios and vulnerabilities used to compromise data and system integrity.

ActiveX Safe for Initialization and Safe for Scripting

ActiveX controls are binary applications run in web pages. Because ActiveX controls may be written for use in trusted desktop applications, developers may fail to consider the security threat of untrusted callers. To mitigate this, IE requires an opt-in declaration by a control in order for that control to run under IE's default security settings. Before instantiating a control, IE attempts to call the `IObjectSafety::SetInterfaceSafetyOptions()` method to force the control to behave safely for untrusted initialization data and callers.

Controls declare themselves safe for initialization by returning `INTERFACESAFE_FOR_UNTRUSTED_DATA`. This constant informs IE that the control can securely handle any initialization data it may be passed (e.g., in the PARAM attributes of an OBJECT tag). Controls may also declare themselves "safe for scripting" by returning INTERFACESAFE_FOR_UNTRUSTED_CALLER. This constant informs IE that the control's methods and properties may be called or set by JavaScript or VBScript.

If a control fails to implement the SetInterfaceSafetyOptions() method, or fails to indicate that it is safe for untrusted data or untrusted callers, IE will immediately unload the object.

ActiveX Opt-In

Except for ActiveX controls installed directly through the browser, and a select number of widely used, Internet-targeted controls such as Flash and RealPlayer, all ActiveX controls are blocked from instantiation in IE by default. Users may opt into using an ActiveX control in the browser by using the information bar.

Because some common development tools will automatically implement IObjectSafety, some controls overpromise their ability to safely be used by the browser. This could lead to exploitable crashes or other security threats. By forcing users to verify a control before it can run in IE, ActiveX Opt-In significantly reduces the attack surface against ActiveX controls.

ATL SiteLock Template and Per-Site ActiveX

The ATL SiteLock template and Per-Site ActiveX offer a combination of explicit and implicit ways that an ActiveX control can be bound to one or many domains. By restricting where and in what context ActiveX controls can run, developers and users can minimize the risk of control repurposing.

ATL SiteLock is an explicit mechanism for restricting what domains and zones may load a given ActiveX control. Control developers who wish to use this restriction can apply the SiteLock template to their ATL-based ActiveX controls. Instead of implementing IObjectSafety, ActiveX controls should instead implement IObjectSafetySiteLockImpl; this interface is derived from IObjectSaftey, and allows developers to declare a list of allowed domains (or zones) that are checked at runtime.

SiteLock is the most reliable mechanism to prevent ActiveX repurposing attacks, whereby a malicious site attempts to abuse a control designed for use on another site. If a site attempts to load a control that SiteLock does not allow, the instantiation of the object will be blocked. No information bar or override is presented.

Because SiteLock requires some effort on the part of control developers, it is not utilized by as many controls as it should be. To that end, Microsoft added a new feature to IE 8 to provide some of the benefits of SiteLock.

The Per-Site ActiveX feature allows users to decide what domains a control is permitted to run on. By default, a control installed through the browser may run only on the site that installed the control. When an installed control is instantiated by a different web site, the user is presented with an information bar asking if a control should be allowed to run on the current domain or all domains (Figure 1–25).

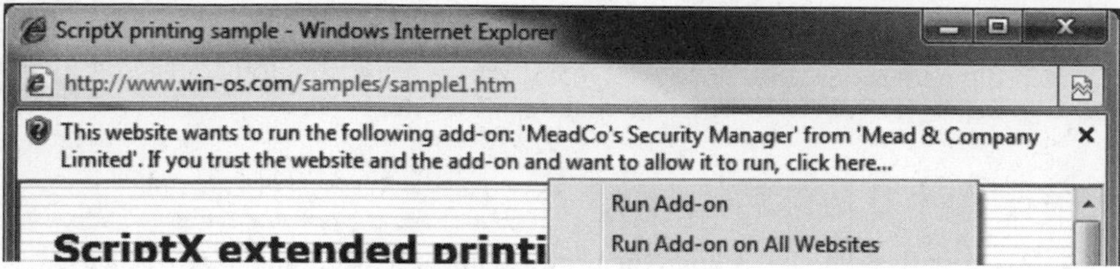

Figure 1–25. Per-Site ActiveX information bar for ScriptX

This list of domains can be managed through the Manage Add-Ons UI or via Group Policy.

Per-User (Non-Admin) ActiveX

Per-User ActiveX (also called Non-Admin ActiveX) enables ActiveX control packages (CABs) to be installed within a user account rather than machine-wide. Developers wishing to turn their CABs into per-user installers can set the `InstallScope` and `RedirectToHKCU` flags to do so in their package's INF file.

Per-machine installations such as CABs typically place files in the Downloaded Program Files folder and write to the `HKEY_LOCAL_MACHINE` hive of the registry. In contrast, per-user applications place files in the current user-owned folders and write registry entries to `HKEY_CURRENT_USER`. Per-user applications aren't new, nor are they limited to CAB files. Any installer script or executable can turn an extension or application into a per-user one by limiting installation to nonsystem folders and registry entries. For example, Google Chrome places itself in the user's Application Data folder instead of the machine-wide Program Files folder.

■ **Note** Prior to Per-User ActiveX, IE explicitly checked to see if a user had administrative privileges before attempting to install ActiveX controls on a web page.

Killbits and Phoenix Bits

Killbits are registry flags that tell IE and its components not to load a control with a specified CLSID. Microsoft typically issues killbits for vulnerable controls or those that, for one reason or another, should never load inside the browser. Third parties use this mechanism as well for security and end-of-support purposes.

Killbits are an effective way to block a control from loading, but can cause compatibility problems with existing content (e.g., HTML burned onto a DVD). To mitigate the compatibility impact of killbits, phoenix bits were devised. These flags redirect requests for a control with a killbitted CLSID to an alternative CLSID, effectively allowing a new control to replace an old one, maintaining compatibility with existing content.

■ **Note** While I originally thought phoenix bits were named after the capital of Arizona, it turns out they were named after a bird from Phoenician, Egyptian, and Greek mythology.

Compatibility Warnings

Add-ons that are known to hang or crash IE can be blocked using compatibility warnings. These add-ons may not be exploitable, but loading them could create security vulnerabilities or impair the user's browsing experience. To protect against these types of add-ons, IE disables and informs users of known incompatible add-ons through a modal dialog shown at startup.

Privacy and Social Engineering Protections

Not all attackers are elite hackers; some simply try to trick users into making bad trust decisions. IE institutes a number of measures to mitigate social engineering attacks against users through the use of UI notifications, file and download blocking, privacy restrictions, and client-side script protections.

Window and Frame Restrictions

In order to protect users from UI spoofing, scripts are prevented from performing certain actions that could potentially trick users and hurt the overall integrity of the browser, data, and system. For instance, scripts cannot turn off the status bar or address bar, pop up a window over the browser UI (such as the address bar), or place windows offscreen.

Malware and Phishing Filters

As pages are loaded and files are downloaded from the Internet zone, IE sends URLs to its SmartScreen service to check for known phishing web sites and malware. In the page load scenario, positive hits will result in a blocked page; for downloads, files will be blocked through an Unsafe Download dialog box (Figure 1–26).

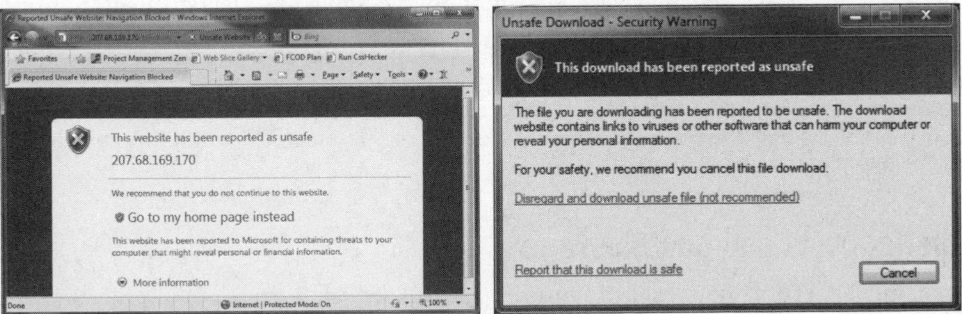

Figure 1–26. SmartScreen blocked site and download warnings

In each case, users can override IE's recommendation, though the ability to override requires extra effort, and overrides can be disabled via Group Policy. As of IE 8, there is no public API that gives access to SmartScreen filter results.

Platform for Privacy Preferences

The Platform for Privacy Preferences (P3P) from the W3C is an opt-in approach toward matching web site cookie policies with a user's or organization's privacy requirements. Essentially, P3P is an XML version of a privacy policy found on many pieces of software, but one only pertaining to how and where a web site will use personally identifiable information (PII) through cookies. If a user or organization implements P3P requirements for web sites, any web site visited returning P3P XML that conflicts with these requirements will have offending cookies blocked. These settings are zone-specific.

Add-ons that modify cookies should do so through the `InternetSetCookieEx()` API; this method ensures that P3P settings found on the system are respected.

Pop-Up Blocker

As of IE 6 on Windows XP SP2, the browser includes a mechanism for preventing non–user-initiated pop-ups from being opened from Internet zone pages. IE uses a proprietary algorithm for determining which pop-ups are allowed and blocked. Users and developers can add or remove sites from an exception list, and the feature itself can be toggled using a URLAction or feature control key.

SSL, EV-SSL, and Identify Information

IE provides a mechanism of positive feedback when users navigate using secure protocols such as HTTPS instead of HTTP. The browser frame displays a lock icon in the address bar for SSL pages, and turns the address bar green when the connection is secured with an Extended Validation SSL certificate. Users can get more information on the certificate displayed through a flyout window.

Domain Highlighting and IDN Spoofing Notifications

The IE 8 address bar provides two features to aid in the identification of phishing web sites: domain highlighting and IDN spoofing notifications.

Domain highlighting is a method for differentiating the domain portion of a URL from the rest of the address using text color. The domain is rendered in black, while the remainder of the URL is gray. This allows users to see the actual domain being navigated to; for example, showing a clear distinction between `bankofamerica.com` and `banko.famerica.com`.

IDN spoofing notifications inform users when a domain attempts to use character sets outside the currently registered browser-accept languages. For instance, a phisher could register `http://fαcebook.com/` with the Latin Unicode character "ɑ" rather than an ASCII "a" in order to trick users into thinking their web site is the real `http://www.facebook.com`. These notifications are displayed using an address bar flyout and icon.

Cross-Domain Requests and postMessage

Web browsers implement a security policy called *same-origin policy*, which restricts communication between content from different domains. To enable legitimate uses of cross-domain communication, IE has instituted two features: the `XDomainRequest` object, which allows client/server communication, and the `window.postMessage()` API, which enables cross-document communication.

InPrivate Browsing and InPrivate Filtering

IE 8's InPrivate browsing feature allows users to access content through IE in a way that disables history, cookies, and other persistent data. Running IE in InPrivate mode also disables toolbars and BHOs by default; these extensions often themselves track browsing information. Users can enable toolbars and BHOs in InPrivate mode through the Internet Control Panel UI. Developers can use the `IEIsInPrivateBrowsing()` API to detect if their control is running in InPrivate mode and react accordingly—for example, by downgrading persistent data to expire at the end of the session.

InPrivate filtering is a feature that detects third-party HTTP requests and optionally allows the user to block such requests. (A *third-party request* is a request targeted to a different domain than the page containing the markup that issues the request.) When a domain is blocked by InPrivate filtering, the browser will not make requests for third-party content from that domain. As of IE 8, there is no supported API for a browser add-on to detect whether a given domain is blocked by InPrivate filtering.

As of IE 8, neither InPrivate browsing nor InPrivate filtering is available for use by hosts of the WebBrowser control.

Cross-Site Scripting Filter

Cross-site scripting (XSS) attacks attempt to inject malicious script into cross-origin web pages. Ultimately, attackers use this vector to steal user information, circumvent access controls, or bypass same-origin policy.

IE 8's XSS filter runs during navigation sequences. If the XSS filter detects that a script sent in the URL or POST body of a cross-origin request has been returned in an HTML document, it sanitizes that portion of the document and informs the user via an information bar.

High-Integrity Brokers

As mentioned before in this chapter, IE 8 on Windows Vista and above uses UAC to separate data access and commands based on ILs and permission sets. Most of these features are part of Protected Mode.

Since per-machine ActiveX controls require binaries and registry settings to be written to high-integrity (system-level) locations, the browser launches separate broker processes to handle these installations. When ActiveX controls are to be installed, IE launches ieinstal.exe and, in certain cases, axinstsv.exe to request permissions (typically in the form of a UAC dialog) and continue the installation process.

ActiveX Installation Broker (ieinstal.exe)

The ActiveX Installation Broker is an out-of-process COM object that installs and registers per-machine ActiveX control packages. After a downloaded ActiveX library or CAB package is checked for a valid Authenticode signature, URLMon instantiates this broker and passes the package to it. When the broker requests elevation to a high-integrity MIC level, a UAC prompt is displayed.

ActiveX Installer Service (axinstsv.exe)

The ActiveX Installer Service is a service for Windows Vista and higher that enables administration of ActiveX installations in environments implementing Group Policy. Since the IE's ActiveX Installation Broker requires elevation to a high-integrity context, users in the Standard Users group cannot install per-machine controls because they lack administrative privileges. This means that, for example, a user in a controlled enterprise environment cannot install Adobe Flash without an administrator typing their password in. The ActiveX Installer Service solves this problem by allowing administrators to preapprove controls for installation.

Hosting and Reuse

IE is not just a web browser, but also a platform for navigating web content and displaying that content within an application. A wide variety of Microsoft-owned and third-party applications use IE's libraries and APIs to retrieve and render web content without the need to create a custom downloader, parser, layout engine, rendering engine, and so on.

MSHTML

MSHTML is an OLE Active Document that loads, parses, and displays HTML content. Since this object is an Active Document, any application that provides a valid OLE Active Document Container can load MSHTML and display web pages. Other Active Documents wishing to build on MSHTML can use Active Document aggregation to override and overload MSHTML's public methods.

WebBrowser Control

The WebBrowser control is an MSHTML host library that shares select browser interfaces with the IE frame. Since this control both displays pages and wraps functionality from the base browser interfaces of IE such as navigation, cookies, and caching, developers can use this control to provide a near-complete web browser experience in their applications. In fact, many other browsers such as Maxthon use the WebBrowser control to create a completely new browser.

While both MSHTML and the WebBrowser control can be used to display web pages or content in an application, there are many advantages to implementing an instance of the WebBrowser control instead of MSHTML. MSHTML hosting is geared toward highly optimized scenarios where an application simply needs bare-bones HTML parsing; this contrasts WebBrowser control–hosting scenarios, which may require navigation, rendering of non-HTML content, and so on.

HTML Applications

HTML applications (HTAs) are web pages loaded into a premade WebBrowser control container called mshta.exe. HTAs run as fully trusted applications, giving them access to freely write to user profiles, launch applications, and use scripting methods unavailable to normal web pages. Historically, HTAs have been used for setup applications and enterprise tools.

Scripting Interfaces and API Usage

IE and its components expose a number of useful scripting interfaces and generic APIs that give script authors and developers a large tool set for developing a wide range of applications. For instance, enterprise administrators could write a simple VBScript to clear IE's cache whenever a user logs onto a domain. Developers could tap into IE's `IUri` interface to quickly parse URIs rather than write a custom regular expression to do so.

Application Management Tools

Microsoft provides a number of tools that allow users and system administrators to manage IE installations. These tools vary in both purpose and functionality, and not all are installed alongside the browser during upgrades or shipped in Windows by default.

Internet Explorer Administration Kit

The IE base configuration can be customized using the Internet Explorer Administration Kit (IEAK). This toolkit creates customizable IE installers. Administrators, vendors, or partners can create builds of IE with custom branding, specific setting configurations, and add-on sets. IEAK builds can be repackaged and distributed just like normal IE setup install packages.

Setup and the Windows 7 Uninstaller

IE offers two main methods for setup: a Windows Update (WU) package and a setup executable. The separate setup executable can be used for manual upgrade scenarios, unattended installations, installation customization using IExpress, and modification and repackaging of the IE setup executable through the IEAK. Since the IE setup modifies protected system libraries that are loaded by other operating system components, a system restart is required to install the browser.

Windows Error Reporting, Event Logging Infrastructure, and the Customer Experience Improvement Program

When an application crashes, users are sometimes asked if they wish to send crash data to Microsoft. This feature is called Windows Error Reporting (WER), sometimes referred to as Dr. Watson or simply Watson. WER allows product support teams and engineers to receive crash dumps and, hopefully, create patches to fix common problems. WER can be enabled or disabled through the system Control Panel.

IE exposes two event types available for nondevelopment scenarios: Application Compatibility events and Event Tracing for Windows (ETW) events. *Application Compatibility events* are raised to indicate changes in functionality from prior versions of IE. For instance, IT administrators can collect events on intranet web pages to find out if they can upgrade IE without modifying these pages. *ETW events* are performance measurement and profiling events used test IE's performance in targeted scenarios. For example, companies could check if their enterprise add-on significantly slows down IE before they deploy. While these events have applications for end users, they can still be accessed by developers through their respective API sets.

As with many other pieces of Microsoft software, IE integrates with the Customer Experience Improvement Program (CEIP) in order to gather metrics and feedback on feature usage. This data enables product teams to understand real-world usage of the browser (e.g., "What percentage of users run developer tools unpinned?"). Users and organizations can enable and disable CEIP through the system Control Panel or Group Policy.

Windows 7 Troubleshooter

The Windows 7 Control Panel includes system and program troubleshooters that offer self-help panels for fixing common problems. Developers can build their own troubleshooters using the new Windows Troubleshooting Platform. Troubleshooters can be built using XML and PowerShell scripts. This means applications and extensions that use IE could, for example, notify a user of problems with a configuration for an add-on rather than having the user uninstall it to solve issues.

Default Programs

In Windows XP and 2000, the default browser and e-mail programs are machine-wide settings made through the Set Program and Access Defaults (SPAD) interface. Windows Vista and above replace SPAD with Default Programs, a feature that allows the default browser to be set machine-wide as well as per-user. These defaults can be specified through the registry and Group Policy. Developers wishing to programmatically set defaults can do so by using the `IApplicationAssociationRegistration` interface and its APIs on Windows Vista and above; applications wishing to set program defaults in Windows XP must do so through the registry.

Online Services

IE hosts a number of online services that complement browser features. The IE Add-Ons Gallery (`www.ieaddons.com`) allows developers to publish extensions and applications for users who wish to extend IE. Suggested Sites and SmartScreen are proprietary information services that provide data for suggested site matching on the Suggested Sites Web Slice, and data on malicious content, respectively. IE's usage of hosted information services such as the last two examples can be disabled through the IE Control Panel.

Settings Management and Feature Controls

IE offers a number of tools and features for managing browser settings and wider configurations that relate to those settings. These tools include APIs, command-line switches, GUI tools, and system integration pieces that as a whole allow for a wide variety of options.

Internet Options Control Panel (inetcpl.cpl)

IE's Internet Options Control Panel allows users and administrators to control IE settings through a UI pane. Basic settings include home page, search, and appearance configurations. The Control Panel also offers more detailed configuration options, including security and zone management, network and program configurations, and privacy settings.

While not officially documented, it is widely known that inetcpl.cpl exposes a number of APIs to perform common IE tasks. For instance, the `ClearMyTracksByProcessW()` API allows developers to clear browsing, history, and cache information programmatically. Administrators can use these APIs without writing code; most can be processed through rundll32.dll.

Reset Internet Explorer Settings

Reset Internet Explorer Settings (RIES) is a Control Panel option that allows users to reset IE back to its default configuration. RIES handles four main settings groups: browser settings (data in the Control Panel), extensibility (all add-ons are disabled), browsing history (all items are cleared), and manufacturer settings (any changes made by an IEAK configuration are reapplied).

Manage Add-Ons

Manage Add-Ons is an interface for enabling and disabling extensions used by IE. Extensions such as ActiveX controls and accelerators that are installed for use in the browser are listed here and can be disabled using the UI.

Information contained in Manage Add-Ons is gathered from Authenticode and certificate information contained in binary packages, and XML or other metadata that is part of scripted or markup-based extensions. As of IE 8, Manage Add-Ons also lists "load time" for any add-on instantiated in the UI thread, where timing information represents the amount of time elapsed between extension instantiation and release of the UI thread by an extension.

Group Policy

Any IE setting can be customized and controlled over a network using group policies. *Group policies* are essentially distributable configurations that allow Windows-based domains to distribute settings to controlled user, group, machine, and domain profiles. Network administrators wishing to change or modify IE's group policies can do so through the Group Policy Management Console and the Group Policy Inventory tool.

Feature Control Keys

Feature control keys (FCKs) are registry settings that allow developers and users to control the state of certain major IE features and security update packages. While IE typically opts into the most secure and feature-rich setting allowed by FCKs, some applications and system configurations necessitate features being enabled or disabled for the sake of application compatibility. Any application hosting or wrapping IE functionality can list its own set of FCKs in the registry.

FCKs, in general, are read and applied during the startup of MSHTML, the WebBrowser control, or IE. This means FCKs that are to be applied to an application must be set before the process starts, or at least before any IE component is loaded within a process. A few runtime-editable FCKs exist, and those FCKs can be found in the `INTERNETFEATURELIST` enumeration. Developers that wish to change any of the runtime-applicable FCKs in this enumeration can use the `CoInternetSetFeatureEnabled()` function to do so.

When I discussed security zones and the `IInternetSecurityManager` interface, I mentioned that URL actions and URL policies are used to determine whether given actions are allowed, disallowed, and so on. When an FCK is used to disable a feature, its setting is typically given precedence over zone settings and overrides their actions. For instance, if data binding is disabled via an FCK, then all associated URL actions are not consulted.

Summary

IE as a web browser has changed significantly from its inception, in the same way that the Web and its usage have evolved. IE 8 lives in a world where web applications have been stretched farther than was even imaginable 15 years ago when the first version of IE was released; the length and scope of this chapter reflects that well.

Beyond the browser frame, IE is a broad and deep platform that provides a wide range of functionality to applications beyond traditional HTML and CSS. In the following chapters, I will go deep into a number of these topics and provide you with the concise information and practical examples required to build great web and desktop applications. Let the journey begin!

CHAPTER 2

■ ■ ■

Interoperability and Compatibility

Web development is hard. An increasingly broad set of major browsers coupled with millions of configurations and over a billion Internet users has redefined the web development process as a whole. Web developers and browser vendors have attempted to rein in the chaos with modernized web standards such as HTML 4.01, HTML 5, CSS 2.1, and CSS 3. IE 8 includes better support for widely adopted web standards than its prior versions, in many (but not all) cases allowing developers to write one page that works in multiple browsers. In this chapter, I cover those standards and interoperability improvements in IE, detail compatibility features, and ways to handle the oftentimes competing forces between standards and compatibility.

Standards Support and Interoperability

The "standards by default" philosophy expressed by the IE development team throughout the IE 8 release cycle points toward a new product goal of wide-reaching standards support. Notably, IE 8 provides full support for the CSS 2.1 specification and introduces support for new features specified in stable areas of the HTML 5 specification. This section highlights the improvements in IE 8 since the IE 7 time frame, and provides a supportability baseline for developers looking to create interoperable web applications.

HTML 4.01, HTML 5, and DOM Spec Support Improvements

IE 8 introduces a number of improvements in its support of the HTML 4.01 standard; it is the most used and recognized document markup language on the Web today. Using IE 7 as a base, IE 8 offers the following enhancements and fixes to its implementation of the HTML 4.01 specification:

- `<p>` **element closure**: Paragraph elements (`<p>`) are automatically closed whenever one of the following tags precedes its closing tag or its closing tag is not present: `<table>`, `<form>`, `<noframes>`, and `<noscript>`.
- `<object>` **fallback**: When IE fails to load a resource from an `<object>` tag, IE will "fall back" by displaying the content contained within that tag.
- `<object>` **as image**: When IE encounters an `<object>` tag that refers to an image resource, it will render that image as if it were embedded in an `<img>` tag. In prior versions, IE would display an image resource through this tag, but would not offer proper resizing or borders, and would in some cases display scrollbars.

The HTML 5 and various DOM specs from the W3C offer web developers a rich set of tools and events to enhance web pages and increase productivity. IE 8 implements a few portions of these specs already implemented by other browsers:

- **Ajax hash navigation**: Hash-based page navigations (where only the fragment component of the URL changes) are now stored as navigation events. This means users can use the back and forward buttons to "navigate" between states of an Ajax application. This includes support of the `onhashchange` DOM event.
- **DOM storage**: Web applications can access a new storage object to persist data and settings on a user's machine. The `window.sessionStorage` and `window.localStorage` objects offer applications up to 10MB of local storage space for this data.
- **Cross-document messaging**: This enhancement introduces a new communication structure for `<iframe>`-based documents within a browser window, even when the documents originate from different domains. These documents can now use the `postMessage` API to ensure that cross-document data transfers are mutually agreed upon, providing extra protection to users.
- **Online/offline events**: The `onoffline` and `ononline` events can now be used to detect loss and restoration of network connectivity. Using popular Ajax techniques combined with DOM storage, applications can function even while offline.
- CSS 2.1 and CSS 3 Support Improvements

IE 8 provides full support for the CSS 2.1 specification, a widely used standard for defining document styles and building rich web user interfaces. Table 2–1 describes the properties that have been changed or added since IE 7's CSS 2.1 support:

Table 2–1. *CSS 2.1 Improvements from IE 7 to IE 8*

CSS 2.1 Property Set	New and Fully Supported Properties for IE 8
@ rules	@page
Border and layout	border-collapse, border-spacing, border-style, caption-side, empty-cells
Color and background	background-position
Keywords	inherit
Font and text	font-weight, white-space, word-spacing
Functions	counter(), attr()
Generated content	content, counter-increment, counter-reset, quotes
Lists	list-style-type
Positioning	bottom, display, left, right, top, z-index
Printing	orphans, page-break-inside, widows
Pseudoclasses	:active, :focus, :lang(), @page :first, @page :left, @page :right
Pseudoelements	:after, :before
User interface	outline, outline-color, outline-style, outline-width

IE 8 also offers limited support for CSS 3 property sets. CSS 3 extends and enhances CSS 2.1 functionality and offers a richer set of controls over styling and display of documents across a wide range of devices. IE 8 implements the CSS 3 properties shown in Table 2–2.

Table 2–2. *Available CSS 3 Features in IE 8*

CSS 3 Property Set	Support Level	Properties
@ rules	Partial	`@font-face`
Attribute selectors	Full	`Namespaced (ns|attr), Prefix [^=], Substring [*=], Suffix [$=]`
Combinators	Full	`General Sibling (~)`
Font and text	Partial	`ruby-align, ruby-overhang, ruby-position, text-align-last, text-justify, text-overflow, word-break, word-wrap, writing-mode`
Positioning	Partial	`overflow-x, overflow-y`
User interface	Partial	`box-sizing`

Document Modes and Versioning

Not all web pages were designed for the latest web standards, and many implement IE-specific functionality that was broken by IE 8's migration toward interoperability. In this section I describe compatibility features that web applications can utilize to get downlevel IE functionality, allowing developers of those applications to migrate toward standards-based implementations in the time frame of their choosing.

Quirks Mode, Document Modes, and X-UA-Compatible

Markup interpretation changes between web browser versions has occurred since the creation of browsers and web standards themselves. In the aftermath of the first browser wars between IE 4 and Netscape 4, newer browsers were left to cope with a web landscape filled with differing interpretations of what markup and styles were (caused by the competing implementations of browsers in the late 1990s). Without a way to tell what a page was doing and why, further modernization of standards would have been stifled due to the fact that existing pages relied heavily on old behavior. The `DOCTYPE` header was created as a result, allowing web developers to "tell" browsers what standards and implementations pages were originally created for.

This was only a temporary fix. In the mid-2000s, three major events happened: the number of widely used web browsers significantly increased, developers started building more complex web applications, and the push for interoperability and standards among browser vendors strengthened. Newer browsers on the scene, such as Safari and Firefox, adhered more closely to newer standards because of their relatively young age; IE, on the other hand, was left behind supporting legacy and enterprise applications that relied on older standards. IE 8 was the browser's first major attempt at catching up to these newer standards, and just like in the 1990s, the problem of what to do with legacy pages arose.

IE 8 added *document modes* as a second set of directives that developers can use to tell IE how to handle legacy web pages. They can be specified through the `X-UA-Compatible` HTTP response header or corresponding <meta> tag. DOCTYPEs, by default, are not honored, but developers can opt into using this older versioning model.

Document Modes

Document modes are directives that tell IE what legacy compatibility measures, if any, should be applied. Given the functionality changes made in IE's page display and level of standards support since IE 6, many applications were written to target older releases rather than web standards. While standards mode rendering is "on by default" in IE 8 and higher, IE offers a number of modes that pages can opt into, allowing them to be parsed and displayed in a way that they were designed for.

IE 8 includes support for a number of document modes, including Quirks mode (behavior similar to IE 5). These modes aim to emulate targeted IE versions, and each has a different level of DOCTYPE support (see Table 2–3).

Table 2–3. *Available Document Modes in IE 8*

Document Mode	Emulates	Header Value	Definition
Quirks mode	IE 5.0	`IE=5`	Displays a page based on the DOCTYPE specified. This behavior emulates that of IE 5.0.
IE 7 Standards mode	IE 7.0	`IE=7`	Displays a page using IE 7's interpretation of web standards. DOCTYPE is ignored.
IE 8 Standards mode	IE 8.0	`IE=8`	Displays a page using IE 8's interpretation of web standards. DOCTYPE is ignored.
IE 7 Emulation mode	IE 7.0	`IE=EmulateIE7`	Displays a page as if it were run in IE 7 Standards mode, but honors any DOCTYPE specified.
IE 8 Emulation mode	IE 8.0	`IE=EmulateIE8`	Displays a page as if it were run in IE 8 Standards mode, but honors any DOCTYPE specified.
Edge mode	(Latest)	`IE=edge`	Always opts into the most current standards interpretation of an IE version (e.g., IE 9 Standards mode on IE 9).

The header value associated with each document mode is used by web pages to target a specific document mode. I discuss how to use these values in the following sections.

Targeting Quirks Mode and Document Modes in Markup

Web pages can opt into a specific mode by using the X-UA-Compatible <meta> tag within a page's <head> element. Listing 2–1 uses the <meta> tag to inform IE that a page should be loaded in IE 7 Emulation mode (IE=EmulateIE7).

Listing 2–1. *HTML <meta> Compatibility Header Example*

```
<!--  Load page in IE7 Emulation Mode -->
<meta http-equiv="X-UA-Compatible" content="IE=EmulateIE7">
```

Older pages that wish to use older interpretations of standards can use a DOCTYPE header and <meta> tag to inform IE of this decision. Listing 2–2 shows a page that uses the Loose HTML 4.0 specification and that wishes to be displayed in Quirks (IE 5) mode.

Listing 2–2. DOCTYPE and Corresponding X-UA-Compatible <meta> Tag

```
<!DOCTYPE HTML PUBLIC "-//W3C//DTD HTML 4.0 Transitional//EN"
    "http://www.w3.org/TR/html4/loose.dtd">
<html>
   <head>
   <!--  Load page in IE5 (Quirks) Mode -->
   <meta http-equiv="X-UA-Compatible" content="IE=5">
```

Targeting Document Modes from the Server Side

Specifying a document mode using the `X-UA-Compatible` `<meta>` tag is straightforward, but it doesn't fit all scenarios. Large web sites and content management systems (CMSs) can have thousands of web pages, and some servers can host thousands of web sites. Adding the `<meta>` tag to *every* page might not make sense for these types of web sites and hosting constructs.

Developers that wish to apply an IE mode across a web server or web site can do so by adding a new HTTP header to any web server configuration. The header name is `X-UA-Compatible`, and its associated value represents the desired mode of pages hosted within that server configuration. Not only does this apply settings server-wide, it actually causes a bit of a performance gain over the `META` tag (since IE knows the mode before parsing the page rather than afterward).

Adding the X-UA-Compatible Header to IIS

Developers can add the `X-UA-Compatible` header to IIS through Internet Information Services (IIS) Manager (found in Control Panel ➤ Administrative Tools). The HTTP Response Headers configuration, found in global settings or in specific sites, contains a list of response headers sent for every page request. The compatibility header is added through the Add dialog on this configuration page, as shown in Figure 2–1.

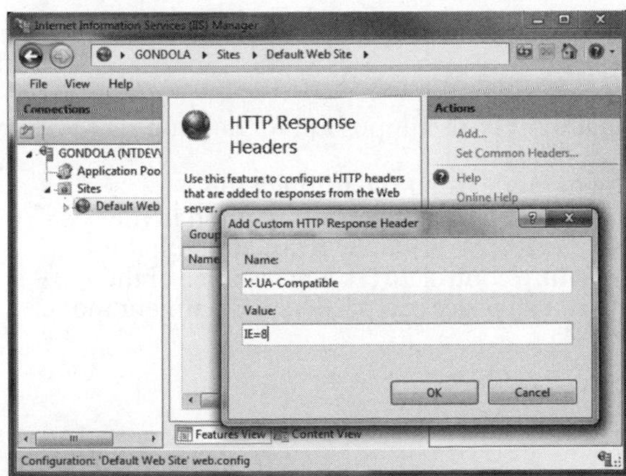

Figure 2–1. Adding the X-UA-Compatible header to an IIS server configuration

This change can be made through the IIS 7 configuration file as well. Developers can add the `<add>` tag in the `<customHeaders>` portion of a `.config` file in `%System32%/inetsev/config` (see Listing 2–3).

Listing 2–3. Adding the X-UA-Compatible HTTP Header to IIS 7 Config XML

```
<?xml version="1.0" encoding="utf-8"?>
...
<configuration> ...a
   <system.webServer> ...
      <httpProtocol> ...
         <customHeaders> ...
            <add name="X-UA-Compatible" value="IE=EmulateIE7" />
```

Adding the X-UA-Compatible Header to Apache

Apache allows custom headers in its global context or within Configuration in its `httpd.conf` configuration file. As in IIS, the `X-UA-Compatible` header can be added to this configuration, allowing developers or server administrators to run a whole site or server in a certain IE mode. Before adding the header, an Apache configuration must load the `mod_headers` module. Once in place, the `Header set` command can be used to indicate the desired IE mode (see Listing 2–4).

Listing 2–4. Adding a Global Header for X-UA-Compatible

```
Header set X-UA-Compatible “IE=EmulateIE7”
```

The previous example shows how to set `X-UA-Compatible` globally. Most complex Apache configurations are set to host multiple web sites using Apache’s Configuration tags. Instead of applying a header globally, developers and administrators can place it within directives like `<Directory>`, `<Files>`, `<Location>`, and `<VirtualHost>` to limit the scope of a header’s application (see Listing 2–5).

Listing 2–5. Adding a Configuration-Based Header for X-UA-Compatible

```
<Directory /var/www/httpd/website>
   Header set X-UA-Compatible “IE=EmulateIE7”
</Directory>
```

Feature Controls for Document Modes

Web sites aren’t the only applications that use IE. Compatibility is also important for desktop applications hosting the WebBrowser control.

Applications wishing to opt into a particular document mode can do so through the `FEATURE_BROWSER_EMULATION` feature control key for a specific process file name. It is found in the `SOFTWARE\Microsoft\Internet Explorer\Main\FeatureControl` key and can be placed in both the `HKEY_LOCAL_MACHINE` and `HKEY_CURRENT_USER` hives. This feature control forces any instance of the WebBrowser control loaded within that process space to run all pages in a particular document mode. The available modes for applications are listed in Table 2–4.

Table 2–4. Feature Control Keys for Compatibility Modes

Compatibility Mode	Feature Control Key	Value (DWORD)
IE 7 Standards mode + DOCTYPE	FEATURE_BROWSER_EMULATION	7000 (0x1B58)
IE 8 Standards mode + DOCTYPE	FEATURE_BROWSER_EMULATION	8000 (0x1F40)
IE 8 Standards mode	FEATURE_BROWSER_EMULATION	8888 (0x22B8)

IE 8 and IE 7 Standards modes are the same modes used within the IE browser. "Forced" IE 8 Standards mode is the same as IE 8 Standards mode except for the fact that DOCTYPE directives that would force Quirks rendering are ignored.

Differences Between IE 7 Standards Mode and True IE 7

Features in IE 8's IE 7 Standards mode were designed to closely mimic the behavior found on pages loaded in IE 7. The rearchitecture of IE 8 in terms of browser interoperability caused a few compatibility breaks that could lead to errors in web applications built for IE 7 and using the IE 7 Standards mode equivalent in IE 8 (see Table 2–5).

Table 2–5. *Differences Between True IE 7 Rendering and IE 8's IE 7 Standards Mode*

Affected Area	IE 7	IE 8's IE 7 Standards Mode	Workaround
Attribute ordering	Item indices of an object's attribute collection were consistently correlated to certain named attributes.	Item indices of an object's attribute collection may not correlate to a specific attribute.	Access object attributes by name; replace instances where an object attribute collection is accessed through array indices.
CSS exception handling	Exceptions were thrown when accessing an invalid CSS object property.	No exceptions are thrown when accessing an invalid CSS object property.	Don't rely on invalid CSS accesses to throw exceptions; only use valid properties from markup and script.

Compatibility View

Compatibility View is a mechanism for displaying web sites designed for older versions of IE without hindering IE's long-term adoption of interoperable web standards. In short, it lets IE move forward without "breaking the Web," as the IE team has stated. Compatibility View is built upon a few basic tenets:

- By default, all web pages run in IE 8 Standards mode ("standards by default").
- Pages loaded through Compatibility View are run in IE 7 Standards mode.
- When loading pages in Compatibility View, the User Agent string and conditional comments indicate the browser is IE 7.
- Compatibility View is applied to an entire domain, including subdomains.

Unless a page has explicitly defined its document mode through the `X-UA-Compatible` `<meta>` tag or HTTP header, a web page will be displayed in Compatibility View if one of the following is true:

- Its domain is present in the user's Compatibility View settings list (added by clicking the Compatibility View button or though manual insertion in Compatibility View Settings)
- Its domain is present in the Compatibility View Group Policy key

- Its domain is present in the Microsoft Compatibility View List
- Its domain is in the Intranet zone, and Compatibility View is enabled for all intranet sites
- Compatibility View is turned on for all web sites

The Microsoft Compatibility View List

At the time of IE 8's release, many commonly used web sites were broken when run in IE 8 Standards mode. Microsoft believed that this would prevent users from everyday browsing once IE 8 was installed on their systems. The Microsoft Compatibility View List was created to mitigate this scenario; this list contains the domains of popular web sites that render better in IE 7 Compatibility mode. Any domain on this list is loaded in Compatibility View until the site owner takes steps to ensure compatibility with IE 8 and/or requests removal.

Microsoft first released the Compatibility View List to users during the IE 8 Release Candidate. This list is sent using Windows Update, and can be downloaded separately through the Microsoft Download Center. Users wishing to download the list must opt into receiving and installing it. Developers should not depend on users doing so, as not all will install the list.

The list itself is an XML document implementing the `ie8compatlistdescription` namespace. Domains placed on the list are stored as strings within `<domain>` tags. The XML document is contained in an IE resource library (`res://iecompat.dll/iecompatdata.xml`) (Listing 2–6).

Listing 2–6. *Selection of Domains from the Compatibility View List (As of October 2009)*

```
<?xml version="1.0" encoding="utf-8" ?>
<ie8compatlistdescription
   xmlns="http://www.microsoft.com/schemas/ie8compatlistdescription/1.0">
   ...
   <domain>americanexpress.com</domain>
   <domain>americangreetings.com</domain>
   <domain>amtrak.com</domain>
   ...
</ie8compatlistdescription>
```

Controlling Compatibility Settings

Domains displayed in Compatibility View can be controlled by users and developers through a number of exposed entry points. This feature is most accessible through the Compatibility View button, a toggle button displayed in the address bar when the feature is available (see Figure 2–2). Compatibility View can be switched on and off for any domain by clicking this button; this event will cause a domain to refresh into the desired state.

Figure 2–2. *Compatibility View button in the IE address bar*

The Compatibility View button will always show up for a web page unless one or more of the following criteria are met:

- The page is an IE resource file (the res:// protocol).
- The page uses the X-UA-Compatible <meta> tag or HTTP header.
- The page resides on the intranet and IE is set to use Compatibility View on all intranet sites.
- IE is set to view all pages in Compatibility View.
- The page's domain is included in the Microsoft Compatibility View List.
- The Compatibility View itself or the button is turned off through the registry or Group Policy.

Developers who do not want this button to display can use the X-UA-Compatible header to explicitly define their page's document mode.

The Compatibility View Settings dialog (Figure 2–3) provides users with control over the use of the Compatibility View feature. Users can manually add and remove entries from this list, control usage of the Microsoft Compatibility View List, and apply Compatibility View throughout the intranet or all web sites.

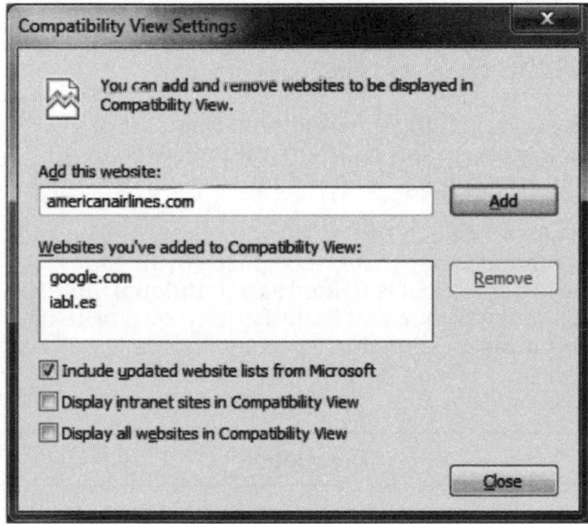

Figure 2–3. *Compatibility View Settings dialog*

Domains added through the Compatibility View Settings dialog are stored in a registry entry constructed as a proprietary binary blob with no public API. Developers wishing to add to this list can do so using the Group Policy key found at `HKEY_CURRENT_USER\Software\Policies\Microsoft\Internet Explorer\BrowserEmulation\PolicyList`. A domain to be included in the list must be a `REG_SZ` string value whose value and data are equal, and must store the domain to be added (e.g., `REG_SZ "mydomain.com"="mydomain.com"`). System administrators can use the same key through their Group Policy Administration applications to apply a preselected list to networked machines.

Version Targeting

Not every page needs to target a document mode to mimic downlevel versions of IE. As developers test their web applications on new IE releases, some may find that their code works properly except in a few areas of script and markup. These testing scenarios also apply to functionality differences between IE and other browsers; portions of code may work in other browsers but not in IE.

Version targeting allows developers to customize sections of script or markup for specific browsers or browser versions. Instead of creating new web pages or web applications for each different scenario, developers can select and target code sections to specific scenarios.

Version Targeting Using Conditional Comments

Markup languages such as HTML and XML aren't designed for functional or conditional programming—their job is to define a document construct. This leads to problems when multiple versions of a markup language exist in the wild; documents would have to exist for every supported version of the markup language itself to provide full compatibility. IE introduced *conditional comments* in order to provide document compatibility within HTML.

Conditional comments are specially formatted HTML comments that IE uses to allow for targeted markup based on conditional logic. Developers wishing to target HTML content toward one or more specific versions of IE and/or non-IE browsers can wrap markup with these comments. When parsing a web page, IE will read any conditional comments present on a page and either use or ignore encapsulated markup based on the condition present.

Every conditional comment begins with an expression describing the condition. Contents of the comment are encapsulated in brackets, and within those brackets lies the `if` keyword followed by an expression. Any HTML to be used conditionally is placed after this tag, followed by a closing comment containing the `endif` keyword in brackets.

There are two main types of conditional comments (described in Table 2–6): *downlevel hidden* and *downlevel revealed.* A downlevel-hidden conditional comment is one that is recognized by IE and ignored by other browsers; the comment starts and ends with `--`, so it is treated as a traditional multiline markup comment. A downlevel-revealed conditional comment is one that is always used by non-IE browsers, but only used by IE versions that meet the conditional expression.

Table 2–6. *Types of Conditional Comments*

Type	Construct	Description
Downlevel hidden	`<!--[if expression]> HTML <![endif]-->`	Content is recognized only by IE versions that match the expression. It is ignored by non-IE browsers.
Downlevel revealed	`<![if expression]> HTML <![endif]>`	Content is recognized by non-IE browsers. Only IE versions matching the expression use enclosed content.

The combination of downlevel-hidden and downlevel-revealed conditional comments allow for one web application to provide both compatible and interoperable markup without the need to build separate applications or use script.

Expressions are conditional statements that consist of features, operators, and values. Features are known product names (e.g., IE and WindowsEdition) or custom feature names defined in the registry (see Table 2–7).

***Table 2–7.** Features for Conditional Commenting*

Feature	Description	Example
IE	Internet Explorer	<!--[if IE 8]>
WindowsEdition	Windows product type from the GetProductInfo() API's pdwReturnedProductType	<!--[if WindowsEdition 1]>
(Custom)	Custom feature defined in a REG_SZ value and placed in the Version Vector registry key located at HKEY_LOCAL_MACHINE\Software\Microsoft\Internet Explorer\Version Vector	<!--[if MyExtension gte 5]>

Operators are logic representations used to compare a value to a feature. Values are numerical representations of a feature version, stored as floats. (See Table 2–8.)

***Table 2–8.** Operators for Conditional Commenting*

<table>
<tr><th>Operator</th><th>Description</th><th>Example</th></tr>
<tr><td>(Empty)</td><td>Equal to or exists</td><td><!--[if IE]></td></tr>
<tr><td>!</td><td>Not equal to</td><td><!--[if ! IE 8]></td></tr>
<tr><td>lt</td><td>Less than</td><td><!--[if lt IE 8]></td></tr>
<tr><td>lte</td><td>Less than or equal to</td><td><!--[if lte IE 8]></td></tr>
<tr><td>gt</td><td>Greater than</td><td><!--[if gt IE 8]></td></tr>
<tr><td>gte</td><td>Greater than or equal to</td><td><!--[if gte IE 8]></td></tr>
<tr><td>&</td><td>And</td><td><!--[if (gte IE 5)&(lt IE 8)]></td></tr>
<tr><td>|</td><td>Or</td><td><!--[if (IE 8)|(gte WindowsEdition 4)]></td></tr>
</table>

An expression can be defined either using a feature alone or as an ordered group of feature, operation, and value; feature-only expressions evaluate to true or false based on the feature's presence. Much like conditionals in traditional programming languages, multiple expressions can be grouped together using parentheses.

Conditional comments can be used anywhere within an HTML document. Common use cases include offering different stylesheets for specific IE versions and displaying messages to users of specific browsers. In the example in Listing 2–7, a web page serves two different CSS files to users: one that uses standards-based CSS that is interoperable in newer browsers such as IE 8 and Firefox 3.5, and another that offers a stylesheet focused on downlevel compatibility with older versions of IE.

Listing 2–7. *Using Conditional Comments to Target Different IE Versions and Browsers*

```
<head>
   <title>Compatible and Interoperable!</title>
   <meta http-equiv="X-UA-Compatible" content="IE=8" />
   <![if gte IE 8]>
      <link rel="stylesheet" type="text/css" href="interoperable.css" />
   <![endif]>
   <!--[if IE 7]>
      <link rel="stylesheet" type="text/css" href="legacyIE.css" />
   <![endif]-->
</head>
```

Users browsing this example web site with IE 7 or IE 6 would be served `legacyIE.css`. All other users (e.g., those running IE 8, Firefox 3.5, and Safari 4) would see styles that were generated from `interoperable.css`.

Just like expressions, conditional comments can be nested. Nested comments are used for comparing multiple features and providing combinatorial markup paths. The sample in Listing 2–8 displays a different messages for users that are running IE 8 on Windows Ultimate, those running IE 8 on other Windows editions, and those users not running IE 8 at all.

Listing 2–8. *Nesting Conditional Comments*

```
<body>
   <!--[if gte IE 8]>
      <![if WindowsEdition 1]>
         <b>You're running IE8+ on Windows Ultimate Edition!</b>
      <![endif]>
      <![if ! WindowsEdition 1]>
         <b>You're running IE8+, but NOT on Windows Ultimate Edition!</b>
      <![endif]>
   <![endif]-->
   <![if ! IE 8]>
      <b>You're not running IE 8 :(</b>
   <![endif]>
</body>
```

User Agent String Sniffing Using JavaScript

User Agent (UA) string sniffing is an unreliable (but often used) mechanism for delivering content for specific browsers, browser versions, or system configurations. Sniffing consists of reading and interpreting the UA string sent by a browser and serving content based on that interpretation. The concept itself is flawed for a few reasons: there are thousands of different configurations (and thus as many UA strings), these strings can be changed or spoofed by any application or person requesting a page, and they are very dynamic between browsers and even between browser versions. IE 8, for instance, even changes the UA string when running in Compatibility View vs. IE 8 Standards mode! If used improperly, the wrong content can be served to the wrong set of users. UA string sniffing should only be used in cases where it is absolutely necessary.

That said, developers can target certain portions of JavaScript to address compatibility issues between IE versions and interoperability issues among all browsers. Version targeting in JavaScript starts with getting the current browser type and version from the UA string. Regular expressions or string-parsing methods can be used to grab the name and version of the browser viewing a page.

In Listing 2–9, the `GetIEVersion()` function provides information on the version of IE the page is loaded in. If the page is loaded in IE and there is a version number present, the function returns the version number. If the browser is not IE or there is no version number, the function returns zero.

Listing 2–9. *Determining the IE Version Using JavaScript Regular Expressions*

```
<script language="javascript" type="text/javascript">
   function GetIEVersion() {
      if (navigator.appName == "Microsoft Internet Explorer") {
         var regEx = new RegExp("MSIE ([0-9]+[\.0-9]*)");
         if (regEx.exec(navigator.userAgent) != null)
            return parseFloat(RegExp.$1);
      }
      else return 0;
   }
</script>
```

Separate code paths can be created to target specific browsers and versions once that data can be determined. The `GetIEVersion()` function from the previous example returns this exact data. In the next sample, the result of calling that function is saved to the variable `ieVersion`. Conditional statements using that variable are created to create separate script paths for different browser and version requirements; in Listing 2–10, there is one path for IE versions before IE 8, and another for IE 8 and all other browsers.

Listing 2–10. *Creating Targeted Code Paths in JavaScript for Compatibility Scenarios*

```
<script language="JavaScript" type="text/javascript">
   var ieVersion = GetIEVersion();
   if(ieVersion > 0 && ieVersion < 8) {
      // Place downlevel IE-compatible code here
      // (IE6, IE7, etc.)
   }
   else {
      // Place interoperable browser code here
      // (IE8, FF3, Chrome 2, etc.)
   }
</script>
```

Targeted script can be as granular as or as broad as required by compatibility and interoperability goals. In the preceding example, code separation using browsers and versioning creates a compatibility path (IE versions before IE 8) to address downlevel issues, and an interoperability path (IE 8 and other browsers) to take advantage of cross-browser web standards. Developers interested in expanding `GetIEVersion()` can do so by parsing the UA string for other browsers and applying the same logic to target code to those versions.

Compatibility View and the UA String

The UA string can be used to determine whether users are accessing web pages in Compatibility View or the most current IE standards mode. The UA strings in Listings 2–11 and 2–12 are generated by IE 8 and IE 8 with Compatibility View, respectively.

Listing 2–11. UA String for IE 8 Running Normally

```
User-Agent: Mozilla/4.0 (compatible; MSIE 8.0; Windows NT 6.0; Trident/4.0;)
```

Listing 2–12. UA String for IE 8 Running in Compatibility View

```
User-Agent: Mozilla/4.0 (compatible; MSIE 7.0; Windows NT 6.0; Trident/4.0;)
```

While pages loaded in Compatibility View report `MSIE 7.0` to be the current browser, the string still reports the rendering and layout engine to be `Trident/4.0`. Thus, developers wishing to gauge user access in IE 8 and compare total views to those using Compatibility View can do so. This metric allows developers to assess the impact and scope of Compatibility View on their application and, if necessary, plan to update them.

To reiterate, Compatibility View and the Microsoft Compatibility List are not designed to be long-term solutions for IE or for web pages. Developers should modify their web applications to migrate toward a more standards-based implementation for handling markup and script whenever possible.

The Web Developer's Dilemma

Compatibility and interoperability are in some cases mutually exclusive; getting the best of both worlds can be a challenge. The "innovator's dilemma," slightly modified for context, is quite relevant in relation to these competing concepts: should developers focus on compatibility and use known products to lower cost and increase profit, or should they embrace disruptive technologies that over time could also lead to attractive cost and profit deltas? Many developers, project managers, and industry leaders are faced with this very question, and each has their own opinions on it. Here are a few ways developers can make intelligent decisions about what route to take and how to ensure that applications will survive the tests of time and economy:

- **Migrate intelligently**: Not every application needs to be migrated to use the latest and greatest web standards. This is especially true in certain enterprise situations, where migration could be costly; for example, many banks still use ages-old applications written in COBOL simply because they still just work. When considering possible routes to take with existing web applications, the costs and benefits of both compatibility and interoperability should be understood before changes are made.
- **Design with templates and frameworks in mind**: Model-View-Controller (MVC) is a great example of how applications and systems can be designed to handle change while minimizing cost. There are a vast number of template systems (often in the form of content management systems [CMSs]) that allow for clear separation between content and structure, allowing a web application to easily change over time. Web frameworks such as jQuery and Dojo offer similar benefits as well; they seek to encapsulate functionality that allows web sites to remain both compatible and interoperable.
- **Develop against an appropriate standards baseline**: HTML 5 is great, and it's packed full of awesome features. For a web site whose user base is filled with IE 6 and IE 7 users, it's not so great. Developers should choose a baseline set of standards that aligns with the goals (business or otherwise) of a web application.

- **Use version targeting wisely**: Version targeting allows applications to remain compatible while pursuing a more interoperable design approach. Web applications using this method can serve content based on context, separate old code from new, and delimit functionality in a way that allows for easy deprecation over time. As discussed in this chapter, IE offers conditional comments that enable this behavior for markup. Outside of IE, developers can target specific browsers or versions through JavaScript and the UA string.
- ***Realistically* push modern browsers**: The time for IE 6 has long past . . . for those who use it without any specific reason. In some cases, there's a legitimate business reason to use an older browser. Developers should recognize that older browsers will represent a percentage of the market share for some time to come, and some may not have the luxury to ignore this constraint. While it's always an option to block users browsing to a site on IE 6, it might not be the best idea for a business that depends on their site to put food on employee's tables.

Clearly, this is not an all-encompassing list of things to consider when developing an application for compatibility and interoperability. Using web standards for the sake of web standards or staying compatible only to support a handful of users are not good reasons to make either decision. Consider the user base, purpose, intended platforms, and risk factors when deciding to develop for compatibility, interoperability, or some combination thereof.

Summary

I'll say it again: web development is hard. Those invested in web applications are in a constant struggle to deliver stellar functionality and meet design goals, all the while flying into a headwind of cost and effort caused by browser differences and endless compatibility scenarios. Web standards are helping to mitigate the problem, and IE 8's improved standards support can reduce the cost of developing sites that are compatible across modern browsers. IE 8 also offers a number of compatibility features that help ensure existing applications continue to work properly, giving you time to migrate applications to a standards-based model as needed.

CHAPTER 3

■ ■ ■

Enriching Web Applications with AJAX and JSON

The XMLHttpPRequest object was introduced IE5 as a way for web applications to download content outside of traditional page navigations. It was quickly adopted by browser vendors and web developers in the its use in conjunction with markup and script was given the term AJAX (Asynchronous JavaScript and XML). Since then, the XMLHttpRequest object and AJAX have become synonymous with dynamic websites, allowing websites to offer functionality and feature sets that were only available in desktop applications.

In this chapter I walk through new and updated features in Internet Explorer that allow you to enhance and streamline your dynamic web applications. I discuss compatibility and interoperability scenarios, highlight IE product changes made in IE that may affect your existing applications, and provide useful and detailed examples that demonstrate how to integrate your website with IE's updated AJAX feature set.

The XMLHttpRequest Object

The XMLHttpRequest object enables web applications to communicate with web servers asynchronously, independent of page navigations; this object is arguably the heart of the AJAX programming model. It was first released as an ActiveX control in the year 2000 as a way for Microsoft Outlook Web Access (the online counterpart to the Microsoft Office Outlook application) to send and receive email data without having to reload a whole webpage. A wide variety of websites have since adopted the object for the same purpose.

The XMLHTTP Library and XMLHttpRequest Object

The Microsoft XML Core Services Library (MSXML) is a set of interfaces that allow applications and scripting languages to easily read and write XML. XMLHTTP is the part of MSXML that contains the XMLHttpRequest object. It facilitates synchronous and asynchronous communication between an application and a remote server (however, synchronous calls should be avoided since they cause applications to hang until a response is received). XMLHTTP is exposed in two ways: through the IXMLHttpRequest interface, accessible to applications wishing to implement or extend the base functionality of this object, or with the XMLHttpRequest ActiveX control, built for use in OLE applications.

Websites running in Internet Explorer 5 and 6 can access the XMLHttpRequest object via this ActiveX control.

Listing 3-1. *Using the XMLHttpRequest ActiveX Object in JavaScript*

```
<html>
   <head>
      <title>Using JavaScript</title>
   </head>
   <body>
      <h3>XMLHttpRequest object loaded? <span id="spanXhrJS">No</span></h3>
      <script type="text/javascript">
         try {

            //  Create a new XMLHttpRequest object and send a GET
            //  request to http://examples.proiedev.com
            var xmlHttp = new ActiveXObject("Microsoft.XMLHTTP");
            xmlHttp.open("get", "http://examples.proiedev.com", true);

            //  Indicate success if the script made it this far
            setText(document.getElementById("spanXhrJS"), "Yes");

         } catch(e) { }

         //  Set element text (cross-browser innerText/textContent)
         function setText(element, text) {
            try {
               if(typeof element.textContent == typeof undefined)
                  element.innerText = text;
               else element.textContent = text;
            } catch(e) { }
         }

      </script>
   </body>
</html>
```

Listing 3-1 demonstrates some JavaScript that loads a new instance of the XMLHTTP library into a variable; the xmlHttp variable is set to grab a new object associated with the "Microsoft.XMLHTTP" ProgID (Programmatic Identifier). IE instantiates the object and sets the variable to an XMLHttpObject instance. This object is not limited to JavaScript.

Any language that supports loading OLE controls, such as VBScript, can use this object. Listing 3-2 demonstrates VBScript code that creates an instance of XMLHttpRequest.

Listing 3-2. *Using the XMLHttpRequest ActiveX Object in VBScript*

```
<html>
   <head>
      <title>Using VBScript</title>
   </head>
   <body>
      <h3>XMLHttpRequest object loaded? <span id="spanXhrVB">No</span></h3>
      <script type="text/vbscript">

         ''  Create a new XMLHttpRequest object
         Set xmlHttp = CreateObject("Microsoft.XmlHttp")
```

```
        ''  Send a GET request to http://examples.proiedev.com
        If Err = 0 Then xmlHttp.open "get", "http://examples.proiedev.com", TRUE

        ''  Indicate success if the script made it this far
        If Err = 0 Then document.getelementbyid("spanXhrVB").innerText = "Yes"

      </script>
   </body>
</html>
```

Native XMLHttpRequest

Internet Explorer 7 introduced a native version of the `XMLHttpRequest` object. This object is a wrapper around the original `XMLHttpRequest` ActiveX that allows JavaScript developers to write a single line of code to instantiate this object across all major browsers. It is only available to JavaScript running in Internet Explorer 7 and higher. Listing 3-3 demonstrates JavaScript that uses the native object instead of ActiveX to instantiate an `XMLHttpRequest` object.

Listing 3-3. *Using the native window.XMLHttpRequest Object in JavaScript*

```
<html>
   <head>
      <title>Native XMLHttpRequest</title>
   </head>
   <body>
      <h3>XMLHttpRequest object loaded? <span id="spanXhrJS">No</span></h3>
      <script type="text/javascript">
         try {

            //  Create a new XMLHttpRequest object and send a GET
            //  request to http://examples.proiedev.com
            var xmlHttp = new XMLHttpRequest();
            xmlHttp.open("get", "http://examples.proiedev.com", true);

            //  Indicate success if the script made it this far
            setText(document.getElementById("spanXhrJS"), "Yes");

         } catch(e) { }

         //  Set element text (cross-browser innerText/textContent)
         function setText(element, text) { /*...*/ }

      </script>
   </body>
</html>
```

Cross-Browser AJAX Compatibility

Although IE7 and above offer a native, cross-browser implementation of `XMLHttpRequest`, websites wishing to support IE6 users must load the ActiveX-based `XMLHTTP` object instead. Listing 3-4 demonstrates JavaScript that attempts to use the native XMLHttpRequest object and, if required, falls back to the ActiveX version. The example uses a cascade of conditionals and exception handling that loads either the native or the ActiveX version into the xhr depending on which is available. Since the native object is simply a wrapper around the ActiveX version, the available properties, methods, and events are the same on each.

Listing 3-4. *Cross-Browser XMLHttpRequest object instantiation*

```
<html>
   <head>
      <title>Cross-Browser AJAX Compatibility</title>
   </head>
   <body>
      <h3>Status of XmlHttpRequest object: <span id="status"></span></h3>
      <script type="text/javascript">

         //  Create a variable to hold the XMLHttpRequest object
         var xhr;

         //  Check to see if the native object exists
         if(window.XMLHttpRequest){
            xhr = new XMLHttpRequest();
            setText(document.getElementById("status"), "Created Native XHR.");
         }

         //  If no native object is found, check for the ActiveX object
         else if(window.ActiveXObject) {
            try {
               xhr = new ActiveXObject("Microsoft.XMLHTTP");
               setText(document.getElementById("status"), "Created ActiveX XHR.");
            } catch(e) {
               setText(document.getElementById("status"), "XHR not supported");
            }
         } else {
            //  Indicate failure to find any XHR object
            setText(document.getElementById("status"), "XHR not supported.");
         }

         //  Set element text (cross-browser innerText/textContent)
         function setText(element, text) { /*...*/ }

      </script>
   </body>
</html>
```

Most web developers will never need to write a script like this; frameworks like jQuery and Dojo abstract this logic and provide a single, cross-browser way of generating XMLHttpRequest objects.

Scripting and DOM Improvements

AJAX applications require a core set of JavaScript and DOM to functionality to deliver dynamic content and features. The next few sections highlight the most important updates to IE's JavaScript engine and object model and discuss how those changes may impact current and future websites.

Native JSON Support

JSON (JavaScript Object Notation) is a lightweight data exchange format, commonly used to pass data between web applications. Much like XML, it encapsulates and compartmentalizes data in a way that can be read, modified, and transferred. Many AJAX developers choose JSON because of its structure; it remains valid JavaScript notation in both serialized and deserialized forms.

Listing 3-5. *An customer record stored in JSON*

```
{
   "firstname"     : "Nick",
   "lastname"      : "Tierno",
   "address": {
      "street"     : "123 Euclid Avenue",
      "city"       : "Cleveland",
      "state"      : "OH",
      "postalCode" : 44106
   },
   "phone": [
      "+1 555 867 5309",
      "+1 555 TIERNOO"
   ]
}
```

Listing 3-5 demonstrates some JSON (in this case, a customer record). It can be interpreted as a JavaScript object literal containing types including `Array`, `String`, `Number`, and `Boolean`, or serialized and transferred as structured markup.

Conversion of a JSON object from a String to JavaScript is trivial with `eval()`; since serialized JSON remains valid JavaScript, this method can convert any valid JSON back into script. The simplicity of JSON conversion using `eval()` hides the fact that `eval()` can be *extremely* dangerous from a security standpoint; since the point of `eval()` is to execute a string as script, its use potentially opens websites to a host of script injection vulnerabilities. Aside from the security issues surrounding `eval()`, JavaScript itself does not provide sufficient built-in functionality to convert a JSON object *back* to a string (besides recursively walking the object).

■ **Note** eval() is dangerous—by definition, it is script injection. While it may be convenient to convert JSON strings into valid JavaScript with eval(), it will turn site security into Swiss cheese unless done properly. Do not use it unless you have to (or you're building a JSON library). Alternatively, use one of the safer options described below: IE's JSON object, JSON libraries, and general JavaScript frameworks that offer such functionality.

The security concerns around `eval()`-based deserialization and lack of good mechanisms for JSON serialization lead to the creation of JSON libraries. The best known (and arguably most optimal) one is json2 (http://link.proiedev.com/json2). Internet Explorer, in versions 8 and above, is host to a native JSON management; it is available to pages rendering in IE8 Standards Mode and above. The native JSON object allows web applications to convert objects to and from the JSON format just like JSON libraries, albeit in a faster and less memory-intensive way.

Objects

- `JSON` **object** - Top-level object that offers conversion methods for JSON objects and strings.
- **(supported objects)** - Boolean, String, Number, and Date JavaScript objects are given a new toJSON() method to convert them into serialized JSON.

Methods

- `(supported object).toJSON()` **method** - Converts supported types (Boolean, String, Number, and Date) to serialize those objects into valid JSON.
- `JSON.parse(source [, reviver])` **method** - Deserializes a JSON object source into a JavaScript array or relevant object. The reviver parameter accepts a callback method, and this callback is raised for each member of the new JSON object as it is converted. This allows for further parsing.
    - `reviver(key, value)` **callback method** - Returns a JavaScript object modified from an original key and value input. This object replaces the object normally returned by JSON.parse() for each member of the original string.
- `JSON.stringify(value [, replacer] [, space])` **method** - Seralizes an existing JavaScript object value into a string. The replacer parameter accepts a callback method, and this callback is raised for each member of the new JSON string as it is converted. This allows for further parsing. The space parameter specifies custom whitespace to be appended between serialization of each object member.
    - `replacer(key, value)` **callback method** - Returns a JavaScript string modified from an original key and value input. This string replaces the string normally returned by JSON.stringify() for each member from thesource array or object.

The structure of IE8's native JSON object was designed to mimic that of the json2 library; applications already incorporating json2 can take advantage of IE's built-in support with minimal code changes.

Listing 3-6 demonstrates IE's native JSON object by deserializing a JSON-formatted string to a JSON object and then re-serializing it back to a string.

Listing 3-6. *Converting between JSON strings and objects*

```
<html>
   <head>
      <title>Native JSON Support</title>
   </head>
   <body>
      <h3>Original String:</h3><span id="original"></span>
      <h3>Parsed JSON:</h3><span id="parsed"></span>
      <h3>Stringified JSON:</h3><span id="result"></span>
```

```
    <script type="text/javascript">

      //  Define a new serialized JSON object
      var contactStr = "{ \"firstname\" : \"Nick\", \"lastname\" : " +
                       "\"Tierno\", \"address\" : { \"street\" : \"123 Euclid " +
                       "Avenue\", \"city\" : \"Cleveland\", \"state\" : " +
                       "\"OH\", \"postalCode\" : 44106 }, \"phone\" : [ " +
                       "\"+1 555 867 5309\", \"+1 555 TIERNOO\" ] }";
      //  Write that string to the page
      setText(document.getElementById('original'), contactStr);

      //  Check if the JSON object exists
      if(window.JSON) {

         // Convert contactStr to a JSON JavaScript object
         var contactObjectJSON = JSON.parse(contactStr);
         var outputFromJSON = "Name: " + contactObjectJSON.firstname + " "
                            + contactObjectJSON.lastname + "\n" +
                            "Address: " + contactObjectJSON.address.street
                            + ", " + contactObjectJSON.address.city
                            + ", " + contactObjectJSON.address.state + " "
                            + contactObjectJSON.address.postalCode + "\n"
                            + "Phone: " + contactObjectJSON.phone[0] + " "
                            + contactObjectJSON["phone"][1];
         setText(document.getElementById('parsed'), outputFromJSON);

         // Convert contactJSON back to a string
         var contactStrRedux = JSON.stringify(contactObjectJSON);
         setText(document.getElementById('result'), contactStrRedux);

      //  Display an error message if the JSON object doesn't exist
      } else {
         setText(document.getElementById("parsed"),
            "Error: window.JSON object does not exist.");
         setText(document.getElementById("result"),
            "Error: window.JSON object does not exist.");
      }

      //  Set element text (cross-browser innerText/textContent)
      function setText(element, text) { /*...*/ }

    </script>
  </body>
</html>
```

The `contactStr` variable represents a string, perhaps received from an `onmessage` handler which fires when an `<iframe>` performs a `postMessage` call (discussed later). The `contactObjectJSON` variable represents a deserialized object output from `JSON.parse(contactStr)`; it is used to display the customer record. Finally, the result of a `JSON.stringify()` is set to the `contactStrRedux` string, which functionally matches the original string `contactStr`.

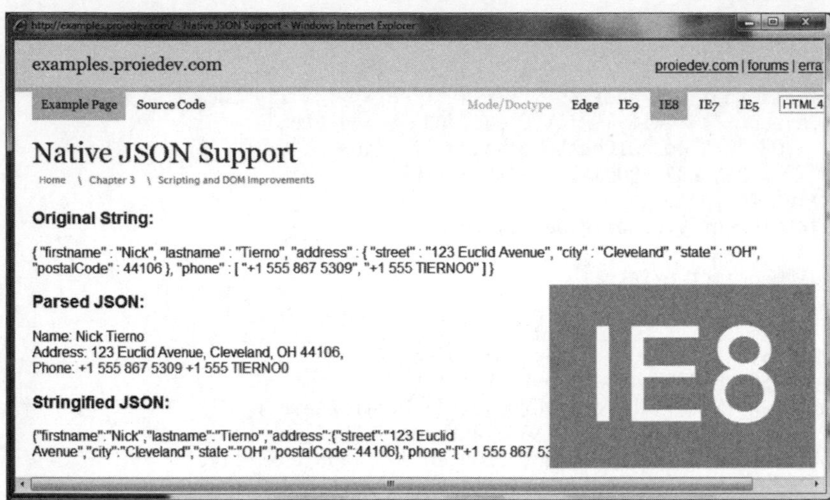

***Figure 3-1.** Webpage that demonstrates the JSON object and serialization/deserialization*

Figure 3-1 is the webpage from the sample code. The `contactStr` and `contactStrRedux` variables are displayed under the "Original String" and "Stringified JSON," respectively. "Parsed JSON" header is followed by data from the deserialized JSON object; this demonstrates that the deserialized `contactStr` can be accessed as any other JavaScript object or array once serialized.

String Sanitization with toStaticHTML

Websites that use JSON libraries or native JSON support are able to block the most trivial instances of malicious JavaScript from tainting potentially-untrusted JSON content even further. The security goodness that these features provide is lost once this content is used to write content to a webpage or transfer that content to another resource (for example, displaying content on a page using an `element` object's `innerHTML` property). IE8 includes a new object, `window.toStaticHTML`, as a second line of defense, allowing scripts to sanitize content before it is used in the context of a page.

Methods

- `toStaticHTML(html)` **object (constructor)** - Returns a sanitized version of the input `html` parameter by removing dynamic objects (certain elements and script) from it.

The code sample in Listing 3-7 uses the `toStaticHTML` object to clean up input coming from an `<input>` textbox. The page was constructed so that input from this object can inject script into the page (when the `sanitizeCheck` checkbox is left unchecked).

***Listing 3-7.** Sanitizing HTML content using toStaticHTML*

```
<html>
   <head>
      <title>Using toStaticHTML</title>
   </head>
```

```
  <body>
    <p>Type some input into the box below.  If "safely handle input" is checked,
    the output will be run through toStaticHTML (if availalable).  If it is
    not, the output will be set as the innerHTML of a div.
    <p><input type="text" id="userInput" name="userInput">
    <input type="checkbox" id="sanitizeCheck" name="sanitizeCheck" checked>
      Safely handle input?
    <button name="displayOutput" id="displayOutput" onclick="processUserInput();">
      Display Output</button>
    <h3>Output:</h3><div id="outputContainer"></div>
    <script type="text/javascript">
      function processUserInput() {

        //  Simulate some evil input, such as script injection
        var evilInput = document.getElementById("userInput").value;
        var sanitizeCheck = document.getElementById("sanitizeCheck").checked;
        var doSanitize = (sanitizeCheck == true) ? true : false;
        var sanitizedInput = "";

        //  Sanitize input text if box is checked
        if(doSanitize) {

          // If toStaticHTML is defined, use it (otherwise, escape)
          if(typeof toStaticHTML == "object") sanitizedInput = toStaticHTML(evilInput);
          else sanitizedInput = escape(evilInput);

          //  Write sanitized input to the webpage
          setText(document.getElementById("outputContainer"), sanitizedInput);

        }

        //  Otherwise, write raw HTML to document
        else document.getElementById("outputContainer").innerHTML = evilInput;

      }

      //  Set element text (cross-browser innerText/textContent)
      function setText(element, text) { /*...*/ }

    </script>
  </body>
</html>
```

The state of the sanitizeInput checkbox determines whether or not this script will clean user input. When sanitization is turned on, the script runs input through toStaticHTML before writing it to the page through the innerText property on the outputContainer element. When this object is not present, it escapes content with escape before writing it to innerText. When this checkbox is disabled, content in the <input> textbox is written to outputContainer through the innerHTML property; this simulates an unsafe use of input data.

Figure 3-2 shows the sample page running in IE8.

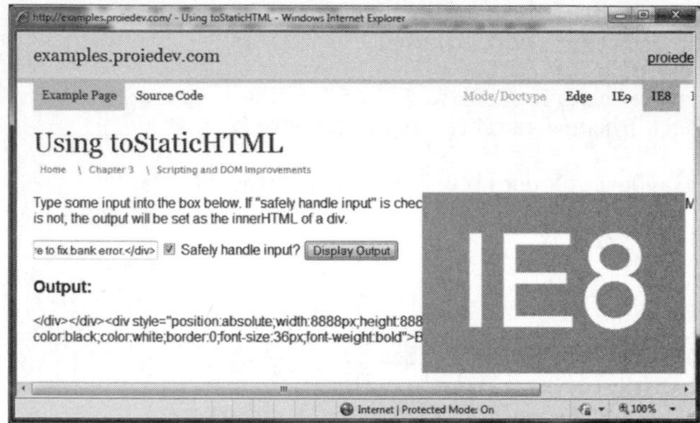

Figure 3-2. Webpage that sanitizes HTML using toStaticHtml()

In this case, the text in Listing 3-8 was passed into the box with sanitization enabled. Even though the input text contains HTML and JavaScript, that data is not added to the DOM nor executed; `toStaticHTML` escapes the content and removes script entries. It is shown as text on the page.

Listing 3-8. Sanitizing HTML content using toStaticHTML()

```
</div></div><div style="position:absolute;width:8888px;height:8888px;z-
index:99;padding:0;background-color:black;color:white;border:0;font-size:36px;font-
weight:bold;" onclick="javascript:window.location.href='http://www.bankofamerica.com'">Bank
error.  Click here to fix bank error.</div>
```

The screenshots in Figure 3-3 show the effect of this same input when written to the page without any sanitization and through the `innerHTML` property of `outputContainer`. In this case, a `<div>` with the text “Bank Error” is placed on top of other page elements. When clicked, this `<div>` launches `bankofamerica.com`; an attacker might do this to entice a user into entering their credentials.

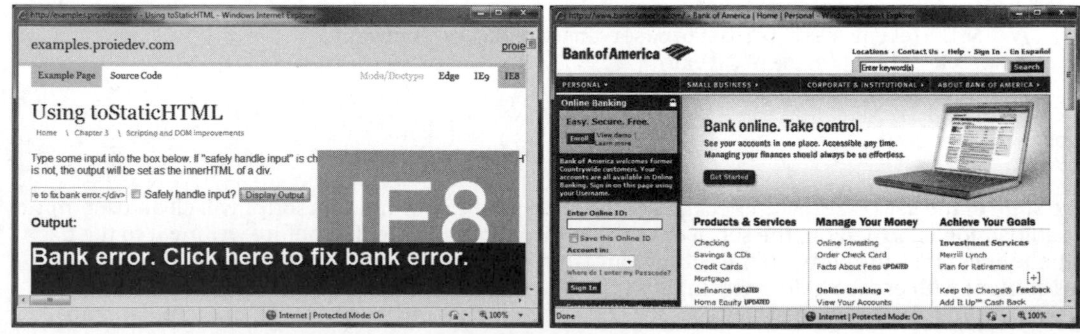

Figure 3-3. Example of script injection from unsanitized input

Standards Compliance Improvements

Internet Explorer 8 introduces a number of changes geared towards conformance with ECMAScript, and W3C specifications. These changes may affect existing AJAX applications, especially those relying upon events and DOM objects such as `element`.

Handling the addEventListener Method

Internet Explorer 8 and older versions do not support the `addEventListener()` method outlined in the W3C DOM Level 2 Events specification. Developers wishing to attach an event to the `window` object can alternatively use the `attachEvent`. Although exposed events may differ between browsers, interoperability can be achieved by first locating `window.addEventListener`; if this is not present, the `window.attachEvent` object can be used as a fallback. Listing 3-9 offers an example of this.

Listing 3-9. *Cross-Browser eventing using either addEventListener or attachEvent*

```
<html>
   <head>
      <title>Handling the addEventListener Method</title>
   </head>
   <body>
      <h3>addEventListenter Support? <span id="supportAEL">No.</span></h3>
      <h3>attachEvent Support? <span id="supportAE">No.</span></h3>
      <h3>Function used: <span id="fallback"></span></h3>
      <script type="text/javascript">

         //  Determine if the browser supports addEventListener()
         if (window.addEventListener)
            setText(document.getElementById("supportAEL"), "Yes!");

         //  Determine if the browser supports attachEvent()
         if (window.attachEvent)
            setText(document.getElementById("supportAE"), "Yes!");

         //  Simulate a fallback chain used by many web applications
         if (window.addEventListener)
            setText(document.getElementById("fallback"), "addEventListener()");
         else {
            if (window.attachEvent)
               setText(document.getElementById("fallback"), "attachEvent()");
            else setText(document.getElementById("fallback"), "-");
         }

         //  Set element text (cross-browser innerText/textContent)
         function setText(element, text) { /*...*/ }

      </script>
   </body>
</html>
```

Figure 3-4 demonstrates this script running in both IE8 and Chrome 3. In IE8, `addEventListener` is not available, thus the script falls back to using `attachEvent`. In Chrome 3, `addEventListener` is available, allowing the script to operate without falling back to `attachEvent`.

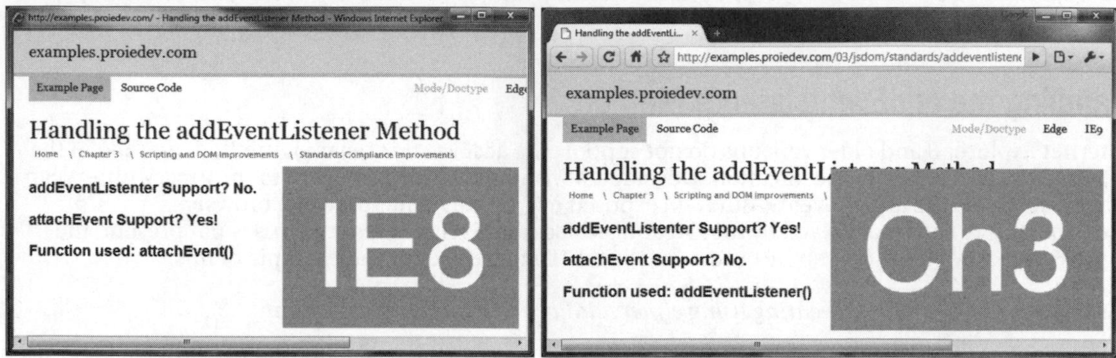

Figure 3-4. *Page showing IE8 using attachEvent() and Chrome 3 using addEventListener()*

While IE does not support `addEventListener`, it can be added to IE8 using DOM prototypes. This method and other DOM work (such as Accessors) are covered in the next chapter.

Case Sensitivity in getElementById

Prior to IE8, the `document.getElementById()` method was case insensitive. Developers building pages in IE8 Standards Mode will discover scripts depending on this trait can no longer find matching elements. IE8 Standards Mode and rendering modes of other newer browsers require the `id` parameter passed to `getElementById()` match the case of a target element's `id`.

Listing 3-10 contains a script that accesses a `<div>` element with the id `testDiv`. In IE7 Standards Mode and lower, the script can access this element by using the lowercase `testdiv` or the camel-case form `testDiv`. The script fails to access the element using the lowercase id `testdiv` in IE8 mode since the case of that string does not match the case of the real `id`.

Listing 3-10. *Example of getElementById case sensitivity*

```
<html>
   <head>
      <title>Case Sensitivity in getElementById</title>
   </head>
   <body>
      <h3>Access element with id "testdiv": <span id="caseInsensitive"></span></h3>
      <h3>Access element with id "testDiv": <span id="caseSensitive"></span></h3>
      <div id="testDiv"></div>
      <script>

         //  Attempt to access element testdiv
         try {
            setText(document.getElementById("testdiv"), " ");
            setText(document.getElementById("caseInsensitive"), "Success!"); }
         catch(e) { setText(document.getElementById("caseInsensitive"), "Error"); }
```

```
        //  Attempt to access element testDiv
        try {
           setText(document.getElementById("testDiv"), " ");
           setText(document.getElementById("caseSensitive"), "Success!"); }
        catch(e) { setText(document.getElementById("caseSensitive"), "Error"); }

        //  Set element text (cross-browser innerText/textContent)
        function setText(element, text) { /*...*/ }

      </script>
   </body>
</html>
```

Figure 3-5 shows the output of the script. Again, the IE7 mode page successfully accesses the `<div>` despite the case difference from the actual element's `id`, indicating success in both cases. In the IE8 mode page, the script can only access the element when the case provided to `getElementById()` matches that of the `id` attribute.

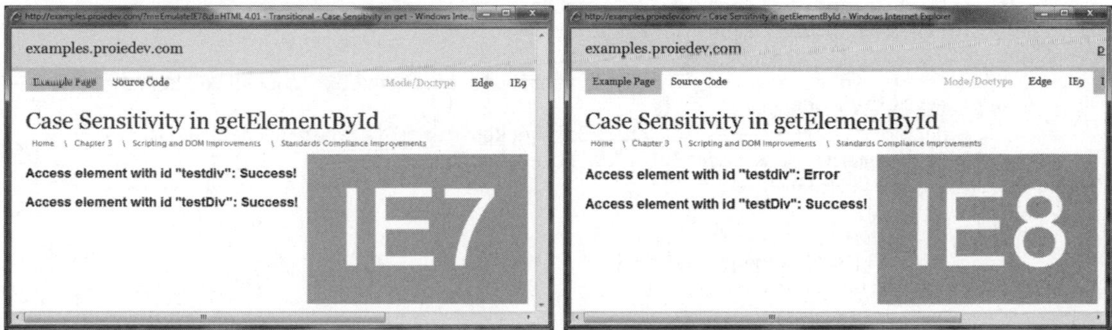

***Figure 3-5.** Webpage that demonstates getElementById case sensitivity*

Attribute Object Changes

A number of changes were made to the way Internet Explorer handles element attributes moving the browser towards more complete standards compliance.

Uninitialized Values and the Attributes Collection

Internet Explorer 8 no longer writes attribute information to an `element` object's attribute collection when those attributes are not given an initial value. Prior to IE8, the browser initialized all attributes and set their value to a default value appropriate for their type.

This behavior affects pages running in all document modes; pages relying on IE7 Standards Mode to emulate IE7 behavior may see exceptions raised by pages accessing unset attributes.

Listing 3-11 is an example of a page that has two `<input>` checkboxes, one without an initial checked state (`checkBox`) and the other with (`checkBoxChecked`).

Listing 3-11. *Code sample showing IE8 not placing uninitialized values into the attributes collection*

```
<html>
   <head>
      <title>Uninitialized Values and the Attributes Collection</title>
   </head>
   <body>
      <h3>Attribute "checked" exists on "checkBox":
      <span id="attrCheckBox"></span></h3>
      <h3>Attribute "checked" exists on "checkBoxChecked":
      <span id="attrCheckBoxChecked"></span></h3>
      "checkBox" Object: <input type="checkbox" id="checkBox"><br>
      "checkBoxChecked" Object: <input type="checkbox" id="checkBoxChecked" checked>
      <script>

         // Attempt to access the "checked" attribute of checkbox "checkBox"
         var attrCheckBox
            = document.getElementById("checkBox").getAttribute("checked");
         setText(document.getElementById("attrCheckBox"),
            (attrCheckBox) ? "True" : "False");

         // Attempt to access the "checked" attribute of checkbox "checkBoxChecked"
         var attrCheckBoxChecked
            = document.getElementById("checkBoxChecked").getAttribute("checked");
         setText(document.getElementById("attrCheckBoxChecked"),
            (attrCheckBoxChecked) ? "True" : "False");

         // Set element text (cross-browser innerText/textContent)
         function setText(element, text) { /*...*/ }

      </script>
   </body>
</html>
```

Script in this example attempts to access the checked attribute of both objects. The first `<input>` object did not have an initial checked state, thus the a null value is applied to `attrCheckBox` when the attempts to set the checked attribute's value to it. The script creates the `attrCheckBox` variable and assigns the checked attribute of the first `<input>` box to it. The `attrCheckBoxChecked` variable, on the other hand, successfully retrieves the value of that parameter on the checkBoxChecked element since that object's checked attribute was initialized in markup.

Figure 3-6 shows the example running in IE7 mode of Internet Explorer 8, conveying the fact that the checked attribute on the element checkBox does not exist since it was not initially set, whereas it does exist on the checkBoxChecked object.

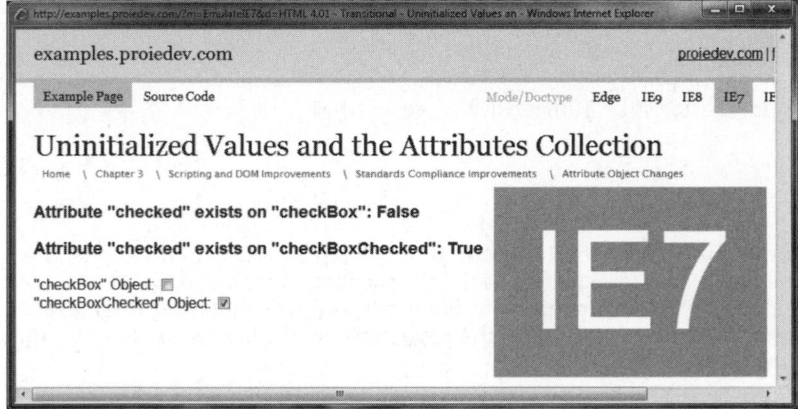

Figure 3-6. *Webpage that demonstrates IE8's behavior regarding uninitialized attributes*

Attributes Collection Ordering

Pages that rely on the order of Internet Explorer's attribute collection may require modifications in order to work properly in IE8 Standards Mode and above. Scripts falling into this category refer to attributes using array notation (e.g. `element.attributes[1]`) instead of using property notation (e.g. `element.style`) or attribute get and set methods (e.g. `element.getAttribute("style")`). This is an effect of the browser's move to no longer pre-initialize unspecified attributes in IE8 Standards Mode and above (as described in the previous section).

The code in Listing 3-12 contains a for loop that looks at the ith attribute of a `<div id="testDiv">` from 0 to 4. This `<div>` has three pre-defined attributes: `class`, `style`, and `id`. is the same code run in both IE7 and IE8 mode, yet the results differ. The results of this loop are written to the page.

Listing 3-12. *Script that demonstrates attribute ordering differences between IE7 and IE8*

```
<html>
   <head>
      <title>Attributes Collection Ordering</title>
   </head>
   <body>
      <div id="resultsDiv"></div>
      <div class="someClass" style="display: none;" id="testDiv"></div>
      <script type="text/javascript">

         //  Return the names of the first 5 attributes on <div>
         var resultHTML = "";
         for(var i = 0; i < 5; i++) {

            //  Attempt to access the ith element of the <div id="testDiv"> attribute
            //  collection
            var attrByArray = document.getElementById("testDiv").attributes[i];
            resultHTML += "<h3>Element [" + i + "] on &lt;div&gt;: "
                        + ((attrByArray) ? attrByArray.name : "&mdash;")
```

```
                        + "</h3>\r\n";
        }

        //  Output results to the screen
        document.getElementById("resultsDiv").innerHTML = resultHTML;

    </script>
  </body>
</html>
```

Figure 3-7 displays the output of this script in both IE7 and IE8 Standards Modes. In IE7 mode, the first five attributes in the attributes collection exist (onresizeend, onrowenter, aria-haspopup, ondragleave, and onbeforepaste), albeit with empty values. In IE8 mode, only the first three exist (class, id, style), with coincide with the attributes explicitly set in the page markup; the last two accesses return null objects instead of empty attributes.

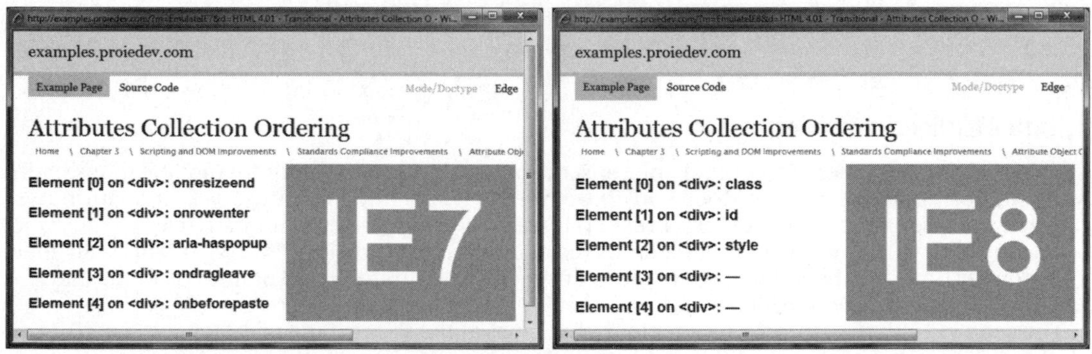

Figure 3-7. *Screenshots verifying attribute ordering changes between IE document modes*

Accessing an Element's Class Information

An element's class information can be obtained in JavaScript via two methods: either through the className property of an element object, or through the getAttribute() method present on that same object. In IE7 and below (as well as in IE8's IE7 Standards Mode), the class attribute was accessible via getAttribute() when the string "className" into it. This did not conform to established standards.

Developers wishing to access the class attribute via getAttribute() must use the string "class" instead of "className" to access an element object's class attribute. The use of "className" will raise a TypeError exception.

The JavaScript in Listing 3-13 attempts to access the class attribute information of <div id="classTest"> three ways: by using the .className property, getAttribute("className"), and getAttribute("class"). The first two methods work properly in IE7 mode, whereas the last throws an exception. IE8 mode results in the same TypeError exception, but when calling getAttribute("className"); the call to getAttribute("class") is successful.

Listing 3-13. Script that accesses element information using the class property and getAttribute() method

```
<html>
   <head>
      <title>Accessing an Element's Class Information</title>
   </head>
   <body>
      <h3>&lt;div&gt; "classTest", getAttribute("class"):
         <span id="attrClass"></span></h3>
      <h3>&lt;div&gt; "classTest", getAttribute("className"):
         <span id="attrClassName"></span></h3>
      <h3>&lt;div&gt; "classTest", property .className:
         <span id="propClassName"></span></h3>
      <div id="classTest" class="testClass"></div>
      <script type="text/javascript">

         //  Get the <div id="testClass"> element
         var divClassTest = document.getElementById("classTest");

         //  Attempt to access the attribute via getAttribute "class"
         try {
            var attrClass = divClassTest.getAttribute("class");
            setText(document.getElementById("attrClass"), attrClass.toString());
         } catch(e) {
            setText(document.getElementById("attrClass"), "-");
         }

         //  Attempt to access the attribute via getAttribute "className"
         try {
            var attrClassName = divClassTest.getAttribute("className");
            setText(document.getElementById("attrClassName"), attrClassName.toString());
         } catch(e) {
            setText(document.getElementById("attrClassName"), "-");
         }

         //  Attempt to access the attribute via property "className"
         try {
            var attrClass = divClassTest.className;
            setText(document.getElementById("propClassName"), attrClass.toString());
         } catch(e) {
            setText(document.getElementById("propClassName"), "-");
         }

         //  Set element text (cross-browser innerText/textContent)
         function setText(element, text) { /*...*/ }

      </script>
   </body>
</html>
```

Figure 3-8 highlights this—the leftmost page, running in IE7 Standards Mode, displays the class attribute value of a `<div>` through the `.className` property as well as through getAttribute("className"). The page running in IE8 mode displays the class value through the .className property as well, but must use "class" to access the it via getAttribute().

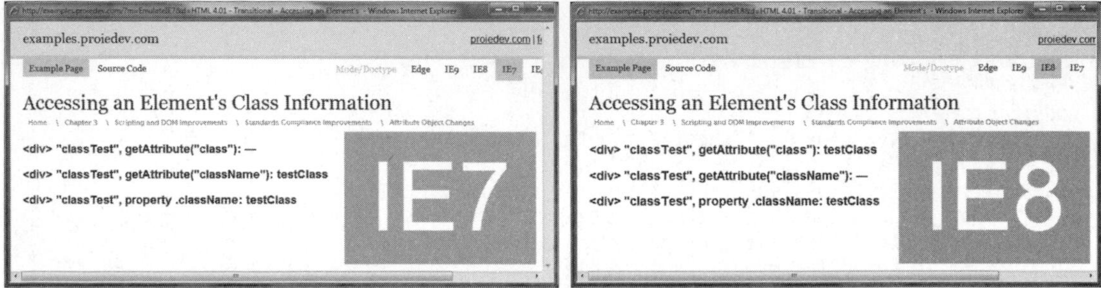

Figure 3-8. *Accessing the class information in both IE7 and IE8 Standards Modes*

Persisting Data with DOM Storage

Implementing interoperable data persistence in a web application is a difficult, especially since no well-adopted standard exists to support it. Traditionally, cookies have been used to achieve such persistent storage. Cookie storage has its drawbacks—there are size limitations for each cookie (4KB for IE7 and below, and 10KB in IE8), domains are limited to a fixed number of cookies, cookies are sent back and forth through every HTTP transaction, and each browser handles cookies in a slightly different way. There has been a number of attempts to fill this void; Flash, Google Gears, and IE5's UserData feature were either created or used to circumvent the limitations of cookies. Each method has major drawbacks and no single one has solved the problem of interoperability.

The HTML 5 specification takes another crack at this problem with its DOM Storage features. Internet Explorer 8 implements these features to all document modes.

Objects

- Storage object - Generic object that defines a storage mechanism. It complies with the HTML 5 DOM Storage specification.
- sessionStorage object - Subclass of the Storage object that stores information for a single browser session.
- localStorage object - Subclass of the Storage object that stores information across multiple browser sessions.

Methods

- getItem(key) **method** - Returns a value in a Storage object identified by a key.
- key(index) **method** - Returns a key located at the specified collection index.
- removeItem(key) **method** - Removes an item from a Storage object specified by key.
- setItem(key, value) **method** - Sets a value into a Storage object identified by a key.
- clear() **method** - Clears all key/value pairs currently set in a Storage object.

Properties

- `length` **property** - Returns the length of a `Storage` object's key/value list.
- `remainingSpace` **property** - Returns the remaining space (in bytes) in a `Storage` object.
- `(expando)` - Returns the value associated from a key, providing that the key name is not the same as a reserved name of a `Storage` object.

Events

- `onstorage` **event** - Fired whenever a key/value pair is created, modified, or deleted.

The `localStorage` and `sessionStorage` objects both derive from the Storage object. They each contain the same methods, properties, and events. They differ only in their level of persistence; `sessionStorage` only persists its contents for the lifetime of a "session." Session in this case does *not* mean a browser session (such as those used by cookies)—it refers to data stored by a page and frames contained within a tab whose persistence lasts only for the lifetime of that tab. `sessionStorage` does not persist data between tabs and there is no reliable way to use this object to share data between frames.

Aside from the length of persistence, these objects are otherwise interchangeable; developers can switch between the two simply by changing the object reference during instantiation.

Most properties and methods on the `Storage` object provide access to data through key/value pairs. Each key can be read from or written to through the get/set methods on a `Storage` object or with an expando; for example, a value under a key "`foo`" in storage object "`myStorage`" can be accessed either by calling `myStorage.getItem("foo")` or via the expando `myStorage.foo`. The `length` property returns the number of key/value pairs on the current subdomain, and the `remainingSpace` property returns the free space remaining in a domain's storage quota (this includes data from subdomains as well). Whenever a key/value pair is added or removed from a `Storage` object, the `onstorage` event is fired.

Listing 3-14 represents a webpage that implements DOM storage to persist data.

Listing 3-14. *An example of cross-browser storage using HTML 5 DOM Storage*

```
<html>
   <head>
      <title>Persisting Data with DOM Storage</title>
   </head>
   <body>
      <h3>Current Value: <span id="curVal"></span></h3>
      <h3>Current Value from <i>expando</i>: <span id="curValExpando"></span></h3>
      Set new text value:  
      <input id="inputVal" size="20" type="text">
      <p><input onclick="setStorageData();" type="submit" value="Save Data">  
      <button onclick="clearItems();">Clear Data</button>
      <h3>DOM Store information for <span id="infoDomain"></span></h3>
      <b>Length:</b> <span id="infoLength"></span> items<br>
      <b>Remaining Space:</b> <span id="infoRemaining"></span> KB<br>
      <script type="text/javascript">

         // Create variables for the storage type
         var storageObject = localStorage;

         // Read DOM Storage data for this domain
         function getStorageData() {
```

```
    //  Get the storage data via getItem. Make sure this value
    //  is string (IE Bug: empty values are returned as VT_NULL
    //  instead of a blank BSTR ("")
    var getItemData = storageObject.getItem('DOMStorageExample');
    if(getItemData == null) getItemData = "";

    //  Sanitize the data with toStaticHTML (if available)
    try { getItemData = toStaticHTML(getItemData); }
    catch(e) { escape(getItemData); }

    //  Write getItem results to the screen
    document.getElementById("inputVal").value = getItemData;
    setText(document.getElementById("curVal"),
       (getItemData == "") ? "-" : getItemData);

    //  Get the value via an expando, again compensating for
    //  the VT_NULL bug
    var expandoData = storageObject.DOMStorageExample;
    if(expandoData == null) expandoData = "-";

    //  Sanitize the data with toStaticHTML (if available)
    try { expandoData = toStaticHTML(expandoData); }
    catch(e) { escape(expandoData); }

    //  Write expando results to the screen
    setText(document.getElementById("curValExpando"), expandoData);

    //  Write domain info
    setText(document.getElementById("infoDomain"), document.domain);

    //  Display length if available
    var remainingSpace = "-";
    try { if(storageObject.remainingSpace != null &&
       typeof storageObject.remainingSpace != typeof undefined)
       remainingSpace = String(Math.round(storageObject.remainingSpace / 1024));
    } catch(e) { }
    setText(document.getElementById("infoLength"), storageObject.length);

    //  Display remainingSpace if available
    var remainingSpace = "-";
    try { if(storageObject.remainingSpace != null &&
       typeof storageObject.remainingSpace != typeof undefined)
       remainingSpace = String(Math.round(storageObject.remainingSpace / 1024));
    } catch(e) { }
    setText(document.getElementById("infoRemaining"), remainingSpace);

}

//  Write data into DOM Storage for this domain
function setStorageData() {

    //  Set the contents of the input box to the storage
    var newValue = String(document.getElementById("inputVal").value);
    storageObject.setItem('DOMStorageExample', newValue);
```

```
            //  Re-display the storage data
            getStorageData();

         }

         //  Clear DOM Storage for this domain
         function clearItems() {

            //  Clear out data in the storage object
            storageObject.clear();

            //  Re-display the storage data
            getStorageData();

         }

         //  Set element text (cross-browser innerText/textContent)
         function setText(element, text) { /*...*/ }

      </script>
   </body>
</html>
```

The following variables and methods are defined in the script:

- storageObject **variable** - References a Storage object. In this example, that object is localStorage; since this and sessionStorage are interchangeable, session storage can be used by changing the reference.
- storageKey **variable** - Represents the key used by the page to save data into the storageObject. While this example only uses one key, webpages can utilize more than one to save site settings.
- getStorageData() **method** - Called to retrieve data in the storage object and display it in the webpage.
- setStorageData() **method** - Called to write data in the page's input box into the storage object.
- clearItems() **method** - Used to clear all data out of the storage object .

When the page is loaded, the <body> onload event triggers the getStorageData() method to retrieve data already in storage. The "Save Data" button triggers the setStorageData() method; it takes the contents of the <input> textbox and saves it to the "DOMStorageExample" key of the storageObject. The "Clear Data" button calls the clearItems() method, which deletes all entries currently in the storageObject.

■ **Note** In IE8, Empty <input> elements return a VARIANT_NULL value rather than a blank BSTR that the storage object expects. When this value is placed directly into DOM Storage, IE crashes. To work around this, always save the value of an <input> box to a string variable or explicitly type it using String(…) before saving it to a storage object.

In addition to using `getItem()` to access a value for a specific key, that value can be accessed via its expando on the `Storage` object. The example demonstrates this in `getStorageData()`, `setStorageData()`, and `clearItems()`; the `innerText` (via `setText`) of `curValExpando` is set using the `storageObject.DOMStorageExample` expando for the key named `DOMStorageExample`. The `getStorageData()` method also grabs and displays information about the current storage object: the domain it's setting data to, the number of keys currently in the object, and the remaining space (if available).

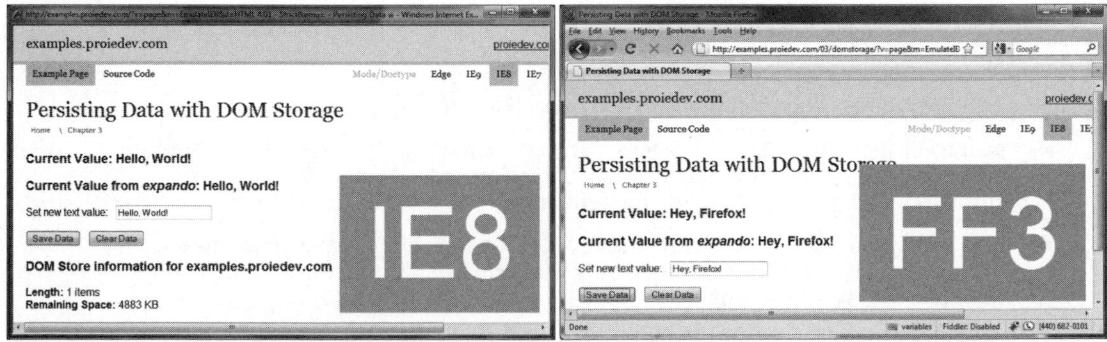

Figure 3-9. *Webpage that uses DOM Storage to persist data*

Figure 3-9 displays a screenshot of the DOM storage example in both IE8 and Firefox 3.5. Contents of the storage object are displayed on the page and, when the `localStorage` object is being used, that data remains available even after the browser is closed and reopened. Data typed into the input box can be saved to the storage object via the "Save Data" button. The storage object can be cleared by clicking on the "Clear Data" button.

DOM Storage and Subdomains

Key/value pairs in `Storage` objects cannot be shared between domains, nor can they be shared between domains and their subdomains. Domains and subdomains do share one storage area even though their respective data is inaccessible to each other; both fall under one limit of 10MB in IE8.

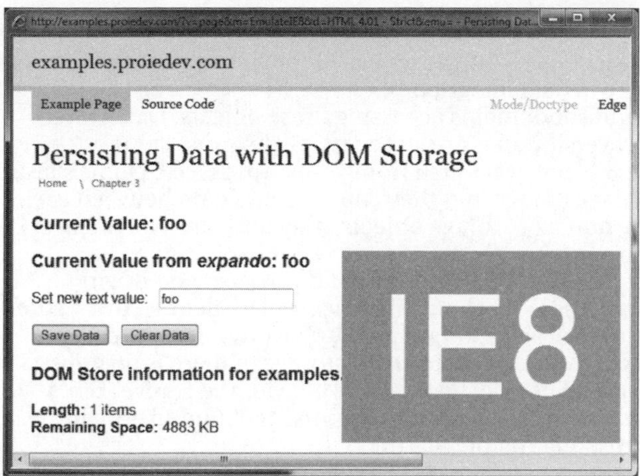

Figure 3-10. Webpage that uses DOM storage to persist data

In Figure 3-10, pages hosted `examples.proiedev.com` and `subdomain.examples.proiedev.com` both write to matching keys in their respective `Storage` objects. Even though they both reside on proiedev.com, they cannot access each other's data even when using the same key. They are, however, restricted to the same amount of shared space; they each must share one 10MB storage area.

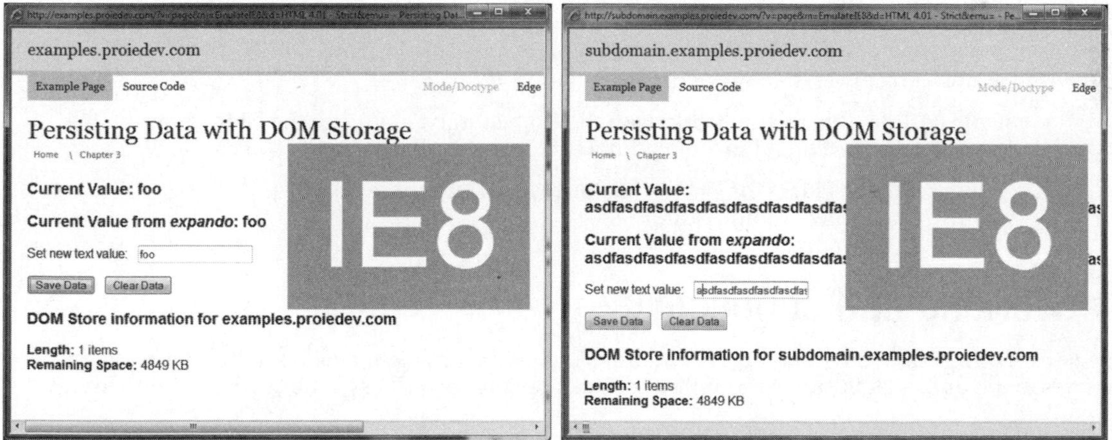

Figure 3-11. Two subdomains that share the same domaion and storage limits yet can't share data

Securing Persisted Storage

Persisted storage is a double-edged sword—while it enables offline scenarios for web applications, it also introduces a new class of security issues pertaining to data integrity.

Storage objects are isolated to the domains and subdomains accessing those objects. Data stored from one domain is not accessible from another, even if values are stored using the same key. For instance, a key/value pair saved from `proiedev.com` is not accessible from `ie-examples.com`. Domains and their subdomains share one 10MB block for data storage, but they cannot share data between each other. These domain restrictions also apply to the quota of Storage objects; only domains which have access to a certain Storage object can save data to that object.

Internet Explorer provides basic data security for storage objects based on context and origin policies. Developers, however, should not rely upon these mechanisms for complete data security; some attacks, such as cross-site scripting exploits, circumvent same-origin policy. Sensitive data (such as personally identifiable information) generally should not be kept in DOM storage; if there is no other option, strong encryption should be used. Data should be selectively removed with the `removeItem()` method or completely deleted using `clear()` if there is no need for it to be persisted. End-users can clear these items through Internet Explorer's Delete Browsing History feature.

Moving towards HTML 5 Storage

HTML 5 DOM Storage finally offers web developers a great option for persistent, cross-browser storage. Unfortunately, older versions of IE and other major browsers don't support this model yet; until these are eventually phased out, developers will need to use older methods to persist data in these scenarios. A number of libraries create an abstraction layer this and older methods of persistent storage. These allow pages to take advantage of HTML 5 Storage when available and fall back to older methods when it isn't. Here are some common frameworks that were available at the time of publication:

- **PersistJS** - Standalone, dedicated persisted storage library. No prerequisites. (http://link.proiedev.com/persistjs)
- **Dojo Offline** - Plugin that works with the Dojo Library. Requires the Dojo library. (http://link.proiedev.com/dojooffline)
- **jQuery jStore** - Plugin for jQuery. Requires the jQuery library. (http://link.proiedev.com/jstore)

Networking and Connectivity

The network and connectivity changes in Internet Explorer 8 and higher consist of new features and updates to old ones that ensure web applications can operate regardless of network connectivity.

Online and Offline Events

The `window.navigator.onLine` property was introduced in Internet Explorer 4 as a way for webpages to know when the browser was running "Offline Mode." This flag did not report the state of network connectivity. AJAX applications that provide offline features have worked around this limitation by "pinging" remote severs with `XMLHttpRequest`, however this method isn't completely reliable. Internet Explorer 8 and higher now use this property to reflect both the state of network connectivity and whether or not the browser is running in Offline Mode.

Properties

- `onLine` **property** - Indicates whether or not the system is connected to the network with a Boolean value. When connected to a network and when IE is not running in "Offline Mode," `true` is returned; `false` is returned otherwise. In IE7 and below, this property indicates only if the browser is running normally (`true`) or in "Offline Mode" (`false`).

Events

- `onoffine` **event** - Fired whenever Internet Explorer detects a loss of network connectivity or the browser has entered "Offline Mode."
- `ononline` **event** - Fired whenever Internet Explorer detects that network connectivity has resumed or the browser has left "Offline Mode."

The events and property changes in the `window.navigator` and `window.clientInformation` objects are available to pages running in any document mode.

The code in Listing 3-15 uses three events to gather and act on connectivity information: `onload`, `ononline`, and `onoffline`. The `onload` event calls the `onLoad()` method; it gathers and displays the initial connectivity state from the `window.navigator.onLine` property. The `onoffline` event calls the `onOffline()` method whenever connectivity is lost; the method in this sample writes "Offline" to the page. `ononline` acts in the opposite manner, calling `onOnline()` when connectivity is restored and, in this case, writing "Online" to the page.

Listing 3-15. *Sample code demonstrating online/offline property and events*

```
<html>
   <head>
      <title>Online/Offline Events</title>
   </head>
   <body ononline="onOnline();" onoffline="onOffline();" onload="onLoad();">
      <h3>Connectivity Status: <span id="status"></span></h3>
      <script type="text/javascript">

         //  When the browser goes online, write "Online" to the page
         function onOnline() {
            setText(document.getElementById("status"), "Online");
         }

         //  When the browser goes offline, write "Offline" to the page
         function onOffline() {
            setText(document.getElementById("status"), "Offline");
         }

         //  When the page loads, display the current connectivity status
         function onLoad() {
            setText(document.getElementById("status"),
               (window.navigator.onLine) ? "Online" : "Offline");
         }

         //  Set element text (cross-browser innerText/textContent)
         function setText(element, text) { /*...*/ }

      </script>
   </body>
```

```
</html>
```

Figure 3-11 shows this sample code running in both IE7 and IE8 Standards Modes. The browser in this scenario initially connected to the internet and running the page in IE8 Standards Mode. The page is reloaded in IE7 mode, quickly followed by a good yank on the CAT-5 cable connected to the client machine. Once the connection is severed, the `onoffline` event is fired and the page reads "Offline."

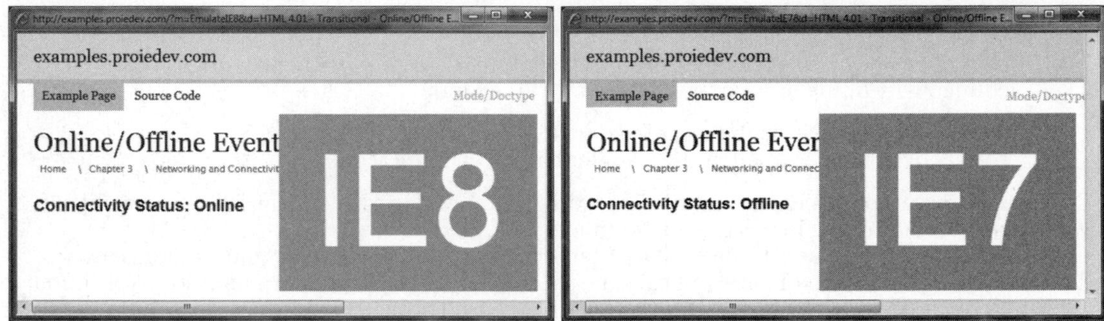

***Figure 3-11.** Webpage that displays current connectivitiy information*

XMLHttpRequest Timeout Events

Internet Explorer 8 and higher include a `timeout` property and `ontimeout` event in the `XMLHttpRequest` object. Scripts using this object can apply a hard limit on the time a request should take using this property, and receive an event when this limit is reached.

Properties

- `timeout` **property** - The amount of time in milliseconds that the `XMLHttpRequest` object should wait for a response from a target. The `ontimeout` event is raised when this limit is reached and the request is aborted.

Events

- `ontimeout` **event** – Fires an associated callback function when time elapsed between the a `XMLHttpRequest.send()` call and the current time is reached.

Listing 3-16 is a webpage that uses server-side script (in this case, PHP) to simulate a webpage taking a long time to load. Whenever a request to this page is received by the server, the script pauses 5 seconds (with `sleep(5)`) before responding with the text "Success!"

***Listing 3-16.** Webpage that forces a server to wait for 5 seconds before responding*

```
<?php

   //  Simulate a page that takes 5 seconds to respond.  Once finished,
   //  return the string "Success!"
   sleep(5);
   echo "Success!";

?>
```

Listing 3-17 demonstrates a script that requests the page in Listing 3-16 using two XMLHttpRequest objects: xhrSmallTimeout and xhrLargeTimeout. The xhrSmallTimeout object requests the above page, but limits the wait time for that request to 2 seconds using its timeout property. The xhrLargeTimeout object attempts to pull down the same page, but allots a maximum of 10 seconds for a response. Each object has two callback methods: one for ontimeout (timeoutRaisedSmall() and timeoutRaisedLarge()), fired if a request's timeout is reached, and the other for onreadystate (readyStateHandlerSmall() and readyStateHandlerLarge()), fired during steps of the request/response process. Exceptions thrown during execution of the onreadystate callbacks are written to <div id="exceptions">.

Listing 3-17. *Code sample using the XMLHttpRequest timeout event*

```
<html>
   <head>
      <title>XMLHttpRequest Timeout</title>
   </head>
   <body>
      <h3>Request with 2s timeout: <span id="xhrSmallStatus"></span></h3>
      <h3>Request with 10s timeout: <span id="xhrLargeStatus"></span></h3>
      <h3>Exceptions:</h3>
      <div id="exceptions"><p></div>
      <script type="text/javascript">

         //  Define the XMLHttpRequest variables, the target page and
         //  elements that will be written to
         var xhrSmallTimeout; var xhrLargeTimeout;
         var targetPage = "http://examples.proiedev.com/03/networking/timeout/result.php";
         var spanXhrSmallStatus = document.getElementById("xhrSmallStatus");
         var spanXhrLargeStatus = document.getElementById("xhrLargeStatus");
         var spanExceptions     = document.getElementById("exceptions");


         function displayException(e, objectName) {
            spanExceptions.innerHTML += "<b>Object:</b> " + objectName + "<br>"
                                     +  "<b>Name:</b> " +  e.name + "<br>"
                                     +  "<b>Message:</b> " + e.message + "<p>";
         }

         //  Timeout callback for request with 2s timeout
         function timeoutRaisedSmall(){
            setText(spanXhrSmallStatus, "Timeout");
         }

         //  Timeout callback for request with 10s timeout
         function timeoutRaisedLarge() {
            setText(spanXhrLargeStatus, "Timeout");
         }

         //  readyState callback for request with 2s timeout.  If an
         //  exception is raised, write it to the screen.
         function readyStateHandlerSmall() {
            if(xhrSmallTimeout.readyState == 4) {
               try {
```

```
                setText(spanXhrSmallStatus, xhrSmallTimeout.responseText);
            } catch(e) { displayException(e, "xhrSmallTimeout"); }
        }
    }

    //  readyState callback for request with 10s timeout.  If an
    //  exception is raised, write it to the screen.
    function readyStateHandlerLarge() {
        if(xhrLargeTimeout.readyState == 4) {
            try {
                setText(spanXhrLargeStatus, xhrLargeTimeout.responseText);
            } catch(e) { displayException(e, "xhrLargeTimeout"); }
        }
    }

    // Create a XMLHttpRequest object with a small (2 second)
    // timeout period
    xhrSmallTimeout = new XMLHttpRequest();
    xhrSmallTimeout.open("GET", targetPage, true);
    xhrSmallTimeout.timeout = 2000;
    xhrSmallTimeout.ontimeout = timeoutRaisedSmall;
    xhrSmallTimeout.onreadystatechange = readyStateHandlerSmall;

    // Create a XMLHttpRequest object with a large (10 second)
    // timeout period
    xhrLargeTimeout = new XMLHttpRequest();
    xhrLargeTimeout.open("GET", targetPage, true);
    xhrLargeTimeout.timeout = 10000;
    xhrLargeTimeout.ontimeout = timeoutRaisedLarge;
    xhrLargeTimeout.onreadystatechange = readyStateHandlerLarge;

    // Sent the XMLHttpRequests
    xhrSmallTimeout.send(null);
    xhrLargeTimeout.send(null);

    //  Set element text (cross-browser innerText/textContent)
    function setText(element, text) { /*...*/ }

  </script>
 </body>
</html>
```

Figure 3-12 shows the sample code being run. The `timeoutRaisedSmall()` method is called and "Timeout" is shown on the page 2 seconds after the `xhrSmallTimeout` object makes a request (since the server won't respond for at least 5 seconds). The `onreadystate` event is raised after the timeout is hit, resulting in an exception—while the request *technically* completed (`readyState == 4`), the `responseText` returns a `null` type rather than a `String`. The second request made by `xhrLargeTimeout` finishes after about 5 seconds, triggering `readyStateHandlerLarge()` to write the associated `responseText` to the page. The method `timeoutRaisedLarge()` is never called since the second request completes before the 10 second limit.

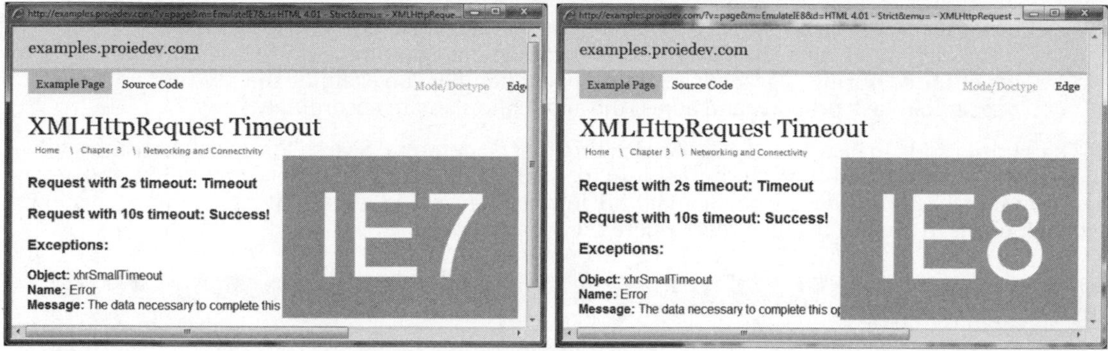

Figure 3-12. Webpage demonstrating the XMLHttpRequest timeout event

This example raises an important point about `XMLHttpRequest` timeouts: transactions that timeout before completion are considered "finished" by the browser, thus `onreadystatechange` callbacks are fired with their `readyState` indicates completion. The `responseXML` and `responseText` properties of those objects, however, are not available. Scripts using the `timeout` property and `ontimeout` event must use `onreadystatechange` event handlers that fail gracefully when these properties are null.

AJAX Navigation Events

Many AJAX applications use in-page navigations (often called hash or fragment navigations) to trigger events or change states. In-page navigations allow pages to update the address bar without making a full navigation request; they give users a way to save a page's state through bookmarks or email a that state to someone else. Mapping sites like Google Maps and MapQuest are great examples—they use in-page navigations to zoom-in on a place or display a window to get directions to a location.

Figure 3-13. Address bar showing in-page AJAX navigations

In older browsers and versions of Internet Explorer prior to IE8, these navigations were never appended to the travel log unless an anchor tag with the same value as the hash existed on the page (for more information on the travel log, see Chapter 1) The back and forward buttons were rendered useless in these cases, and users needed to rely on the web application to provide similar functionality.

IE8 breaks from this old behavior by allowing developers to add in-page navigations to the travel log when necessary. This feature is opt-in—webpages are given a chance to append hash information to the navigation history whenever the `onhashchanged` event is fired. Only pages running in IE8 Standards Mode and above may catch this event and persist navigations.

Properties

- **`location.hash` property** - Returns the fragment component of the current URL, including the leading hash (#) mark. This property is read/write (in IE8 Standards Mode and above).

Events

- **onhashchange event** - Fired when an in-page navigation occurs either by a user (through the IE user interface) or script (through navigation methods). This event is not fired during page load; an `onload` Event handler can examine the `location.hash` property and adjust the application's state accordingly.

The sample code in Listing 3-16 is a "Search Provider Generator." Search Provider extensions, discussed in Chapter 10, add search engines into the search box in Internet Explorer, Firefox, and any other browsers that support the OpenSearch XML format. Figure 3-14 gives a bit more context; it shows the search boxes in both in IE and Firefox where these extensions live.

***Figure 3-14.** Search boxes (top-left input box in each window) of IE8 and Firefox 3.5*

The printed sample here omits the finer details of Search Providers and focuses mainly on how this tool uses AJAX navigation.

Concepts presented here represent a "wizard"-style interface; there are a series of ordered steps represented as panels. These panels either present information or wait for user action, the same concept used by setup applications. In-page navigations are a great solution for wizards; the hash can be used to store a user's current position within the wizard. In this case, there are four steps:

1. Ask the user for the name of a Search Engine.
2. Have the user perform a search query using the word "TEST" and place the URL of the result into a textbox.
3. Ask the user for some metadata.
4. Provide the user with information—in this case, a new Search Provider extension that can be either installed or downloaded to the system.

Figure 3-15 shows each of these four panels.

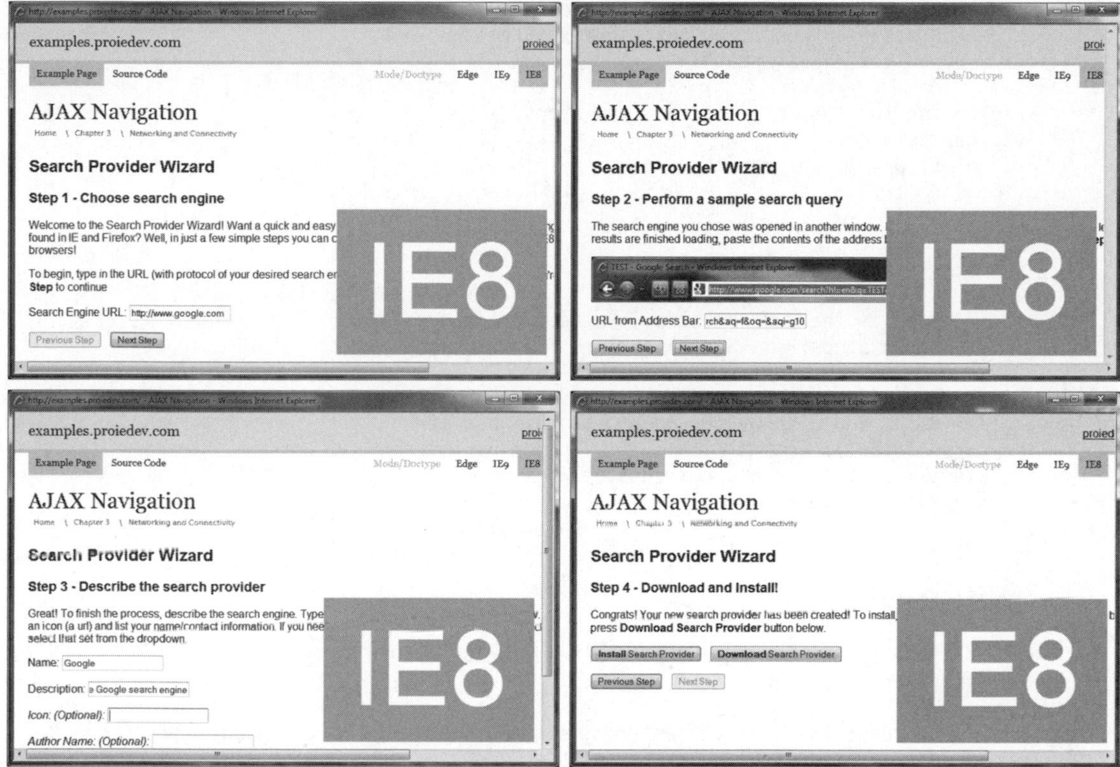

Figure 3-15. Webpage using in-page navigations to display a wizard interface with four steps/panels

Listing 3-18 highlights the code for this example that pertains to in-page navigations. The page begins by throwing the `onload` event, which calls the `onHashChange()` method. This method reads the current hash value; it represents the current position within the wizard (which can range from `minStep` ()1 to `maxStep` (4). If the `window.location.hash` value is empty or outside of this range, the number is set to `minStep`. The `loadPanelForStep()` method is called once the hash is normalized; this method displays the panel `<div>` associated with the current step.

Listing 3-18. Sample code for the Search Provider Generator using in-page navigation

```
<html>
   <head>
      <title>AJAX Navigation</title>
   </head>
   <body>
      <h2 id="title">Search Provider Wizard</h2>
      <div id="stepPanel1"> <!-- ... --> </div>
      <div id="stepPanel2"> <!-- ... --> </div>
      <div id="stepPanel3"> <!-- ... --> </div>
      <div id="stepPanel4"> <!-- ... --> </div>
```

```
<p>
<button id="previousStep" onclick="previous()">Previous Step</button>  
<button id="nextStep" onclick="next()">Next Step</button>
<script type="text/javascript">

   //  Define the current, min, and max steps.
   var currentStep = 1;
   var minStep = 1; var maxStep = 4;

   //  ...

   function next() {

      //  Stop if the current step is already at/above max
      if(currentStep >= maxStep) return;

      //  Increase the current position, set that position to the
      //  hash, and display the panel for this new step
      currentStep++;
      window.location.hash = currentStep;
      loadPanelForStep();

   }

   function previous() {

      //  Stop if the current step is already at/below min
      if(currentStep <= minStep) return;

      //  Decrease the current position, set that position to the hash, and
      //  display the panel for this new step
      currentStep--;
      window.location.hash = currentStep;
      loadPanelForStep();

   }

   function onHashChange() {

      //  Grab the step specified by the hash as an Integer
      var hashStep = parseInt(window.location.hash.substr(1));

      //  If the hash value isn't a valid number, start at the first step. If
      //  it is out of bounds, snap to the closest limit.  Otherwise, set the
      //  current step to be the one specified in the hash
      if(isNaN(hashStep))          currentStep = minStep;
      else if(hashStep < minStep) currentStep = minStep;
      else if(hashStep > maxStep) currentStep = minStep;
      else                         currentStep = hashStep;

      //  Display panel for the current step
      loadPanelForStep();

   }
```

```
        function loadPanelForStep() {

           //  Disable the previous button if on the first panel and
           //  disable the next button of on the last
           document.getElementById("previousStep").disabled
              = (currentStep <= minStep) ? true : false;
           document.getElementById("nextStep").disabled
              = (currentStep >= maxStep) ? true : false;

           //  Show the current panel and hide all others
           for(var i = minStep; i <= maxStep; i++) {
              var display = ((i == currentStep) ? "block" : "none");
              document.getElementById("stepPanel" + i).style.display = display;
           }

           //  ...

        }

        //  ...

      </script>
   </body>
</html>
```

The "Previous Step" and "Next Step" buttons (previousStep and nextStep, respectively) move backwards and forward through the steps in the wizard. When previousStep is clicked, its onclick handler subtracts 1 from the currentStep position if possible and calls loadPanelForStep() to display the panel for this new value. The nextStep button does the same, but instead increases currentStep by 1. Since these panels are located on the same page, the data input into each remains while the user remains within the page context. Finally, each of these methods set the new hash value to window.location.hash—this "registers" the new in-page navigation with the travel log, thus making it available to IE's back and forward buttons as well as navigation history.

The last major piece of AJAX navigation is integration with the browser's forward and back buttons. The onhashchange event handler of the <body> tag is raised whenever these buttons refer back to a location within the page; to grab these events, the same onHashChange() method used for the onload handler is used to catch these events. This method reads the current hash value, normalizes it, and navigates to the step provided by this value.

Concurrent Connections

The HTTP 1.0 and 1.1 specifications suggest limits to the number of concurrent connections a requesting application (in this case, the browser) should make to each host server. These limits were based upon the infrastructure of the era (the 1990s). While the limits were wise at the time, improvements in network infrastructure have caused most browser developers to increase their connection limits.

Current versions of major browsers increased connection limits in order to speed page load and allow AJAX applications to utilize more concurrent connections. Internet Explorer 8 increases this number to 6 connections per domain in non-modem configurations. Comparative values are shown in Table 3-1.

Table 3-1. *Table listing concurrent connections-per-host limits*

	IE <= 7	IE 8
HTTP 1.0 Server over modem	4	4
HTTP 1.1 Server over modem	2	2
HTTP 1.0 Server	4	6
HTTP 1.1 Server	2	6

IE8 also exposes a new property on the `window` object called `macConnectionsPerServer`. Scripts can query this property, potentially offering varying behavior and functionality based on the number of concurrent connections available.

Properties

- `maxConnectionsPerServer` **property** - Returns number of connections available per domain based on the server HTTP version and the connection type. This property is read-only.

The page in Listing 3-19 attempts to download eight images from a server located at `examples.proiedev.com`.

Listing 3-19. *Code sample that highlights how concurrent connections operate*

```
<html>
   <head>
      <title>Concurrent Connections</title>
   </head>
   <body>
      <h3>Maximum connections per host: <span id="maxCon"></span></h3>
      <img src="images/1.jpg"><br>
      <img src="images/2.jpg"><br>
      <img src="images/3.jpg"><br>
      <img src="images/4.jpg"><br>
      <img src="images/5.jpg"><br>
      <img src="images/6.jpg"><br>
      <img src="images/7.jpg"><br>
      <img src="images/8.jpg">
      <script type="text/javascript">

         //  If the number of maxConnectionsPerServer is readable from
         //  script, display that value to the screen
         var spanMaxCon = document.getElementById("maxCon");
         if(window.maxConnectionsPerServer)
            setText(spanMaxCon, window.maxConnectionsPerServer);
         else setText(spanMaxCon, "-");

         //  Set element text (cross-browser innerText/textContent)
         function setText(element, text) { /*...*/ }
```

```
    </script>
  </body>
</html>
```

The page, when running in IE8 and using a broadband connection, can download up to 6 items at a time from the server. In theory, this means the first six images in the sample will start downloading around the same time, and the seventh will begin when the first completes.

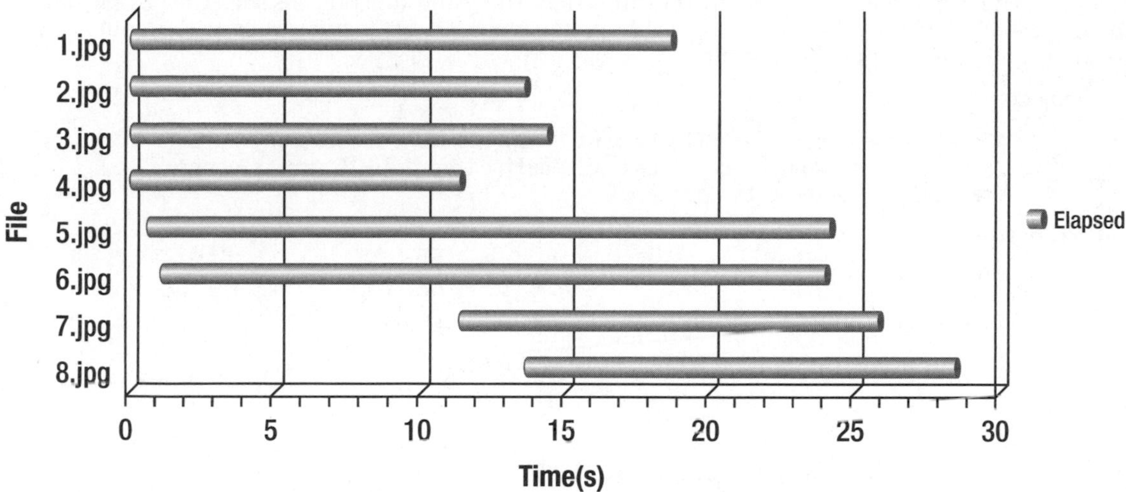

Figure 3-16. *Network timeline highlighting concurrent connections*

Figure 3-16 shows a network request timeline generated with Excel based on timing information captured by the Fiddler Web Debugger. When the example page is loaded, Internet Explorer checks the number of connections per host. Trident's parser subsystem (described in Chapter 1) issues download requests for embedded resources. The download subsystem begins issuing requests until the connections-per-host limit is reached, at which point subsequent requests are queued until a connection becomes free. In this case, six image files are downloading concurrently, and the seventh begins when an earlier request completes and frees a connection slot.

The 6 connection limit is directly tied to a specific hostname. Some websites use this definition to circumvent browser connection limits; by using multiple hostnames or CDNs (Content Delivery Networks), pages can increase the number of available concurrent connections. For example, a page served from the hostname `examples.proiedev.com` could increase the number of images downloaded concurrently by a client browser by serving some content on another hostname like `www.proiedev.com`.

Communicating Across Pages and Domains

The use of mixed content or mixed origins carries with it a risk of cross-site scripting vulnerabilities and request forgeries. Developers must take care to ensure that data transferred between origins is sanitized before it's use. The next few sections outline features of IE8 that help developers build secure cross-domain and cross-site communication channel which such mixing is necessary.

Cross-Domain Requests

The XDomainRequest object (and enhanced versions of XMLHttpRequest found in Firefox 3.5 and Safari 4) provides an asynchronous communication channel for domains with a pre-established trust relationship.

XDomainRequest is similar to XMLHttpRequest in terms of core functionality—one page (the requestee) makes a request to a remote page (the requestor) and, upon receiving and validating the request, the requestor returns a response to the requestee. Unlike XMLHttpRequest, XDomainRequest *assumes* that it's being used by two origins that have a trust relationship. The requestor confirms such trust by including the requestee's domain in a response header. It omits certain security features such as credential handling and cookie support as a result.

Objects

- XDomainRequest object – A lightweight, asynchronous request object that enforces cross-domain access controls defined by the W3C Access Control for Cross-Site Requests standard.

Properties

- contentType property – Same as XMLHttpRequest.contentType.
- responseText property – Same as XMLHttpRequest.responseText.
- timeout property – Same as XMLHttpRequest.timeout.

Methods

- abort **method** – Same as XMLHttpRequest.abort().
- open **method** – Same as XMLHttpRequest.open().
- send **method** – Same as XMLHttpRequest.send().

Events

- onload **event** - Raises a callback method when the requested server returns a response. This is similar the onreadystatechange event in XMLHttpRequest, but it only fires when a transaction is complete (thus there is no readyState property).
- onerror **event** – Same as XMLHttpRequest's onerror event.
- onprogress **event** – Same as XMLHttpRequest's onprogress event.
- ontimeout **event** – Same as XMLHttpRequest's ontimeout event.

The XDomainRequest object does not have an onreadystatechange event. Instead, the onload event is fired when a transaction is finished. This coincides with the "completed" state (or readyState == 4) of the XMLHttpRequestObject's onreadystatechange event.

Asynchronous, origin-restricted communication is not limited to IE8. Firefox 3.5 and Safari 4 have also added this functionality. Instead of using the XDomainRequest object, this functionality was placed directly on the XMLHttpRequest object. This topic is discussed in-depth in the following sections.

■ **Note** When writing scripts that are expected to run in all browsers that support Cross-Domain Requests, use the XDomainRequest object in IE8 and XMLHttpRequest for other browsers such as Firefox 3.5+ and Safari4+.

Building the Request

The sample page in Listing 3-20 attempts to access origin-restricted resources found at both `examples.proiedev.com` and `www.ie-examples.com`. The origin of the requesting page is `http://examples.proiedev.com`. Script in this sample uses either Internet Explorer 8's `XDomainRequest` object or origin-controlled versions of `XMLHttpRequest` (in browsers that support it) to attempt a trusted connection with the server. The proper object is chosen by detecting the browser with the Peter-Paul Koch's BrowserDetect.js script; it can be downloaded from http://link.proiedev.com/browserdetect.

Listing 3-20. *Code sample using Cross-Domain Requests*

```
<html>
   <head>
      <title>Cross-Domain Requests</title>
   </head>
   <body>
      <div id="resultDiv">
         <h3>Request to examples.proiedev.com: <span id="xdrAllowed"></span></h3>
         <h3>Request to www.ie-examples.com: <span id="xdrBlocked"></span></h3>
      </div>
      <!-- Include PPK's BrowserDetect script from QuirksMode.org -->
      <script type="text/javascript" src="browserdetect.quirksmode.js"></script>
      <script type="text/javascript">

         //  Create variables to hold XDomainRequest or instances of
         //  XMLHttpRequest that offer origin header support
         var xdrAllowed = null;
         var xdrBlocked = null;

         //  Callback functions for onload and onerror events in
         //  XDomainRequest/XMLHttpRequest
         function onLoadAllowed()  { displayEvent("xdrAllowed", xdrAllowed.responseText); }
         function onLoadBlocked()  { displayEvent("xdrBlocked", xdrBlocked.responseText); }
         function onErrorAllowed() { displayEvent("xdrAllowed", "Error") }
         function onErrorBlocked() { displayEvent("xdrBlocked", "Error") }

         //  Create XDomainRequest objects (or XMLHttpRequest objects
         //  if not IE and on a browser that offers origin header support)
         if(window.XDomainRequest) {
            xdrAllowed = new XDomainRequest(); xdrBlocked = new XDomainRequest();
         } else if((BrowserDetect.browser = "Firefox" && BrowserDetect.version > 3.5) ||
                   (BrowserDetect.browser = "Safari"  && BrowserDetect.version > 4)) {
            xdrAllowed = new XMLHttpRequest(); xdrBlocked = new XMLHttpRequest();
         }

         //  Only proceed if cross-domain protections are available
```

```
        //  otherwise write a "not-available" message to the page
        if(xdrAllowed != null && xdrBlocked != null) {

           //  Point the xdrAllowed object to examples.proiedev.com
           xdrAllowed.onload  = onLoadAllowed;
           xdrAllowed.onerror = onErrorAllowed;
           xdrAllowed.open("GET",
              "http://examples.proiedev.com/03/xcomm/xdr/alloworigin/allow.php",
              true
              );

           //  Point the xdrAllowed object to www.ie-examples.com
           xdrBlocked.onload  = onLoadBlocked;
           xdrBlocked.onerror = onErrorBlocked;
           xdrBlocked.open("GET",
              "http://www.ie-examples.com/03/xcomm/xdr/alloworigin/block.php",
              true
              );

           //  Send requests to each domain
           xdrAllowed.send(null);
           xdrBlocked.send(null);

        } else displayNotAvailableMessage();

        //  Display a message on the page indicating origin header support
        //  isn't available on the current browser
        function displayNotAvailableMessage() {
           var resultDiv = document.getElementById("resultDiv")
           resultDiv.innerHTML = "<h3>XDomainRequest and origin-restricted XMLHttpRequest "
                               + "are not available in this browser.</h3>";
        }

        //  Generic function to display data in an element
        function displayEvent(id, text) {
           var element = document.getElementById(id);
           setText(element, text);
        }

        //  Set element text (cross-browser innerText/textContent)
        function setText(element, text) { /*...*/ }

      </script>
   </body>
</html>
```

The xdrAllowed and xdrBlocked objects are initialized to either an XDomainRequest or an XMLHttpRequest object. They each register onload and onerror event handlers and open a GET request to http://examples.proiedev.com and http://www.ie-examples.com, respectively.

After the page loads, the xdrAllowed and xdrBlocked objects open a connection with their respective servers. If a given request is successful, the onload event callback is executed; the onerror callback is run if that request is denied.

Building the Response

Webpages that receive a request via XDomainRequest or access-control-enabled XMLHttpRequest objects may use the Access-Control-Allow-Origin HTTP response header to indicate whether or not a resource is accessible. The header may contain one of two values pertaining to allowed origins: either an asterisk (*), which indicates the response page is intended for all origins, or a specific origin containing a protocol and domain (e.g. http://examples.proiedev.com). This header does not support multiple URLs, but a web application can simulate this functionality by serving different headers through logic switching using the HTTP request's Origin value.

***Listing 3-21.** Response allowing requests from examples.proiedev.com*

```
<?php
     header('Access-Control-Allow-Origin: http://examples.proiedev.com');
   header('Content-Type: text/plain');
   echo "Success!";
?>
```

Listing 3-21 is a sample response page requested by the xdrAllowed object in Listing 3-20. In this case, the server includes an Access-Control-Allow-Origin-Header header in its response, pointing to http://examples.proiedev.com. Since the requesting page matched this origin, IE displayed the response data after reading the server headers.

Listing 3-22 is the same exact response page that was used in the prior example. Unlike the other response, this page is hosted on the domain www.ie-examples.com and requires the origin of any request derive from http://www.ie-examples.com. The xdrBlocked object throws an error once IE sees that the allowed origin doesn't match the page making the request.

***Listing 3-22.** Response allowing requests from www.ie-examples.com*

```
<?php
   header('Access-Control-Allow-Origin: http://www.ie-examples.com');
   header('Content-Type: text/plain');
   echo "Success!";
?>
```

Putting it Together: The Request/Response Sequence

Examples in Listings 3-20, 3-21, and 3-22 represent a sample a request/response sequence using the cross-domain request object.

The example page in Figure 3-17 is a screenshot of the request page in Listing 3-20. On load, the page makes two Cross-Domain Requests from the URL http://examples.proiedev.com. The first request made is by the xdrAllowed object to a page hosted on the same domain, http://examples.proiedev.com. The response handler in Listing 3-21 allows for requests originating from http://examples.proiedev.com, thus the transaction is successful and the transaction's responseText value is displayed after xdrAllowed's onload even is raised.

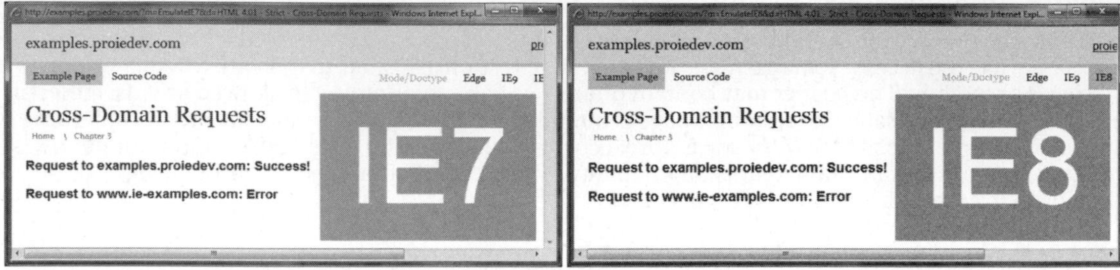

***Figure 3-17.** Webpage demonstrating Cross-Domain Requests in IE8*

The second request is made by `xdrBlocked` to a response page hosted on a different domain, `http://www.ie-examples.com`. The second response page from Listing 3-22 only allows for requests originating from `http://www.ie-examples.com`, thus it denies the access request. The `xdrBlocked` object raises its `onerror` event upon rejection, and the callback displays the word "Error" on the screen.

Building Interoperable Cross-Domain Requests

The relatively recent introduction of the `W3C Access Control for Cross-Site Requests` (the standard covering cross-domain request functionality) means that current cross-browser support is limited. At the time of IE8's release, Firefox 3.5 and Safari 4 supported this specification as an extension of the `XMLHttpRequest` object, whereas IE uses a separate `XDomainRequest` object. IE and other browsers also differ in the access control headers they support; IE, for instance, only recognizes the `Access-Control-Allow-Origin` header, whereas Firefox and Safari implement most if not all headers outlined in the W3C's specification.

Listing 3-23 provides some sample code that demonstrates a cross-browser implementation of cross-domain access control in JavaScript.

***Listing 3-23.** Cross-Browser compatible Cross-Domain Request sample*

```
<html>
   <head>
      <title>Building Interoperable Cross-Domain Requests</title>
   </head>
   <body>
      <div id="resultDiv">
         <h3>XDR over XDomainRequest? <span id="useXDR">No</span></h3>
         <h3>XDR over XMLHttpRequest? <span id="useXHR">No</span></h3>
      </div>
      <!-- Include PPK's BrowserDetect script from QuirksMode.org -->
      <script type="text/javascript" src="browserdetect.quirksmode.js"></script>
      <script type="text/javascript">

         //  Create variables to hold XDomainRequest or instances of
         //  XMLHttpRequest that offer origin header support
         var xdrAllowed = null;
         var xdrBlocked = null;
```

```
      //  Create XDomainRequest objects (or XMLHttpRequest objects
      //  if not IE and on a browser that offers origin header support)
      if(window.XDomainRequest) {
         xdrAllowed = new XDomainRequest(); xdrBlocked = new XDomainRequest();
         setText(document.getElementById("useXDR"), "Yes");
      } else if((BrowserDetect.browser = "Firefox" && BrowserDetect.version > 3.5) ||
                (BrowserDetect.browser = "Safari"  && BrowserDetect.version > 4)) {
         xdrAllowed = new XMLHttpRequest(); xdrBlocked = new XMLHttpRequest();
         setText(document.getElementById("useXHR"), "Yes");
      }

      //  Set element text (cross-browser innerText/textContent)
      function setText(element, text) { /*...*/ }

    </script>
  </body>
</html>
```

The sample itself implements only those features of cross-domain access control that are interoperable: the existence of an object that supports access control, and the `Access-Control-Allow-Origin` header.

■ **Note** In addition to a having a different object name versus other browsers (XDomainRequest versus XMLHttpRequest), Internet Explorer 8 only supports the Access-Control-Allow-Origin HTTP header.

Cross Frame Messaging with postMessage()

Cross-frame communication (that between a page and `<iframe>`) is been a pain point for developers building pages that contain multiple origins—commonly known as "mashups." IE and other browsers have put some strict security measures in place around what `<iframe>` objects and their hosts can do and how they can communicate. This isolation, however necessary, neuters communication between them. Developers have worked around this limitation by treating the `document.location.hash` as a mutual data store.

The HTML5 spec addresses establishes `postMessage()`and the `onmessage` event as a way for parents and their child `<iframe>` object to communicate. They can send and receive data between each other using this method as well as force the host browser to enforce origin-based restrictions on request.

Internet Explorer 8 implements this feature—the `postMessage()` method and `onmessage` event— for all document modes.

Objects

- `postMessage(msg [, targetOrigin])` **method** - Sends a message specified in the string `msg`. Further restrictions are placed through `targetOrigin`, which restricts the origin of content permitted to receive the message.

Events

- `onmessage` **event** - Fired when a target window object receives a message sent using the `postMessage()` method. The message itself is stored in a property on the event object.

- `origin` **property** - Returns the Origin of the document that sent the message.
- `data` **property** - Returns the message sent by the `origin` document.
- `type` **property** - The type of event, in this case `message`.

The code sample in Listing 3-24 shows a parent document that hosts an `<iframe>`. In IE8, these two documents can send messages to each other with `postMessage`. This page contains an `<input>` textbox and a submit button; the `onclick` event on the submit button sends the content of the `<input>` textbox to the iframe through `postMessage` located on the `<iframe>`'s `contentWindow` instance.

***Listing 3-24.** Code for a document parent hosting a frame object and communicating with postMessage*

```
<html>
   <head>
      <title>Cross Frame Messaging with postMessage</title>
   </head>
   <body>
      <h3>Parent Document (examples.proiedev.com)</h3>
      Post message to remote document (www.ie-examples.com):  
      <input id="postDataInput" size="25" type="text">  
      <input onclick="postToRemote();" type="submit" value="Post Message"><br><br>
      <iframe id="remoteFrame"
              src="http://www.ie-examples.com/03/xcomm/xdm/remote"
              width="400px" height="200px" class="highlightBorder"
              frameborder="no"></iframe>
      <script type="text/javascript">

         //  Post contents of an input box to a remote page
         function postToRemote() {

            //  Grab the input value from the box (explicitly type as a string to
            //  avoid pulling in a VT_NULL (IE Bug) and quit if empty
            var postData = String(document.getElementById("postDataInput").value);
            if (postData == "") return;

            //  Use postMessage to send the string message over to the remote page
            var remote = document.getElementById("remoteFrame");
            remote.contentWindow.postMessage(postData, "http://www.ie-examples.com");

         }

      </script>
   </body>
</html>
```

The parent page uses `postMessage`'s `targetOrigin` parameter to restrict what page can receive the message; even if an injected script manages to change the location of the parent's `<iframe>`, IE will only transport the message to a target at `http://www.ie-examples.com`.

Listing 3-25 is the code for the "receiver" document hosted in the parent's `<iframe>`. The script opts-in to messages from the parent by attaching itself to the `onmessage` event handler; using `attachEvent()` in IE and with `addEventListener()` in other browsers. When script on the parent page calls `postMessage()`, the `onmessage` event is fired in this page and the `receiveData()` callback is executed. Script writes data from the event to the screen whenever a message is received.

Listing 3-25. *Code sample for child frame using the onmessage event*

```
<html>
   <head>
      <title>Cross Frame Messaging with postMessage (Receiver)</title>
   </head>
   <body>
      <h3>Remote Page (www.ie-examples.com)</h3>
      Message Origin (e.origin): <span id="receivedDataOrigin"></span><br>
      Message Contents (e.data): <span id="receivedDataContents"></span><br>
      Message Type (e.type): <span id="receivedDataType"></span><br>
      <script type="text/javascript">

         //  Point the onmessage event callback to receiveData, either by
         //  using addEventListener or attachEvent
         if(window.addEventListener)
            window.addEventListener("message", receiveData, false);
         else window.attachEvent("onmessage", receiveData);

         //  Grab messages from the parent through this callback/event e
         function receiveData(e) {

            //  Make sure that the origin server is examples.proiedev.com
            if (e.data != "" && e.origin == "http://examples.proiedev.com") {

               //  Write message data to the webpage
               setText(document.getElementById("receivedDataOrigin"), e.origin);
               setText(document.getElementById("receivedDataContents"), e.data);
               setText(document.getElementById("receivedDataType"), e.type);

            }

         }

         //  Set element text (cross-browser innerText/textContent)
         function setText(element, text) { /*...*/ }

      </script>
   </body>
</html>
```

Figure 3-18 shows the pages described in the prior two code samples. The parent document, located at examples.proiedev.com, hosts an <iframe> that loads a page from www.ie-examples.com.

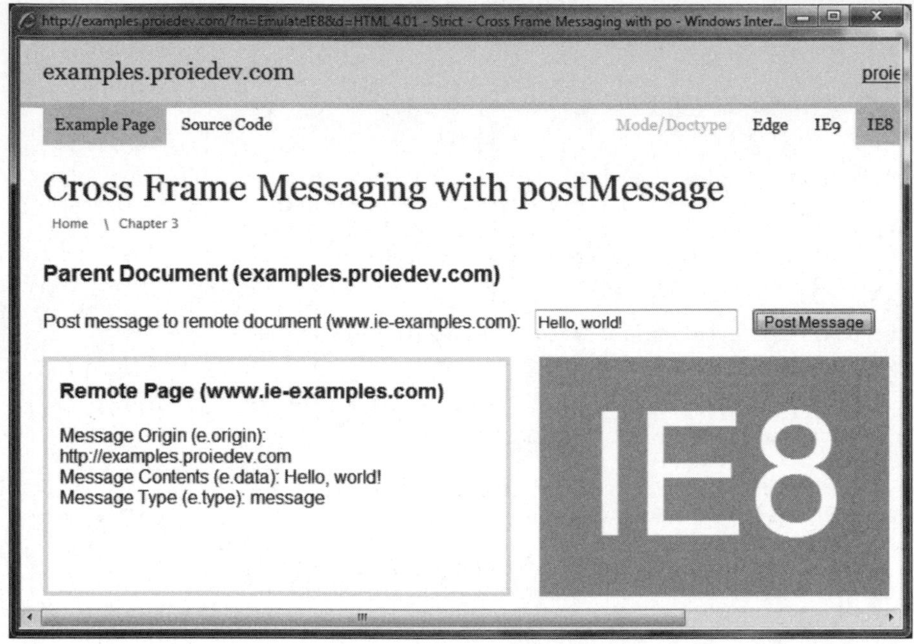

Figure 3-18. Sample page demonstrating Cross-Document Messaging with postMessage

A The parent calls `postMessage()` method to send a message (the contents of an `<input>` box) to the child frame when the "Post Message" `<input>` is clicked. The child frame receives notification of the message from the `onmessage` event, and promptly displays that message to the user.

■ **Note** IE does not permit webpages to communicate with popup windows or tabs through postMessage(), even those created by a webpage itself; Firefox and other browsers are more lenient.

Tips and Tricks for Secure Communication

The following tips and tricks provide insight into building websites that communicate across documents and domains securely.

- **Don't mix protocols.** Ensure that HTTPS pages do not rely on content served over HTTP. Mixed content is more than just an annoying dialog; trusted connections could be compromised if insecure content is added to a secure document.
- **Sanitize incoming data.** Web applications should sanitize all input being used by the web server. Data should be sanitized using server-side code and client-side methods such as `toStaticHTML()`.

- **Use postMessage() to communicate between documents.** It's reliable, broadly supported, and allows for mutually-suspicious cross-origin communication..
- **Protect against threats on both sides.** Insecure connections are subject to man-in-the-middle attacks, and servers must not assume that the browser is a trustworthy client.

Summary

IE8's changes with respect to AJAX and JSON allow developers to take advantage of some more advanced scenarios that simplify development of dynamic web applications. I used the samples to provide ways of using these features in an interoperable way and have highlighted some of the pitfalls and quirks that you could encounter when testing these features in IE. In the next chapter, I'll focus on some more interoperability scenarios regarding the Document Object Model and IE's JavaScript engine.

CHAPTER 4

■ ■ ■

Connecting Services with Accelerators

Accelerators were introduced in IE 8 as a way to reduce the number of steps required for targeted access to web services. They provide developers with a way to make page content actionable without constructing binary extensions. IE makes a number of Accelerators available during the first-run experience, linking users to Microsoft web services such as Windows Live Search and Bing Maps.

In this chapter I discuss how you can build rich Accelerators that provide a seamless link between page content with web services. I begin with some basics—the purpose, basic techniques, and technical overview of tags, variables, and structure needed to define them. I demonstrate how you can link these models with new or existing services, offer users the opportunity to install and manage Accelerators, and develop some interesting and compelling scenarios that were quite difficult prior to IE 8.

The What and Why of Accelerators

Accelerators are context menu extensions that integrate common online activities into the browser (see Figure 4–1 for an example Accelerator. Accelerators make use of the HTTP GET and POST requests, forwarding selected web page content to web services. Users decide which Accelerator to use based on a set of categories defined by the Accelerators they have installed.

Accelerators provide some unique advantages over binary context menu extensions and Browser Helper objects (BHOs). Namely, they offer a streamlined install experience, a good end-user management story, consistent UI behavior, good performance and reliability, and a simpler security model.

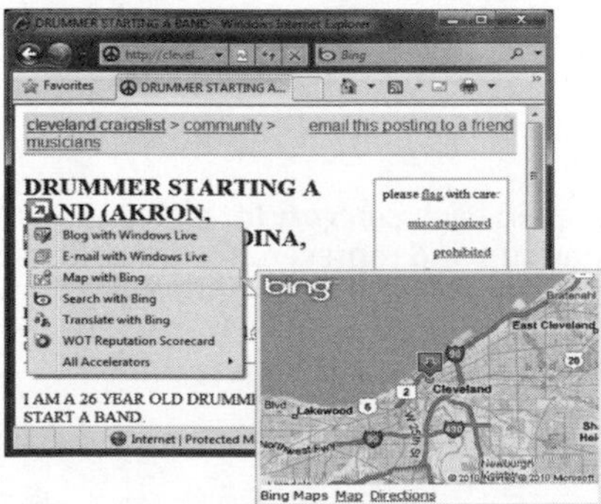

Figure 4–1. Example of an Accelerator that handles map content

Accelerators cannot execute binary code, nor can they directly access the DOM. Given their markup-based nature, the browser handles interpretation and execution. Downloaded Accelerators are stored in the registry and copied to users' Application Data folders.

■ **Note** Accelerators were originally called "activities" when they were introduced for IE 8 beta 1. Using both names when searching for more information or code snippets can help improve the result set.

User Experience and Data Flow

Accelerators are listed in two menus: the Accelerator menu (accented with a blue "gleam" icon) and the context menu. These menus are shown in Figure 4–2.

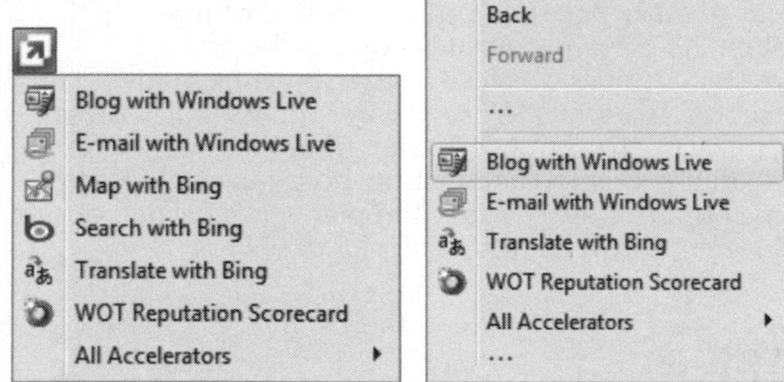

Figure 4–2. *Accelerator entry points: The Accelerator menu (left) and the context menu (right)*

The Accelerator gleam is only shown after a text selection. The icon, displayed in Figure 4–3, is shown near the text selection. This icon cannot be suppressed by web content.

Figure 4–3. *The Accelerator gleam icon, responsible for launching the Accelerator menu*

When either menu is triggered, IE displays the default Accelerators in each *category* for a given *context*. Categories are defined by Accelerators themselves in their markup and represent the general use cases they cover, and the defaults are the user-selected default Accelerators in each category. Accelerators not marked as category defaults are listed in the All Accelerators submenu.

There are three Accelerator contexts: selection, link, and document. Table 4–1 lists these three contexts for posterity.

***Table 4–1.** Data Contexts Within Accelerators*

Context	Description
Selection	Text selection on a document (either text or HTML)
Link	A link within a document, represented by text or objects encapsulated by an <a> tag
Document	The document itself or any scenario not covered by the other contexts

The selection context refers to any time text is selected on a document. The link context refers to a situation where a context menu is triggered over a link or the text selected is a link. The document context covers all other cases, when Accelerators are called without selected text or a targeted link. Categories, defaults, and context are covered in more detail later in this chapter.

An Accelerator with *preview* support will receive events when a user scrolls over it in either the context menu or the Accelerator menu. This action will launch a small preview window, as shown in the previous example (Figure 4–1). Preview windows allow Accelerators to provide some initial information about how their associated web service will react to the input content.

Once clicked, IE will trigger an *execute* event on a given Accelerator. This navigates to a web service specified in the Accelerator's definition file. Navigations are opened in a new tab, and a tab group is formed between the original link and the new Accelerator navigation (or merged with the original page's existing tab group). The Accelerator definition XML, described in subsequent sections, can pass a wide variety of data to a web service based on the context an Accelerator was run in.

The OpenService XML Schema

The OpenService XML schema, discussed in the previous section, provides a way for Accelerators to be defined using simple markup. This schema is made up of two main elements: *tags* and *variables.* OpenService tags are used to both define metadata describing the extentsion itself and specify that the browser should perform when certain events occur. OpenService variables are used to inform IE what data should be sent to a web service during an action.

Tags

Accelerator tags are used to instruct IE how to use, display, and execute a specific extension. Table 4–2 outlines the tags that can be used in constructing an Accelerator XML definition file and their individual descriptions.

***Table 4–2.** Tags in the OpenService Specification*

Tag	Description
<os:openServiceDescription>	Root tag of the Accelerator
<os:homepageUrl>	Specifies the home page of the Accelerator's web service
<os:display>	Parent tag for display information such as a name and icon
<os:name>	Specifies the name of the Accelerator
<os:icon>	Specifies a link to a 16×16-pixel icon in icon (ICO) format
<os:description>	Specifies the description of the Accelerator

Tag	Description
<os:activity>	Parent tag for actions in an Accelerator
<os:activityAction>	Defines an action within an Accelerator
<os:preview>	Specifies a web service for previewing content
<os:execute>	Specifies a web services for handling content
<os:parameter>	Specifies data to be sent to a web service

The `<os:openServiceDescription>` tag is the root tag in an extension's XML definition. The set of tags directly following the root (`<os:homepageUrl>`, `<os:display>`, `<os:name>`, `<os:icon>`, and `<os:description>`) represents metadata that explains what the control is and does.

`<os:activity>` contains action tags that inform IE *how* to send page content to one or many web services. It also contains one metadata element—the `category` attribute—allowing developers to specify the type of the add-on (such as Mail, Maps, or Search).

Actions (`<os:activityAction>`) define the context or contexts in which the Accelerator can be run: `selection` (representing content highlighted on a page), `document` (representing the document itself), and `link` (an `<a>` tag referring to a URL).

The last tags, *execute* and/or *preview*, define the events an action will respond to. The execute tag (`<os:execute>`) handles the `onClick` event, fired when a user clicks an Accelerator's context menu item. The preview tag (`<os:preview>`) is used for the `onHover` event of that same object (when a user places their mouse over that same item). One or both of these tags must be present in an action.

Variables

The OpenService XML definition provides variables as a way for IE to know what page content it should send to a web service. They represent items such as the source URL, content that was highlighted, and information about a link. They are only permitted within `<os:preview>`, `<os:execute>`, and `<os:parameter>` tags—the tags ultimately responsible for instructing IE how to talk to web services.

Table 4–3 outlines the variables IE can pass to a web service.

Table 4–3. *Variables in the OpenService Specification*

Variable	Context(s)	Return Types	Description
{documentUrl}	All	Text	The entire URL of the active page
{documentTitle}	All	Text	The title of the active page
{documentDomain}	All	Text	The domain of the active page
{documentHost}	All	Text	The fully qualified domain of the active page
{selection}	Selection	Text, HTML	The selected content on the current page
{link}	Link	Text	The entire URL of the selected link
{linkText}	Link	Text	The inner text of the selected link
{linkRel}	Link	Text	The object relationship of the selected link
{linkType}	Link	Text	The MIME type of the link (if specified)
{linkDomain}	Link	Text	The domain of the selected link
{linkHost}	Link	Text	The fully qualified domain of the selected link

Security and privacy mitigations prevent variables from being used in all cases. The following rules are in place to limit the amount of potentially private data leaked to a web service:

- The `{selection}` variable is only available in the selection context.
- The `{selection}` variable cannot be used by a preview except in the selection context.
- No variables will be transmitted between insecure and secure protocols (for instance, between HTTP and HTTPS contexts).
- Variables will not be transmitted from a less-restrictive security zone to one with more restriction (for instance, from the intranet zone to the Internet zone).
- Accelerators that do not pertain to the current context will not be shown (for instance, an Accelerator that doesn't implement the link context will not be displayed when a user accesses the context menu over an `<a>` tag).

Creating Basic Accelerators

The most basic Accelerator has two parts: first, an XML file defining when, why, and how it should operate; and second, a web service that handles and displays when a user interacts with it.

The following sections walk through the construction of an Accelerator called Tweet This! The first version lets users post text selected on a page to Twitter as a *tweet*. A tweet is a 140-character string posted to Twitter, describing what a person is doing for a given moment in time (aka microblogging). Figure 4–4 shows the first iteration of the extension.

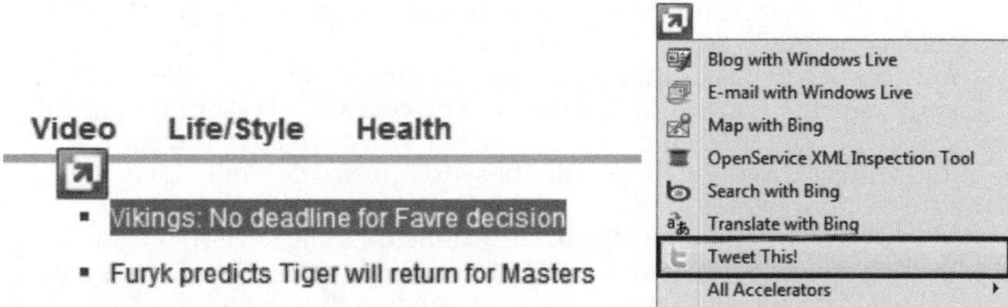

Figure 4–4. *Screenshot of the Tweet This! Accelerator example*

Constructing an Accelerator's XML File

The XML file that defines Tweet This! is used by IE to create a new context menu UI element and access the web service. The code sample in Listing 4–1 shows this markup.

Listing 4–1. *XML Definition for the First Iteration of Tweet This!*

```
<?xml version="1.0" encoding="UTF-8" ?>
<os:openServiceDescription
   xmlns:os="http://www.microsoft.com/schemas/openservicedescription/1.0">
   <os:homepageUrl>http://examples.proiedev.com/04/basic/xmlservice/</os:homepageUrl>
   <os:display>
      <os:name>Tweet This!</os:name>
```

```
        <os:icon>http://examples.proiedev.com/04/basic/xmlservice/favicon.ico</os:icon>
        <os:description>Tweet website content to your Twitter account.</os:description>
    </os:display>
    <os:activity category="Twitter">
        <os:activityAction context="selection">
            <os:execute
                action="http://examples.proiedev.com/04/basic/xmlservice/service.php"
                method="get">
                <os:parameter name="mode" value="execute" type="text" />
                <os:parameter name="type" value="selection" type="text" />
                <os:parameter name="documentUrl" value="{documentUrl}" type="text" />
                <os:parameter name="selection" value="{selection}" type="text" />
            </os:execute>
        </os:activityAction>
    </os:activity>
</os:openServiceDescription>
```

■ **Note** This and the remaining examples in this chapter use XML tags and variables described in Tables 4–2 and 4–3. Refer back to those tables for detailed information on how each portion of the XML file works.

The definition begins by creating a root `<os:openServiceDescription>` tag. The home page of the Accelerator is set in `<os:homepageUrl>` tags. Display information is defined in the `<os:display>` tag: the name is Tweet This, the icon is an ICO file residing on the same domain as the `<os:homepageUrl>`, and the description reads "Tweet website content to your Twitter account."

The `<os:activity>` defines how IE will call the Twitter web service handler. This example uses the `category` attribute tag to state that its category is a Twitter extension. The `<os:activityAction>` tag tells the browser to send the currently selected content to the web service if it's being used in the context of a `selection`. (Since only the selection context was defined, IE will not send information or display the Accelerator when nothing on the current page is selected).

The `<os:execute>` tag binds the `<os:activityAction>` tag to the extension's click event. It also specifies the web service URL with the `action` attribute and the HTTP method in the `method` attribute. `<os:execute>` has four child `<os:parameter>` tags, each defining a piece of data that IE will send to Twitter. The first two are hard-coded variables that indicate the initiating event (`execute`) and the context (`selection`). The last two parameters surface the source document's URL `{documentURL}` and the text selected on that page `{selectedText}`.

Constructing a Web Service Handler

The Tweet This! Accelerator uses a server-side script (shown in Listing 4–2) to convert data sent from IE into a Twitter post. The script submits a string no longer than 140 characters and one that contains plain text. In addition to the posting requirements, this script includes a link to the source page that is minified through a URL-shortening service.

Listing 4–2. *Web Service Handler for the Tweet This! Accelerator*

```
<?php

   //  Include some necessary functions (truncateString, getHTTPVar, ...)
   require_once('functions.php');

   //  Set the HTTP method used for passed variables
   $method              = METHOD_GET;

   //  Get values from HTTP variables
   $documentUrl         = getHTTPVar("documentUrl",    $method);
   $selection           = getHTTPVar("selection",      $method);

   //  Function to build a tweet (minify a URL and truncate a string
   //  to 140 characters)
   function buildTweet() {

      global $documentUrl;
      global $selection;

      //  Minify the URL (e.g., TinyURL)
      $minifiedURL = minifyURL($documentUrl);

      //  Truncate the text + URL to 140 characters or less
      $output  = truncateString($selection, 140 - strlen($minifiedURL));
      $output .= " " . $minifiedURL;

      //  Return the output (urlencoded if specified)
      return  urlencode($output);

   }

   //  Execute the Accelerator
   header('Location: http://twitter.com/home?status=' . buildTweet(true));

?>
```

The web service begins by reading the document URL and the page selection sent to it via an HTTP GET request. The page uses a special function for this (`getHTTPVar()`) that sanitizes the string for safe use. The document URL is then made into a short string (minified) through TinyURL.

The script takes selected content and minified URL and uses them to create a new message that is 140 or less characters in length. This value is sent to Twitter through an HTTP redirect, posting the string to a user's account (one opened in the same session context as the Accelerator).

Handling Accelerator Contexts

Accelerators can handle three basic contexts, or types of data: selections, links, and documents. When the Accelerator icon or the context menu is triggered on a page, IE displays the Accelerators that are registered for a specific context. For instance, if the context menu is triggered over a text selection, only those Accelerators registered for the selection context are available.

The following sections describe each of these contexts and how they can be handled by Accelerators and their related web services.

Using the Selection Context

The selection context represents content selected on a web page. Selected content can be text or a combination of text, images, and other content. Data from the selection context is served to a web service via the {selection} variable as either text or HTML. Listing 4–3 shows an XML definition that registers for the selection context.

***Listing 4–3.** Accelerator XML for the Selection Context*

```
...
<os:activityAction context="selection">
   <os:execute
      action="http://examples.proiedev.com/04/basic/post/service.php"
      method="post">
      <os:parameter name="mode" value="execute" type="text" />
      <os:parameter name="type" value="selection" type="text" />
      <os:parameter name="documentUrl" value="{documentUrl}" type="text" />
      <os:parameter name="selection" value="{selection}" type="text" />
   </os:execute>
</os:activityAction>
...
```

An action registers for the selection context through the context attribute of <os:activityAction>, setting its value to selection. The content can be passed to a web service through the {selection} variable previously mentioned. You can set web services to receive text contained within a selection by setting the type attribute of the parameter using the {selection} variable to text. You can set them to receive HTML from this variable by setting the same attribute to html.

Listing 4–4 shows the Tweet This! Accelerator handling content from the selection context.

***Listing 4–4.** Tweet This! Web Service Handler for the Selection Context*

```
//  Set the HTTP method used for passed variables
$method              = METHOD_POST;

//  Get values from HTTP variables
$documentUrl         = getHTTPVar("documentUrl",   $method);
$selection           = getHTTPVar("selection",     $method);

//  Function to build a tweet (minify a URL and truncate a string
//  to 140 characters)
function buildTweet() {

  global $documentUrl;
  global $selection;

  //  Minify the URL (e.g., TinyURL)
  $minifiedURL = minifyURL($documentUrl);

  //  Truncate the text + URL to 140 characters or less
  $output  = truncateString($selection, 140 - strlen($minifiedURL));
```

```
  $output .= " " . $minifiedURL;

  //  Return the output (urlencoded if specified)
  return  urlencode($output);

}
```

In this example, the web service grabs the values from {documentUrl} and {selection} through the HTTP request. It proceeds to build a new Twitter message whose content is based on the {selection} text and that creates a link to the value stored in {documentUrl}.

Special care should be used when accepting HTML from the {selection} variable. Content in this context could contain script intended for cross-site scripting attacks. IE's XSS filter will trigger if the browser detects script being displayed directly from this context in a web service; however, it will not catch all instances. Web services intending to receive raw HTML content from a selection context should properly sanitize this content before using it for internal functionality or displaying it to users.

■ **Note** Web services that receive HTML content from an Accelerator's {selection} context should take care to sanitize return values before using it for internal functionality or displaying it to users. IE's XSS filter may trigger if this content is used improperly, but it should not be relied upon to secure users or sites in all cases.

Using the Link Context

The link context represents Accelerators run when a link is the target of Accelerator execution. Links include any object (text, image, or otherwise) that is encapsulated in an <a> tag. Accelerators opting into this context have a number of link-specific variables available to them: {linkText}, {linkRel}, {linkType}, {linkDomain}, and {linkHost}. Listing 4–5 shows the Tweet This! Accelerator opting into the link context.

Listing 4–5. *Accelerator XML for the Link Context*

```
...
<os:activityAction context="link">
   <os:execute
      action="http://examples.proiedev.com/04/content/link/service.php"
      method="post">
      <os:parameter name="link" value="{link}" type="text" />
      <os:parameter name="linkText" value="{linkText}" type="text" />
   </os:execute>
</os:activityAction>...
```

An action registers for the link context through the context attribute of <os:activityAction>, setting its value to link. The content can be passed to a web service through any of the {link...} variables. These variables can only be transmitted via text formatting (unlike {selection}, which can be sent as either text or HTML).

Listing 4–6 shows the Tweet This! web service extended to handle the link context. In this case, the service uses the {linkText} passed from the Accelerator as the message content and the {link} variable as the target URL.

Listing 4–6. *Tweet This! Web Service Handler for the Link Context*

```
//  Set the HTTP method used for passed variables
$method              = METHOD_POST;

//  Get values from HTTP variables
$link                = getHTTPVar("link",         $method);
$linkText            = getHTTPVar("linkText",     $method);

//  Function to build a tweet (minify a URL and truncate a string
//  to 140 characters)
function buildTweet() {

  global $link;
  global $linkText;

  //  Minify the URL (e.g., TinyURL)
  $minifiedURL = minifyURL($link);

  //  Truncate the text + URL to 140 characters or less
  $output  = truncateString($linkText , 140 - strlen($minifiedURL));
  $output .= " " . $minifiedURL;

  //  Return the output (urlencoded if specified)
  return  urlencode($output);

}
```

Using the Document Context

The document context represents execution of an Accelerator without a clear target—essentially, it is the catchall case, covering everything besides selection or link targeting. For instance, right-clicking any space in a document or on an image will trigger Accelerators opting into the document context. The {documentUrl}, {documentTitle}, {documentDomain}, and {documentHost} variables are available in this context. Listing 4–7 shows the Tweet This! Accelerator handling the document context.

Listing 4–7. *Accelerator XML for the Document Context*

```
...
<os:activityAction context="document">
   <os:execute
      action="http://examples.proiedev.com/04/content/link/service.php"
      method="post">
      <os:parameter name="documentUrl" value="{documentUrl}" type="text" />
      <os:parameter name="documentTitle" value="{documentTitle}" type="text" />
   </os:execute>
</os:activityAction>
...
```

An action registers for the document context through the context attribute of <os:activityAction>, setting its value to document. The content can be passed to a web service through any of the {document...} variables. These variables can only be transmitted via text formatting.

Listing 4–8 shows the Tweet This! web service handling the document context. In this case, the service uses the `{documentTitle}` as the Twitter post content and the `{documentUrl}` as the target link.

***Listing 4–8.** Tweet This! Web Service Handler for the Document Context*

```
//  Set the HTTP method used for passed variables
$method             = METHOD_POST;

//  Get values from HTTP variables
$documentUrl        = getHTTPVar("documentUrl",   $method);
$documentTitle      = getHTTPVar("documentTitle", $method);

//  Function to build a tweet (minify a URL and truncate a string
//  to 140 characters)
function buildTweet() {

  global $documentUrl;
  global $documentTitle;

  //  Minify the URL (e.g., TinyURL)
  $minifiedURL = minifyURL($documentUrl);

  //  Truncate the text + URL to 140 characters or less
  $output  = truncateString($documentTitle, 140 - strlen($minifiedURL));
  $output .= " " . $minifiedURL;

  //  Return the output (urlencoded if specified)
  return  urlencode($output);

}
```

Implementing Previews

Accelerators have the option to provide content previews without having to make a full navigation to a web service. Previews are displayed as small windows (320×240 pixels) to the right or left of the context menu. They become visible when the mouse enters an Accelerator's menu UI and disappear when it leaves that same area. An example of the preview can be seen in the Map with Bing Accelerator, shown in Figure 4–5.

Adding a preview to an Accelerator requires two changes be made to it: the insertion of an `<os:preview>` tag into its XML definition and the inclusion of a web service that provides a page supporting the size and security constraints of the preview window.

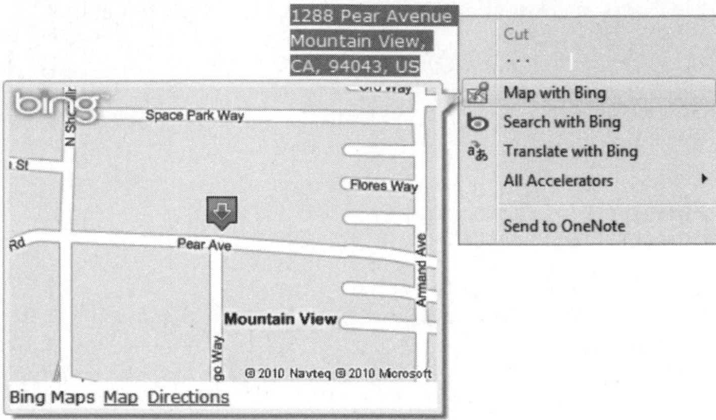

Figure 4–5. Bing Maps Accelerator preview window

Adding a preview window the Tweet This! Accelerator follows the same process. First, `<os:preview>` tags are added to any `<os:activityAction>` where a preview window is desired. In this case, a preview window will be added to all the contexts (`selection`, `document`, and `link`). Listing 4–9 shows the result of this change.

***Listing 4–9.** Tweet This! XML Definition with Preview Support*

```
...
   <os:activityAction context="document">
      <os:preview
         action="http://examples.proiedev.com/04/twitter/service.php"
         method="post">
         <os:parameter name="mode" value="preview" type="text" />
         <os:parameter name="type" value="document" type="text" />
         <os:parameter name="documentUrl" value="{documentUrl}" type="text" />
         <os:parameter name="documentTitle" value="{documentTitle}" type="text" />
      </os:preview>
   ...
   </os:activityAction>
   <os:activityAction context="selection">
      <os:preview
         action="http://examples.proiedev.com/04/twitter/service.php"
         method="post">
         <os:parameter name="mode" value="preview" type="text" />
         <os:parameter name="type" value="selection" type="text" />
         <os:parameter name="documentUrl" value="{documentUrl}" type="text" />
         <os:parameter name="selection" value="{selection}" type="text" />
      </os:preview>
   ...
   </os:activityAction>
   <os:activityAction context="link">
      <os:preview
         action="http://examples.proiedev.com/04/twitter/service.php"
```

```
            method="post">
            <os:parameter name="mode" value="preview" type="text" />
            <os:parameter name="type" value="link" type="text" />
            <os:parameter name="link" value="{link}" type="text" />
            <os:parameter name="linkText" value="{linkText}" type="text" />
        </os:preview>
    ...
    </os:activityAction>
...
```

Each <os:preview> tag needs to pass the same information as the <os:execute> tags in each action. To do this, the <os:parameter> tags in each sibling <os:execute> are copied over, the only change to the copies being the value of the mode tags.

The second half of the change is shown in Listing 4–10. The update adds HTML to the web service that is specially formatted to display in the preview window. Logic is added to the server side, which either displays the preview content or calls into Twitter based on whether the preview or execute mode was used.

Listing 4–10. *Web Service Handler for the Tweet This! Accelerator with Preview Support*

```
<?

  ...

  //  Execute the Accelerator if the mode is set to MODE_EXECUTE
  if($mode == MODE_EXECUTE) {
     header('Location: http://twitter.com/home?status=' . buildTweet(true));
     exit();
  }

  //  Otherwise, display the preview!

?>

<html>
  <head>
     <meta http-equiv="X-UA-Compatible" content="IE=edge">
     <meta http-equiv="Pragma" content="no-cache">
     <title>Tweet This! Preview</title>
              <link type="text/css" rel="stylesheet" href="styles/preview.css">
  </head>
  <body>
     <div id="container">
     <div id="container">
        <div id="logo">
           <img src="images/logo.png">
        </div>
        <div id="preview"><img id="shadow" src="images/shadow.png"></div>
        <div id="content"><? echo(buildTweet()); ?></div>
     </div>
  </body>
</html>
```

Figure 4–6 shows the Tweet This! Accelerator being used to preview content before sending data to the Twitter web service.

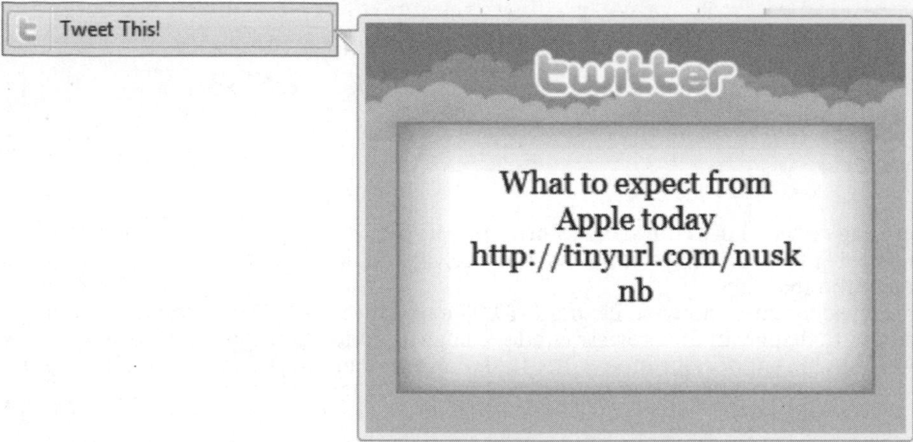

Figure 4–6. The Tweet This! Accelerator preview window

Installation and Deployment

IE provides a simple model for deploying Accelerators inside or outside of the browser. The following sections review script-based and COM-based interfaces that can be used to install and deploy Accelerators onto user accounts.

Installing and Deploying via JavaScript

The most common method for installing and deploying Accelerators is through a web page using markup and JavaScript. Accelerators can be installed using the `AddService()` function, located on the `window.external` JavaScript object (see Listing 4–11).

Listing 4–11. The window.external.AddService() Method

```
window.external.AddService('twitter.Accelerator.xml');
```

This call can be tied to any user-initiated object or event such as the `onClick` event of a `<button>`. Listing 4–12 shows a link that allows a user to install the Tweet This! Accelerator when clicked.

Listing 4–12. Using AddService in an <a> Tag

```
<a href="javascript:window.external.AddService
  ('twitter.Accelerator.xml'); return false;">
  Install the Tweet This! Accelerator
</a>
```

Invocation of `AddService()` presents a user with an installation dialog (see Figure 4–7). The dialog contains an Accelerator's name, source web site, destination, and category. A user may set the new Accelerator as the default service provider for a specific category.

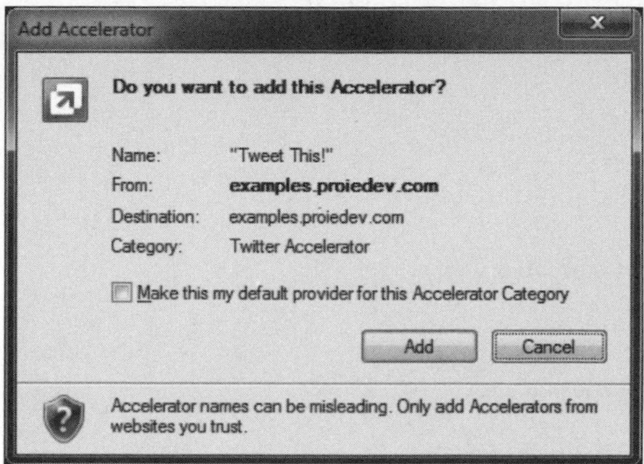

Figure 4–7. The Accelerator installation dialog

Users can access the new Accelerator through the context menu immediately after installation.

Checking for Installed Accelerators

The `isServiceInstalled()` method (see Listing 4–13) allows developers to check if an Accelerator is already installed. Web services may invoke `isServiceInstalled()` to control the display of Accelerator installation buttons on web pages. They may also call it to provide specially formatted content for those users that have a given Accelerator installed.

Listing 4–13. The window.external.isServiceInstalled() Method

```
window.external.isServiceInstalled('twitter.Accelerator.xml');
```

This API may only be called on pages from the Accelerator's domain; for example, it cannot be called to determine if a competitor's Accelerator is installed.

Installing and Deploying via Desktop Applications

Accelerator installation is not limited to web sites; binary applications that wish to install Accelerators can do so through public OpenService COM interfaces. These interfaces expose functionality that mimics that found in the JavaScript functions, allowing Accelerators to be installed by pointing IE to the URL of their XML definition. The following sections demonstrate these interfaces and detail how Accelerators are stored in the registry and user-owned folders after installation.

Using the OpenService COM Interfaces

IE exposes a number of interfaces that handle the installation and management of Accelerators. Exposed OpenService interfaces may be found in the `openservice.idl` definition file.

Binary applications installing Accelerators will use two interfaces and one coclass to do so: `IOpenServiceManager`, `IOpenService`, and the `OpenServiceManager` coclass. Listing 4–14 shows a C# interop file that defines the existence of these items for use in a .NET application.

Listing 4–14. C# Interop Definition for Interfaces Used in Accelerator Installation

```
[Guid("098870b6-39ea-480b-b8b5-dd0167c4db59")]
[ComImport, ClassInterface(ClassInterfaceType.None)]
public class OpenServiceManager
{
   //  Coclass exposed through IEOpenServiceObjects
}

[Guid("5664125f-4e10-4e90-98e4-e4513d955a14")]
[ComImport, InterfaceType(ComInterfaceType.InterfaceIsIUnknown)]
public interface IOpenServiceManager
{
   void InstallService(
      [MarshalAs(UnmanagedType.LPWStr)] string pwzServiceUrl,
      out IOpenService ppService);

   void UninstallService(
      IOpenService pService);

   void GetServiceByID(
      [MarshalAs(UnmanagedType.LPWStr)] string pwzID,
      out IOpenService ppService);
}

[Guid("C2952ED1-6A89-4606-925F-1ED8B4BE0630")]
[ComImport, InterfaceType(ComInterfaceType.InterfaceIsIUnknown)]
public interface IOpenService
{
   void IsDefault(
      [MarshalAs(UnmanagedType.Bool)] out bool pfIsDefault);

   void SetDefault(
      [MarshalAs(UnmanagedType.Bool)] bool fDefault,
      IntPtr hwnd);

   void GetID(
      [MarshalAs(UnmanagedType.BStr)] out string pbstrID);
}
```

A sample project—the Manage Accelerators application—was created to highlight the use of the OpenService COM definitions. The sample shown in Figure 4–8 is a simple form containing a text box, a check box, and a button.

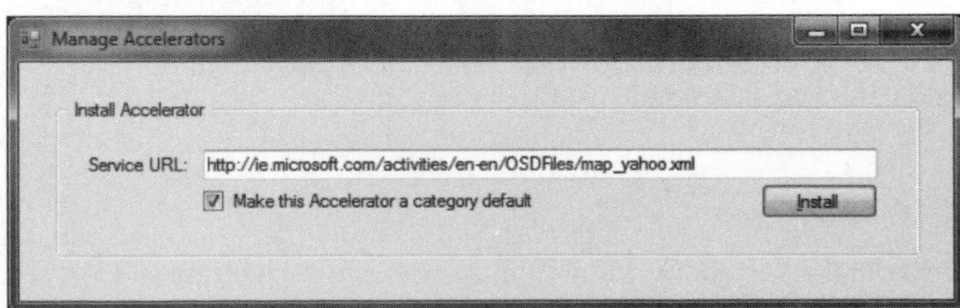

Figure 4–8. The Manage Accelerators sample application

The text box accepts a URL pointing to an Accelerator's XML definition file. The check box tells the sample to either request that the Accelerator be installed as a default for its category (checked) or install without requesting default status (unchecked). The button handles the installation process through its mouse click event handler.

The installation process, shown in Listing 4–15 through an event handler, begins with the definition of IOpenServiceManager and IOpenService objects. The openServiceManager variable is set to a new instance of the OpenServiceManager coclass, based on the IOpenServiceManager interface. The openService variable is defined as an IOpenService type but is left uninitialized; the installer function will use this variable to reference a new IOpenService object created during the installation process.

Listing 4–15. *Button Event Handler That Triggers an Accelerator Installation*

```
//  Handle the onClick event of the Install button
private void buttonInstallAccelerator_Click(object sender, EventArgs e)
{

   //  Create the OpenServiceManager and IOpenService objects
   IOpenServiceManager openServiceManager = (IOpenServiceManager) new OpenServiceManager();
   IOpenService openService;

   //  Install the service and have an object representation saved to
   //  the openService placeholder
   openServiceManager.InstallService(
      this.textServiceURL.Text,      // URL of the Accelerator
      out openService                // Created OpenService object
      );

   //  If instructed to set as default, do so by calling the SetDefault
   //  function on the openService object.  Send this form's window handle
   //  in case a modal dialog needs to be thrown
   if (this.checkDefault.Checked)
      openService.SetDefault(true, this.Handle);

}
```

The InstallService() function is called from the openServiceManager variable to initiate an Accelerator installation. This function accepts a URL pointing to an XML file (in this case, the string is found in the sample application's text box) and a variable to write a newly created IOpenService object (the uninitialized openService variable in Listing 4–15). If this function successfully installs the Accelerator, the openService variable will be set to a valid object using the IOpenService interface.

Successfully installed Accelerators can be set as the default extension in their category through the SetDefault() method on an IOpenService object. The Manage Accelerators example provides a check box allowing a user to decide if an Accelerator should be installed as a default. The SetDefault() function is called on the openService variable when this option is selected. This function accepts two parameters: a Boolean setting the Accelerator to the default (true) or not (false), and a window handle (HWND) of a visible window owned by the calling application.

Accelerators and the Registry

The registry and user folders can be used to install an Accelerator outside of IE. Data is stored in the HKEY_CURRENT_USER\Software\Microsoft\Windows\CurrentVersion\Internet Settings\Activities registry key. Local copies of an Accelerator's XML definition are saved in IE's Application Data folder for a given user. Listing 4–16 highlights the structure of the registry key.

Listing 4–16. *Example of an Accelerator That Passes a Version Value*

```
HKEY_CURRENT_USER\
    Software\
        Microsoft\
            Windows\
                CurrentVersion\
                    Internet Settings\
                        Activities\
                            (Category)\
                                (Domain)\
                                    (Action1)\
                                        preview\
                                            (Parameter1)\
                                            ...
                                            (Parametern)\
                                        execute\
                                            (Parameter1)\
                                            ...
                                            (Parametern)\
                                    (Action2)\
                                        ...
                                    (Action3)\
                                        ...
```

Accelerators are stored in keys based on their category (Map, Email, etc.). Each category specifies the default Accelerator for itself in the `DefaultActivity` value. Under each category is a folder for the Accelerator's host domain; note the limitation of one host domain per category, as mentioned in the previous section on categories and defaults. Table 4–4 highlights these keys and values, as well as their corresponding mapping in the OpenService XML schema.

Table 4–4. *Keys and Values for a Category Key ...\Activities\(Category)*

	Name	Value Type	XML Mapping	Description/Range
Value	(Default)	REG_SZ	-	Not used
Value	DefaultActivity	REG_SZ	<os:activityAction>	String representing the link
Key	{Domain}	-	-	Registry key representing a preview action and parameters

The `{Domain}` key under a `{Category}` represents an Accelerator. Most of the values under this key directly map to values specified in the metadata of the XML definition file, with a few notable exceptions. The `Description`, `DisplayName`, `HomepageUrl`, `Icon`, and `Verb` values map directly to attributes and values found in the OpenService XML schema. Of the remaining values, `ContentMask` presents the most unique construct; its value must be a bitmask of all supported contexts whose values map to the `OpenServiceActivityContentType` enumeration in Listing 4–17.

Listing 4–17. *The OpenServiceActivityContentType Enum, Used for the ContentMask Bitmask*

```
public enum OpenServiceActivityContentType
{
   ActivityContentNone = -1,      // Ignore
   ActivityContentDocument,       // 1
   ActivityContentSelection,      // 2
   ActivityContentLink,           // 4
   ActivityContentCount           // Ignore
};
```

Table 4–5 details all the values associated with this key in further detail.

Table 4–5. *Keys and Values for a Domain Key ...\Activities\(Category)\(Domain)*

	Name	Value Type	XML Mapping	Description/Range
Value	(Default)	REG_SZ	-	Not used
Value	ActionCount	REG_DWORD	-	Integer from 1 to 3, representing the number of actions handling each context
Value	ContentMask	REG_DWORD	-	Integer bitmask of all contexts handled by actions; values map to the OpenServiceActivityContentType enum
Value	Deleted	REG_DWORD	-	Integer representing deletion state; either 0 (present) or 1 (deleted)
Value	Description	REG_SZ	<os:description>	String used as the description
Value	DisplayName	REG_SZ	<os:name>	String used as the display name
Value	Domain	REG_SZ	-	String indicating the Accelerator's source domain
Value	DownloadUrl	REG_SZ	-	String representing the Accelerator's URL origin
Value	Enabled	REG_DWORD	-	Integer representing enabled state; either 0 (disabled) or 1 (enabled)
Value	HomepageURL	REG_SZ	<os:homepageUrl>	String representing the home page of the Accelerator's creator
Value	Icon	REG_SZ	<os:icon>	String pointing to the Accelerator's identifying icon

	Name	Value Type	XML Mapping	Description/Range
Value	Type	REG_DWORD		Integer; value must equal 1
Value	Verb	REG_SZ	<os:activity>	String representing the Accelerator's category
Value	XML	REG_SZ	-	String representing the local file system location of the Accelerator's XML definition
Value	XMLUrl	REG_SZ	-	String representing the Accelerator's XML URL
Key	Action{1..3}	-	<os:activityAction>	Registry keys representing up to three actions associated with an Accelerator; each action covers a specific context

The Domain key also contains subkeys that define actions (supported contexts and their web service definitions) for the Accelerator. One to three action keys can exists (one is required), and each is sequentially numbered from one to three (e.g., Action1, Action2, Action3). Contents of these keys are described in the following paragraphs.

An Accelerator can have at least one and up to three Action{1..3} keys. These keys represent Accelerator actions that handle one of the three available contexts: selection, link, or document. The Context value represents this information, whose value is the same as that contained in the context attribute of the <os:activityAction> tag. HasPreview is a Boolean DWORD, where 0 means there is no preview associated with an Accelerator and 1 indicates there is one (which means a corresponding preview key must exist). The execute and preview keys represent the execute and preview methods defined in an Accelerator's <os:execute> and <os:preview> tags, respectively. Table 4–7 highlights the details of these attributes and keys.

Table 4–6. *Keys and Values for an Execute or Preview Key ...\(Domain)\(Action#)*

	Name	Value Type	XML Mapping	Description/Range
Value	(Default)	REG_SZ	-	Not used
Value	Context	REG_SZ	<os:activityAction>	String representing the Accelerator's context (selection, document, link)
Value	HasPreview	REG_DWORD	-	Integer representing whether an Accelerator has a preview (1) or doesn't (0)
Key	execute		<os:execute>	Registry key representing an execute action and parameters
Key	preview	-	<os:preview>	Registry key representing a preview action and parameters

The execute and preview keys map to the <os:execute> and <os:preview> tags, respectively, in an Accelerator's XML definition. All values under this key, save for ParamCount, directly map to the attributes in each tag. Parameters are stored as sequentially numbered child keys, the total number of which is reflected in the ParamCount value. Detailed information can be found in Table 4–7.

Table 4–7. *Keys and Values for an Execute or Preview Key ...\(Domain)\(Action#)\(execute|preview)*

	Name	Value Type	XML Mapping	Description/Range
Value	(Default)	REG_SZ	-	Not used.
Value	Action	REG_SZ	<os:execute> <os:preview>	String representing the web service to be called.
Value	Method	REG_SZ	<os:execute> <os:preview>	String specifying the HTTP request type, either get or post.
Value	Enctype	REG_SZ	<os:execute> <os:preview>	String specifying the MIME type of the request sent to a web service.
Value	Accept-charset	REG_SZ	<os:execute> <os:preview>	String specifying the character set of the web service request.
Value	ParamCount	REG_DWORD	-	Integer representing the number of parameters defined for this method.
Key	Parameter{1..n}		<os:execute> <os:preview>	Registry key representing parameters for this method. The key count must match the number in ParamCount.

Parameters for execute and preview methods each have a key named in sequential order starting with Parameter1. These keys and their values directly map to the structure found in the OpenService <os:parameter> tag. The name value represents the parameter name, the same value found in the name attribute of <os:parameter>; the type and value values also map to attributes with the same names in this tag. Detailed information can be found in Table 4–8.

Table 4–8. *Keys and Values for a Parameter Key ...\(Domain)\(Action#)\(execute|preview)\(Parameter#)*

	Name	Value Type	XML Mapping	Description/Range
Value	(Default)	REG_SZ	-	Not used.
Value	Name	REG_SZ	<os:parameter>	String representing the name of a parameter to be sent to a web service.
Value	Type	REG_SZ	<os:parameter>	String representing format of replacement variables such as {selection}. Accepted values are text or html.
Value	Value	REG_SZ	<os:parameter>	String representing the value of the parameter to be sent to a web service.

Listing 4–18 aims to clarify the preceding tables. The following registry script represents an export of the Tweet This! Accelerator. The file begins with the category key (in this case, "Twitter") and continues on to the definition of individual parameters; the export demonstrates the structure of an Accelerator's registry entry and the hierarchy of its data.

***Listing 4–18.** Registry Export of the Tweet This! Accelerator*

```
Windows Registry Editor Version 5.00

[HKEY_CURRENT_USER\Software\Microsoft\Windows\CurrentVersion\Internet
Settings\Activities\Twitter]

[HKEY_CURRENT_USER\Software\Microsoft\Windows\CurrentVersion\Internet
Settings\Activities\Twitter\proiedev.com]
"Icon"="C:\\Users\\mattcrow\\AppData\\LocalLow\\Microsoft\\Internet
Explorer\\Services\\Twitter_proiedev.com.ico"
"Description"="Tweet website content to your Twitter account."
"HomepageURL"="http://examples.proiedev.com/04/twitter/"
"Domain"="proiedev.com"
"Verb"="Twitter"
"DisplayName"="Tweet This!"
"XMLUrl"="http://examples.proiedev.com/04/twitter/twitter.xml"
"XML"="C:\\Users\\mattcrow\\AppData\\LocalLow\\Microsoft\\Internet
Explorer\\Services\\Twitter_proiedev.com.xml"
"DownloadUrl"="http://examples.proiedev.com/04/twitter/"
"Type"=dword:00000001
"Enabled"=dword:00000001
"Deleted"=dword:00000000
"ActionCount"=dword:00000003
"ContentMask"=dword:00000007

[HKEY_CURRENT_USER\Software\Microsoft\Windows\CurrentVersion\Internet
Settings\Activities\Twitter\proiedev.com\Action1]
"Context"="document"
"HasPreview"=dword:00000001

[HKEY_CURRENT_USER\Software\Microsoft\Windows\CurrentVersion\Internet
Settings\Activities\Twitter\proiedev.com\Action1\execute]
"Action"="http://examples.proiedev.com/04/twitter/service.php"
"Method"="post"
"Enctype"="application/x-www-form-urlencoded"
"Accept-charset"="utf-8"
"ParamCount"=dword:00000004

[HKEY_CURRENT_USER\Software\Microsoft\Windows\CurrentVersion\Internet
Settings\Activities\Twitter\proiedev.com\Action1\execute\Parameter1]
"Name"="mode"
"Value"="execute"
"Type"="text"

...
```

There are a myriad of settings that are set in the Accelerator installation process. While some use of the registry is unavoidable, developers should use either the script-based or COM versions of the OpenService APIs for installation and management of Accelerators.

Working with Categories and Defaults

Accelerators specify a category in their XML definition that best describes their activity. The default Accelerator for each category is chosen either by the user through web-based installation and Manage Add-Ons, or by a binary application run under user consent. If an Accelerator is installed as a default service provider, or if it is the only Accelerator in a given category, it will be shown on the top level of its context menu; otherwise, it will be in the second-level Accelerator submenu (see Figure 4–9).

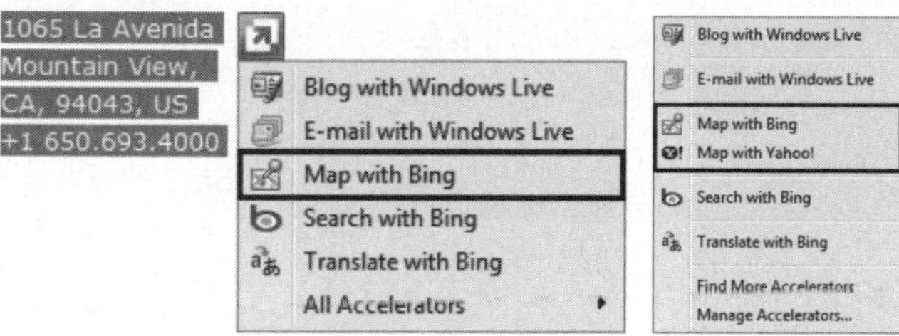

***Figure 4–9.** The Accelerator menus*

The lack of a fixed set of categories lends itself to abuse. Accelerators can "automatically" become a default provider and earn better placement by creating unique category names. Although the results are tempting, developers must avoid creating unique categories for every Accelerator offered. Not only does this add to clutter in a user's context menu, too many Accelerators may turn off users to a brand. Since Manage Add-Ons offers an easy way for users to remove them, Accelerators for a specific brand can easily be uninstalled if they provoke a user to do so.

Managing Accelerators

Accelerators must be uninstalled from the Manage Add-Ons interface within IE (see Figure 4–10). Developers cannot uninstall Accelerators from a web page via JavaScript.

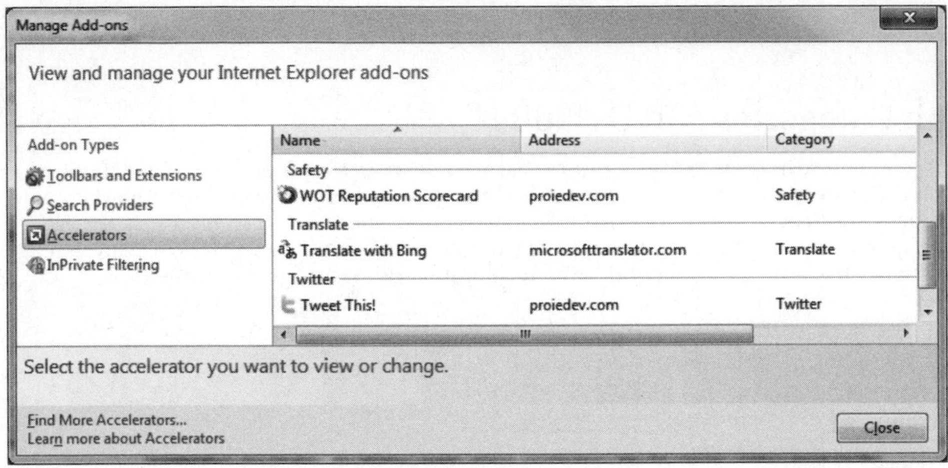

Figure 4–10. The IE Manage Add-Ons interface

Users can disable an Accelerator by selecting an Accelerator and clicking the Disable button in the information pane, as shown in Figure 4–11.

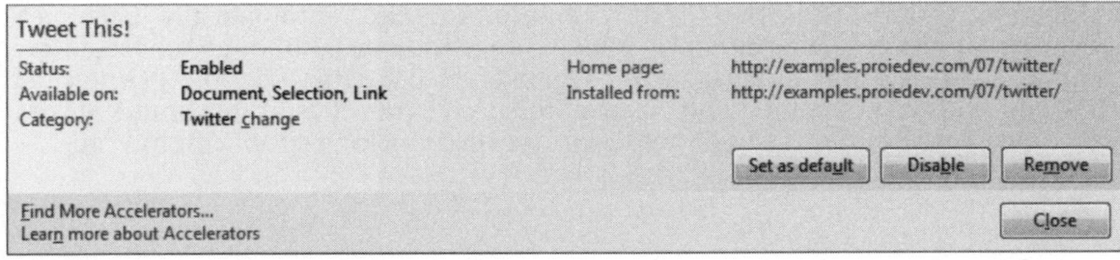

Figure 4–11. Disabling an Accelerator

This pane also allows for two more actions: "Remove as default" removes an Accelerator as the default for its category, and Remove uninstalls the Accelerator.

Advanced Topics

Developers may come across a number of issues outside of the ones outlined here. The following sections cover some more advanced topics, such as using Accelerators for third-party services and localization.

Updating Installed Accelerators

Accelerators can be upgraded in the same way they are installed—using the `AddService()` method. Instead of being given a standard installation dialog, users are asked if they wish to replace the existing Accelerator, as shown in Figure 4–12.

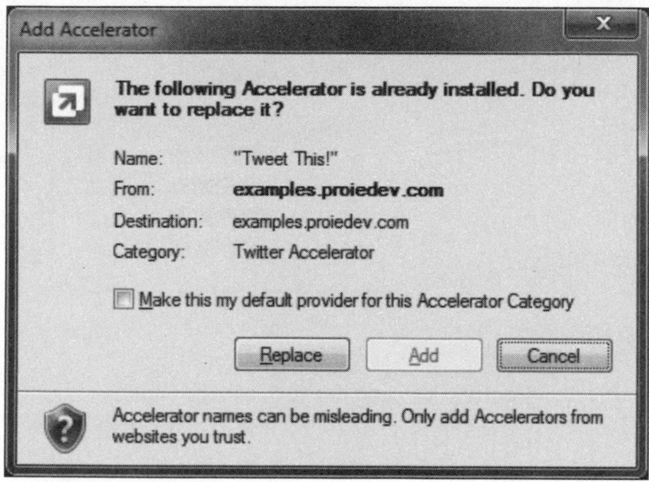

Figure 4–12. *The Accelerator replacement and upgrade dialog*

There is no automatic, push-down mechanism whereby a web service can upgrade previously installed Accelerators. Accelerators can, however, be designed to pass a version number to a web service via a `<parameter>` tag. Users can then be prompted to upgrade an Accelerator from that service.

Listing 4–19 shows an Accelerator that passes version information to its web service. On receipt of the `version` variable, a web service may return a notice to a user that an upgrade is necessary through the preview window or the target page.

Listing 4–19. *Example of an Accelerator That Passes a Version Value*

```
...
<activityAction context="selection">
    <execute
      action="http://examples.proiedev.com/book/examples/flip/flip.html"
      method="get">
        <parameter name="t" value="{selection}" type="text" />
        <parameter name="version" value="1.0" type="text" />
    </execute>
</activityAction>
...
```

Building Rich Previews

Accelerators don't need to defer to a new window or even implement the execute method in their definition. Preview windows can be used to create rich experiences without the need to navigate to a web service. Figure 4–13 demonstrates an Accelerator called the WOT Reputation Scorecard, and an extension that uses APIs provided by the Web-of-Trust link reputation service. This Accelerator allows users to learn the reputation of a URL before navigating to it.

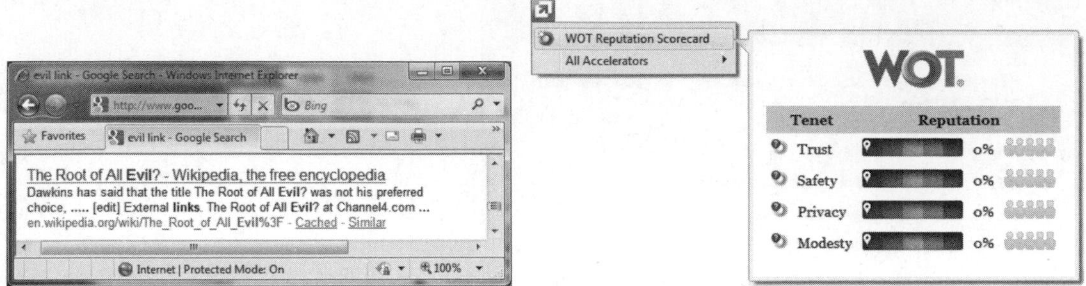

Figure 4–13. The WOT Reputation Scorecard Accelerator

Listing 4–20 shows the XML definition for this Accelerator. For each context, the only method is available is preview, which routes link information back to a web service. There is no execute method.

Listing 4–20. XML for the WOT URL Reputation Accelerator

```
<?xml version="1.0" encoding="UTF-8" ?>
<os:openServiceDescription
   xmlns:os="http://www.microsoft.com/schemas/openservicedescription/1.0">
   <os:homepageUrl>http://examples.proiedev.com/04/advanced/mixed/</os:homepageUrl>
   <os:display>
      <os:name>WOT Reputation Scorecard</os:name>
      <os:icon>http://examples.proiedev.com/04/advanced/mixed/favicon.ico</os:icon>
      <os:description>The WOT community has rated millions of websites.
         Use their warnings to protect yourself from online scams, sites
         with adult content and spam.
      </os:description>
   </os:display>
   <os:activity category="Safety">
      ...
      <os:activityAction context="link">
         <os:preview
            action="http://examples.proiedev.com/04/advanced/mixed/service.php" k
            method="post">
            <os:parameter name="mode" value="document" type="preview" />
            <os:parameter name="type" value="document" type="link" />
            <os:parameter name="documentDomain" value="{documentDomain}" type="text" />
            <os:parameter name="linkDomain" value="{linkDomain}" type="text" />
         </os:preview>
      </os:activityAction>
   </os:activity>
</os:openServiceDescription>
```

Listing 4–21 is the web service for this Accelerator. Unlike the Tweet This! example, the main focus of this page is to display content in the preview window without navigating to a web service.

***Listing 4–21.** XML for the WOT URL Reputation Accelerator*

```
<html>
   <head>
      <meta http-equiv="X-UA-Compatible" content="IE=edge">
      <meta http-equiv="Pragma" content="no-cache">
      <title>WOT URL Reputation Service</title>
            <link type="text/css" rel="stylesheet" href="styles/preview.css">
   </head>
   <body topmargin="0" leftmargin="0">
      <div id="logo"><img src="images/logo.png" width="100px" height="38px"></div>
      <table border="0" cellpadding="0" cellspacing="0" align="center">
         <thead>
            <tr>
               <td width="71px" colspan="2" align="center">Tenet</td>
               <td width="171px" colspan="3" align="center">Reputation</td>
            </tr>
         </thead>
         <tbody>
            <? foreach($components as $k => $v) { ?>
            <tr>
               <td width="16px"><img src="images/<? echo(getReputationIcon($k)); ?>"></td>
               <td width="55px"><? echo(getComponentName($k)); ?></td>
               <td width="100px" class="testimony"><img src="images/marker.png"
                  style="margin-left: <? echo(getMarkerPos($k)); ?>px;"></td>
               <td width="20px"><? echo(getReputationValue($k)); ?>%</td>
               <td width="51px"><img src="images/<? echo(getConfidenceIcon($k)); ?>"></td>
            </tr>
            <? } ?>
         </tbody>
      </table>
   </body>
</html>
```

When this service receives link information, it queries the WOT API for information on that link. It uses the preview window to format the results of this API call into content consumable by an end user.

Localizing Accelerators

The OpenService schema does not provide for the built-in localization of Accelerators. Developers may localize Accelerators by creating an XML definition for each supported language. Listings 4–22 and 4–23 show an Accelerator localized in English and Spanish, respectively.

***Listing 4–22.** The Tweet This! Accelerator Localized in English*

```
<?xml version="1.0" encoding="UTF-8" ?>
<os:openServiceDescription
   xmlns:os="http://www.microsoft.com/schemas/openservicedescription/1.0">
   <os:homepageUrl>http://examples.proiedev.com/04/basic/xmlservice/</os:homepageUrl>
   <os:display>
      <os:name>Tweet This!</os:name>
      <os:icon>http://examples.proiedev.com/04/basic/xmlservice/favicon.ico</os:icon>
```

```
      <os:description>
         Share and discover what's happening right now,
         anywhere in the world.
      </os:description>
...
```

Listing 4–23. The Tweet This! Accelerator Localized in Spanish

```
<?xml version="1.0" encoding="UTF-8" ?>
<os:openServiceDescription
   xmlns:os="http://www.microsoft.com/schemas/openservicedescription/1.0">
   <os:homepageUrl>http://examples.proiedev.com/04/basic/xmlservice/</os:homepageUrl>
   <os:display>
      <os:name>¡Publique su selección con Twitter!</os:name>
      <os:icon>http://examples.proiedev.com/04/basic/xmlservice/favicon.ico</os:icon>
      <os:description>
         Comparte y descubre qué está pasando ahora mismo
         en cualquier lugar del mundo.
      </os:description>
...
```

A localized Accelerator may point to a localized web service. A variable can be passed to a web service indicating a desired localization for that service. Listing 4–24 is an example of this—a service receives a locale parameter that it can use to render the page—in this case, en-us for US English.

Listing 4–24. Passing a Target Language to a Web Service Using Parameters

```
...
<activityAction context="selection">
   <execute
      action="http://examples.proiedev.com/book/examples/flip/flip.html"
      method="get">
      <parameter name="t" value="{selection}" type="text" />
      <parameter name="version" value="1.0" type="text" />
      <parameter name="locale" value="en-us" type="text" />
   </execute>
</activityAction>
...
```

Cross-Browser Integration

Other applications and browsers are free to use the Accelerator model in their platforms under the Creative Commons license. While no browsers have implemented Accelerators as of this book's publication, a Firefox add-on is available. Michael Kaply's IE8 Accelerators for Firefox places Accelerators into the Firefox context menu in the same way as IE. It can be downloaded from the Firefox Add-Ons site (http://addons.mozilla.org).

Best Practices for Building Accelerators

Accelerators can be used to create extensions that link a wide variety of services to IE's context menu. Despite the wide range of potential Accelerators, there are a common set of best practices that should be followed during the design, development, and deployment process.

Providing Relevant Information

Users are provided with Accelerator information—its name, description, category, and so on—during the installation process and later on through the Manage Add-Ons interface (see Figure 4–14). This metadata is defined in the XML definition file for each Accelerator.

Tweet This!			
Status:	Enabled	Home page:	http://examples.proiedev.com/07/twitter/
Available on:	Document, Selection, Link	Installed from:	http://examples.proiedev.com/07/twitter/
Category:	Twitter change		

Figure 4–14. *Accelerator information pane in Manage Add-Ons*

Providing relevant information allows users to make informed decisions about Accelerators and stay in control of their browsing experience.

Designing Secure Accelerators

Security is an important aspect of Accelerator design. Accelerators offer users and developers a new way of associating web content to web services, but along with this comes an increased attack surface. Developers must take a careful look at what data will be sent to a web service and how that web service handles data—this includes controlling how data is integrated into a web service. Thorough planning can prevent malicious activity such as script injection and denial-of-service attacks.

To protect users from denial-of-service and drive-by attacks, the web browser instance shown in preview mode places limits on active content. ActiveX controls can run, but the controls must be already installed and approved to run on the service's domain before they can be used by the preview; no information bar will be shown.

Developers must also be mindful of script injection attacks when designing Accelerators. An example of this form of attack is shown in Listing 4–25, in which the script is sent through a `GET` variable.

Listing 4–25. *An Example Script Injection Attack Using GET Variables*

```
http://www.example.com/action.php?t=%3Cscript%3Ealert(%22Pwnd.%22)%3B%3C%2Fscript%3E
```

Other forms of XSS attacks, such as DOM-based and persistent script injection via `GET` and `POST` variables, are not mitigated by the browser. Despite built-in protections such as IE's XSS filter and Firefox's NoScript extension, it's always a good idea to sanitize input of variables from an Accelerator (or other input methods). Client-side Accelerator code may use the `window.toStaticHTML()` sanitization method in IE 8 to mitigate against script injection. When using server-side languages such as PHP, Ruby, and ASP.NET, developers should take advantages of built-in or library-based sanitization functions before rendering untrusted input. The Microsoft Anti-XSS library is a great starting point for developers looking to help fight against this problem.

Designing Performant Accelerators

Performance of web pages belonging to a service can also impact the experience of using an Accelerator. IE allows users to determine their own tolerance for slow controls by displaying a "Loading . . ." screen during an Accelerator's loading process. Fast-loading pages will avoid such an experience. Tooling applications like the IE Developer Tools, Fiddler, and Firebug can be used to ensure page load time is kept to a minimum.

Designing Preview Web Pages

The preview window is 320 pixels in width by 240 pixels in height on a 96-dots-per-inch (dpi) display. Any content rendered in the preview pane will be trimmed to this size; scrollbars are disabled as well.

High DPI mode (120 or 144 dpi) should be considered when creating Accelerators. When IE is running in High DPI mode, the preview windows will be expanded by appropriate measure (e.g., 120 percent for 120 dpi).

An Accelerator Design Checklist

The following checklist highlights some best practices developers can use to design, build, and deploy quality Accelerators:

- Provide concise and relevant information in the Accelerator XML definition.
- Create a deployment, installation, and upgrade plan for an Accelerator.
- Ensure that web services handling content from an Accelerator do so securely.
- Design preview pages to work for the 320×240 preview window.
- Optimize the performance of pages that are rendered as Accelerator previews.

Summary

Accelerators offer a simple way to bridge the gap between web services and the browser user interface. In this chapter, I discussed the Accelerator platform and how you can easily expose web services for use on any pages your users visit.

The subjects covered in this section are relevant for more than just Accelerators; the concepts of XML definitions and restrictive security models are recurring themes in IE extensions. As I move ahead, keep these concepts and their roles in the overall browser programming model in mind.

CHAPTER 5

■ ■ ■

Debugging and Inspecting Pages with Developer Tools

In-browser development tools are all about experimentation—while most of your development might take place in Dreamweaver, Aptana, or vi, those development environments don't always provide enough insight into how your page will behave in an *actual* browser. That's where the IE developer tools come in: they ensure your pages look, feel, and act the way you intended. A wide variety of tools are included in the package, covering a number of important scenarios in the development process: a markup inspector for analyzing HTML, a layout and styles inspector for CSS and element positioning, a JavaScript debugger for deducing problems with script, a script profiler for analyzing script performance, and more. This chapter highlights the features and functionality provided by the IE developer tools.

Navigating the IE Developer Tools

The IE developer tools can be launched in one of three ways: from the Developer Tools icon in the command bar, from the Developer Tools entry in the Tools menu, and by pressing F12 on a web page (only F12 is available for pop-up dialogs). Figure 5–1 shows this UI.

Figure 5–1. *The Developer Tools command button (left) and its Tools menu entry (right)*

Once launched, the tools may be docked to IE (as an explorer bar), or may be *unpinned* and displayed as a separate window. These display modes are controlled through the icons in the top-right corner of the toolbar (Figure 5–2).

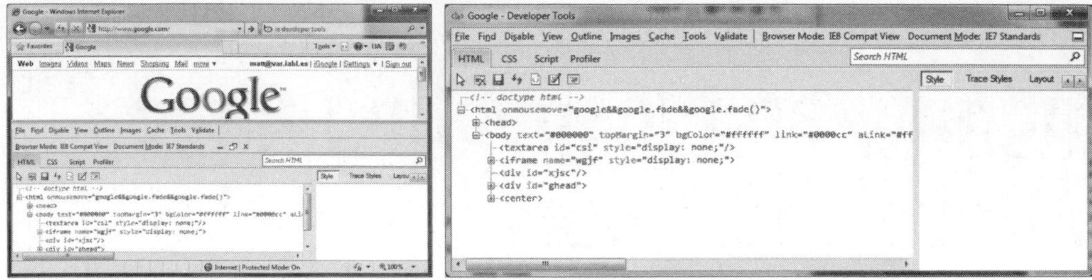

Figure 5–2. *Developer tools pinned (left) and unpinned (right)*

Each tool has its own tab, and in each the search box in the tab strip allows developers to search data in the current tab. The menu above the developer tools provides links to utilities that aren't specific to the tabs (Figure 5–3).

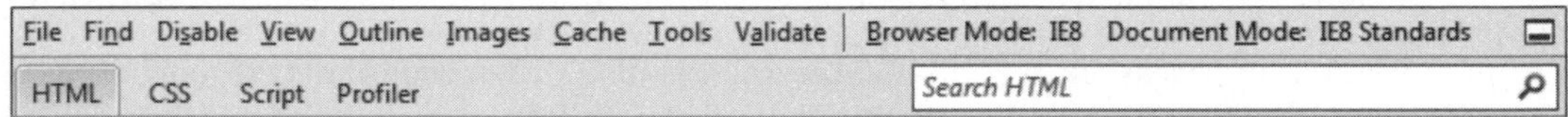

Figure 5–3. *Developer tools tab interface and search box*

View Source

IE 8 includes a View Source window that displays a web page's source, complete with syntax highlighting and line numbering (see Figure 5–4). View Source reflects the original document downloaded by IE; changes made through the developer tools are not reflected in the View Source window.

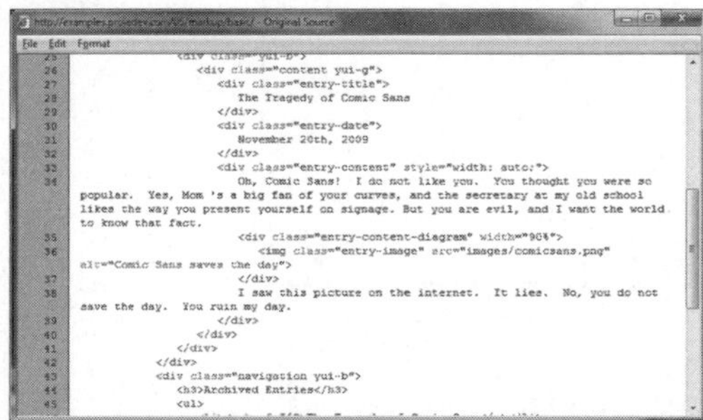

Figure 5–4. *The View Source window, introduced in IE 8*

Prior to IE 8, IE opened Notepad to display the source of a web page by default; this option could be changed to open source in another external application. Developers wishing to change the default source viewer can do so through the developer tools; as in prior versions, source viewing can be redirected to any external application that supports it.

The File Menu

The File menu offers access to basic developer tools settings. The Undo All command reverts markup, layout, styling, and script changes back to those of the original page. Developers can customize the web page source viewer in the next option; instead of using the View Source window provided with IE, you can set the browser to open an external application. Last, the Exit option closes a Developer Tools session (Table 5–1).

***Table 5–1.** File Menu Entries*

Button	Shortcut	Description
Undo All	-	Reverts a document to its original state (undoes all changes made to markup, script, and styles through the developer tools)
Customize Internet Explorer View Source…	-	Allows developers to specify a default source viewer (either IE or an external application)
Exit	F12	Closes the developer tools

Inspecting Markup

The IE developer tools offer a number of utilities for inspecting, editing, and analyzing page markup. The following sections describe the markup tools and provide some examples of how they are used.

The HTML Tab and the DOM Explorer

The HTML tab allows for real-time inspection and editing of page markup. Almost all aspects of page markup can be changed, including element attributes, values, and overall markup structure.

Table 5–2 highlights the top-level UI commands.

***Table 5–2.** HTML Tab Buttons*

Button	Shortcut	Description
Select Element by Click	Ctrl+B	Navigates to an element's definition in the HTML tab's DOM Explorer when it is clicked in the current web page.
Clear Browser Cache	Ctrl+R	Clears the browser cache for all domains and sessions.
Save HTML	Ctrl+S	Saves the current markup in the DOM Explorer to a file. This includes edits made within the developer tools.
Refresh	F5	Syncs the DOM Explorer's markup to be that of IE's current DOM for a page.

Button	Shortcut	Description
Element Source with Style	Ctrl+T	Displays the HTML source hierarchy and applied styles for the currently selected element in a View Source window.
Edit	Alt+E	Toggles the display of a text editor containing the DOM Explorer's current markup.
Word Wrap	Alt+W	Toggles word-wrap for the DOM Explorer's text editor.

When a page is loaded, the hierarchy in the DOM Explorer represents IE's interpretation of a page's markup. This hierarchy is placed into a tree view. Parent elements can be expanded to show their children and element attributes can be edited inline. When an element is selected using Select Element by Click, the tree is expanded to reveal the element within the DOM Explorer hierarchy.

The Edit button ( ) toggles the DOM Explorer between a tree view and a text editor. Developers can modify the current markup (as parsed and interpreted by IE) as when running in Edit mode (as shown in Figure 5–5). When Edit mode is switched off, changes are applied to the document and are reflected both on the current web page and the DOM Explorer's tree (Figure 5–6).

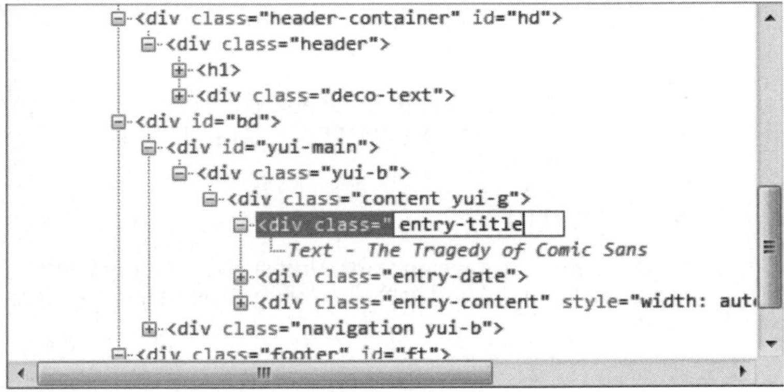

Figure 5–5. DOM Explorer with editing box

```
<DIV style="WIDTH: auto" class=entry-content>Oh, Com
<DIV class=entry-content-diagram width="90%"><IMG cl
<DIV class="navigation yui-b">
<H3>Archived Entries</H3>
<UL>
<LI><A href="#">The Tragedy of Comic Sans</A></LI>
<LI><A href="#">Just Another First Post</A></LI></UL
<H3>Font Blogs I Read</H3>
<UL>
<LI><A href="#">California Serif'n</A></LI>
<LI><A href="#">Sans Restraint</A></LI>
<LI><A href="#">Hiram Glyphics</A></LI>
<LI><A href="#">Dithering Heights</A></LI>
<LI><A href="#">Subpixel Underground</A></LI></UL></
```

Figure 5–6. DOM Explorer in Edit mode

If the current page makes changes to its own markup (e.g., with script or through Ajax calls), those changes are *not* reflected in the DOM Explorer. Those changes can be loaded by clicking the Refresh button. Conversely, changes made in the DOM Explorer *are* immediately applied to the current page. Developers wishing to edit the most recent version of the markup should click the Refresh button *before* making changes in the DOM Explorer.

■ **Note** Markup and other data in the IE developer tools does not automatically update when a web page makes changes through JavaScript or Ajax. Developers looking to get the most up-to-date information on a document should click the Refresh button; this will force the tools to resync their representation of the DOM.

The Attributes Pane

The DOM Explorer allows for inline editing of attribute values; however, it does not allow attributes to be added, removed, or renamed. The Attributes pane (Figure 5–7) allows the remaining actions to happen for the currently selected element in the DOM Explorer.

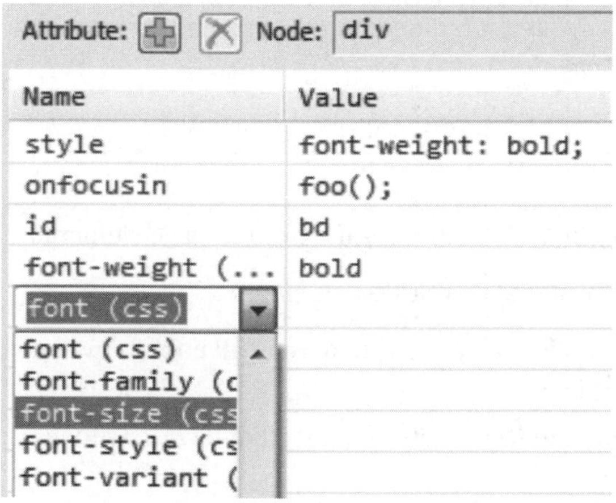

Figure 5–7. *Attributes pane and attribute name drop-down*

Figure 5–7 shows an example of an element's attributes being edited in this pane. The current element type is shown at the top alongside UI elements for adding and removing attributes. Each attribute on the current element is displayed in the list box. You can change an attribute name by clicking its name and either typing it or selecting an attribute from a drop-down. Values associated with a named attribute can be changed by editing the corresponding entry in the Value column. Changes made to attributes are immediately reflected in the current document.

The Find, View, and Outline Menus

Locating specific elements on large pages can be hard using the DOM Explorer by itself. The Find, View, and Outline tools help lessen this burden by helping locate, access, and position page elements.

The Find menu (see Table 5–3) offers only one entry: Select Element by Click. This command—also found in the top-level buttons of each developer tool's tab—navigates to any element that is selected in the current web page when activated.

***Table 5–3.** Find Menu Entries*

Menu Item	Shortcut	Description
Select Element by Click	Ctrl+B	Navigates to an element's definition in the HTML tab's DOM Explorer when it is clicked in the current web page.

Commands in the View menu (see Table 5–4) provide detailed information about the context of page elements. The first set of view commands are for reporting: developers can overlay class, ID, link path, tab index, and access key information onto elements. Reporting tools in this menu allow developers to correct issues such as incorrect class, ID, and link references. A number of source viewers in this menu display page markup in a number of contexts.

***Table 5–4.** View Menu Entries*

Menu Item	Shortcut	Description
Class and ID Information	Ctrl+I	Overlays class and ID information onto all page elements
Link Paths	-	Overlays link paths on relevant elements
Link Report	-	Generates a new web page with a list of all links found on the current page
Tab Indexes	-	Overlays tab indexes on all elements that have a defined `tabindex` attribute
Access Keys	-	Overlays access key information onto all elements that have a defined `accesskey` attribute
Source ➤ Element Source with Style	-	Displays markup and applied styles for the currently selected element in a new View Source window
Source ➤ DOM (Element)	-	Displays markup and applied styles for the currently selected element in a new View Source window
Source ➤ DOM (Page)	-	Displays markup and applied styles for the current page through a new View Source window
Original	-	Displays markup for the original web page or last refreshed source data in the HTML tree in a new View Source window

The Outline menu (Table 5–5) surfaces commands that outline elements based on type or property. Borders drawn by these tools are temporary; they are drawn over the web page, are not added to markup or CSS, and are removed when the developer tools are closed.

***Table 5–5.** Outline Menu Entries*

Menu Item	Shortcut	Description
Table Cells	-	Outlines all table cell elements in the current document.
Tables	-	Outlines all table elements in the current document.
DIV Elements	-	Outlines all `<div>` elements in the current document.
Images	-	Outlines all image elements in the current document.
Any Element…	Ctrl+O	Displays the Outline Elements dialog. This dialog allows custom elements to be outlined with a custom color.
Positioned Objects ➤ Relative	-	Outlines all elements that have relative positioning.
Positioned Objects ➤ Absolute	-	Outlines all elements that have absolute positioning.
Positioned Objects ➤ Fixed	-	Outlines all elements that have fixed positioning.
Positioned Objects ➤ Float		Outlines all elements that have float positioning.
Clear Outlines	Ctrl+Shift+O	Clears all outlines.

Figure 5–8 shows the Outline Elements dialog. This figure demonstrates a scenario where `<h1>` elements are assigned a red border and `<h3>` elements are given a green one.

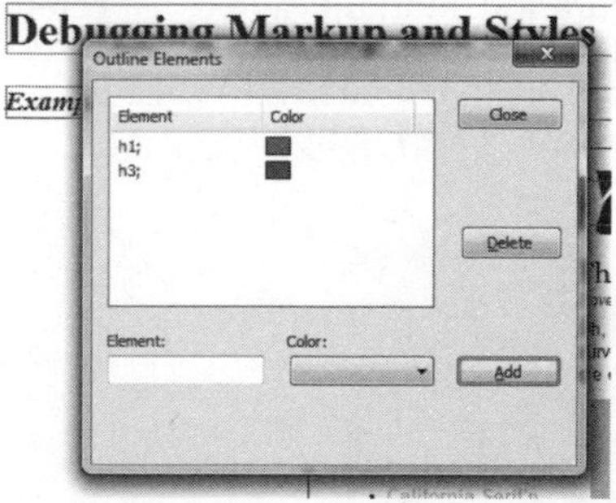

***Figure 5–8.** The Outline Elements dialog*

Exporting Changes

Changes made to markup can be saved to a new file through the Save As icon (💾) (or Ctrl+S). By default, saved markup is given the `.txt` extension; this prevents the original file from being overwritten if it was loaded from the local filesystem.

Markup Inspection in Action

The Joy of Fonts blog is a sample web page for demonstrating markup inspection (see Figure 5–9). The page's CSS layout was constructed using the Yahoo UI Builder; this tool created a page with a header, navigation column, content column, and footer.

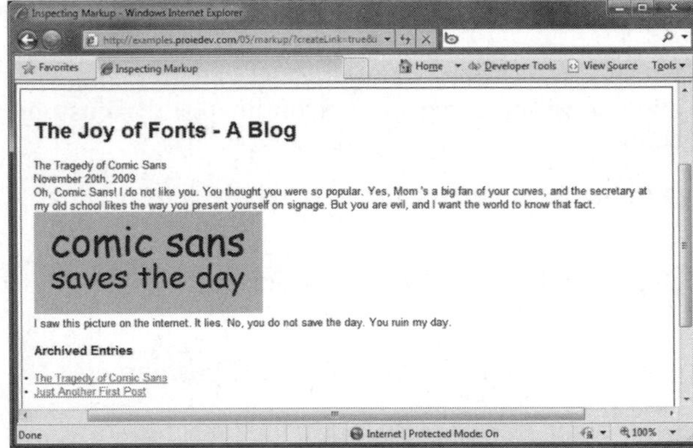

Figure 5–9. The Joy of Fonts blog example

The document did not place the content in the right locations—instead of displaying the two-column format the page was supposed to be in, it stacked the parts on top of one another. (For reference, the correct result is shown in Figure 5–12.)

Markup inspection can help to shed light on the offending configuration. Markup can be inspected by opening the developer tools after the page is loaded. An analysis of the markup in the DOM Explorer (shown in Figure 5–10) shows that the main `<div>` on the web page (the one that contains the header, navigation, content, and footer) omitted the CSS class `yui-t1` required by the Y!UI template.

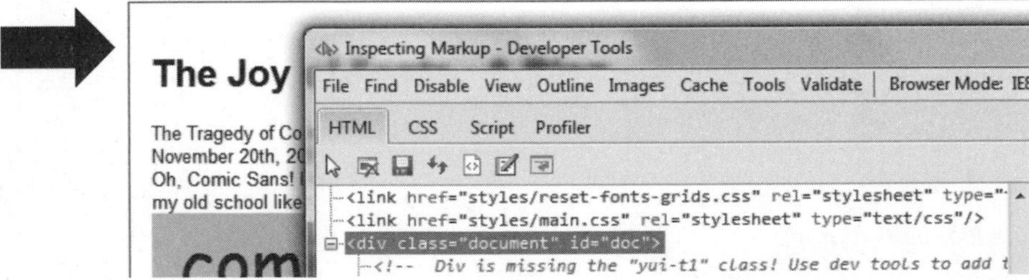

Figure 5–10. Accessing the document <div> using Select Element by Click

The attributes on this element can be edited through the DOM Explorer to determine if this is the root cause. The `class` attribute on this `<div>` can be modified by clicking the current attribute value in the DOM Explorer and changing the value through an inline text box. Figure 5–11 demonstrates this inline box and, in this scenario, the addition of the token `yui-t1`.

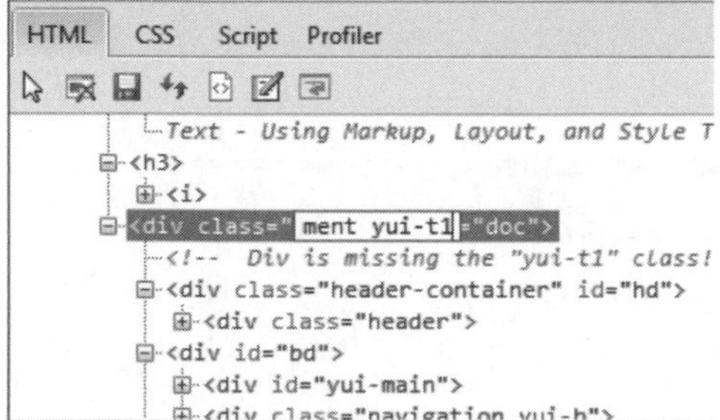

***Figure 5–11.** Inline editing of attributes in the DOM Explorer*

The new class value is applied to the `<div>` as soon as the inline editing box is closed (when you press Enter or change focus). The results are immediately reflected on the current page. Figure 5–12 shows the result of this markup change—the header, navigation, content, and footer are correctly placed.

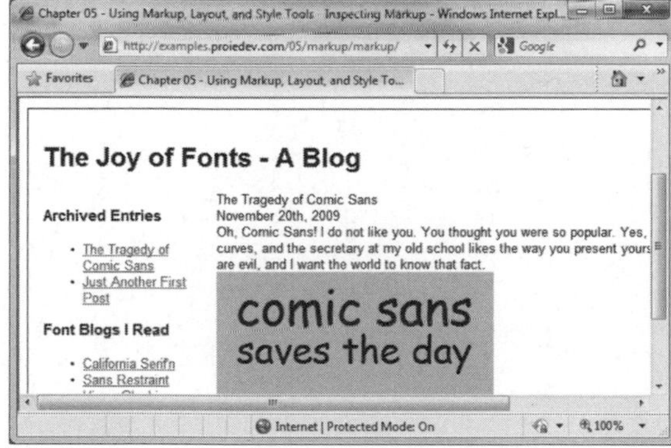

***Figure 5–12.** Modified sample web page using markup inspection*

Changes made through the developer tools can be saved to disk. The Element Source with Styles tool could be used instead to only save those elements and styles used by the document `<div>`.

Inspecting Layout and Styles

The IE developer tools not only allow for inspection of markup, but also for real-time manipulation of element layout and styles (Figure 5–13).

Figure 5–13. *Style, Trace Styles, Layout, and Attributes panes on the HTML tab*

The Style Pane

The Style pane (Figure 5–14) lists CSS rules applied to an element. Properties applied to an element are organized by the rule they came from—inherited, inline, or directly from a selector.

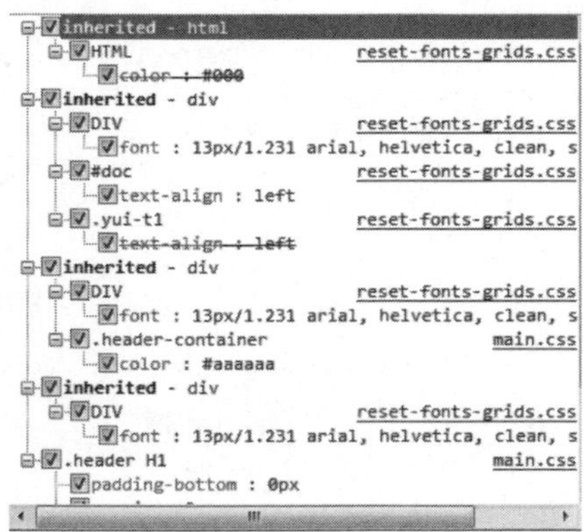

Figure 5–14. *The Style pane*

Properties are displayed alongside a link to their corresponding files. Property values can be edited, enabled, or disabled; changes made to each of these are immediately reflected in the current page. Entries shown with a strikethrough represent those ignored by the browser.

The Style pane is not meant to convey the ordering of rules applied to an element; the Trace Styles pane, described next, is better suited to determining the ordering of rule application.

The Trace Styles Pane

The Trace Styles pane displays an element's styles based on order and precedence of application. Since an element can inherit styles from its ancestors, multiple (and sometimes conflicting) properties may be applied to an element. Unfortunately, developers cannot easily determine which styles were applied to an element without more information from the browser.

Figure 5–15 shows the traced styles of an example element. Each applied style is shown here, and those styles that have been overridden during the cascade are struck through. The source of each CSS property is shown next to it, and clicking it will navigate to its definition in the Source pane of the CSS tab (described later in this chapter).

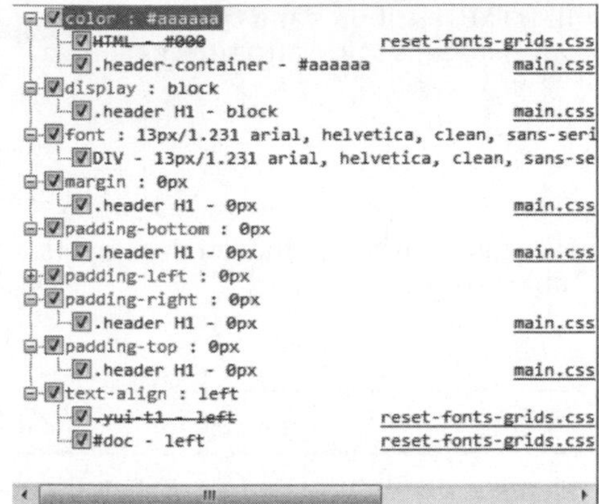

***Figure 5–15.** The Trace Styles pane*

The Layout Pane

The Layout pane (Figure 5–16) displays layout information of elements that occupy space on a page. The offset, margin, border, padding, size, position, and z-index properties are available here.

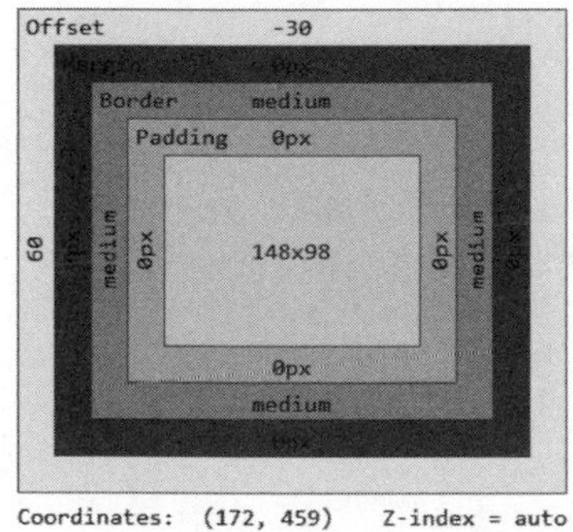

***Figure 5–16.** The Layout pane*

Developers can edit the layout values displayed in this view by clicking a value and making changes in the edit box that appears. Inline elements (such as <span>) that do not use certain layout properties will show all layout values even though IE's layout engine may ignore some of them.

■ **Note** Not all element types use layout properties like padding or margins. Developers should consider the element type being modified when adjusting properties in the Layout pane.

The Attributes Pane

The Attributes pane, described previously in the "Inspecting Markup" section, is useful for CSS properties as well. The drop-down list of attributes contains both HTML attributes and CSS properties; CSS properties added through the Attributes pane are added to an element's `style` attribute, as shown previously in Figure 5–7.

The CSS Tab

The CSS tab displays CSS files used on a page. Its toolbar includes a few commands that let developers access and navigate CSS files loaded by IE; these are shown in Table 5–6.

***Table 5–6.** CSS Tab Toolbar Buttons*

Button	Shortcut	Description
Select Element by Click	Ctrl+B	Navigates to an element's definition in the HTML tab's DOM Explorer when it is clicked in the current web page. This will switch focus away from the CSS tab.
Clear Browser Cache	Ctrl+R	Clears the browser cache for all domains and sessions.
Save CSS	Ctrl+S	Saves all changes made in the CSS tab to a file.
Stylesheet list	-	A drop-down list of files used by the current page that contain styles. Accessing an entry in this list will change the CSS displayed in the source pane of the CSS tab.

The CSS Source pane (Figure 5–17) displays the styles present in the document selected in the Stylesheet list. Styles and properties of a document are shown in a format similar to a stylesheet or `<style>` tag. All properties are shown under their owner selector (e.g., a tag, class, ID, or other selector type).

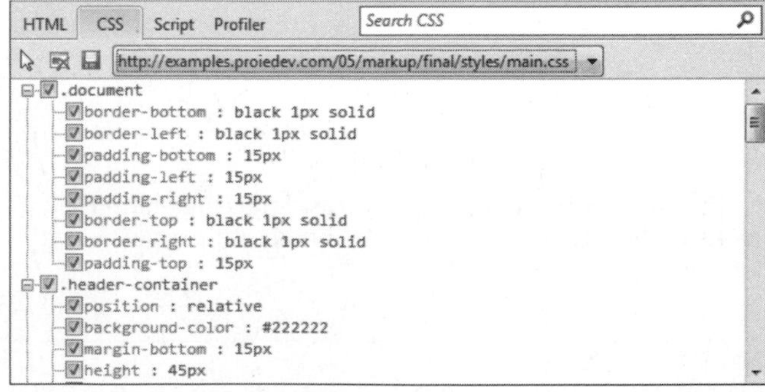

***Figure 5–17.** The CSS Source pane*

Each property and selector can be enabled or disabled through a check box, much like the check boxes in the Style and Trace Styles panes of the HTML tab. Each entry in the list may be edited by clicking a targeted item. Changes made to list entries, either through value changes, enabling, or disabling, are immediately reflected in the document. The rules of each file, disabled or otherwise, may be searched and highlighted using the Search CSS box.

CSS and Layout Inspection in Action

The Joy of Fonts blog presented in the "Inspecting Markup" section is built and ready to go from an HTML standpoint, but it lacks visual appeal. CSS styles have been added to spice up the page elements in a way that is fitting for a blog; Figure 5–18 shows the new blog page with styles applied. There are a few problems with the application of these styles; the developer tools are used in the following examples to find and mediate the root causes.

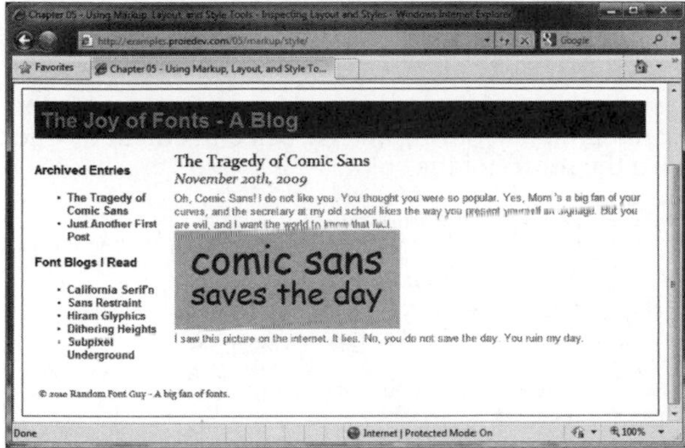

Figure 5–18. The Joy of Fonts sample page with added CSS

The first problem with this page is the font size of the blog entry date. The sample page's date, "November 20th, 2009," is significantly larger than the `.9em` value set in its `entry-date` CSS class. Using the Select Element by Click command, the date is clicked and its corresponding markup is shown in the DOM Explorer (shown in Figure 5–18). Trace Styles reveals that this element has inherited the font of the parent element's class, `entry-title`. Since the `em` unit is relative to the inherited font size, the font shown on the screen will be larger than intended (since the basis font is that of the parent, not the page). This style is changed to an absolute size of 14 pixels using the inline edit box; the results are shown in Figure 5–19.

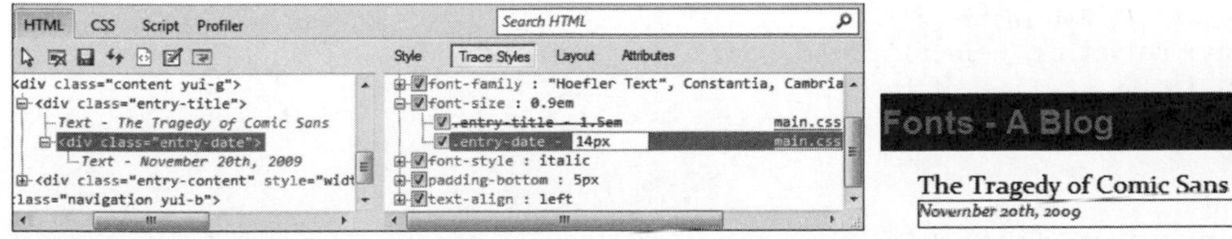

Figure 5–19. Modifying the font size of the .entry-date class

The image in the content pane presents the next problem: it is lacking proper padding. Figure 5–18 shows a "Comic Sans saves the day" banner that is pressed up against the content text. Padding can be added to the image through the Layout pane in the HTML tab; Figure 5–20 shows the layout values of the image object in this view. The padding values are changed through inline edit boxes in the layout window; in this case, 10 pixels of padding have been added to each side of the image.

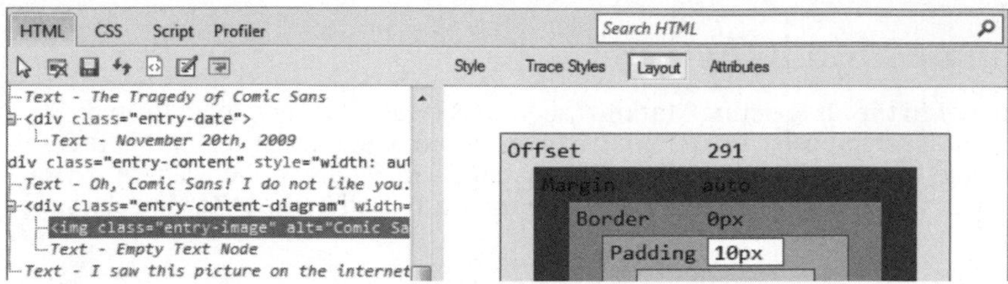

Figure 5–20. Editing padding using the Layout pane

The font color is the only major issue remaining with the Joy of Fonts blog. Figure 5–21 reveals why the blog content has been colored in red, something not intended during design. Select Element by Click and Trace Styles can be used once again to track down the source of the color.

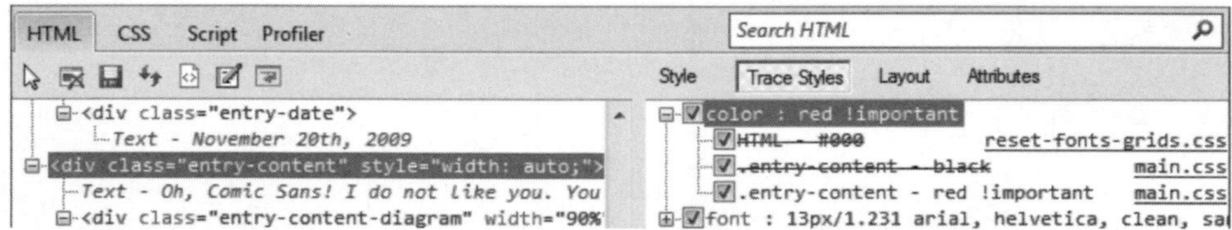

Figure 5–21. Removing the color property overrides with the Trace Styles pane

The Trace Styles value in Figure 5–21 show that there is an `!important` color style being applied to the element, overriding the `color: black` style intended for the element. Analysis of the source code in Listing 5–1 reveals that a development artifact was carried over: a duplicate definition for `.entry-content` exists with a style of `!important color`, thus it is given precedence (despite the fact that it was declared earlier in the file).

Listing 5–1. *Using String Substution in the Console Object*

```
/* Blog Entries */

.entry-content {  /* For Testing */
   font-family: Helvetica, Helvetica Neue, Arial, sans-serif;
   font-size: 1em;
   color: red !important;
}
...
.entry-content {
   font-family: Helvetica, Helvetica Neue, Arial, sans-serif;
   font-size: 1em;
   color: black;
}
```

Once this reference is removed from the stylesheet, the font displays correctly in black.

These fixes can be exported to a new CSS file through the CSS tab's Save button, or to an Element Source with Style file, as is done in the markup inspection example. Figure 5–22 shows the final result of these changes on the page, including the correct font for the blog entry date, proper padding on the image, and the correct font color for blog content.

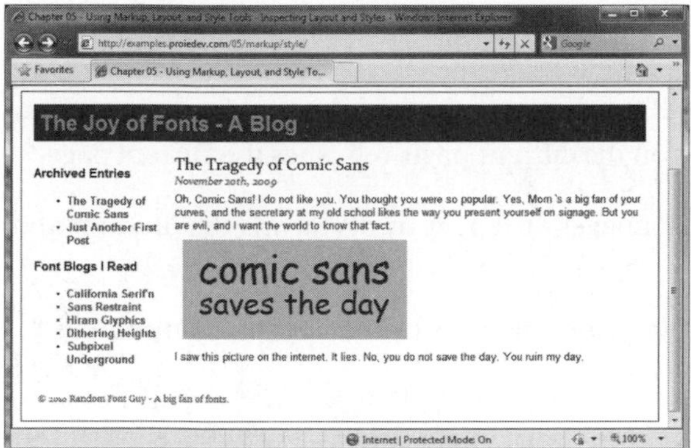

Figure 5–22. Joy of Fonts blog after style and layout corrections

Using the Extended Toolset

The Extended Toolset is a grab bag of tools that are helpful in the web development process but are not necessarily used in everyday development work.

The Disable Menu

Items in the Disable menu (see Table 5–7) do just what you would expect: they disable certain features in IE. Disabling or hiding certain portions of the browser or a web page allows developers to potentially exclude those items as root causes of a bug. Developers may block script and CSS from running through this menu; they also have the ability to toggle the IE Pop-Up Blocker on and off. Images can be disabled as well; this feature is located in the Images menu (discussed in the next section).

Table 5–7. Disable Menu Entries

Menu Item	Description
Script	Disables JavaScript when developer tools are open
Pop-Up Blocker	Disables the Pop-Up Blocker when developer tools are open
CSS	Disables CSS when developer tools are open

Disabling the Pop-Up Blocker is useful when debugging JavaScript. The Pop-Up Blocker's algorithm checks to see if a pop-up was spawned through a user-initiated action. Breakpoints and other debugging steps could cause such checks to fail.

The Images Menu

The Images menu provides access to those tools related to images and image management in web pages. They exist to help developers gather the right information (size, description, source location, etc.) for layout and design decisions. Table 5–8 outlines these in more detail.

Table 5–8. *Images Menu Entries*

Menu Item	Description
Disable Images	Disables loading of images on the current page; refreshes the current page
Show Image Dimensions	Shows the dimensions of all images on a page by overlaying that information onto them with a label
Show Image File Sizes	Shows the file sizes of all images on a page by overlaying that information onto them with a label
Show Image Paths	Shows the paths of all images on a page by overlaying that information onto them with a label
View Alt Text	Shows the Alt text of all images on a page by overlaying that information onto them with a label
View Image Report	Opens a new page displaying a report of all images on the current web page, including their path, size, and Alt text

The Tools Menu

IE developer tools contain a few extra goodies that don't fit into any major category, yet do provide some useful functionality. There are three such tools that fall into this category: a browser resizer, rulers, and a color picker. Table 5–9 outlines Tools menu.

Table 5–9. *Tools Menu Entries*

Menu Item	Shortcut	Description
Resize ➤ 800×600	Ctrl+Shift+1	Resizes the current browser window to 800 pixels in width by 600 pixels in height.
Resize ➤ 1024×768	Ctrl+Shift+2	Resizes the current browser window to 1024 pixels in width by 768 pixels in height.
Resize ➤ 1280×768	Ctrl+Shift+3	Resizes the current browser window to 1280 pixels in width by 768 pixels in height.
Resize ➤ 1280×1024	Ctrl+Shift+4	Resizes the current browser window to 1280 pixels in width by 1024 pixels in height.

Menu Item	Shortcut	Description
Resize ➤ Custom…	-	Opens a dialog containing custom browser size configurations. These custom browser sizes are persisted after the developer tools are closed.
Show Ruler	Ctrl+L	Opens the Ruler tool, allowing ruled lines to be placed on top of an HTML document to measure pixel offsets and distances.
Show Color Picker	Ctrl+K	Displays the Color Picker tool, allowing the reading of onscreen colors and the copying of those colors to the clipboard.

The Resize Browser tool literally sets the IE window to a specific size. This is useful for projects that require support for an exact, minimum, or maximum resolution (e.g., screen sizes on netbooks). The custom size dialog allows for custom window sizes beyond the four preset values, as shown in Figure 5–23.

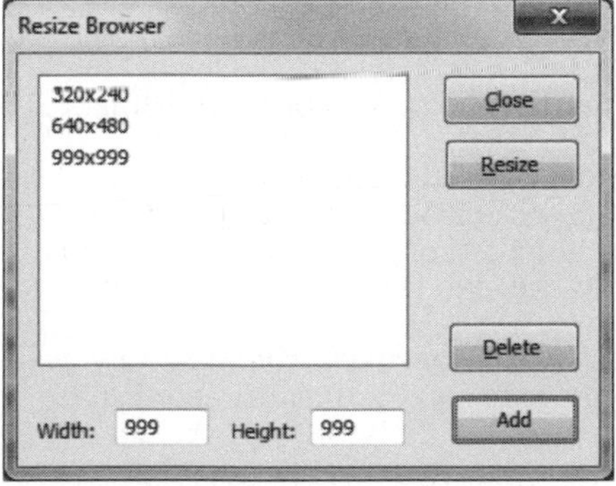

Figure 5–23. Resize Browser tool

The Ruler (see Figure 5–24) allows elements to be measured with metered lines. The Styles, Trace Styles, and Layout panes provide developers with WYSIWYG functionality in terms of element positioning, but these tools rely upon a developer supplying a value either from a guess or from work done outside of the developer tools.

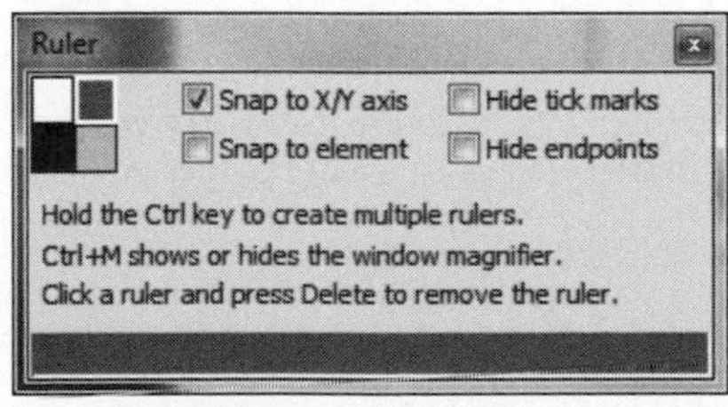

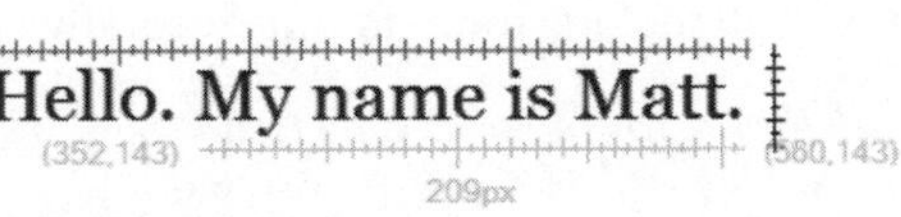

Figure 5–24. The Ruler tool, and a measurement example

The Color Picker is a simple dialog that displays the current color underneath the mouse cursor. Since the tool is run under the context of a tab (as described in the architecture portion of Chapter 1), it can only pick up colors from locations within the tab: the status bar, the explorer bars, the scrollbars, and the page itself. A selected color can be copied to the clipboard through the "Copy and close" button, as shown in Figure 5–25.

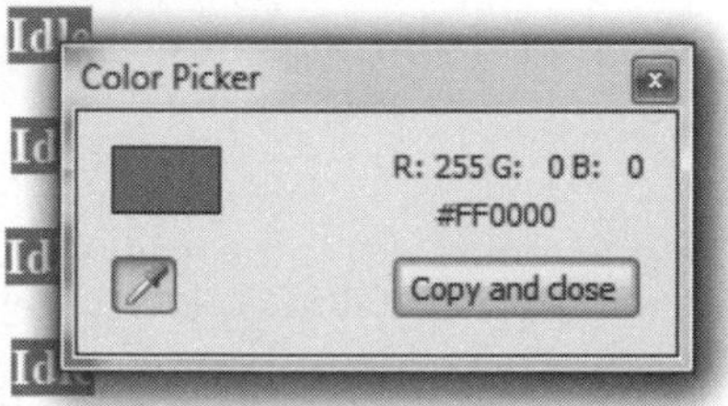

Figure 5–25. *The Color Picker tool*

The Extended Toolset in Action

The HTML and CSS tools were used in the previous sections to fix layout and styles of the Joy of Fonts blog. This example demonstrates how the IE developer tools' Extended Toolset can be used to finalize the fit and finish of a page.

The Joy of Fonts blog will be given a decorative header. The header used in the preceding two examples consisted of gray text ("The Joy of Fonts—A Blog") with a dark background. The header is modified in this example; the word "Joy" is made to stand out from the rest of the header text—in this case, it will have different CSS styles than the rest of the title (jump ahead to Figure 5–29 to see the result).

Listings 5–2 and 5–3 show changes made to the markup and styles, respectively; the word "Joy" was removed from the header and placed in a `<span>`. A transparent image file was added to create a space between "The" and "of."

Listing 5–2. *New Markup for the Joy of Fonts Blog Header*

```
<div class="header">
   <h1>
      The
      <img class="spacer" src="images/spacer.gif" alt="(blank)">
      of Fonts - A Blog
   </h1>
   <span class="deco-text">JOY</span>
</div>
```

A new `<span>` is placed in the header to create the intended effect. The CSS `z-index` property will let the word "Joy" be overlaid atop the existing header, and the image will be resized to create a space between the other header text, making room for the decorative word.

Listing 5–3. *New Markup for the Joy of Fonts Blog Header*

```
.spacer {
   height: 5px;
}
.deco-text {
```

```
    position: absolute;
    font-family: Baskerville, Times, Times New Roman, serif;
    font-size: 80px;
    color: white;
    margin: 0;
    padding: 0;
    font-weight: bold;
    font-style: italic;
    top: -25px;
}
```

Figure 5–26 shows the changes made to the markup. Unfortunately, the `<span>` is displayed too far left of the intended location.

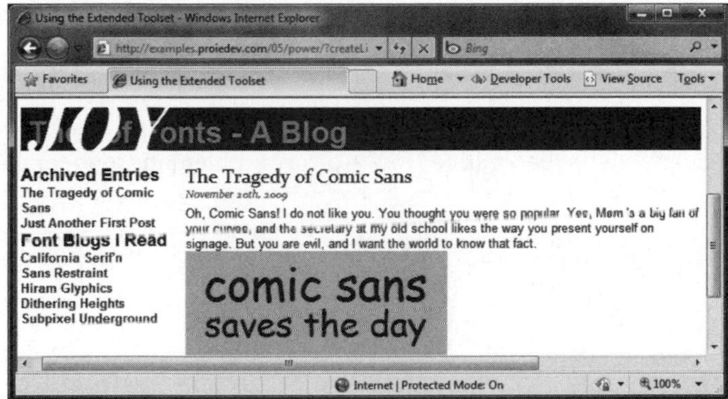

Figure 5–26. The Joy of Fonts blog with incorrectly positioned decorative text

The Ruler tool can be used here to determine the best positioning values for the new stylesheet entries. Two measurements are made (in Figure 5–27). The first is that of the distance between the start of the word "Joy" and the end of the word "The"; this represents how many pixels the decorative text should be moved to the right. Next is the width of the word "Joy," representing the space it will need to occupy in the header (thus the desired width of the spacer image).

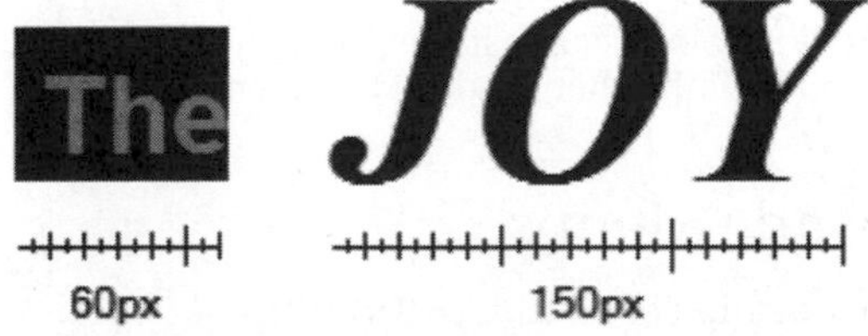

Figure 5–27. Ruler tool being used to measure object size

These two measurements indicate that the span needs to be aligned 60 pixels to the right of its current position and the spacer image needs to be 150 pixels in width.

Figure 5–28 demonstrates the next step in this process: setting the property values with information gathered from the Ruler. The CSS `left` property for the `<span>` is set to `60px` and the width of the spacer `<img>` element is set to `150px`.

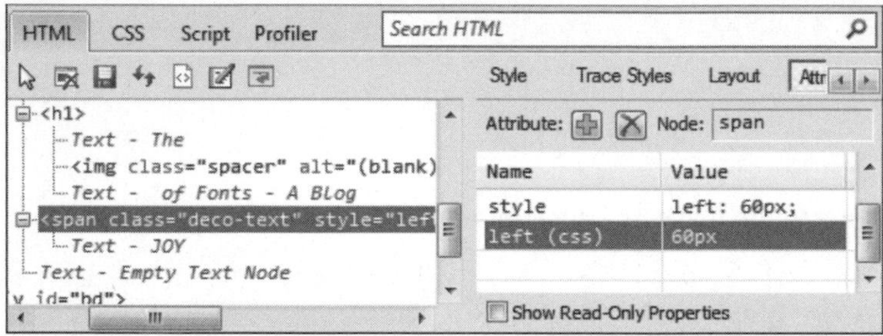

Figure 5–28. Adjusting positioning with the Attributes pane

The text is now in its proper position, and its color is changed to white to blend in with the page background. Figure 5–29 shows the new header with the decorative "Joy"—a very emblematic logo for a font blog.

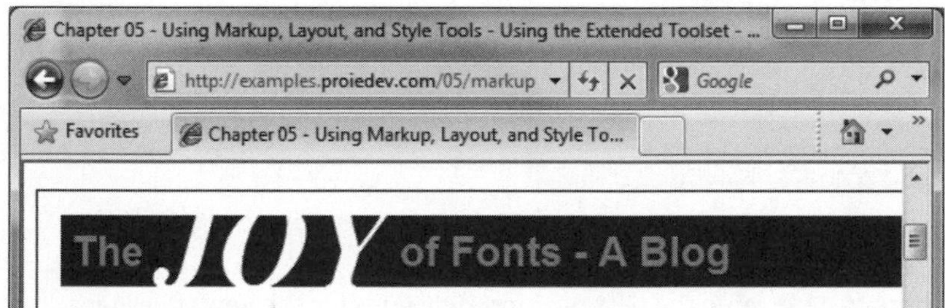

Figure 5–29. Decorative text placed within the Joy of Fonts sample web page

Testing for Compatibility and Interoperability

The developer tools offer a number of ways designers and developers can test their web sites for compatibility with older versions of IE and for interoperability with other modern browsers.

The Browser Mode and Document Mode Menus

The Browser Mode menu enables developers to simulate a version of IE: IE 7, IE 8, and IE 8 Compatibility View. This is not browser virtualization; instead, a browser mode tells IE to masquerade as a specific version. Different information is sent back to web sites based on the browser mode chosen through the developer tools:

- **User Agent (UA) string**: The version of IE specified in the UA string sent to a web site (e.g., the IE 7 browser mode will report back `IE7` to web sites)
- **Version vector**: The number used by the browser when evaluating conditional comments (e.g., the IE 7 browser mode will return `7` for the version value of `IE` in conditional comments)

Each browser mode is associated with a set of document modes (see Table 5–10). The available document modes are the same ones accessible through `<meta>` tags, HTTP headers, and the browser UI. For instance, IE 8 Standards mode isn't available in IE 7, and thus is not available in the IE 7 browser mode.

Table 5–10. *Browser Mode Options and Their UA, Version Vector, and Document Mode Settings*

Browser Mode	UA Version	Version Vector	Available Document Modes
IE 7	IE 7	IE = 7	Quirks (IE 5), IE 7
IE 8	IE 8 + Trident/4.0	IE = 8	Quirks (IE 5), IE 7, IE 8
IE 8 Compatibility View	IE 7 + Trident/4.0	IE = 7	Quirks (IE 5), IE 7, IE 8

The Validate Menu

The Validate menu links to online services that validate a web page against known standards in markup, styles, and accessibility. For HTML and other forms of markup, specific standards noted in a page's `DOCTYPE` header will be used during the validation process. Table 5–11 outlines the available validation services in the IE developer tools.

Table 5–11. *Validate Menu Entries*

Menu Item	Description
HTML	Sends the current URL to the W3C Markup Validation service for HTML validation.
CSS	Sends the current URL to the W3C CSS Validation service for CSS validation.
Feed	Sends the current URL to the `http://feedvalidator.org` FEED Validator service.
Links	Sends the current URL to the W3C Link Checker validation service.
Local HTML…	Opens a new tab to the W3C Markup Validation service for customized HTML validation runs. No data is sent from the current page.

Menu Item	Description
Local CSS…	Opens a new tab to the W3C CSS Validation service for customized CSS validation runs. No data is sent about the current URL or developer tools data.
Accessibility ➤ WCAG Checklist	Sends the current URL to the HiSoftware Cynthia Says WCAG Checklist service for WCAG accessibility compliance validation.
Accessibility ➤ Section 508 Checklist	Sends the current URL to the HiSoftware Cynthia Says Full Reporting service for Section 508 compliance validation. The service is opened in a new web page.
Multiple Validations…	Opens a dialog that allows a developer to load multiple validators for the current URL. Each validator chosen loads in a new web page.

These tools work by sending URLs to online services. Pages located on a local filesystem or a corporate intranet will not work with these tools.

Debugging JavaScript

The IE developer tools include a built-in JavaScript debugger used to catch errors, watch execution, and dynamically modify script. The next sections detail these tools and provide a real-world example of the tools in action.

The Script Tab

The Script tab, shown in Figure 5–30, consists of command buttons that control the most used features in the debugger, a toggle switch for debugging, a drop-down list that permits access to all JavaScript files loaded for a given document, and a number of panels that expose the UI of the debugger itself.

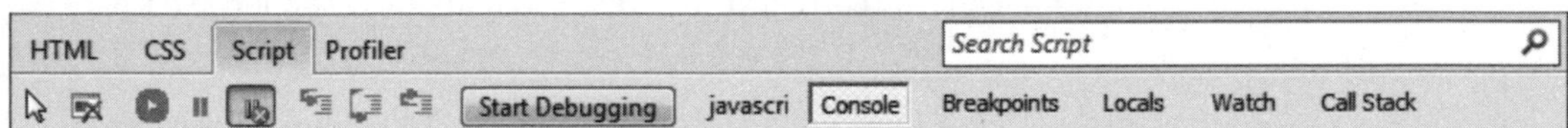

Figure 5–30. *The JavaScript Debugger UI*

Developers can also use the search box to search loaded script for matching text. Table 5–12 highlights the commands, buttons, and tabs available.

Table 5–12. JavaScript Debugger Buttons

Button	Shortcut	Description
Select Element by Click	Ctrl+B	Navigates to an element's definition in the HTML tab's DOM Explorer when it is clicked in the current web page. This will switch focus away from the Script tab.
Clear Browser Cache	Ctrl+R	Clears the browser cache for all domains and sessions.
Continue	F5	Restarts a script after a breakpoint has been hit, and continues running the script until another breakpoint is reached.
Break All	Ctrl+Shift+B	Pauses script execution immediately.
Break on Error	Ctrl+Shift+E	Pauses script execution when an error is reached, even if no breakpoint is set. This is on by default when the developer tools are open.
Step Into	F11	Executes the next line of script after a breakpoint.
Step Over	F10	Executes the next line of script within the current function (steps over script lines that would leave the current function).
Step Out	Shift+F11	Leaves the current function and breaks at the next line of script in the function's caller (if any).
Start/Stop Debugging	F5 (Shift+F5)	Starts/stops debugging.
Script list	-	A drop-down list of scripts used by the current page. Accessing an entry in this list will change the script displayed in the source pane of the Script tab.

The panes to the right of the command buttons and drop-down give access to more detailed information regarding script execution and debugging events, such as the console and call stack.

The Source Pane

The Source pane, shown in Figure 5–31, displays syntax-highlighted contents of each file containing script loaded in the current page. Developers can switch between files using the Script list in the main Script tab UI. Beyond viewing source, the pane is used to set, modify, and remove breakpoints for running script.

```
        .Complete { background-color: green; color: white;
        .noInput  { background-color: #cccccc; }
    </style>
    <script id="jsUtilities" src="scripts/utilities.js" t
    <script type="text/javascript">

        // Define function states
        var idle        = "Idle";
        var progress    = "Running";
        var complete    = "Complete";

        // Add a switch to turn off everything but
        // function calls
        var callsOnly  = false;

        // Initialize function call delay values
        var bDelay      = 3000;
```

***Figure 5–31.** The Script tab Source pane*

Breakpoints and the Breakpoints Pane

Breakpoints can be set on lines of script (statements, functions, and event handlers) after the JavaScript debugger has been started. When the JavaScript engine encounters a breakpoint, script execution will pause until action has been taken to stop or continue the script. Breakpoints can be set in three ways:

- By clicking the leftmost area of the source pane, inline with the targeted line number
- Through the context menu on a statement in the Source pane
- Through the F9 key, when a statement in the Source pane is selected

Breakpoints on specific lines of code can be modified through the same context menu used to set them in the Source pane (see Figure 5–32). These can be deleted or disabled, or a condition can be placed on their execution.

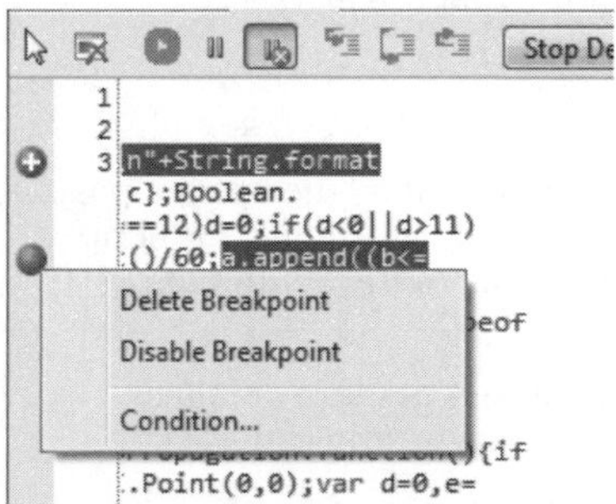

***Figure 5–32.** Existing breakpoint context menu in the Source pane*

Conditional breakpoints allow more granular control over when a breakpoint is triggered. Through this same context menu (or through the Breakpoints pane discussed later), logical conditions can be set on a given breakpoint using variables and functions of the loaded script (see Figure 5–33). The next time the JavaScript debugger reaches the breakpoint, the script will only be paused if the condition placed on it evaluates to `true`.

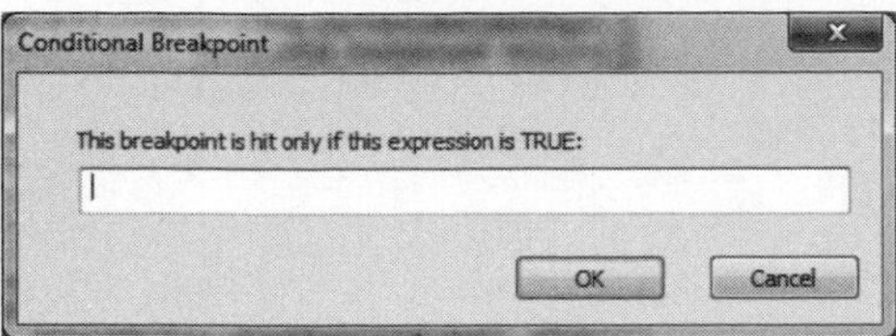

***Figure 5–33.** Conditional Breakpoint dialog*

The Breakpoints pane displays currently selected breakpoints and their status, and allows users to enable, disable, or remove them. Double-clicking a breakpoint will open the script file associated with that breakpoint and navigate to the statement it was set on. Just like the Script pane, each entry in the breakpoints pane provides a context menu that can be used to manage breakpoints already set for a page (see Figure 5–34).

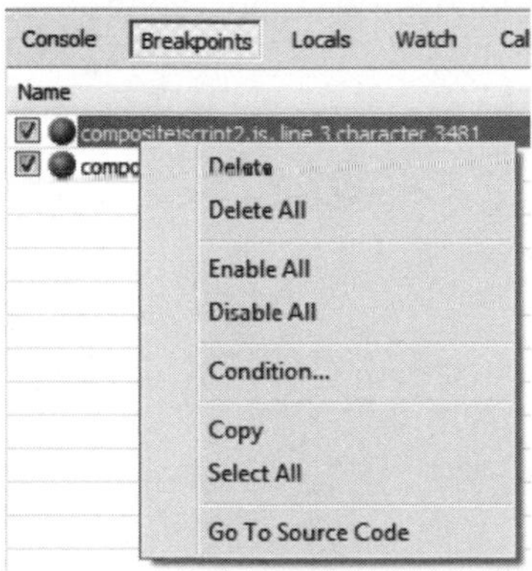

***Figure 5–34.** Breakpoints pane context menu*

The Locals, Watch, and Call Stack Panes

The Locals, Watch, and Call Stack panes allow developers to see activity in functions and variables at a given point in time. The Locals pane displays objects local to a function and their values. The Watch pane displays the same for a list of objects that have been chosen by a developer. The Call Stack pane represents an ordered list of functions called to reach the current statement. To view the call stack, script execution must be paused. Items in the call stack can be added to the Locals and Watch panes while script execution is paused during a breakpoint.

Objects can be added to the Watch list during breakpoints; the context menu for a given breakpoint exposes a command to add a specific object to the list (see Figure 5–35).

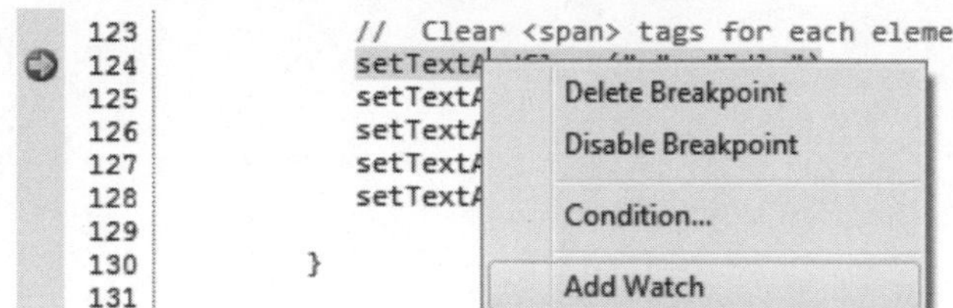

Figure 5–35. Active Breakpoint context menu with Add Watch menu option

The Debugging Console Pane and the console Object

The Debugging Console pane allows developers to inject single- or multiline JavaScript statements into the current page without the need to modify the original source (see Figure 5–36). It also provides a number of logging functions that can be used to debug scripts running within the web application.

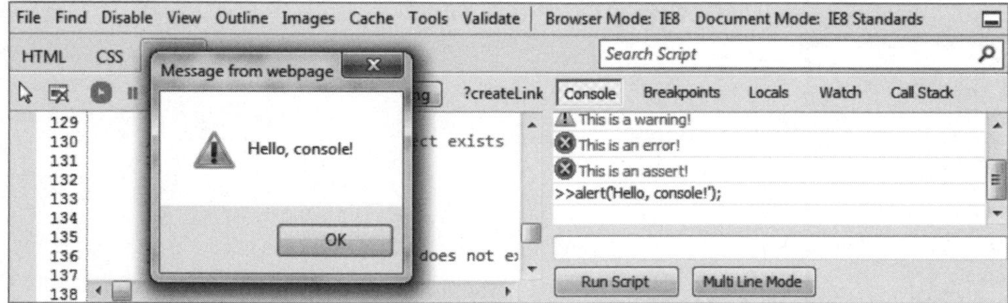

Figure 5–36. Web page running script input in the Debugging Console pane

The context menu on the Debugging Console pane also allows messages to be filtered by types defined in the following functions and UI notification elements.

The Debugging Console pane can be accessed from a web page through the `console` object in JavaScript. This object handles one-way communication from a page to the console. There are a number of predefined functions that provide different types of console messaging; these functions can be expanded through expandos on the `console` object itself.

- `console` **object**: Object that handles communication between a web page and the Developer Tools JavaScript Debugger Console.
- `log(message [,substitution])` **function**: Writes a string `message` to the console pane. Substitution strings in `message` will be replaced by a matching number of `substitution` parameters.
- `info(message [,substitutions])` **function**: Writes a string `message` to the console pane. These messages have a custom "information" icon. Substitution strings in `message` will be replaced by a matching number of `substitution` parameters.
- `warn(message [,substitutions])` **function**: Writes a string `message` to the console pane. These messages have a custom "warning" icon. Substitution strings in `message` will be replaced by a matching number of `substitution` parameters.

- `error(message [,substitutions])` **function**: Writes a string `message` to the console pane. These messages have a custom "error" icon. Substitution strings in `message` will be replaced by a matching number of `substitution` parameters.
- `assert(statement, message [,substitutions])` **function**: Writes a string `message` to the console pane only if the `statement` evaluates to `false`. These messages have a custom "error" icon. Substitution strings in `message` will be replaced by a matching number of `substitution` parameters.
- `clear()` **function**: Clears out all entries in the `console` object.
- (expando) **functions**: Function objects that handle custom log messages, passing information into another function on the `console` object.
- : `console.info()` notification icon.
- : `console.warn()` notification icon.
- : `console.error()` and `console.assert()` notification icons.

The `console` object is only available when the developer tools are open, and is not available in IE 7 and earlier releases. This applies to IE 8 and higher; the object may be available in other browsers under different conditions. Scripts using the `console` object should check for the object's existence before using it.

All console logging functions, save for the `clear()` function, can accept an arbitrary number of parameters given that those parameters match substitution tokens in the message parameter. This means that the `console` object can handle type conversion automatically, much like C's `printf()`, but in a limited capacity. The tokens used in substitutions are

- `%d`: Double type
- `%i`: Integer type
- `%f`: Float type
- `%o`: Object type
- `%s`: String type

Unlike the substitution style present in `printf()`, these tokens cannot be modified to convert a substituted value further; for instance, `%d` cannot be rewritten as `%02d` to pad the integer value with zeros until it is at least two digits wide.

Listing 5–4 demonstrates the basic usage of the `console` object.

Listing 5–4. *Using the Basic console Message Functions*

```
//  Check if the console object exists
if(window.console) {

   //  Write entries to the console
   console.log("This is a log entry!");
   console.info("This is information!");
   console.warn("This is a warning!");
   console.error("This is an error!");
   console.assert(false, "This is an assert!");

} else alert("Console object does not exist!");
```

When the code from this example is run, the console will display the messages with their respective icons, as shown in Figure 5–37.

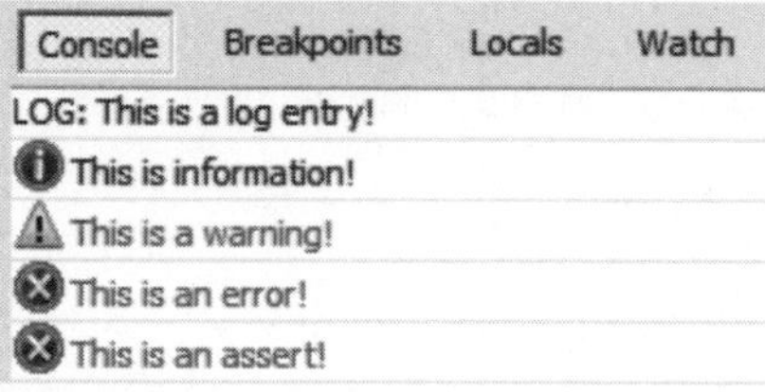

***Figure 5–37.** Basic console logging and message types*

■Note The `console` object (in IE) is only available when the developer tools are open; scripts that don't check to see if this object exists first will trigger an error. Always check to see if this object exists before using it.

Console messages can be simplified using substitution tokens. The `message` parameter itself is a `String` type; thus, some other types might require conversion to place it in the message. Developers can depend on the JavaScript engine for such a conversion by placing a token into the message where data of another type should reside and appending that variable as an additional parameter. Listing 5–5 demonstrates this.

***Listing 5–5.** Using String Substution in the console Object*

```
//  Check if the console object exists
if(window.console) {

   //  Define some variables
   var u = 3.14159;      //  Double (Float)
   var v = 8675309;      //  Float
   var x = 42;           //  Integer
   var y = new Date();   //  Object
   var z = "Marmite";    //  String

   //  Write to the console
   console.log("Double: %d", u);
   console.info("Floats: %f %f", v, u);
   console.warn("Integer: %i", x);
   console.error("Object: ", y);
   console.assert(false, "String: %s", z);

} else alert("Console object does not exist!");
```

This code outputs the result, as shown in Figure 5–38.

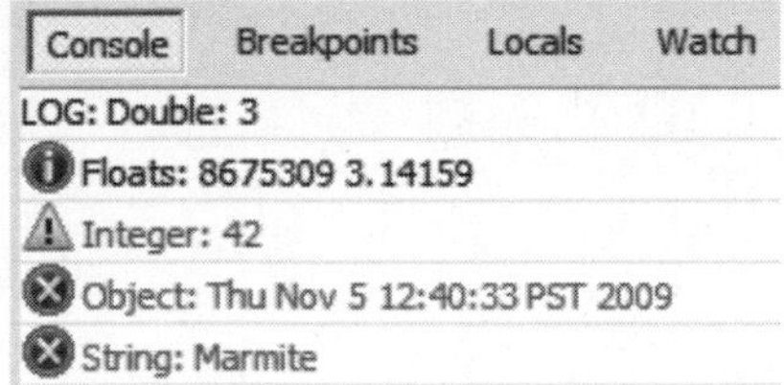

Figure 5–38. *Console logging using string substitution*

Finally, Listing 5–6 is an example of a custom function created to send data to the Debugging Console pane. Developers wishing to create a customized logging function can place that function onto the `console` object itself. This allows for a single point of conversion from a custom `console` logging string into one that can be displayed in the Debugging Console pane.

Listing 5–6. *Creating Custom Functions*

```
// Check if the console object exists
if(window.console) {

   // Create a new method on the console object
   console.debug = function() {

      // Get all the arguments and concat them
      var concatArguments = arguments.join(" ");

      // Grab the current date object
      var now = new Date();

      // Construct a new message format that uses the
      // "Debug: " prefix and appends a time to the end
      // of the message
      console.info("Debug: " + concatArguments +
                   " - " + now.toTimeString().split(" ")[0] +
                   " " + String(now.getUTCMilliseconds()) + "ms");

   }

   // Write to the console
   console.debug("This is a custom method!");
   console.debug("This is a custom method...", "with multiple input parameters");

} else alert("Console object does not exist!");
```

The code here outlines the creation of a new function on the `console` object: `console.debug()`. This function appends a custom message (`Debug:`) and a timestamp to every string being sent to the Debugging Console pane. Once the final string is concatenated, the function places the new string into the console through the `console.log()` function. Figure 5–39 demonstrates the result of this, displaying the two calls made into the new function at the end of the code sample.

Figure 5–39. *Console logging using custom functions/expandos*

JavaScript Debugging in Action

JavaScript debugging varies in difficulty based on the size and complexity of a web site. This section uses a web page found on the companion web site to highlight the features of the JavaScript debugger found in the IE developer tools. There's a catch, though: the example won't work right off the bat. This is where the JavaScript debugger comes in.

The code in Listing 5–7 is a buggy script in the aforementioned example. The script has two functions: `foo()`, which contains a string variable called `bar`, and `displayBar()`, which pops up an alert dialog containing the string contained in `foo()`'s `bar` variable. When the script is executed, it attempts to show the alert dialog by calling `display()` (hint: that's the first problem).

Listing 5–7. *Some Buggy JavaScript Functions*

```
<script type="text/javascript">

   //  Create a foo object that contains
   //  a variable bar
   function foo() {

      this.bar = "golden";

   }

   //  A function to display the current value of bar
   function displayBar() {

      try{

         //  Display the value of bar
         alert(foo.bar);

      } catch(exception) { }

   }

   //  Display the bar variable
   display();

</script>
```

JavaScript debugging is turned on with the Start Debugging button on the Script tab, and the page is reloaded. When the script is run, the debugger throws a balloon on the line of code that encountered an error: the call to `display()`. The error raised was "Object expected," which is shown both in the information balloon and the console (Figure 5–40).

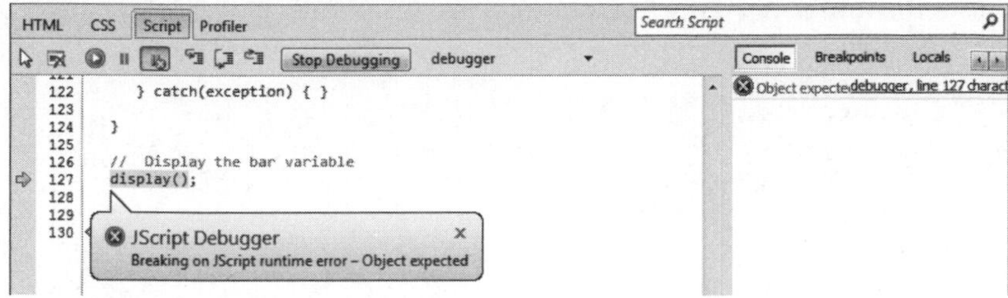

Figure 5–40. The JavaScript debugger breaking on an error

The error makes sense: there is no function named `display()` in the script. The script does, however, contain a function called `displayBar()`, which happens to be the code that call was intended for. Once the error is fixed, the page is reloaded and the debugger won't break on any more critical errors. The problem remains, however: no alert dialog is shown.

Breakpoints can be used to debug defects in script that don't cause breaking errors. The `displayBar()` function is responsible for showing the dialog. A breakpoint on this function will allow for analysis of what is causing the failure. Figure 5–41 shows this breakpoint.

```
HTML  CSS  Script  Profiler
Start Debugging   debugger

        } catch(exception) { }

    }

    // Display the bar variable
    displayBar();

</script>
        </div>
```

Figure 5–41. Setting a breakpoint on a line of JavaScript

The `displayBar()` function is called as the page is reloaded. The JavaScript debugger, upon entering this function, triggers the breakpoint set on the `displayBar()` call, as shown in Figure 5–42.

```
HTML  CSS  Script  Profiler
Stop Debugging   debugger

        } catch(exception) { }

    }

    // Display the bar variable
    displayBar();
```

Figure 5–42. The JavaScript debugger pausing on a set breakpoint

The call was reached, so the problem may lie *within* the function. The Step Into command steps into and pauses on the first line of the function. Figure 5–43 shows this pause, and it also displays the offending line of code: a call to an element.

HTML CSS Script Profiler

Stop Debugging debugger

```
// A function to display the current value of bar
function displayBar() {

   try{

      // Display the value of bar
      alert(foo.bar);

   } catch(exception) { }

}
```

***Figure 5–43.** Using the Step Into command to pause inside a called function*

Stepping through the debugger reveals that `alert(foo.bar)` didn't work; the debugger didn't break, however, because there was a `try...catch` statement surrounding the call. This is where the debugger stops working and the developer begins thinking (again, the developer tools are not a catchall toolset). The problem here is with the use of `foo.bar` to display the string "golden"; `foo` is the *name* of a function that is treated like an object, but it can only be used as an *object* if a new instance of it is created.

The variable `myFoo` was created and instantiated to be `new foo()`, a new instance of the `foo` object. Listing 5–8 shows this code change. After a reload, a dialog pops up with the word "golden," showing that the script errors were fixed correctly and the page is now, in fact, golden (Figure 5–44).

***Listing 5–8.** Corrected Version of the Buggy JavaScript Functions*

```
<script type="text/javascript">

   // Create a foo object that contains
   // a variable bar
   function foo() {

      this.bar = "golden";

   }

   // A function to display the current value of bar
   function displayBar() {

      try{

         // Create a new instance of foo
         var myFoo = new foo();

         // Display the value of bar
         alert(myFoo.bar);

      } catch(exception) { }
```

```
    }

    // Display the bar variable
    displayBar();

</script>
```

Figure 5–44. A message box emitted from a correctly working script

JavaScript Measurement and Optimization

The JavaScript profiler, along with competitive tools in Firebug (and its extension Y!Slow), Dragonfly, and WebKit give web developers a way to get the raw data needed to assess potential performance pain points. The next few sections highlight the performance tools in IE and some real examples of how to use them.

The JavaScript Profiler

The profiler collects data on the time spent in each JavaScript function as script executes, and displays a report after it is stopped. It may be started and stopped at any time, and does not require the page to be reloaded (however, since most script runs during page load, it is most effective when profiling during the page load process). There is no minimum time the profiler must run to collect data.

The Profiler UI

The Profiler tab consists of top-level UI elements (shown in Figure 5–45) that toggle the profiler and enable developers to view reports from profiler runs within the current session.

Figure 5–45. The JavaScript Profiler UI

Table 5–13 outlines the functionality of these elements.

Table 5–13. JavaScript Profiler Buttons

Button	Shortcut	Description
Select Element by Click	Ctrl+B	Navigates to an element's definition in the HTML tab's DOM Explorer when it is clicked in the current web page. This will switch focus away from the Profiler tab.
Clear Browser Cache	Ctrl+R	Clears the browser cache for all domains and sessions.
Export Data	-	Exports data from a currently selected report to a comma-separated value (CSV) file that can be loaded by most spreadsheet and database applications.
Start/Stop Profiling	F5 (Shift+F5)	Begins or ends the JavaScript profiler session.
Current View drop-down	-	Determines the format profile data should be displayed in.
Current Report drop-down	-	Selects a profile result set to be viewed.

Profile Views

After a profile has been collected, the results can be viewed in the tool itself. There are two main ways of viewing this data: Function view and Call Tree view.

- **Function view**: A list of all JavaScript functions called during a profiling session and associated data regarding call counts and elapsed time
- **Call Tree view**: An expansion of Function View that displays called functions in groups of trees based upon functions' caller/callee relationships

Each view of a profile run displays the same basic information: functions called, the number of calls made, the time it took to run those functions, and metadata such as the resource location and the line number for a specific function in that resource. By default, IE displays the gathered data in Function view (shown in Figure 5–46). Developers can add and remove data points from the display and results may be ordered by any column. The available data points are

- **Function**: Name of a function
- **Count**: Total number of calls made to a function
- **Inclusive Time (msec)**: Time spent in a function and its callees (in milliseconds)
- **Inclusive Time (%)**: Percentage of overall time spent in a function and its callees
- **Exclusive Time (msec)**: Time spent in a function (in milliseconds)
- **Exclusive Time (%)**: Percentage of overall time spent in a function

- **Average Time (msec)**: Average time spent in a function and its callees (in milliseconds)
- **Max Time (msec)**: Maximum time spent in a function and its callees (in milliseconds)
- **Min Time (msec)**: Minimum time spent in a function and its callees (in milliseconds)
- **URL**: URL of the file where a function is defined
- **Line Number**: Line number within the source URL where a function is defined

Function view displays a list of timing data by function name. Developers looking for raw timing information will find Function view most useful—the functions that are detrimental to performance can be quickly identified.

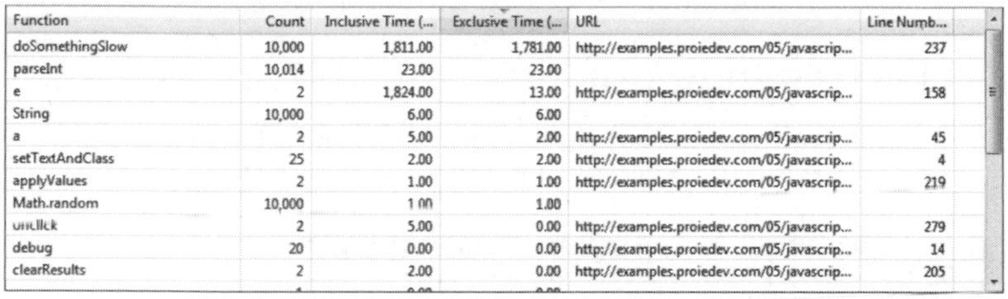

Function	Count	Inclusive Time (...	Exclusive Time (...	URL	Line Numb...
doSomethingSlow	10,000	1,811.00	1,781.00	http://examples.proiedev.com/05/javascrip...	237
parseInt	10,014	23.00	23.00		
e	2	1,824.00	13.00	http://examples.proiedev.com/05/javascrip...	158
String	10,000	6.00	6.00		
a	2	5.00	2.00	http://examples.proiedev.com/05/javascrip...	45
setTextAndClass	25	2.00	2.00	http://examples.proiedev.com/05/javascrip...	4
applyValues	2	1.00	1.00	http://examples.proiedev.com/05/javascrip...	219
Math.random	10,000	1.00	1.00		
onclick	2	5.00	0.00	http://examples.proiedev.com/05/javascrip...	279
debug	20	0.00	0.00	http://examples.proiedev.com/05/javascrip...	14
clearResults	2	2.00	0.00	http://examples.proiedev.com/05/javascrip...	205

Figure 5–46. Function view of a profile

Inline blocks are not well represented in the profiler's data. In order to get accurate timing information for a block of code, developers should "name" that block of code by wrapping it in a function call.

Call Tree view, shown in Figure 5–47, contains all the data provided by Function view. Instead of being organized by name, it is organized by functional relationships.

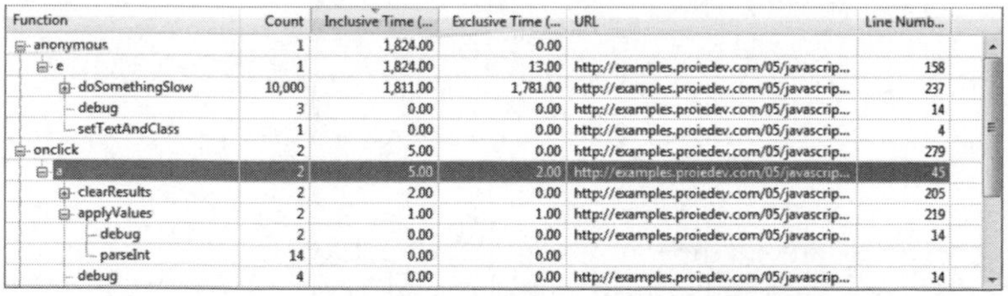

Function	Count	Inclusive Time (...	Exclusive Time (...	URL	Line Numb...
⊟ anonymous	1	1,824.00	0.00		
⊟ e	1	1,824.00	13.00	http://examples.proiedev.com/05/javascrip...	158
⊞ doSomethingSlow	10,000	1,811.00	1,781.00	http://examples.proiedev.com/05/javascrip...	237
debug	3	0.00	0.00	http://examples.proiedev.com/05/javascrip...	14
setTextAndClass	1	0.00	0.00	http://examples.proiedev.com/05/javascrip...	4
⊟ onclick	2	5.00	0.00	http://examples.proiedev.com/05/javascrip...	279
⊟ a	2	5.00	2.00	http://examples.proiedev.com/05/javascrip...	45
⊞ clearResults	2	2.00	0.00	http://examples.proiedev.com/05/javascrip...	205
⊟ applyValues	2	1.00	1.00	http://examples.proiedev.com/05/javascrip...	219
debug	2	0.00	0.00	http://examples.proiedev.com/05/javascrip...	14
parseInt	14	0.00	0.00		
debug	4	0.00	0.00	http://examples.proiedev.com/05/javascrip...	14

Figure 5–47. Call Tree view of a profile

The call tree format provides insight into the overall performance impact of function relationships.

Exporting Data

The Export Data tool ( ) allows developers to export profile data as a CSV file. This file may be loaded in a number of spreadsheet and database applications for further analysis. Figure 5–48 shows an exported data set being displayed in Microsoft Excel.

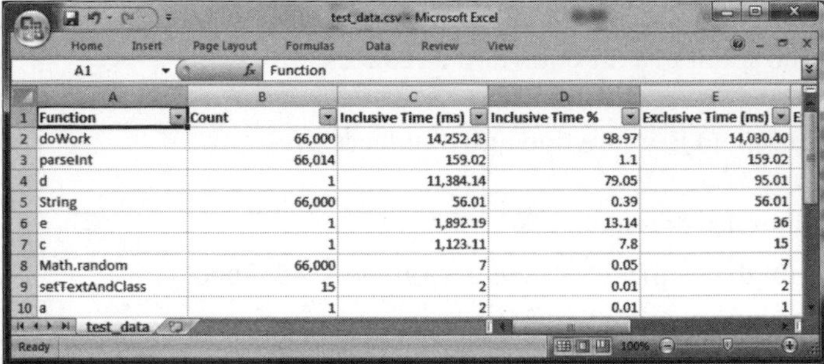

Function	Count	Inclusive Time (ms)	Inclusive Time %	Exclusive Time (ms)
doWork	66,000	14,252.43	98.97	14,030.40
parseInt	66,014	159.02	1.1	159.02
d	1	11,384.14	79.05	95.01
String	66,000	56.01	0.39	56.01
e	1	1,892.19	13.14	36
c	1	1,123.11	7.8	15
Math.random	66,000	7	0.05	7
setTextAndClass	15	2	0.01	2
a	1	2	0.01	1

Figure 5–48. Exported profiler data loaded into Microsoft Excel

JavaScript Performance Testing in Action

The sample web page for this section (on the companion web site) demonstrates how to use the JavaScript profiler to time data flows and function calls (Figure 5–49).

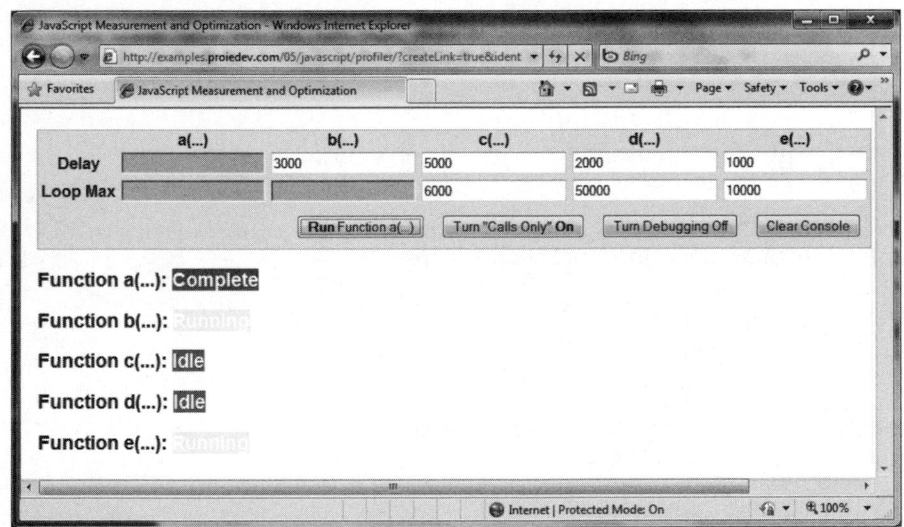

Figure 5–49. Example web page for modeling JavaScript performance

To start the performance demo, a user clicks the Run Function a(...) button at the top of the page. This kicks off a series of function calls (named "a" through "e") and simulated "work" that ultimately result in a set of timing data. While a function is running, its status is reflected on the page as either Idle, Running, or Complete. Once all functions are complete, the time it took to process each function call and the work done by each can be seen in the profiler's report viewer.

There are five worker functions present on the web page, again named alphabetically "a" through "e." Function `a()` starts a cascade that calls each of the other functions once. All functions except `a()` are started after a certain delay specified in milliseconds; these delays can be modified in a set of input boxes at the top of the page. Functions c() through e() run some nonperformant tasks a set number of times (the Loop Max input boxes indicate how many times this task is performed by each function).

The flow diagram in Figure 5–50 shows how each function is called.

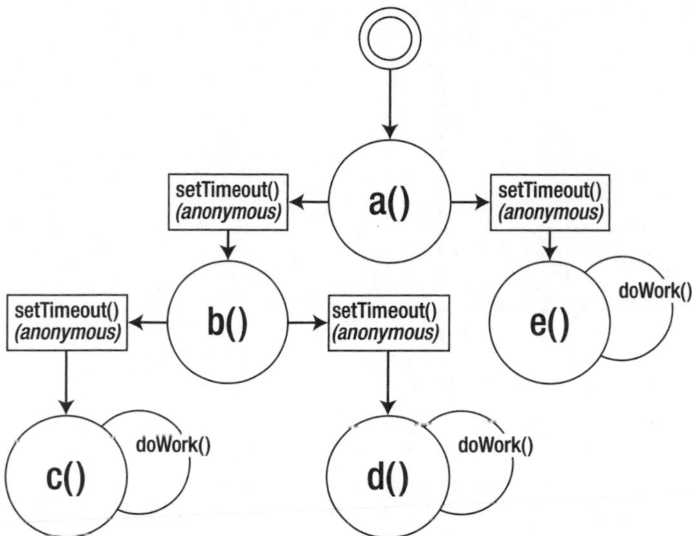

Figure 5–50. Call graph of the sample web page

When the onclick event of the Run Function a(...) button is triggered, function a() is called by the JavaScript engine. Functions b() and e() are called after their respective delays; function b() proceeds to trigger functions c() and d() after a delay as well. Functions c(), d(), and e() each call a doWork() function (whose code is shown in Listing 5–9) the number of times indicated in the Loop Max input boxes.

Listing 5–9. A Slow JavaScript Function: doWork()

```
// A function whose sole purpose is to waste time.
function doWork() {
   // Do some really random, wasteful work.
   var containerDiv = document.getElementById('container');
   var newDiv = document.createElement("div");
   newDiv.setAttribute('id', "tempDiv" + String(parseInt(Math.random() * 1000000)));
   newDiv.innerHTML = "   ";
   containerDiv.appendChild(newDiv);
   containerDiv.removeChild(newDiv);
}
```

The raw results from the profile run are shown in Call Tree view in Figure 5–51. The results show that d() ran for the greatest length of time, followed by e(), c(), a(), and b().

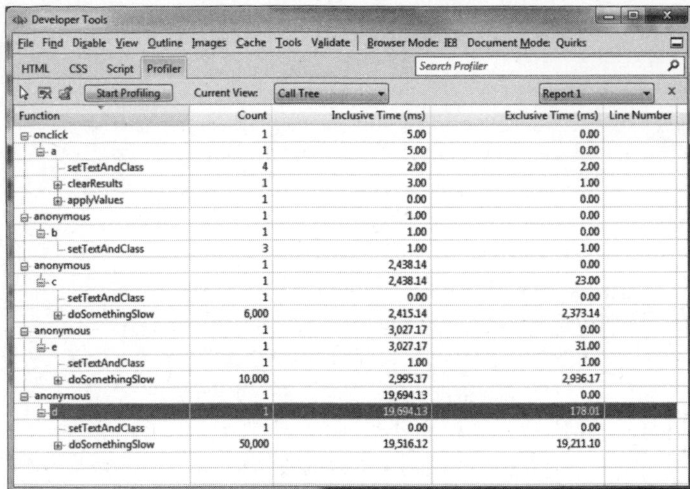

Function	Count	Inclusive Time (ms)	Exclusive Time (ms)	Line Number
onclick	1	5.00	0.00	
a	1	5.00	0.00	
setTextAndClass	4	2.00	2.00	
clearResults	1	3.00	1.00	
applyValues	1	0.00	0.00	
anonymous	1	1.00	0.00	
b	1	1.00	0.00	
setTextAndClass	3	1.00	1.00	
anonymous	1	2,438.14	0.00	
c	1	2,438.14	23.00	
setTextAndClass	1	0.00	0.00	
doSomethingSlow	6,000	2,415.14	2,373.14	
anonymous	1	3,027.17	0.00	
e	1	3,027.17	31.00	
setTextAndClass	1	1.00	1.00	
doSomethingSlow	10,000	2,995.17	2,936.17	
anonymous	1	19,694.13	0.00	
d	1	19,694.13	178.01	
setTextAndClass	1	0.00	0.00	
doSomethingSlow	50,000	19,516.12	19,211.10	

Figure 5–51. *Results from profiling the sample page*

Clearer results can be seen using external tools and charting software. The results here were imported into Excel and placed into a chart (Figure 5–52) showing when each function started and ended.

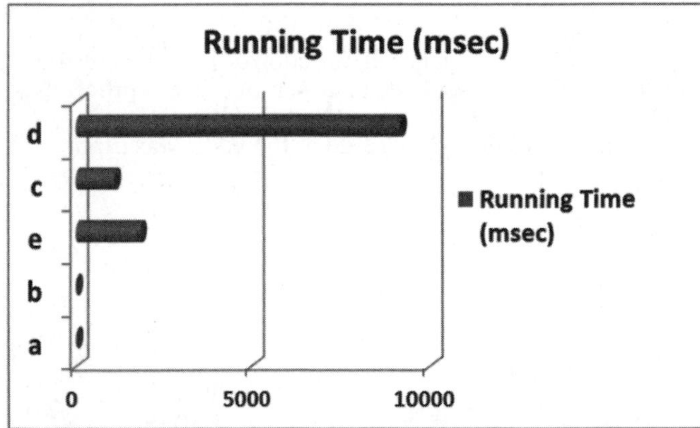

Figure 5–52. *Charted results highlighting each function's running time*

Managing Cookies and the Cache

The developer tools contain tools for cleaning up and inspecting cookies and cache information. Commands include operations to clear the cookies and the cache, to disable cookies and caching, and to view cookies. See Table 5–14 for details.

Table 5–14. Cache Menu Entries

Menu Item	Shortcut	Description
Always Refresh from Server	-	Ignores the cache and always downloads content for each page load
Clear Browser Cache…	Ctrl+R	Clears the browser cache
Clear Browser Cache for this Domain…	Ctrl+D	Removes files from the current domain from the browser cache
Disable Cookies	-	Disables cookies browser-wide
Clear Session Cookies	-	Clears nonpersistent (session) cookies
Clear Cookies for Domain	-	Clears session and persistent cookies associated with the current domain
View Cookie Information	-	Displays a list of all cookies in a new web page

This implementation, shown in Figure 5–53, is quite basic; it does not offer granularity of information further than that of the current domain or session. Developers are encouraged to use other tools for deeper analysis, such as a network and HTTP debugger.

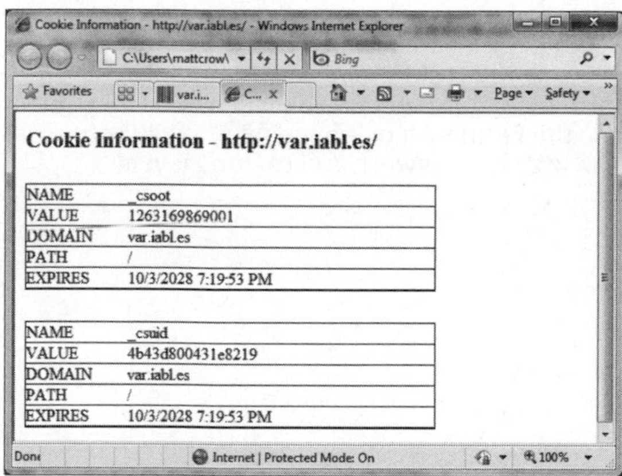

***Figure 5–53.** Data displayed by the View Cookie Information command*

Tips for Debugging and Inspecting Web Sites

The following tips and tricks can help developers get the best results when using the developer tools:

- **Don't use developer tools to *code* web sites**: The IE developer tools are meant to aid developers in fixing bugs or developing interoperable pages. They are not replacements for a traditional development environment. They are not a text editor. It would take much longer for a developer to code a page using the developer tools than using traditional web development practices.
- **Treat page inspection as a feedback loop**: Just like informational tooltips and debugger feedback in many IDEs, script errors thrown by browsers, and error and warning log files, the information provided by in-browser tools is meant to provoke a reaction. Developers should expect to jump back and forth between tools and the web page development process until a page reaches a satisfactory state.
- **Use complementary tools**: There are a lot of features packed into the IE developer tools, but they aren't all-encompassing. There is no HTTP inspector or network debugger. There isn't a color profile manager. There is no mobile emulator. Developers should use the IE developer tools as a part of a wider developer workflow.

Summary

The developer tools provide a wide variety of utilities that can help you inspect and debug markup, layout, styles, and script in your pages. These tools aren't designed to replace a full development environment—they are, however, a great way to ensure your pages display and behave the way you intended. Beyond the inspection and debugging capabilities of the HTML, CSS, and Script tabs, the JavaScript profiler provides some great insight into performance improvements you can make to your pages as well. In the next chapter I cover ways you can use the Fiddler web debugging proxy to gain further insight into the way your web application interacts with IE's network and caching layers.

CHAPTER 6

■ ■ ■

Scripting with Mutable DOM Prototypes

Customization of the Document Object Model (DOM) is a powerful concept, especially when used with dynamic languages like JavaScript. Prototype and property modification can solve important compatibility and interoperability issues without requiring changes to existing code. While older IE releases do not support a mutable DOM, IE 8 has added mutable prototype support enabling these important scenarios. In this chapter, I will detail how you can apply these concepts to your projects and provide some examples you can reuse on your own web sites.

A Primer: Prototypes, Properties, and the DOM

JavaScript has many traits of an object-oriented programming (OOP) language; however, it lacks the traditional class structure expected in most OOP contexts. JavaScript is classified as a *prototypal* language—an OOP language in which objects inherit behaviors (functions, properties, etc.) rather than object definitions (classes).

Prototypes

Objects in prototypal languages form inheritance hierarchies by inheriting sets of behavior rather than building on base structures. These sets of behaviors are called *prototypes*. Put simply, prototypes are blueprints for what an object can do and the information it can store.

Objects maintain an object-oriented inheritance hierarchy by way of prototype inheritance, also called *prototype chaining*. Instead of object definitions declaring their relationship to a base or superclass object, JavaScript objects extend their base or parent object by inheriting their prototype and (optionally) building or overriding its behavior.

Figure 6–1 shows an inheritance diagram relating a chain of general to specific representations of an automobile to each other in a hierarchy. In this case, the hierarchy begins with the `Auto` object (representing a general automobile); as the relation grows, objects represent more specific (and detailed) automobile classifications (e.g., a 2008 Jeep Wrangler).

Class-based languages would represent this hierarchy using only the objects on the left side; the objects, represented through classes, would inherit from each other. In JavaScript, each object instead references a set of behaviors, or a prototype. These prototypes chain off of each other, extending their behavior from the base prototype to the more specific prototype later in the hierarchy.

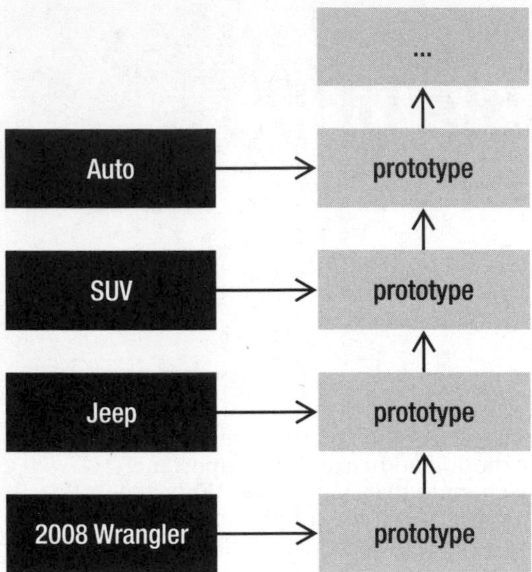

Figure 6–1. *Example of JavaScript prototypes and prototype chaining*

Properties (Getters and Setters)

JavaScript addresses the most important principles of an OOP system even though it doesn't implement a class-based OOP structure. Encapsulation (protection of private data via filtered accessibility) is one area that modern JavaScript implementations address (as of the ECMAScript 5 specification). Private data protection is ensured through the use of *properties* (commonly known as mutator methods). (Note that JavaScript has no true concept of access modifiers, so the use of *public* and *private* should be taken in an illustrative context.)

JavaScript properties encapsulate two basic activities: the reading of an object (*get*) and the writing to an object (*set*). A *getter* represents a function that handles the former action, and a *setter* is a function representing the latter.

There are two types of properties: data properties and accessor properties. Data properties are basic storage variables that can store and emit a value. The JavaScript engine handles the *get* and *set* actions for these objects. For example, you can set a value to the document object's data property through `document.data`.

Accessor properties are properties where a developer has *explicitly* defined the getter and setter for that property. Developers can define the set of actions that take place whenever a value is set to that property or when that property is read. For instance, a developer can customize the `innerHTML` property in such a way that the contents of that object are sanitized whenever it is read from or written to.

Developers can use property descriptors to define whether an object is a data property or an accessor property. Table 6–1 describes these descriptors; use of these descriptors is described later in this chapter.

Table 6–1. Property Descriptor Attributes

Descriptor Attribute	Description	Property Type
`writable`	Attribute indicating that the property can be changed	Data
`enumnerable`	Attribute indicating that the property may be enumerated off the owner object	Data, accessor
`configurable`	Attribute indicating that the property may be changed or deleted from the owner object	Data, accessor

JavaScript and the DOM

The DOM is an API for accessing markup-based documents. This API projects a web page's hierarchical, node-based structure onto JavaScript objects using prototypes and prototype chaining.

The W3C DOM Level 1, 2, and 3 specifications together represent the standard model for representing documents in JavaScript. Interfaces, such as a `Document`, `Element`, and `Attribute`, represent *actual* constructs found on a page; the `Document` object, for example, represents a web page's document container; an `Element` object represents any HTML element in that document; and so on. These objects derive from the `Node` object's prototype—the `Node` object being the W3C DOM specification's atomic representation of a markup entity. Figure 6–2 demonstrates a small cutaway of the W3C DOM for context.

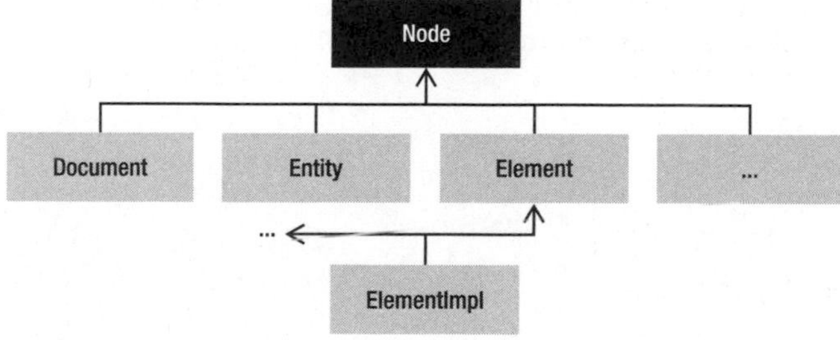

Figure 6–2. Partial heirarchy of the W3C DOM

IE exposes markup objects to JavaScript via a DOM; however, the DOM in IE 8 and below loosely resembles the W3C recommendation. Figure 6–3 shows the base structure and an example object chain.

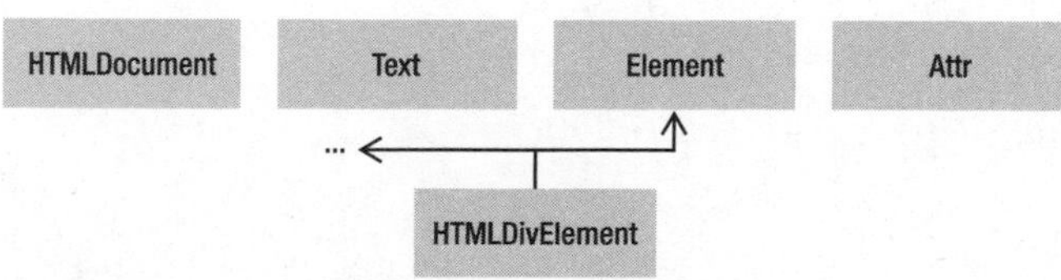

Figure 6–3. Partial heirarchy of the IE DOM

Unlike the W3C DOM, IE's DOM does not have an atomic object that represents a basic markup entity. Instead, the IE DOM contains similar—many identical—loosely connected objects that form a markup-based document's representation to JavaScript.

This difference is unimportant from a functionality standpoint; however, it does mean that in IE versions up to 8, scripts that use DOM functionality may *not* be fully interoperable between IE and other browsers.

Mutable Prototypes and Properties in IE 8

Mutable prototypes and properties were extended to DOM objects as of IE 8. This allows developers to modify and change IE's DOM behavior by overriding objects and properties of DOM object prototypes. The following sections outline how prototype objects and properties can be manipulated.

Manipulating DOM Objects

Creation, modification, and deletion of DOM objects is available in IE 8 and above. Prior to this version, DOM objects in IE were specially cased and could not have their prototypes modified in the way custom object prototypes could. Opening prototype modification to these objects allows for some great compatibility, interoperability, and augmentation scenarios that other browsers have enjoyed for quite some time.

Adding New Functions

New functionality can be added to objects by way of an object's prototype. For example, one can add a function to the `Element` interface by adding it to `Element.prototype`; objects using objects on the `Element` interface will automatically have this available to them, even if they were created before the new functionality was added. Listing 6–1 shows an example of this, adding two functions on the `Element` interface that control the case of an instance's text content.

***Listing 6–1.** Adding Functionality via DOM Prototypes*

```
<script type="text/javascript">

Element.prototype.toUpperCase = function() {

   //  Create a new toUpperCase function on the Element interface
   this.innerText = this.innerText.toUpperCase();

}

Element.prototype.toLowerCase = function() {

   //  Create a new toLowerCase function on the Element interface
   this.innerText = this.innerText.toLowerCase();

}
```

Accessing and Storing Built-In Functions

Built-in (default) functions stored in object prototypes can be saved to variables. This is useful for extending existing functionality. For example, the `setAttribute()` function can be saved to a variable and later called through that variable. Listing 6–2 provides a simple illustration.

***Listing 6–2.** Storing a Default Function in a Variable*

```
<script type="text/javascript">

   //  Save the default setAttribute function to oldSetAttribute
   var oldSetAttribute = Element.prototype.setAttribute;
```

Wrapping Existing Functions

Existing functions can be replaced in the same way that new functions are defined. Setting a function value to an object's prototype will "hide" the existing function value, resulting in the new function being executed in response to future calls. The old function can be saved to a variable and called within the new function as well, essentially allowing for function overriding.

The example in Listing 6–3 shows the `Element` interface's `setAttribute()` function being overridden after the old functionality is saved to a variable.

***Listing 6–3.** Wrapping the setAttribute() function*

```
<script type="text/javascript">

   //  Save a copy of the default setAttribute function
   var defaultSetAttribute = Element.prototype.setAttribute;

   Element.prototype.setAttribute = function (attr, value) {

      //  Support the use of classname as a reference to class
      if (attr.toLowerCase() == "classname") {

         //  Pass to the original setAttribute as "class"
         defaultSetAttribute.call(this, "class", value);

      }
      else
        defaultSetAttribute.call(this, attr, value);
   };

</script>
```

Deleting Custom Functions

Custom functions can be deleted using the `delete` keyword. It is used by calling `delete` followed by the object and function names. Listing 6–4 demonstrates the removal of a custom `getElementById` function from the document element.

Listing 6–4. *Removing the Custom getElementById Function*

```
<script type="text/javascript">

   try {

      //  Delete the custom innerText property on Element
      delete document.getElementById;

   } catch(e) {
      /*  Ignore exceptions thrown when no custom properties  */
      /*  exist on the object                                 */
   }

</script>
```

If a default function is overridden by a custom one, its original functionality is restored. Listing 6–4 is a good example of this; a custom version of `getElementById` was removed from the `document` object; thus, subsequent calls to `document.getElementById()` will use the default function. Default functions cannot be removed using the `delete` command.

Manipulating DOM Object Get and Set Properties

Properties, like objects, can be modified for DOM objects as of IE 8. Each can have a getter and setter that can be applied in an interoperable fashion (one defined in the ECMAScript 5 specification). The following sections outline how DOM objects such as `Element` can have new properties and even have existing ones such as `innerText` extended. More detailed examples are provided later in this chapter.

Creating New Properties

New properties can be created on both existing DOM objects and custom objects. They are appended through the `Object.defineProperty()` function, which takes three parameters: the DOM object prototype that will house the property, the name of the property in string format, and a property object containing either a getter, a setter, or both. Listing 6–5 shows an example of adding a new property.

Listing 6–5. *Adding a New Property*

```
<script type="text/javascript">

   //  Create a variable for storage
   var varData = "";

   //  Create a property to get and set varData
   Object.defineProperty(Element.prototype, "myProperty", {

      //  Property setter: Set varData to be contents of value
      //  and signal it was called with an alert
      set: function(value) {

         varData = value;
         alert("Set - varData: " + value);
```

```
        },

        //  Property getter: Get and return contents of varData
        //  and signal it was called with an alert
        get: function ()
        {

           alert("Get - varData:" + varData);
           return varData;

        }

    });

</script>
```

A number of descriptor attributes are available for properties. Descriptor attributes allow developers to define how a property works and what it does.

Accessing and Storing Built-In Properties

Built-in properties can be stored to a variable for later use. New properties applied to DOM objects can pass along data to these properties in order to modify or enhance the functionality of the original properties. Listing 6–6 demonstrates the `Object.getOwnPropertyDescriptor` function, used to return the property object for a given property on a DOM object.

Listing 6–6. *Storing a Default Property*

```
//  Get the innerText property on Element
var defInnerText = Object.getOwnPropertyDescriptor(Element, "innerText");
```

This function takes two arguments: the DOM object being targeted and the property being targeted (in that order). The first should point to an object; the second should be a string containing a property name available to that object.

Tread carefully—storing built-in properties by reading them directly will lead to an unpleasant surprise. When property values are referenced in this way (e.g., `var foo = bar.myProperty`), only the *getter* is saved to the variable. This means any calls into the saved version of `myProperty` will fail if the setter is accessed. Developers looking to store a full property (both a *getter* and a *setter*) should do so by using the `getOwnPropertyDescriptor()` function shown in the preceding code.

Wrapping Existing Properties

Existing properties can be wrapped and replaced with new ones. They can be overridden by using the process described in the last section—copying the original property to a variable before replacing it. Property wrappers can pass information back and forth between saved properties; Listing 6–7 offers an example of this.

Listing 6–7. *Wrapping a Property*

```
<script type="text/javascript">

   //  Get the innerText property on Element
   var defInnerText = Object.getOwnPropertyDescriptor(Element, "innerText");
```

```
   // Define a new property for innerText
   Object.defineProperty(Element.prototype, "innerText",
   {
      // Return the value held by the original innerText property
      // and prepend a test string
      get: function () { return "Test Get: " + defInnerText.get.call(this); }

      // Map the setter to the original innerText property setter and
      // call it after prepending a text string
      set: function (content) {
              defInnerText.set.call(this, "Test Set: " + content); }

   });

</script>
```

The script begins by saving the innerText property of the Element interface to the variable defInnerText. Next, the Object.defineProperty() function is called; the Element interface's prototype, the string innerText, and the code for a new property are passed to it. The new property consists of a getter and a setter. The new getter calls the original getter and returns the value on the original prepended with Test Get:. The new setter also prepends the value, but this time before it is run through the original setter.

Deleting Custom Properties

Custom properties can be deleted using the delete command. Listing 6–8 demonstrates the removal of a custom innerText property from the Element interface's prototype.

Listing 6–8. *Removing a Property*

```
<script type="text/javascript">

   try {

      // Delete the custom innerText property on Element
      delete Element.prototype.innerText;

   } catch(e) {
      /* Ignore exceptions thrown when no custom properties  */
      /* exist on the object                                 */
   }

</script>
```

Just like deletion of custom objects, deletion of custom properties reverts those properties to DOM defaults if they existed before. The delete command cannot remove default properties.

Using Property Descriptors

Property descriptors can be used to specify whether a property acts like a data property or an accessor property. There are three attributes described at the beginning of this chapter, in Table 6–1: writable, enumerable, and configurable.

Developers can specify one or more of these attributes when defining a property with `defineProperty()`. Each attribute is specified as a Boolean array value and appended as the last parameter of this function (Listing 6–9).

Listing 6–9. *Using Property Descriptors with defineProperty()*

```
<script type="text/javascript">

   // Get the innerText property on Element
   var defInnerText = Object.getOwnPropertyDescriptor(Element, "innerText");

   // Define a new property for innerText
   Object.defineProperty(Element.prototype, "innerText",
   {
      // Return the value held by the original innerText property
      // and prepend a test string
      get: function () { return "Test Get: " + defInnerText.get.call(this); }

      // Map the setter to the original innerText property setter and
      // call it after prepending a text string
      set: function (content) {
              defInnerText.set.call(this, "Test Set: " + content); }

   },
   {
      enumerable: true,
      configurable: true
   });

</script>
```

IE Improvements in Practice

The usefulness of IE's DOM improvements may not be obvious for developers who have never used this functionality before. The following sections provide a selection of examples of how IE mutable DOM prototypes and support for getters and setters can enhance pages run in IE 8 and above.

Downlevel IE Compatibility

Microsoft made changes between IE 7 and 8 to bring IE closer to standards recommendations and cross-browser interoperability. Some of these changes, however, caused compatibility breaks between IE 8 and downlevel versions. Mutable DOM prototype support added in IE 8 can be used to simulate legacy functionality, allowing older scripts to run until they can be upgraded or rewritten for standards-compliance.

Example: Reenabling Support for the className Attribute

IE 8 dropped support for accessing an element's `class` attribute using the `className` moniker within the `Element` interface's `getAttribute()` and `setAttribute()` functions. This change removed the need for scripts to create special cases when accessing this attribute in IE. Solving this interoperability problem for a wide swath of the JavaScript development community caused breakage in another set of scripts: those designed for use in IE 7 and below.

Mutable DOM prototypes can be used to reinsert support for the class attribute's className moniker by overriding the default behavior of getAttribute() and setAttribute(). Listing 6–10 shows a script that does just this.

***Listing 6–10.** Script Overriding get/setAttribute to Support class Attribute Access via the className Moniker*

```
<script type="text/javascript">

   //  Create variables to hold the default set and get
   //  attribute functions
   var defaultSetAttribute = Element.prototype.setAttribute;
   var defaultGetAttribute = Element.prototype.getAttribute;

   //  Overwrite the default setAttribute function
   Element.prototype.setAttribute = function (attr, value) {

      //  Support the use of classname as a reference to class
      if (attr == "className") {

         //  Pass to the original setAttribute as "class"
         defaultSetAttribute.call(this, "class", value);

      }
      else
        defaultSetAttribute.call(this, attr, value);
   };

   //  Overwrite the default getAttribute function
   Element.prototype.getAttribute = function (attr) {

      //  Support the use of classname as a reference to class
      if (attr == "className") {

         //  Pass to the original getAttribute as "class"
         return defaultGetAttribute.call(this, "class");

      }
     return defaultGetAttribute.call(this, attr);
   };

</script>
```

The example begins with two variables, defaultSetAttribute and defaultGetAttribute; respectively, they point to the original implementation of the setAttribute() and getAttribute() functions on the Element interface. The script proceeds to specify a new implementation of Element.prototype.setAttribute—one that accepts a value of className and converts it to the IE 8's required "class" value; all other inputs are left alone. This value is passed to the original implementation saved in the defaultSetAttribute variable. The same is done for Element.prototype.getAttribute, converting "className" to "class" and passing the request to the defaultGetAttribute variable.

Cross-Browser Interoperability

IE 8 does not offer full support in areas such as DOM Level 2 and 3 APIs, forcing web developers to create workarounds for some functionality until future releases of the browser. DOM prototypes, in many cases, offer a solution for interoperability scenarios left unfulfilled in current releases of IE. Developers looking to add or replace APIs on base DOM objects can do so through this method and, in doing so, use one script that works across browsers instead of sprinkling workarounds for IE throughout their code.

Example: Supporting Both textContent and innerText

The `innerText` property is used in IE to get or set the inner text within a markup node (be it HTML or some generic XML). `innerText`, however, is not interoperable across all browsers. Firefox, for instance, uses the W3C-recommended `textContent` property instead. While these two properties perform the exact same task, the difference in naming can cause scripts to fail, frustrating developers trying to build interoperable pages.

Listing 6–11 demonstrates some HTML and script that would cause errors in this scenario—in IE, the call to `textContent` would not work as expected since the property does not exist; in Firefox, the call to `innerText` would yield a similar failure.

Listing 6–11. *Script Testing Browser Support for Both innerText and textContent*

```
<div id="testInnerText"></div>
<div id="testTextContent"></div>

<script type="text/javascript">

   //  Access the two test divs
   var divInnerText   = document.getElementById("testInnerText");
   var divTextContent = document.getElementById("testTextContent");

   //  Attempt to write to the innerText property of divInnerText
   divInnerText.innerText = "This element supports innerText.";

   //  Attempt to write to the textContent property of divTextContent
   divTextContent.textContent = "This element supports textContent.";

</script>
```

Getter and setter support in IE 8, in combination with its handling of DOM prototypes, may be used to abstract this difference. The example in Listing 6–12 demonstrates a script that brings support for the `textContent` property to IE 8.

Listing 6–12. *Creating a textContent Property on the Element Interface, Aliasing innerText*

```
<script type="text/javascript">

   //  Get the innerText property on the Element interface
   var defInnerText = Object.getOwnPropertyDescriptor(Element, "innerText");


   //  Define a new property for all elements called textContent
   Object.defineProperty(Element.prototype, "textContent",
```

```
{

    //  Map the getter to the original innerText property getter
    get: function () { return defInnerText.get.call(this); }

    //  Map the setter to the original innerText property setter
    set: function (content) {defInnerText.set.call(this, content); }

});

</script>
```

The example begins with the defInnerText variable being set to the Element interface's implementation of innerText (through the getOwnPropertyDescriptor() function). Next, a new property called textContent is appended to Element. The script then defines a getter and setter for the textContent property; the getter calls the getter from the innerText reference, and the setter invokes the setter on this same reference, passing along the content parameter to be set as the text content of the element.

This approach can be used to address some other important scenarios. For example, many HTML 5 functions, such as getElementsByClassName(), and DOM functions currently unsupported by IE, such as addEventListener(), can help build interoperable web applications.

■ **Note** Remember, storing built-in properties by reading them directly will result in only their getters being saved to a variable. Developers should use getOwnPropertyDescriptor() to store both the getter and setter of a property.

Security and Sanitization

The threat of cross-site scripting attacks means that developers should build multiple layers of protection against injection into their web applications. The safe use of client-side script can be seen as one of these defenses, providing a first line of defense and a first chance to immobilize threats. The following examples highlight the use of IE's DOM improvements to streamline the mitigation of injection attacks.

Example: Disabling document.write

The document.write() function permits script to override the content within the document object. A script may pass data to this function in order to completely replace page content. Although pages may intentionally use this function, malicious code injected into the page could also use this to emit misleading or dangerous content into the current session. Using the innerHTML property as a replacement for this is ineffective—it is no safer than document.write. Targeted writes using innerText provide a safer approach to dynamic content, but their use does not disable nor preclude the use of document.write().

The sample in Listing 6–13 demonstrates one possible solution: completely disabling document.write() by replacing it with an innocuous function.

Listing 6–13. *The disableWrite() Function and Its Replacement of document.write()*

```
<script type="text/javascript">

   //  Create a function that does "nothing" except write
   //  a message to the console (or pop an alert if the console
   //  object doesn't exist
   function disableWrite(data) {
      var message = "There seems to be a bug in this page!";
      if(console) console.write(message);
      else alert(message);
   }

   //  Set the the disableWrite function as document.write
   HTMLDocument.prototype.write = disableWrite;
   HTMLDocument.prototype.writeln = disableWrite;

</script>
```

A new, empty function called `disableWrite()` is created; the intention of this function is to do nothing at all. The `write()` function on the `HTMLDocument` object prototype is set to this function; any calls to `document.write()` or `document.writeln()` are redirected to `disableWrite()` where they hit a dead end. Since `disableWrite()` does nothing with the input parameter data, the value is never written to the document as intended.

Listing 6–14 demonstrates the new, useless function in action. A form is created containing a text box whose value is intended for the `document.write()` function. On submit, the form calls the `writeToDocument()` function, which in turn passes input from the form text box into `document.write()`. Again, since `write()` was overridden by a dummy `disableWrite()` function, no data is ever written to the document, and the page remains the same after the Submit button is clicked.

Listing 6–14. *Form Whose Action Tests the document.write() Override via Prototypes*

```
<script type="text/javascript">

   //  Write the current value of data to the document
   function writeToDocument() {
      document.write(document.getElementById("data").value);
   }

</script>


<form action="javascript:writeToDocument()">
   <p>
   Data to write:<br />
   <input type="text" id="data" name="data" />
   </p>
   <input type="submit" id="submit" name="submit" value="Write text" />
</form>
```

■ **Note** Pages allowing calls to `document.write()` are most likely vulnerable to script injection in the first place. This method doesn't prevent script injection and is not meant to mitigate threats of that type.

Example: Automatically Sanitizing innerHTML Reads and Writes

The `innerHTML` property of the `Element` interface is widely used to provide dynamic user experiences. Data applied to this variable is assumed to be HTML and applied as a child tree to a target `Element` (the one whose `innerHTML` was set). Not only does it allow for changing HTML content, but it also allows scripts to capture the child DOM of a specific element—a scenario very important to Ajax-based systems. Unfortunately, the HTML content get and set using this property is far from safe—markup, styles, and script all remain active. Active content, especially script placed into an element through this function, poses a threat to the integrity of a web application due to script injection attacks.

Prototypes, getters, and setters can be used to sanitize incoming and outgoing content on `innerHTML`, avoiding case-by-case data sanitization (and thus avoiding those missed cases). Listing 6–15 shows a script that sanitizes content passing in and out of this property using another new IE 8 feature: `toStaticHTML()`.

Listing 6–15. *Script Overriding the innerHTML Getter/Setter, Adding HTML Sanitization Using toStaticHTML*

```
<script type="text/javascript">

   //  Get the innerHTML property on the Element interface
   var defInnerHTML = Object.getOwnPropertyDescriptor(Element, "innerHTML");
   var defInnerText = Object.getOwnPropertyDescriptor(Element, "innerText");

   //  Define a new property for innerText
   Object.defineProperty(Element.prototype, "innerHTML",
   {

      //  Map the getter to the original innerHTML property getter and
      //  return sanitized content using toStaticHTML
      get: function () {
         if(typeof toStaticHTML == "object") {
            return toStaticHTML(defInnerHTML.get.call(this));
         } else {
            return defInnerText.get.call(this);
         }
      }

      //  Map the setter to the original innerText property setter and
      //  call it after sanitizing the input content using toStaticHTML
      set: function (content) {
         if(typeof toStaticHTML == "object") {
            defInnerHTML.set.call(this, toStaticHTML(content));
         } else {
            defInnerText.set.call(this, content);
         }
      }
```

```
});
</script>
```

This script begins by referencing the default innerHTML and innerText properties held by the Element interface prototype. Next, Object.defineProperty() is used to create a *new* innerHTML property on the Element interface. A new getter is created that returns a sanitized version of the original innerHTML property's getter value using toStaticHTML; if the toStaticHTML object does not exist, the getter returns a sanitized value through innerText. The new setter follows the same paradigm; the parameter passed to the new innerHTML property is sanitized using toStaticHTML(), whose result is passed along to the Element interface's original innerHTML property. If toStaticHTML does not exist, innerText is used to set a sanitized version of the input content.

Input Validation

Input validation scenarios can be streamlined by appending validation functions to target elements and input. Forms, for example, often submit to server-side validation scripts that are distinct from the markup and script of the original page. Prototypes can streamline this workflow by making validation a seamless part of the input process.

Example: Input Validation for Forms

The following example demonstrates how input validation can be implemented as prototype functions on target elements. Figure 6–4 displays a screenshot of a sample form that gathers three pieces of user information: a person's name, their e-mail address, and the URL of their home page.

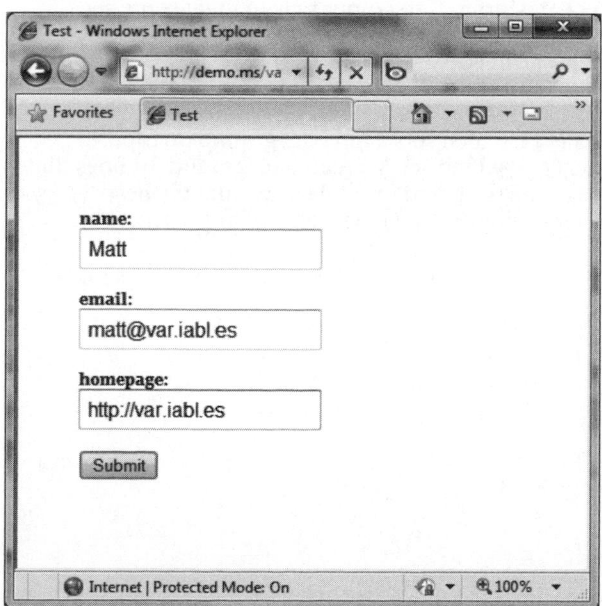

Figure 6–4. Basic form requesting a name, e-mail address, and home page URL

The form shown here is constructed using basic <span>, <input>, and <label> tags. Listing 6–16 shows the markup for this form. The <span> tags house the label headers for each form element, the <input> text boxes receive input for each requested area, and the <label> tags are used by the validation script to display form validation errors (explained later in this section).

***Listing 6–16.** Code for the Form Shown in Figure 6–4*

```
<form action="">
   <p>
      <span class="label">name:</span><br />
      <input type="text" id="name" name="name" class="text" /><br />
      <label for="name" id="nameLabel"></label>
   </p>
   <p>
      <span class="label">email:</span><br />
      <input type="text" id="email" name="email" class="text" /><br />
      <label for="email" id="emailLabel"></label>
   </p>
   <p>
      <span class="label">homepage:</span><br />
      <input type="text" id="homepage" name="homepage" class="text" /><br />
      <label for="homepage" id="homepageLabel"></label>
   </p>
   <input type="submit" id="submit" name="submit" value="Submit" />
</form>
```

Form validation is a flow of validation and feedback, repeated until an input set fits some criteria. A user begins the process by visiting a page with a form, typing in required information, and submitting it. The form then calls a number of functions that check the input. If the input fails to meet some set criteria, the form and its values are passed back to the user. Well-designed validation systems highlight errors in user input and offer suggestions on how a user can correct his or her entry.

To begin, some CSS is used to create visual "pass" and "fail" markers. Validation functions in this example use visual cues alongside textual instructions to inform a user of input validity. Listing 6–17 defines two classes for <input> elements: `validationFail`, which sets a red background on input elements that do not pass validation, and `validationPass`, which sets a green background for ones that do. The `validationFail` and `validationPass` classes are also created for <label> elements; these elements will be used to display errors related to their partner <input> elements (if any exist).

***Listing 6–17.** CSS Defining Visual Feedback for Validation Pass and Fail Cases*

```
<style>

   input.validationFail {
      background: #ffdddd;
   }

   input.validationPass {
      background: #ddffdd;
   }

   label.validationFail {
      font-family: "Georgia", serif;
      font-style: italic;
      margin-top: 15px;
```

```
        padding: 7px;
        border-left: 3px solid red;
        background: #ffdddd;
        display: block;
    }

    label.validationPass {
        display: none;
    }

</style>
```

Validity of elements in this example is determined through the use of *regular expressions.* JavaScript uses Perl-style regular expressions for text comparison. These expressions allow for text analysis without requiring complex use of the JavaScript `string` object or iterative evaluations of input text. Listing 6–18 defines two key parts of this validation system: first, a function that returns `true` or `false` based on whether a given regular expression matches an input string, and second, an associative array (object) containing validation expressions and their metadata.

Listing 6–18. *Script Defining Regular Expressions for Validation and a Utility Function for Matching*

```
<script type="text/javascript">

    //  A function to determine if a source contains one or more matches of
    //  a pattern based on PREGs
    function regexMatch(source, pattern) {

        //  Create a new regular expression from the pattern
        var regEx = new RegExp(pattern);

        //  Execute that pattern against the source (use the test method
        //  since all validation strings start with ^ and end with $
        var matches = regEx.test(source);

        //  Return false if there are no matches, true if one or more exist
        return !(matches === null);

    }

    //  Array that defines different validation classes, their error strings,
    //  and their associated regular expressions
    var regexValidators = {
        '.validateName'      : [
            'This item may only contain letters and spaces.' ,
            /^[\w ][^0-9_]+$/],
        '.validateNumeric'       : [
            'This item may only contain numbers.' ,
            /^[0-9]+$/, ],
        '.validateAlphanumeric' : [
            'This item may only contain numbers and letters.' ,
            /^[0-9a-zA-Z]+$/ ],
        '.validateEmail'         : [
            'This item must be a valid email address' ,
            /^[a-zA-Z0-9._%+-]+@[a-zA-Z0-9.-]+\.[a-zA-Z]{2,4}$/ ],
```

```
        '.validatePhoneNumber'  : [
            'This item must be a valid phone number.',
            /^(([0-9]{1})*[- .(]*([0-9]{3})*[- .)]*[0-9]{3}[- .]*[0-9]{4})+$/ ]
    };

</script>
```

The regexValidators object contains keys defining different validation types. Each key is linked to a value array whose 0th element is an error description for invalid input and whose 1st is a regular expression defining how all valid input should be formed.

Keys defined in the regexValidators object aren't arbitrary—they represent valid CSS class name selectors. The validate() function, discussed later, maps <input> elements declaring these selectors in their class attribute to these keys. Elements that use one or more of these selectors will be subject to the regular expression validation associated with each.

Listing 6–19 shows the form defined in Listing 6–16, this time with inputs opting into validation rules. The name text box, for instance, requires that input only be alphabetical characters; it selects this rule by using the validateName class. The email text box requires, through the validateEmail class, input matching the general format of an e-mail address.

Listing 6–19. *Original Form with Class Selectors Opting into Input Validation Constructs*

```
<form action="">
   <p>
      <span class="label">Name:</span><br />
      <input type="text" id="name" name="name" class="text validateName" /><br />
      <label for="name" id="nameLabel"></label>
   </p>
   <p>
      <span class="label">email:</span><br />
      <input type="text" id="email" name="email" class="text validateEmail" /><br />
      <label for="email" id="emailLabel"></label>
   </p>
   <p>
      <span class="label">homepage:</span><br />
      <input type="text" id="homepage" name="homepage" class="text" /><br />
      <label for="homepage" id="homepageLabel"></label>
   </p>
   <input type="submit" id="submit" name="submit" value="Submit" />
</form>
```

Listing 6–20 defines some utility functions used by the validation function. The first set of functions is built to manage the addition, removal, and existence checking of CSS classes on the Element interface. The addClass() function adds a CSS class to the Element interface if it isn't already present on that object. Conversely, the removeClass() function removes a CSS class from the Element interface if that selector is present on it. Both of these functions use the hasClass() function, used to return the existence (true) or nonexistence (false) of a class on the Element interface. All three of these functions are placed into the Element interface's prototype.

Listing 6–20. *Utility Functions for CSS Class Management and Label Access, Used As Object Prototypes*

```
<script type="text/javascript">

   //  If a class does not exist on an element, add it
   function addClass(cn) {
      if(!this.hasClass(cn)) {
         try {
            var attrClass = this.getAttribute("class");
            this.setAttribute("class", attrClass + ' ' + cn);
         } catch(ex) { return false; }
         return true;
      } else { return true; }
   };

   //  If a class exists on an element, remove it
   function removeClass(cn) {
      if(this.hasClass(cn)) {
         try {
            var attrClass = this.getAttribute("class");
            this.setAttribute("class", attrClass.replace('/\b' + cn+ '\b/',''));
         } catch(ex) { return false; }
         return true;
      } else { return true; }
   }

   //  Indicate whether or not an element specifies a certain class
   function hasClass(cn) {
      var attrClass = this.getAttribute("class");
      return regexMatch(attrClass, '/\b' + cn+ '\b/');
   }

   //  The getLabel function finds a label tag associated with
   //  the current element
   function getLabel() {

      //  Get all labels in the document
      var labels = document.getElementsByTagName("label");

      //  Loop through all document labels
      for(i = 0; i < labels.length; i++){

         //  If the associated "for" id is the id of this
         //  element, return it
         if(labels[i].htmlFor == this.id) { return labels[i]; }
      }

      //  If no label is found, return null (so we can differentiate
      //  between this and an HTMLInputElement interface)
      return null;

   }
```

```
   //  Assign the addClass, removeClass, and hasClass functions
   //  to the Element interface
   Element.prototype.addClass = addClass;
   Element.prototype.removeClass = removeClass;
   Element.prototype.hasClass = hasClass;

   //  Assign the getLabel function to the HTMLInputElement interface
   HTMLInputElement.prototype.getLabel = getLabel;

</script>
```

The last function, getLabel(), uses the for attribute of <label> tags to associate a label object with an <input> tag. This function is bound to HTMLInputElement so that when it is called from an instance of an <input> element, it can return an associated instance of the HTMLLabelElement interface (if one exists).

The heart of this example lies in the validate() function; shown in Listing 6–21, it iterates through every input that specifies a validation selector in its class attribute.

Listing 6–21. *The validate() Function, Used to Validate Input Boxes Against a Set of Rules*

```
<script type="text/javascript">

   function validate() {

      //  Create a variable to mark validation progress
      var isOk = true;

      //  Loop through each validation type
      for (key in regexValidators) {

         //  Get the error message and regex for this validation type
         var errorMessage   = regexValidators[key][0];
         var regexValidator = regexValidators[key][1];

         //  Grab all elements opting into this validation type
         var inputs = document.querySelectorAll(key);

         //  Loop through each element and check if its value passes
         //  validation. If it doesn't, ensure overall validation progress
         //  fails and this element's label indicates failure type
         for (i = 0; i < inputs.length; i++) {
            if (!regexMatch(inputs[i].value, regexValidator)) {
               isOk = false;
               try {
                  associatedLabel = inputs[i].getLabel();
                  if(associatedLabel != null) {
                     inputs[i].removeClass("validationPass");
                     inputs[i].addClass("validationFail");
                     associatedLabel.innerText = errorMessage;
                     associatedLabel.removeClass("validationPass");
                     associatedLabel.addClass("validationFail");
               } } catch(ex) { }
            }
            else {
               try {
```

```
                associatedLabel = inputs[i].getLabel();
                if(associatedLabel != null) {
                   inputs[i].removeClass("validationFail");
                   inputs[i].addClass("validationPass");
                   associatedLabel.innerText = "";
                   associatedLabel.removeClass("validationFail");
                   associatedLabel.addClass("validationPass");
             } } catch(ex) { }
          }
       }

    }

    //  Return the overall validation status
    return isOk;

  }

  //  Customize the DOM by accessing HTMLDocument's
  //  prototype and extend its functionality
  //  to include the validate() method.
  HTMLDocument.prototype.validate = validate;

</script>
```

The function begins by looping through each of the validation selectors. For each selector, `validate()` queries the document object for all child elements using the current selector through `document.querySelectorAll()`. A secondary loop begins, iterating over the results of that function call; text content of matching elements are compared to the regular expression associated with the current validation selector. If the validation pattern is matched, the form element and its associated label denote success. If a match is not found, a CSS class for failure is applied to the element, and an error notification is written to the element's label.

The `validate()` function is applied to the `HTMLDocument` object, allowing it to be accessed anywhere in the document context through `document.validate()`.

The final step in this example consists of linking the validation prototypes with the target form. Listing 6–22 shows two parts to this: the `document.validate()` function is called by a form submission handler, `submitForm()`, which is set as the target form's action.

Listing 6–22. *Function Handling Form Submission and Updated Form Action Referring to It*

```
<script type="text/javascript">

  //  Function that calls validation on the document object
  function submitForm() {

    //  Validate forms in the document
    document.validate();

  }

</script>  <!-- ... -->

<form action="javascript:submitForm()">
  <p>
```

```
<span class="label">Name:</span><br />
<input type="text" id="name" name="name" class="text validateName" /><br />
```

Validation methods on this form are now defined, with validation occurring every time a user submits the form. Figure 6–5 shows a running example of the validation engine.

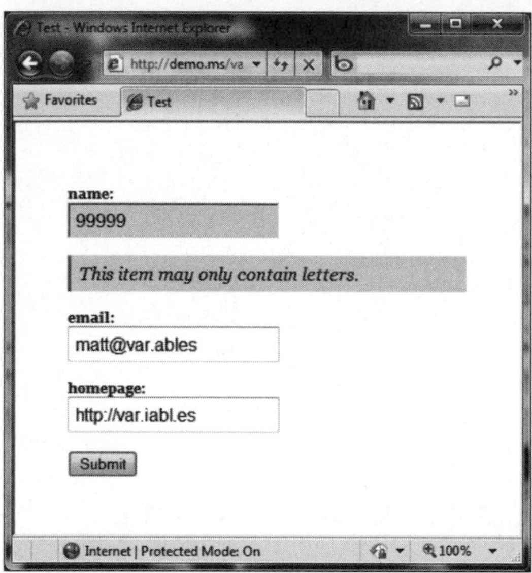

***Figure 6–5.** Updated form showing prototype-based script validation techniques*

In this figure, numbers were input into the name field. Since the name field opted into accepting alphabetical characters only (*A* through *Z*, case insensitive), the submission of numbers triggers an error. The validation function changes the color of the offending input box and error label. The text of the error label referencing the name input box is set to the error associated with the `validateName` error text. The form displays without error messages once all values submitted by a user meet the validation criteria.

Summary

The DOM provides a powerful mechanism for making broad changes to your web site with minimal effort and changes to your existing design. As older versions of IE fade away, DOM scripting will become both a realistic and simple way to support interoperable functionality without sacrificing downlevel compatibility.

I began this chapter with a primer on the relevant portions of JavaScript programming and properties as they apply to DOM scripting. After that, you saw a number of examples of how DOM scripting can be used to solve real-world web programming challenges. I encourage you to use this chapter as a springboard for investigating and using these powerful features in your web applications.

CHAPTER 7

■ ■ ■

Debugging and Inspecting Pages with Fiddler

Developers looking to make solid, performant applications must design, develop, and test not only applications but the interactions between applications, the messages sent between a server and clients, and how each uses that information. Enter Fiddler.

Fiddler is a *web-debugging proxy*, an application that lets you monitor and tamper with HTTP and HTTPS traffic being sent between a client computer and a server.

I begin this chapter by describing how to install Fiddler, run it for the first time, and perform basic session inspection. Following that, we'll walk through the process of setting filters and tampering with request/response sequences. Methods for using Fiddler in performance tuning follow, and the chapter closes with basic information on setting Fiddler up for HTTPS debugging and using the lightweight capture tool FiddlerCap.

Getting Started with Fiddler

Fiddler provides developers with a powerful way to tap into HTTP and HTTPS communication between browsers and web sites, clients, and servers.

Fiddler, at its heart, is a stand-alone proxy that automatically registers itself as the system proxy using the WinINET library. WinINET (discussed in Chapter 1) is used by IE, Office, and countless other Microsoft-owned and third-party applications for communication over standard Internet protocols. Fiddler intercepts all requests sent and responses received by this system so they may be both monitored and tampered with. Because most other browsers (except Firefox) adopt WinINET's system proxy setting by default, they too will work with Fiddler without additional configuration.

Installing and Running Fiddler

Fiddler can be downloaded as a setup file from `www.fiddler2.com`. The installation process is straightforward and will install the Fiddler application, Start menu items, and button and toolbar extensions inside of IE (see Figure 7–1).

Figure 7–1. The Fiddler Start menu icon, IE toolbar button, and IE Tools menu item

Firefox does not adopt the WinINET proxy settings by default, so the setup application will also install the FiddlerHook plug-in for Firefox. This plug-in will detect when Fiddler is capturing and configure Firefox's proxy settings to point to the proxy (see Figure 7–2).

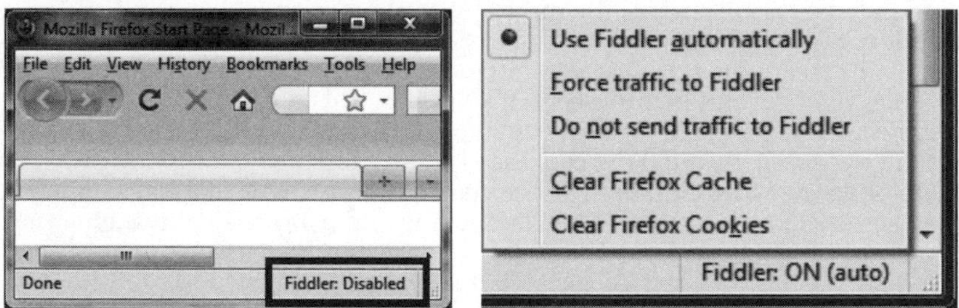

Figure 7–2. The FiddlerHook plug-in's status bar and context menu for Firefox

Running Fiddler from any of these locations simply takes a click of the mouse. Once loaded (see Figure 7–3), Fiddler will begin monitoring and intercepting HTTP traffic.

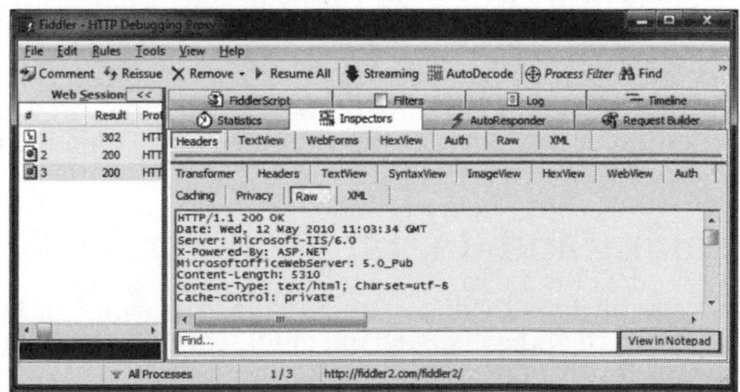

Figure 7–3. The Fiddler splash screen and main window

Navigating the Fiddler User Interface

Fiddler provides an extensive base of features in a very compact user interface. Figure 7–4 shows an example of Fiddler being used to debug a large web site; this UI can be daunting for the first-time user.

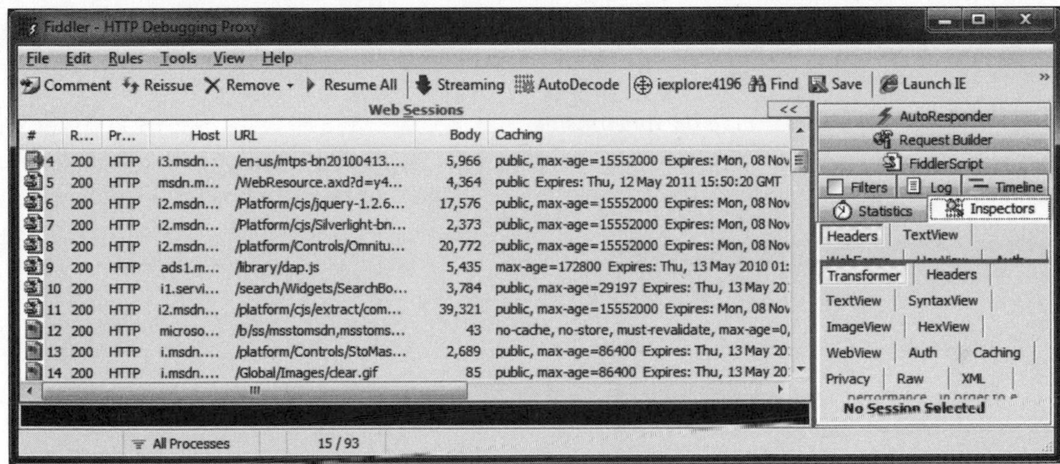

Figure 7–4. *The Fiddler application window in full use*

The application layout is fairly simple. At the top are menus and toolbars; they surface the most commonly used application commands.

The list taking up most of the window and positioned along the left is the session list; this stores *sessions*, or *request-response sequences* seen by Fiddler. The tabs directly to the right of the session list are the tools; these are used to analyze and modify the data summarized in the session list.

The black box below the session list is the QuickExec box. This box is used to execute simple commands; this chapter discusses it in the context of breakpoints later on. The status bar, at the bottom of the window, provides up-to-date information on Fiddler, including the capture and filtering status (clicking these items also toggles their state).

Scripting Fiddler with Rules

Fiddler exposes much of its core functionality to .NET-based scripts importing the Fiddler namespace. The aptly named FiddlerScript provides a way for developers to extend the functionality of Fiddler using JScript .NET. Developers can create rules that tell Fiddler what to do during session events. For example, script can be notified before requests are sent or when responses are received in order to perform tasks related to each event.

The source for Fiddler's rules can be accessed and modified by selecting the Customize Rules item in the Rules menu. Figure 7–5 shows this menu.

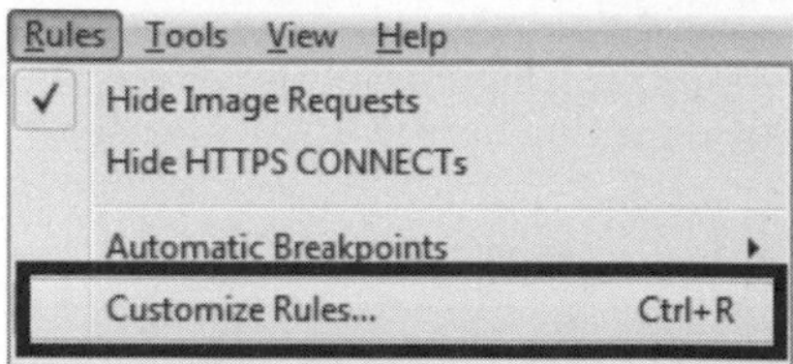

Figure 7–5. The Customize Rules item in the Rules menu

The Customize Rules item will launch Fiddler's rule file, `CustomRules.js`. On machines with only Fiddler installed, this will open `CustomRules.js` in a user's default text or JavaScript editor (Figure 7–6).

```
import System;
import System.Windows.Forms;
import Fiddler;

// GLOBALIZATION NOTE:
// Be sure to save this file with UTF-8 Encoding if using any non-AS
// in strings, etc.
//
// JScript Reference
// http://www.fiddler2.com/redir/?id=msdnjsnet
//
// FiddlerScript Reference
// http://www.fiddler2.com/redir/?id=fiddlerscriptcookbook
//
// FiddlerScript Editor:
// http://www.fiddler2.com/redir/?id=fiddlerscripteditor

class Handlers
{
        // The following snippet demonstrates a custom-bound column
        // See http://www.fiddler2.com/fiddler/help/configurecolumns
        //public static BindUIColumn("Method", 60)
        //function FillMethodColumn(oS: Session){
        //      if ((oS.oRequest != null) && (oS.oRequest.headers !=
        //      return oS.oRequest.headers.HTTPMethod; else return S
```

Figure 7–6. The Customize Rules item in the Rules menu

Developers looking for a richer environment for developing with FiddlerScript may download the Fiddler ScriptEditor (Figures 7–7 and 7–8), which runs as a stand-alone application or a tab inside Fiddler itself. This optional extension for Fiddler adds a small development environment that can be used to streamline the development of rules. It provides syntax highlighting as well as useful information on the Fiddler namespaces exposed classes and methods.

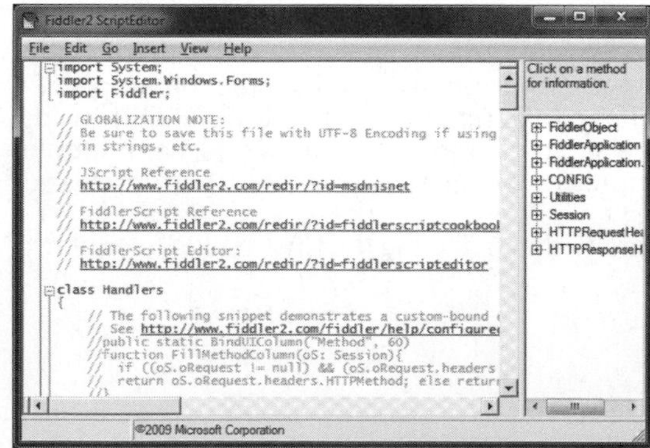

Figure 7–7. The Fiddler ScriptEditor

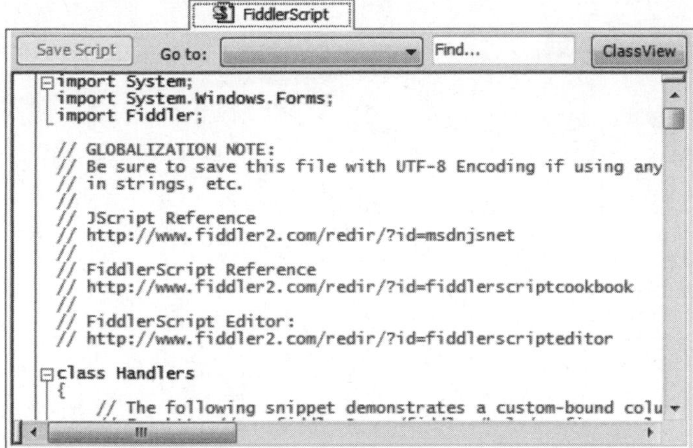

Figure 7–8. A lightweight FiddlerScript editor added to Fiddler's tabs

Viewing and Inspecting Sessions

By default, Fiddler does a version check on startup; since the version check uses HTTP, you can inspect the version using Fiddler itself. Similarly, when you open an IE window, you will find that its traffic appears in Fiddler's Web Sessions list (Figure 7–9).

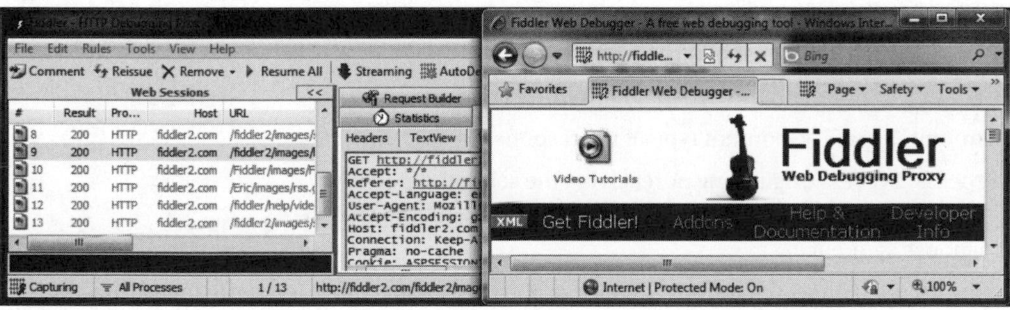

Figure 7–9. Fiddler in action viewing request-response sequences from www.fiddler2.com

The following sections introduce the session list, inspectors, and other information necessary to perform efficient and quality analysis of session data using Fiddler.

Deciphering the Session List

Every transaction seen by Fiddler is added as a new session in the session list. Each entry contains detailed metadata pertaining to the nature, content, and result of the session. Figure 7–10 shows an example of a session list built during navigation to `www.fiddler2.com`.

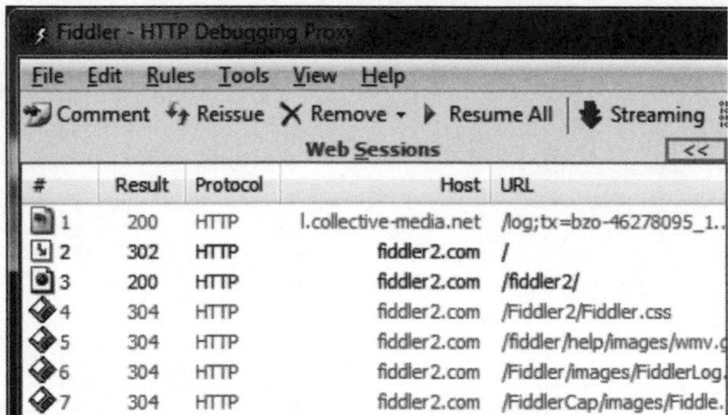

Figure 7–10. *The session list*

Metadata associated with captured request-response sequences is shown in the session list alongside each session entry. The columns in this list are

- #: Incremental ID of the session entry, starting from 1 (used by Fiddler; not part of the request-response sequence)
- **Result**: The HTTP response code received
- **Protocol**: The protocol used to transfer session data
- **Host**: The target host specified in the request header
- **URL**: The URL target of the request
- **Body**: The size (in bytes) of the response body
- **Caching**: Cache settings used in determining the response
- **Content-Type**: The content type of the response
- **Process**: Process originating or receiving the session data
- **Comment**: User-specified comment (used by Fiddler; not part of the request-response sequence)

The details provided here are far from exhaustive and are not meant to answer detailed questions about each transaction. Instead, developers can use this data as a way to triage potential sessions to investigate further using the Inspectors tab.

Inspecting the Request-Response Sequence

Fiddler captures request and response data for each item in the session list. Users may view and inspect this data using the Inspectors tab by selecting this tab and selecting a session from the session list. Figure 7–11 shows this tab in action.

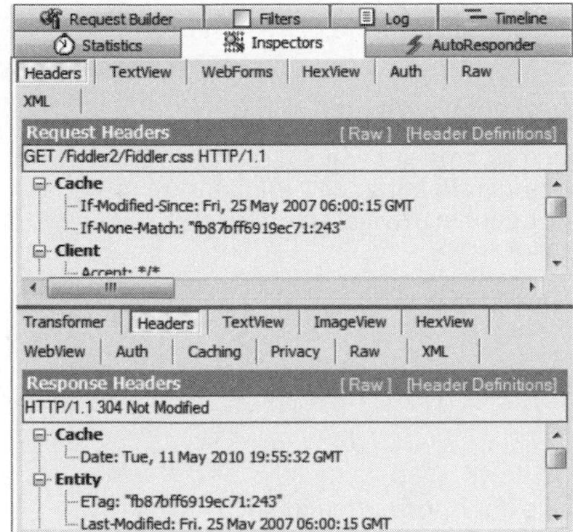

Figure 7–11. Inspectors tab showing the Headers inspector

The Inspectors tab is separated into two regions: Request Headers (top) and Response Headers (bottom). Each region represents the headers gathered during the request sequence sent to the server and those gathered during the response sequence returned from it, respectively. Figure 7–12 displays screenshots of some select inspectors.

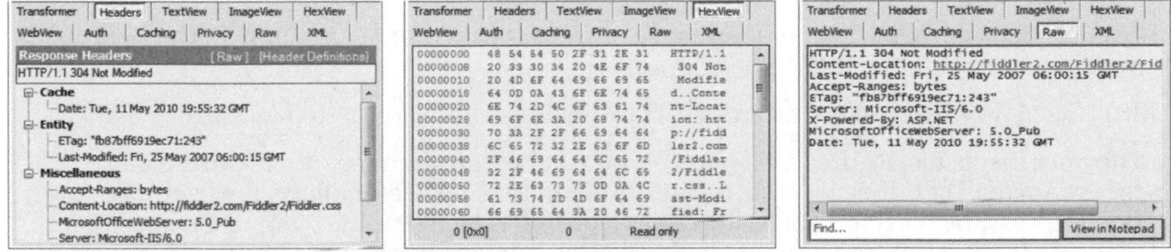

Figure 7–12. The Headers, HexView, and Raw inspectors

Both the request and response headers contain a number of inspectors. These inspectors provide different views or analysis of the data gathered in each request or response. For instance, if a certain request sequence included a query string, the WebForms inspector would provide the ideal view of this query string using a key-value pair layout. If a response turned out to be an image, a developer could use the ImageView inspector to view the image that was sent via the response body (instead of viewing a somewhat useless hexadecimal representation).

The following are the default request inspectors:

- **Headers**: Displays a hierarchal tree view of the HTTP request headers from a client
- **TextView**: Displays the request body as plain text
- **WebForms**: Displays the key-value pairs contained in a request's query string
- **HexView**: Displays the request in hexadecimal format

- **Auth**: Displays information from any authentication request headers
- **Raw**: Displays the request headers and body as raw text (as it would be seen sent over the wire)
- **XML**: Displays a hierarchical tree view of any request body formatted as XML

The Response Headers region offers a similar set of inspectors, some of which are the same as those just described. There are, however, a number of unique inspectors reflecting the broad nature of responses and settings that a server may return (e.g., caching or cookie privacy statements).

The following inspectors are available for the response headers:

- **Transformer**: Displays the HTTP-level encoding of response data and allows for the removal (or addition) of compression or chunking
- **Headers**: Displays a hierarchical tree view of the HTTP response headers from a server
- **TextView**: Displays the response body as plain text
- **ImageView**: Displays the response body as an image if it is formatted as such
- **HexView**: Displays the response in hexadecimal format
- **WebView**: Displays the response body as a web page loaded into a Web Browser object
- **Auth**: Displays information from any authentication response headers
- **Caching**: Displays caching information used by the server in its response
- **Privacy**: Displays cookie and P3P privacy information related to the response
- **Raw**: Displays the headers and body as raw text (as it would be seen sent over the wire)
- **XML**: Displays a hierarchical tree view of any response body formatted as XML

The Transformer inspector (Figure 7–13) plays a more active role than the others during the debugging process. Instead of simply viewing the information, this inspector allows the user to compress or decompress the HTTP response for easier viewing. For instance, a plain text response compressed using GZIP for faster transmission will need the Transformer to decompress it for viewing.

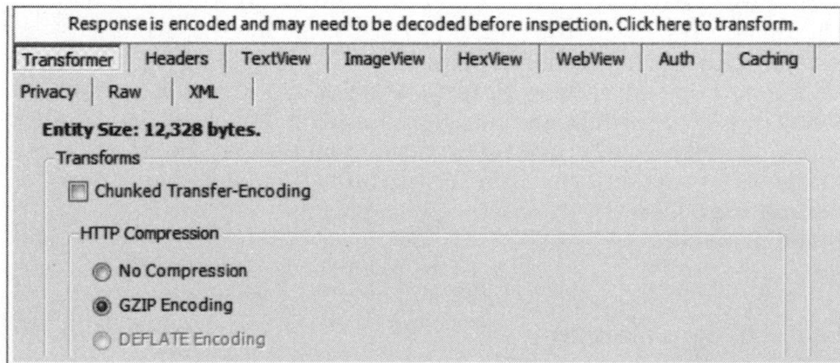

***Figure 7–13.** The Transformer inspector, part of the Inspectors tab's Response Headers section*

This inspector is useful for more than simply trying to read encoded data; developers can use it to gauge the impact such compression may have on the overall performance of a web application.

Comparing Sessions

Some HTTP debugging scenarios may call for the comparison of two or more sessions with each other. Difference comparisons can help to uncover a number of issues, from potential vulnerabilities to server-caching problems.

Fiddler offers a simple way to compare sessions through the session list's context menu. You can compare two sessions by selecting both, right-clicking the selection, and clicking the Compare menu item (see Figure 7–14).

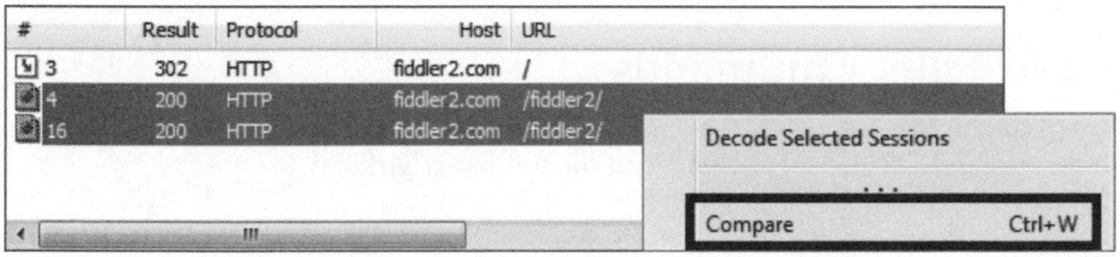

***Figure 7–14.** The Compare context menu option, allowing for comparison using WinDiff*

Fiddler will attempt to compare the two sessions by outputting them as text files to a temporary directory and calling the WinDiff comparison tool on them. If WinDiff is installed, these files will open in a comparison views and unique elements will be highlighted, as in Figure 7–15. Users who do not have WinDiff installed can find it by searching for the term at the Microsoft Download Center.

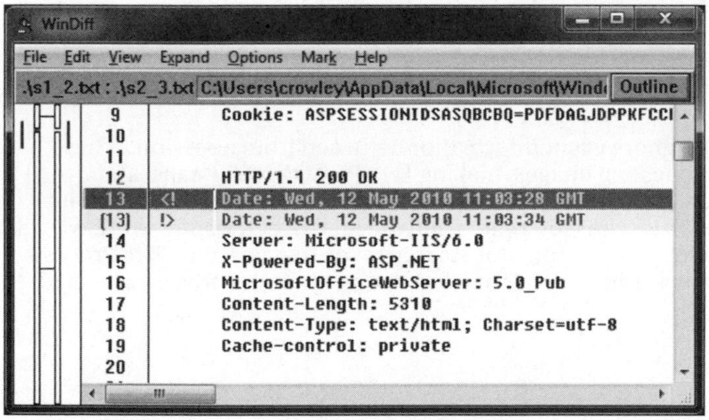

***Figure 7–15.** Two requests made to www.fiddler2.com being compared using WinDiff*

Data collected through WinDiff can be used to point out headers, variables, or other data that differs between two sessions' request-response sequences.

Filtering Sessions

Narrowing down the number of sessions displayed in the session list can expedite the debugging process. Developers targeting a specific site or scenario will find that the session list can become rather busy since Fiddler will display all communications made through WinINET by all running processes. Multiple browser windows and Ajax-based web pages can contribute to the noise.

Fiddler offers a number of ways to filter the information displayed in the session list. A handful of out-of-the-box commands can help to weed out messages that may not pertain to an issue being researched. The Filters tab offers even more control over this, giving developers a chance to include or exclude sessions based on commonly targeted data points. Developers looking to completely customize filtering can do so through script-based rules. The following sections highlight each of these methods in detail.

Using the Top-Level Filter Commands

The Rules menu and the Fiddler toolbar provide a handful of basic commands for session filtering. Figure 7–16 shows those entries in the Rules menu (left) and the toolbar (right).

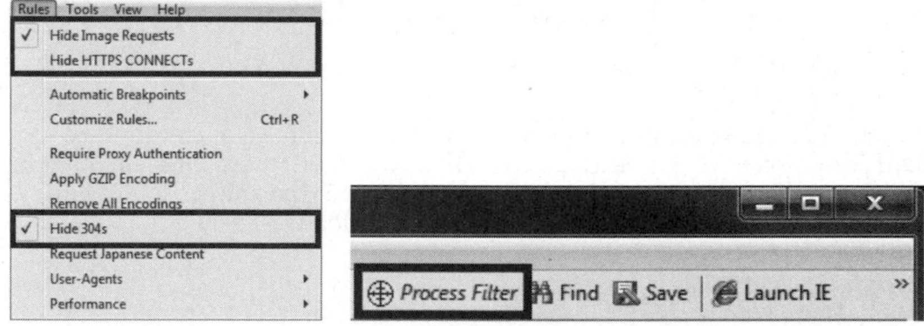

Figure 7–16. *Basic filtering commands in the Fiddler Rules menu and toolbar*

Developers can use the Rules menu to ignore event information returned from a session. These include events raised while a browser is requesting images, making HTTPS CONNECT calls, and receiving 304 (Not-Modified) response headers (common when caching is in use). The Fiddler toolbar surfaces one command, the *Process Filter.* This is an icon that, when dragged over a visible window, will show only those sessions originating from or going to the process that owns that window. The Process Filter icon is quite useful when dealing with a large number of windows or when the process associated with a specific window is unknown.

Using the Filters Tab

The Filters tab (Figure 7–17) surfaces commonly used filtering scenarios for HTTP debugging. It provides developers with a quick way to reduce the number of displayed sessions, trigger actions during important events during a session, or modify the request and response headers for all sessions. Filter settings can be modified when the Use Filters check box, in the top-left corner of the tab, is checked.

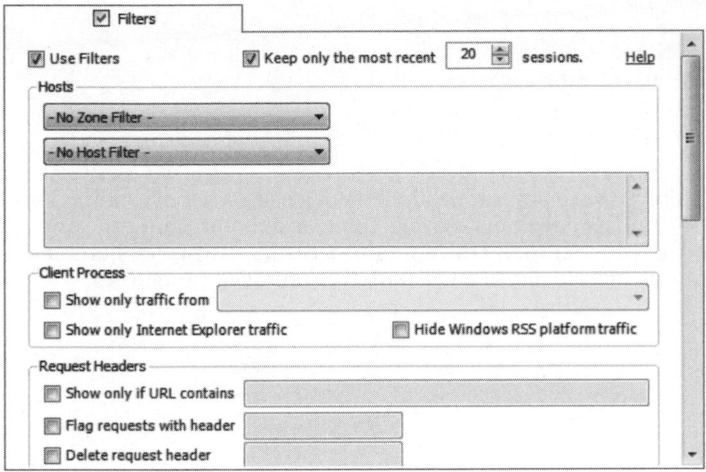

Figure 7–17. *The Filters tab*

The filters provided here may not provide the fine granularity required by specific debugging or tampering scenarios. Custom filters can be created using FiddlerScript, a method discussed in later sections.

The first filter provided in this tab restricts the number of recent sessions in the Session List. Developers looking to limit the number of items shown there can specify that amount in the selection box at the top of the Filters tab.

The Hosts group restricts the display of sessions based on the name of the host requested and/or the IE zone that the host is a member of. Developers can restrict hosts to either the Internet or intranet zone using the topmost drop-down. Fiddler can hide or exclusively show sessions containing a set of one or more hosts, whose list can be provided in a text box (Figure 7–18).

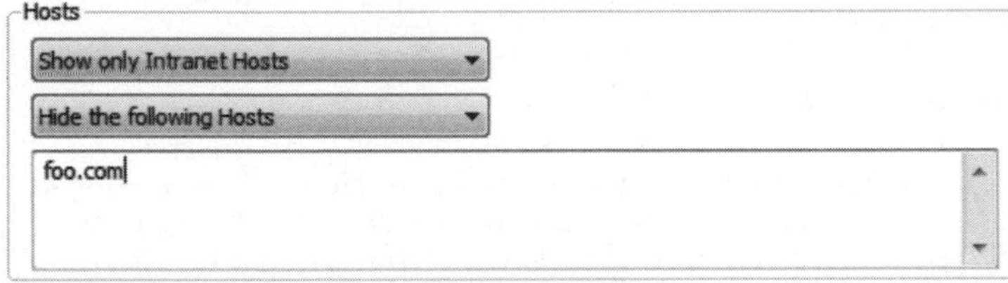

Figure 7–18. *The Hosts group on the Filters tab*

Sessions can be filtered based on the process they originate from. The Client Process group (Figure 7–19) provides three basic settings to do so. The first permits the developer to limit sessions that originate from one currently running process; the current processes and their PIDs (process identifiers) are shown in a drop-down list. The second option allows a user to show only those sessions that originate from an IE process. Last, developers may hide all sessions that originate from the Windows RSS Platform; this can reduce chatter from Windows-based and third-party RSS clients, as well as IE's Web Slice update service.

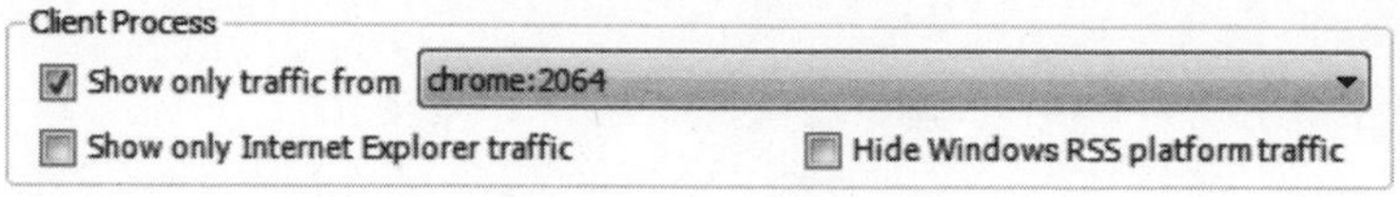

Client Process
Show only traffic from chrome:2064
Show only Internet Explorer traffic
Hide Windows RSS platform traffic

Figure 7–19. The Client Process group on the Filters tab

The Request Headers pane filters sessions whose request headers meet a certain set of criteria. The basic filtering options, shown in Figure 7–20, allow developers to flag, filter, and modify requests. The first option shows or hides sessions based on whether their URL contains a certain string. Sessions can be flagged if their header contains a certain string. Headers can be added or removed from every request.

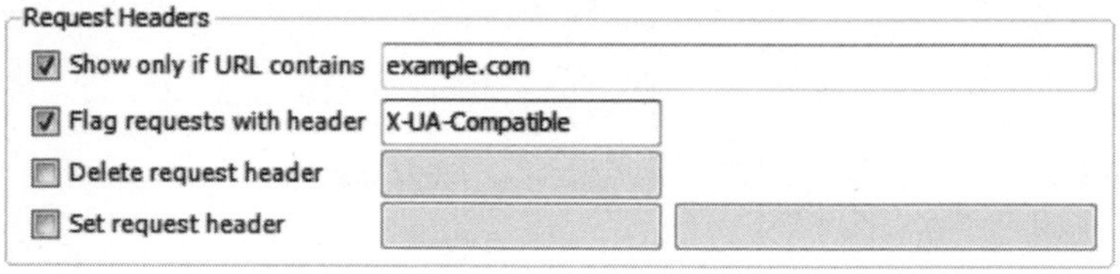

Request Headers
Show only if URL contains example.com
Flag requests with header X-UA-Compatible
Delete request header
Set request header

Figure 7–20. The Request Headers group on the Filters tab

The Breakpoints group (see Figure 7–21) enables developers to trigger automatic breakpoints on requests or responses meeting common criteria. Like in other debuggers, breakpoints "pause" the flow of execution and allow the user to modify data before execution proceeds. The simple controls in this pane allow you to break whenever an HTTP POST request occurs, an HTTP GET containing a query string is seen, or a response matches a certain Content-Type.

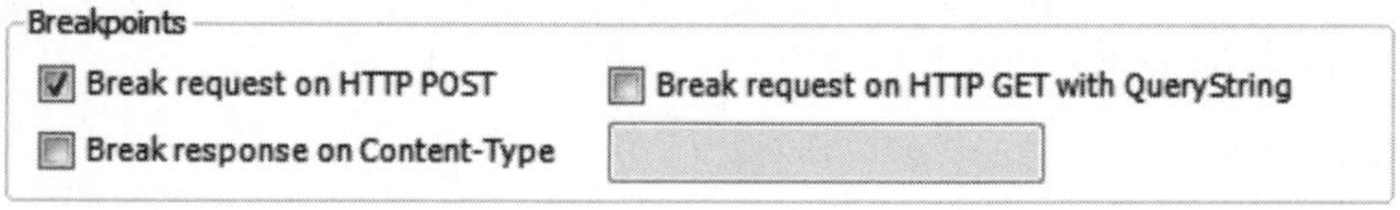

Breakpoints
Break request on HTTP POST
Break request on HTTP GET with QueryString
Break response on Content-Type

Figure 7–21. The Breakpoints group on the Filters tab

The Response Status Code pane (Figure 7–22) permits developers to hide sessions whose response header matches a specific HTTP response code or range of codes. The options available through the Filters tab represent the more commonly used filtered types, such as success codes, authentication request headers, redirections, and not-modified notifications. These are not the only status codes that can be used to filter sessions; later sections discuss how FiddlerScript can be used to create custom rules and filters.

Response Status Code
Hide success (200,204,206)
Hide Authentication demands (401)
Hide redirects (300,301,302,303,307)
Hide Not Modified (304)

Figure 7–22. The Response Status Code group on the Filters tab

Figure 7–23 demonstrates the Response Type and Size filters. These settings instruct Fiddler to ignore sessions whose response data is either of a specific type or size. Developers can select from a number of preset configurations from a drop-down list; these presets include scenarios where all image sessions are ignored or only sessions containing HTML payloads are shown. Sessions can be ignored by response size, limiting them by their lower or upper bounds. Requests for scripts, images, Flash animations, and CSS scripts can also be blocked altogether through this pane.

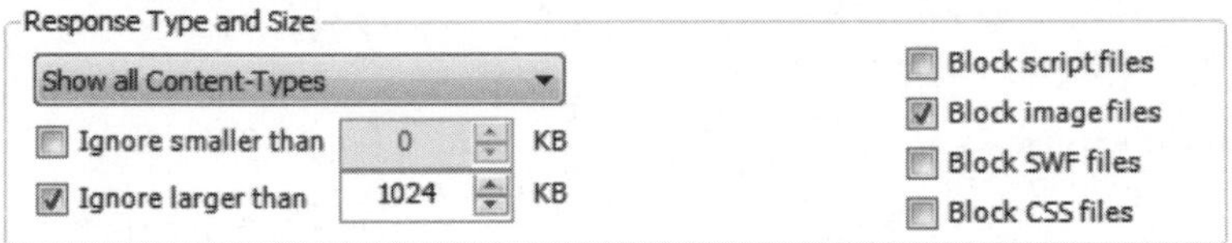

Figure 7–23. *The Response Type and Size group on the Filters tab*

The Response Headers group, shown in Figure 7–24, enables sessions to be flagged based on contents found in the response headers of a session. Sessions can be flagged based on whether they contain cookies or whether they contain a certain string. This pane can be used to remove or append an additional response header.

Figure 7–24. *The Response Headers group on the Filters tab*

The entries contained on the Filters tab are by no means the limit to which sessions can be filtered. Developers who wish to customize or extend filtering functionality can do so by writing custom rules in FiddlerScript.

Debugging and Manipulating Sessions

Fiddler provides powerful mechanisms for manipulating a session's request-response sequence. Developers can use a number of tools to create new requests, add and delete headers, and even pause transactions to append changes as they occur. Fiddler provides session manipulation by employing the same techniques it uses for session monitoring, by acting as a proxy for all inbound and outbound web traffic.

Using the Request Builder

The Request Builder allows developers to build HTTP requests either from scratch or by modifying previously captured requests. These requests can then be executed and sent directly from Fiddler without using a browser. Figure 7–25 shows the Request Builder tab used to do this.

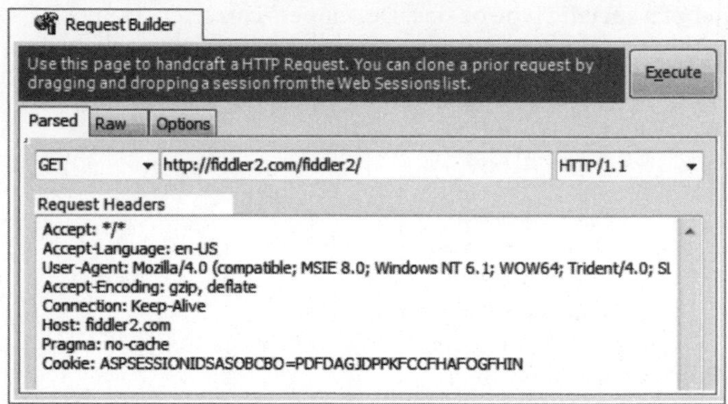

Figure 7–25. *Creating an HTTP request using the Request Builder*

A new request can be created simply by typing a request string into the text box. Developers hardly ever write requests from scratch, however. Instead, Fiddler makes it easy to reuse and, if necessary, modify existing requests. Items in the session list can be dragged into this text box for reuse; the request header data associated with the selected session is placed into the text box as a string. The copied request can be modified before execution. When everything is ready, the Execute button sends the text box contents onto the wire as a new request.

Using the Filters Tab to Modify Session Data

As noted in a prior section, the Filters tab offers a few simple options that allow developers to globally delete or set headers on sessions. This means that, when these filters are set, headers are added or removed during all request-response sequences.

Figure 7–26 shows the Request Headers and Response Headers filter groups printed earlier in this chapter. Headers can be set or deleted globally using the respective settings in each filter group.

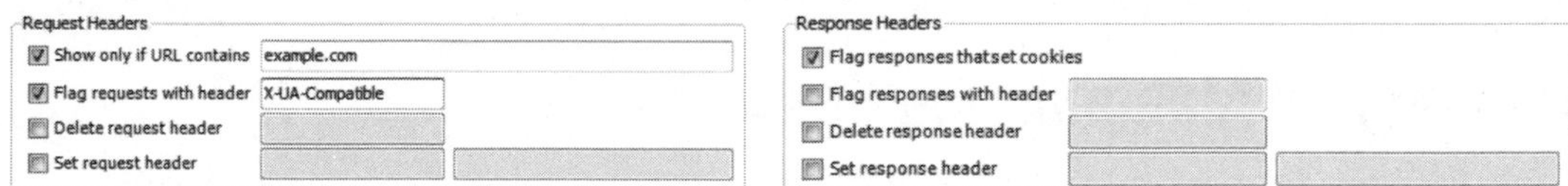

Figure 7–26. *Request and Response groups on the Filters tab*

Setting and Using Breakpoints

Developers can use breakpoints as a way to manipulate a live session. Similar to traditional breakpoints, the term used here means a signal that forces Fiddler to pause a transaction, awaiting human input before continuing. Breakpoints can be set via the Rules menu using automatic breakpoints, using settings on the Filters tab, through the QuickExec box, or through customized rules written in FiddlerScript.

The Filters tab allows for a handful of broadly scoped breakpoints to be set during a capture. Figure 7–27 shows these options, including breaking on all HTTP POST requests, breaking on HTTP GET requests containing a query string, and breaking on a response whose content type matches a specified string.

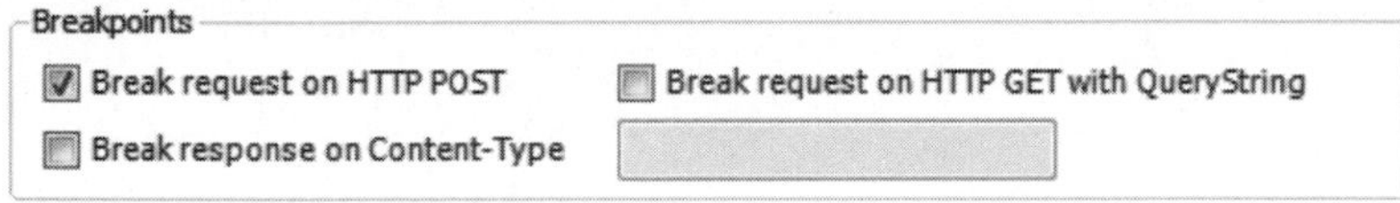

Figure 7–27. *The Breakpoints group on the Filters tab*

A few automatic breakpoint configurations are built into the Automatic Breakpoint submenu under Rules. Only one may be used at a time. Fiddler can be set to break before requests or after responses, or to never automatically break. This menu, shown in Figure 7–28, also provides a way to ignore images when automatically breaking.

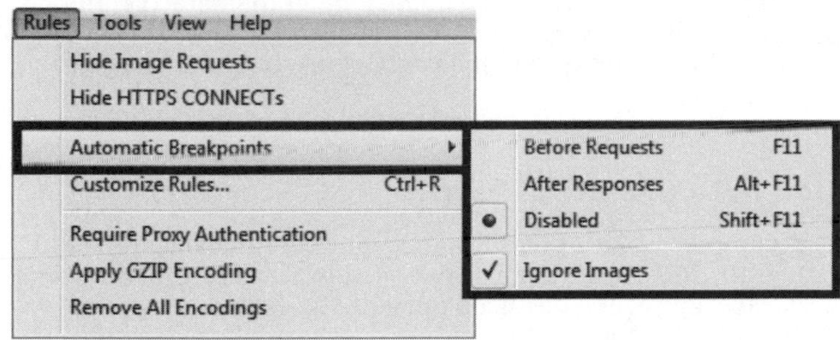

Figure 7–28. *Automatic Breakpoints submenu of the Rules menu*

The QuickExec box can also be used to get or clear more specific breakpoints. The following QuickExec commands and parameters are available:

- `bpu [str]`: Break whenever a request URI is encountered containing a certain string. If no string is provided, running this command clears the breakpoint.
- `bpafter [str]`: Similarly to `bpu`, this command will break responses whose request URI contains a certain string. If no string is provided, running this command clears the breakpoint.
- `bps [integer]`: Break whenever a status code matches a certain integer. If no integer is provided, running this command clears the breakpoint.
- `bpm [HTTP_METHOD]`: Break whenever a specified HTTP method is used (e.g., POST, GET). If no string is provided, running this command clears the breakpoint.

Analyzing Site Performance

Fiddler provides a number of powerful tools for assessing a page's ability to perform under different stresses, situations, and user profiles. The following sections discuss methods for improving the performance of both server- and client-side systems via Fiddler's detailed and thorough analysis tools.

As the sections progress, it should be noted that the use of Fiddler's performance tools depends on true HTTP transfers. Caching can be a huge performance win for web applications, but it is important to understand that, as a proxy, Fiddler only sees requests that are sent over the network. Before using Fiddler to capture performance data, developers should clear both the WinINET cache and cookie stores using the Tools menu (Figure 7–29).

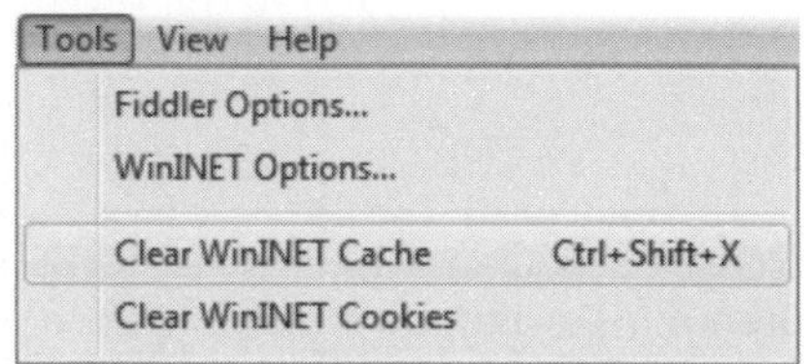

Figure 7–29. Tools menu items to clear WinINET cache and cookies

Developers should also enable *streaming mode* using the button in the Fiddler toolbar to get the most accurate results. By default, Fiddler operates in *buffering mode*, which collects the entire HTTP response before returning it to the client; this enables breakpoint-style debugging, but interferes with progressive rendering of pages.

Quantifying Request Items, Types, and Times

The Statistics and Timeline tabs provide developers with raw performance numbers and statistics (and some useful graphs to boot). Numbers and estimates shown in these two sections act as a good indicator of how a site will perform in the real world, especially when balanced out with the estimated speeds presented on the Statistics tab.

The Microsoft Developer Network (MSDN) site (`http://msdn.microsoft.com`) was loaded and its sequences captured by Fiddler to demonstrate how Fiddler quantifies performance. This section is intended to cover the data emitted by Fiddler, not the analysis of that data. Figure 7–30 really sets the mood here.

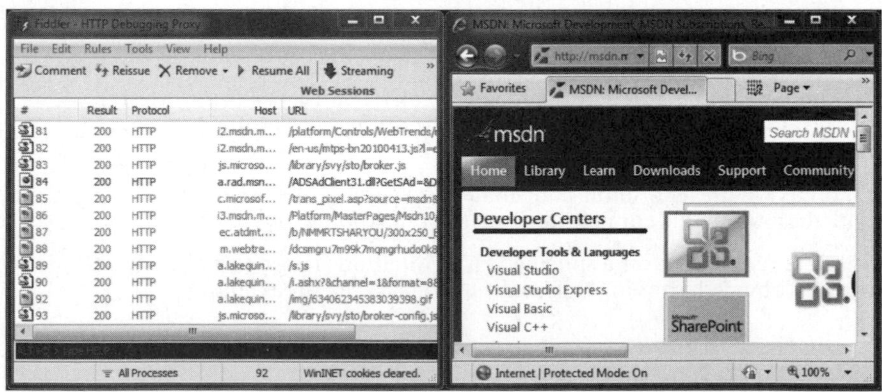

Figure 7–30. Fiddler capturing traffic from IE loading http://msdn.microsoft.com

You can display the statistics of the overall transaction by selecting all sessions in the session list and then opening the Statistics tab. Figure 7–31 shows the run results from the MSDN web page: 92 files received, 93KB sent, 456KB received, and an elapsed time of about 13 seconds.

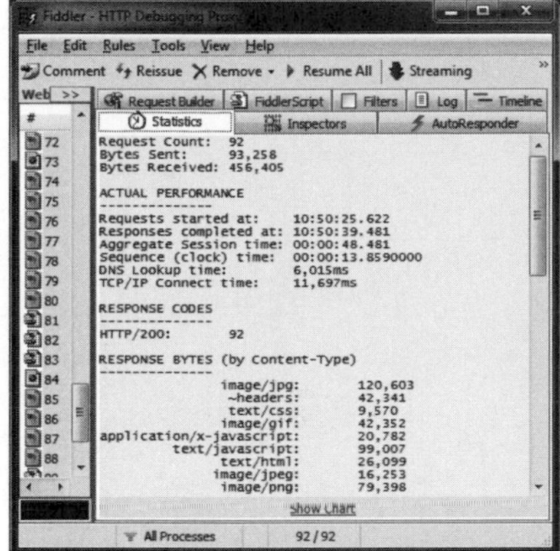

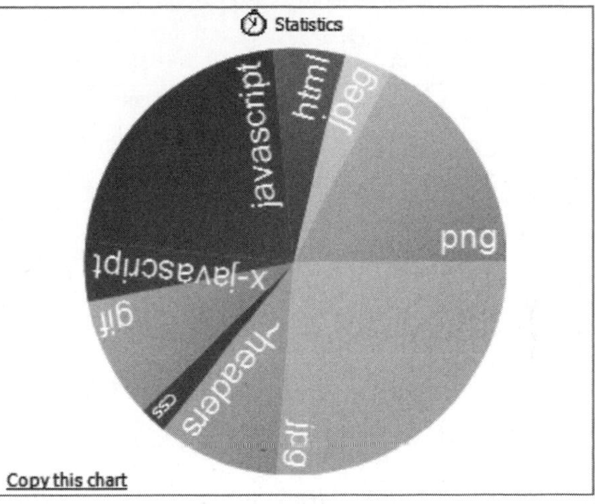

Figure 7–31. Fiddler showing basic request/response stats and content chart for http://msdn.microsoft.com

Figure 7–31 also shows the content breakdown, or what content types made up what percentage of the bytes transferred. In this case, it is clear that JavaScript is the largest content type transferred, followed by JPG, PNG, and GIF image types.

The Statistics tab provides rough estimates about what this same scenario would look like in different locales and at different bandwidths. Figure 7–32 shows a screenshot of Western US and Asia round trip and elapsed time estimates, the maximum estimate capping out at 132 seconds (over 2 minutes!)

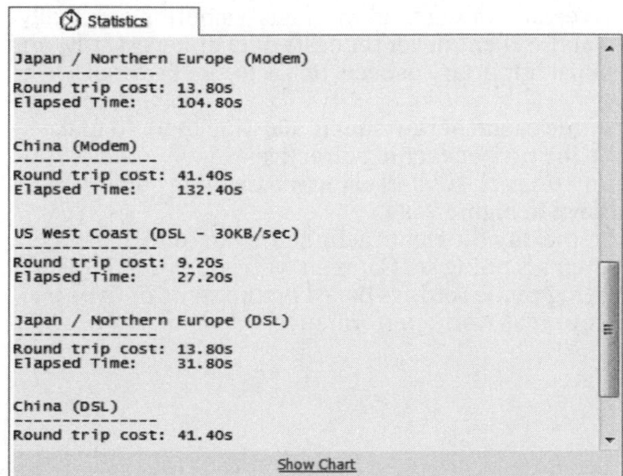

Figure 7–32. Estimated round trip and elapsed time costs for http://msdn.microsoft.com (original request made from a tethered phone in Queen Anne, Seattle, Washington)

Last but definitely not least is a high-level view of what objects were transferred when and for how long. The Transfer Timeline, found on the Timeline tab, provides a timeline chart that shows the start, end, and duration of requests and responses. This timeline helps developers get a feel for how their server is working, how clients are requesting items, and what the order of items through the pipe is (see Figure 7–33).

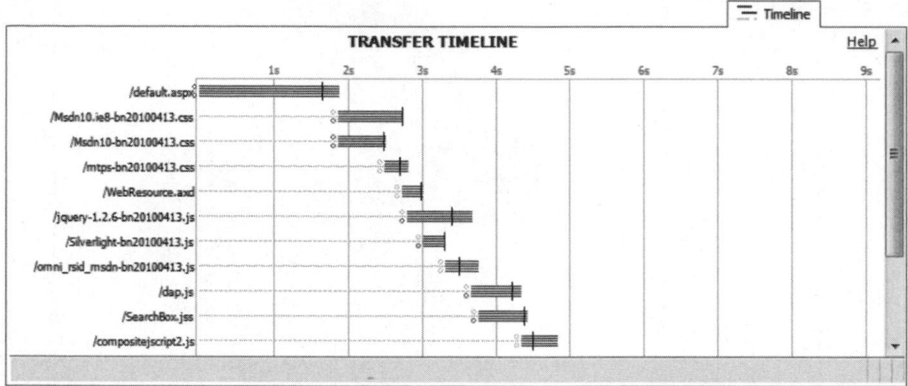

Figure 7–33. *The Timeline tab presents a Transfer Timeline graph, showing the start, duration, and end of all request-response sequences in chronological order*

Fiddler provides a lot of meaningful data that developers can use to analyze their sites. These next sections provide some insight on how this data can be applied to specific yet important areas that greatly impact the performance of sites.

Evaluating Cache Performance

Site performance is oftentimes more about what a server isn't doing than what it is—a notion especially true in the case of caching. Proper caching ensures that the client never requests data unnecessarily, and thus having proper cache performance is one of the most important aspects of a web site's overall performance experience.

Fiddler provides information to help developers tune cache performance, allowing them to make sure that their servers are marking each response with the proper caching directives.

The session list provides basic caching information on each session using the Caching column. A sample of this from `http://msdn.microsoft.com` is shown in Figure 7–34.

While Fiddler doesn't provide a "magic bullet" for picking the right cache setting to send, it does offer a way to visualize what a server is serving and when it's doing so. Coupled with good practice (such as emitting cache headers whenever possible and varying cache settings based on the static or dynamic nature of content), this information may greatly improve real-world performance.

#	R...	Pr...	Host	URL	Body	Caching
79	200	HTTP	i.msdn....	/ee402630.Security_sm(e...	1,316	public, max-age=86400 Expires: Thu, 13 May 2010 16:09:58 GMT
80	200	HTTP	i.msdn....	/ee402630.Global_sm(en-...	5,801	public, max-age=86400 Expires: Thu, 13 May 2010 17:19:07 GMT
81	200	HTTP	i2.msdn...	/platform/Controls/WebTr...	6,403	public, max-age=15552000 Expires: Mon, 08 Nov 2010 15:43:30 GMT
82	200	HTTP	i2.msdn...	/en-us/mtps-bn20100413....	11,693	public, max-age=15552000 Expires: Mon, 08 Nov 2010 16:02:31 GMT
83	200	HTTP	js.micro...	/library/svy/sto/broker.js	4,663	public,max-age=7200
84	200	HTTP	a.rad.m...	/ADSAdClient31.dll?GetSA...	917	no-cache, must-revalidate Expires: Fri, 01 Jan 1990 00:00:00 GMT
85	200	HTTP	c.micro...	/trans_pixel.asp?source=...	44	
86	200	HTTP	i3.msdn...	/Platform/MasterPages/Ms...	49	public, max-age=86400 Expires: Thu, 13 May 2010 16:33:11 GMT
87	200	HTTP	ec.atd...	/b/NMMRTSHARYOU/300x...	16,253	Expires: Thu, 13 May 2010 16:27:55 GMT
88	200	HTTP	m.webt...	/dcsmgru7m99k7mqmgrhu...	67	no-cache Expires: -1
89	200	HTTP	a.lakeq...	/s.js	1,450	max-age=86400
90	200	HTTP	a.lakeq...	/i.ashx?&channel=1&form...	401	private
92	200	HTTP	a.lakeq...	/img/63406234538303939...	41,135	
93	200	HTTP	js.micro...	/library/svy/sto/broker-co...	1,278	public,max-age=7200

Figure 7–34. *Caching information for items download from http://msdn.microsoft.com*

Optimizing Compression Settings

Compression allows a server to send smaller files over the wire. Clients that can handle compressed responses decompress them in the background unbeknownst to the user. IE and other modern browsers accept two main types of compression over the wire: GZIP and Deflate.

Servers sending uncompressed content to clients could receive a performance boost (and smaller bandwidth usage bill) by compressing those files that would most benefit from it. Fiddler provides a tool to test the possible gain (or lack thereof) using these two and other compression methods via the Transformer inspector (Figure 7–35).

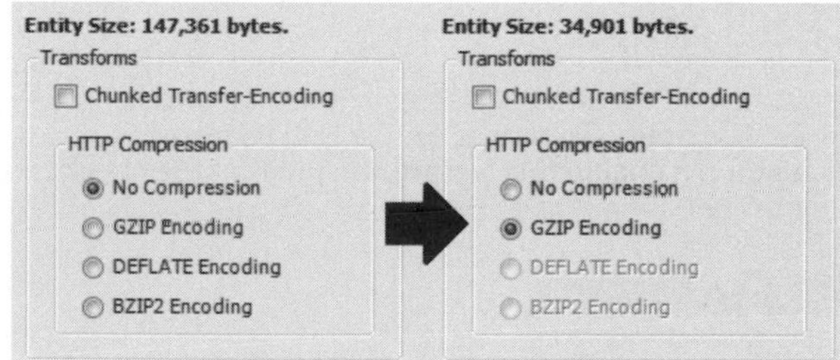

Figure 7–35. *JavaScript file being tested for significant size change under GZIP compression*

Looking for files that would benefit from compression can be tricky. When looking in Fiddler, developers should locate uncompressed, text-based files such as HTML, CSS, and JavaScript. These files are generally very compressible; they contain many repeat characters, strings, and other patterns that are optimized by compression algorithms. Images and other files that are already compressed (e.g., GIF, JPG, PNG, etc.) are not good candidates for compression, and could even grow larger if recompressed with GZIP or Deflate.

Simulating Performance Scenarios Using Built-In Rules

The Rules menu offers a number of simulation scenarios that may prove helpful to developers looking to tweak server settings or see best- and worst-case performance scenarios out of the box.

Performance rules geared toward time simulation and information can be found in the Performance submenu of the Rules menu. Figure 7–36 shows a screenshot of this menu and the available items.

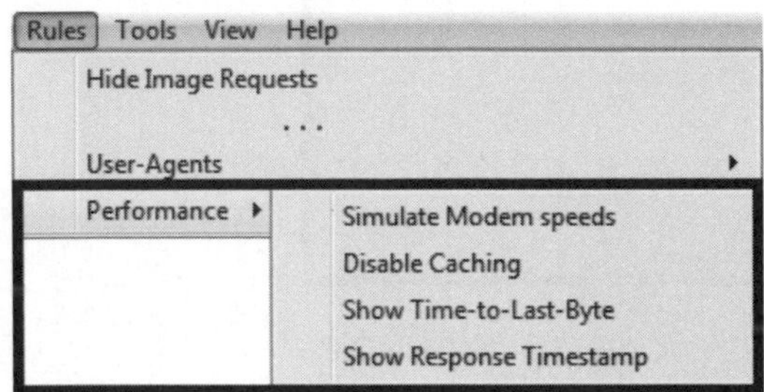

Figure 7–36. *Performance item and submenu within the Rules menu*

Simulate Modem Speeds helps to demonstrate how a site would perform if being loaded from far-away locations or from a very low-bandwidth pipe. Putting the name "modem" aside, this setting provides a way for developers to see which objects take the longest to load and why. It does this by stretching out the transaction time, essentially acting like a 56k modem connection.

Disable Caching does just that—it marks all responses as uncacheable. This setting, when used in conjunction with the Statistics tab, can flesh out possible worst-case performance scenarios for a given site.

Using Fiddler to Decrypt HTTPS Traffic

Fiddler can decrypt traffic sent over the HTTPS protocol. This feature is disabled in its out-of-the-box configuration; however, turning it on is fairly simple. The option is located on the HTTPS tab of the Fiddler Options dialog, accessible from the Tools menu. To enable this feature, ensure that the check box for "Decrypt HTTPS traffic" is checked (see Figure 7–37).

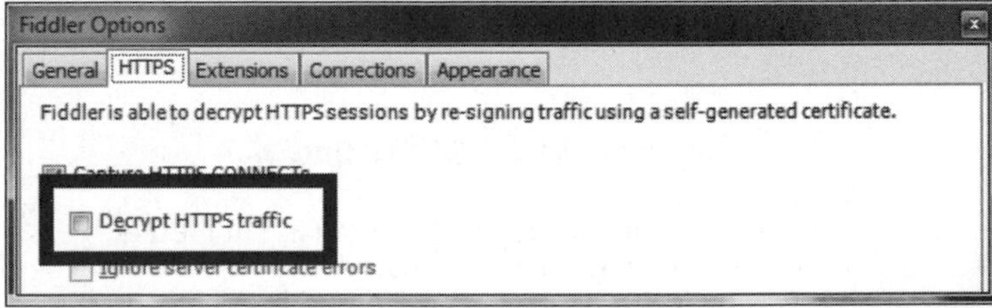

Figure 7–37. *The "Decrypt HTTPS traffic" settings in Tools ➤ Fiddler Options ➤ HTTPS*

Fiddler doesn't decrypt HTTPS messages silently. Instead, it intercepts and re-encrypts traffic using its own certificate; when used for more nefarious means, this process is referred to as a *man-in-the-middle (MITM) attack.*

At this point, Fiddler can properly encrypt and decrypt traffic, displaying sessions sourced from HTTPS alongside those from HTTP. Figure 7–38 highlights some of the messages, both neutral and negative, that developers might receive when navigating to HTTPS pages in any browser on the system.

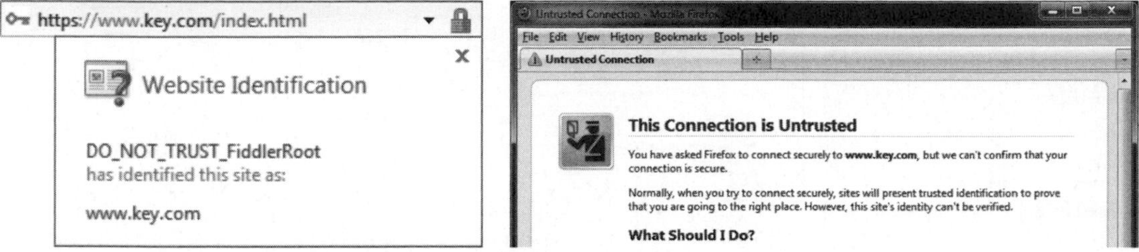

Figure 7–38. *IE (left) and Firefox (right) HTTPS information*

When this setting is enabled, two dialogs (Figure 7–39) will display to notify you that Fiddler will be adding certificates to the Trusted Root Certificate store. In sum, these dialogs warn users not to pass out the keys to anyone and to realize that, when running, the real HTTPS certificate information for sites is obscured. Users interested avoiding warnings from their browser about Fiddler's untrusted root certificate may click Yes twice.

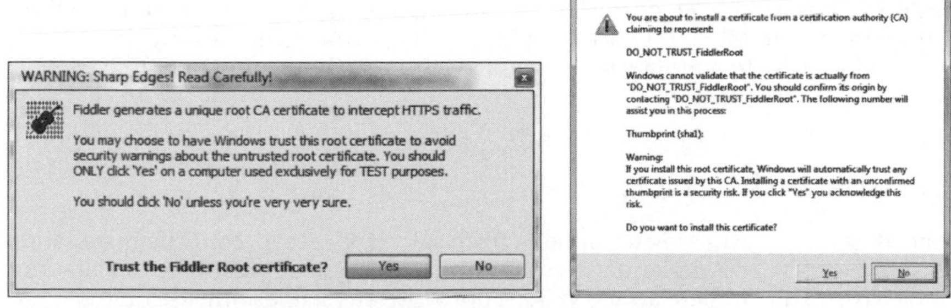

Figure 7–39. *Fiddler certificate installation warning dialogs*

Even with the root certificate installed to the Windows certificate store, Firefox still does not recognize it as a root authority. The HTTPS tab of the Fiddler Options dialog provides a way to export the root certificate so that it can be imported into Firefox (Figure 7–40).

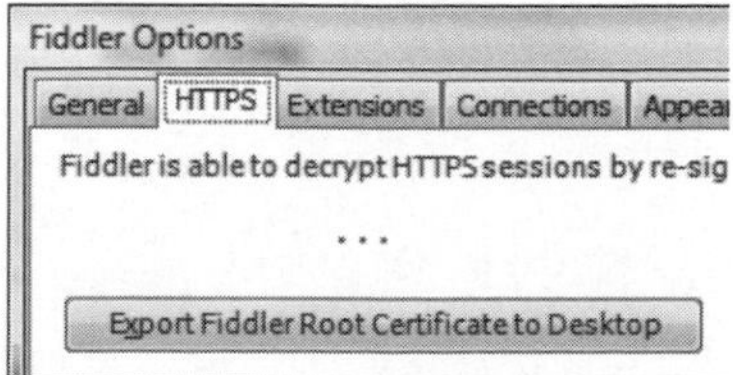

Figure 7–40. *The Export Root Certificate to Desktop button in the Fiddler Options dialog*

Once this file is exported, you can import into Firefox by first clicking the Options item in the Tools menu. Clicking the View Certificates button on the Encryption tab in the Advanced section (Figure 7–41) will open the Certificate Manger dialog. You can import the Fiddler certificate as an authority by selecting it from the Import button's dialog.

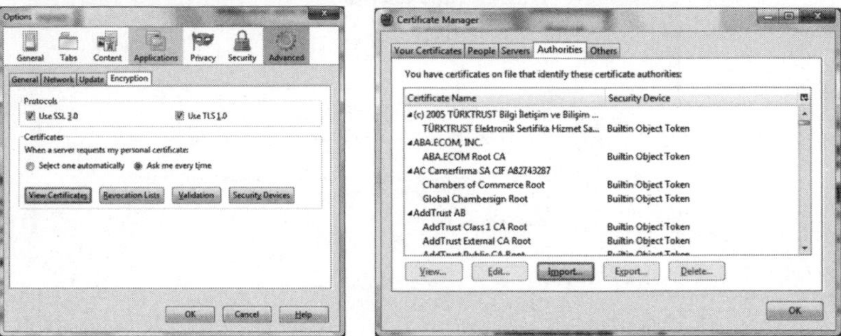

Figure 7–41. Importing the Fiddler root certificate into the Firefox certificate store

Grabbing Simple Captures with FiddlerCap

FiddlerCap is a lightweight utility for capturing HTTP and HTTPS traffic without requiring Fiddler to be installed. FiddlerCap gives developers a lightweight solution for those users willing to participate in the debugging process. FiddlerCap installs to one folder, leaves a limited footprint, requires only the .NET 2 Framework, and provides a way for users to submit capture data valuable to debugging processes, customer impact assessment, and defect triage.

Installing and Running FiddlerCap

FiddlerCap can be downloaded as a self-extracting executable from `www.fiddlercap.com`. The installation process, by default, places all of FiddlerCap's dependencies into one folder and suggests the installation folder as the current user's desktop. The FiddlerCap setup does not write any values outside of this folder, allowing it to be a reliable and safe stand-alone capture tool. Running the FiddlerCap executable will load up the application (as no Start Menu icon is created during installation).

Figure 7–42 shows an instance of FiddlerCap running for the first time. The application waits to capture information until the Start Capture button is clicked.

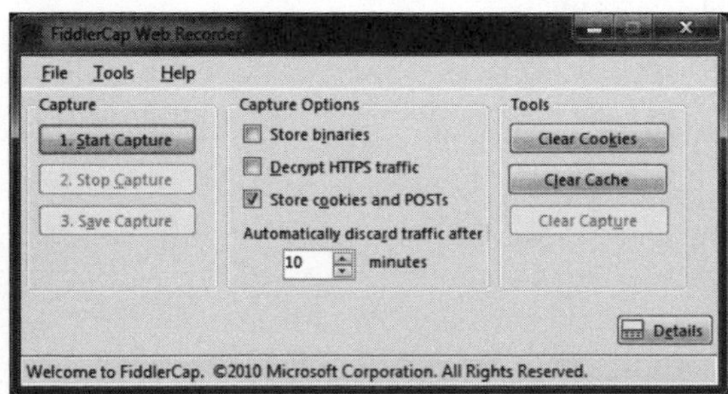

Figure 7–42. The FiddlerCap application

Capturing Traffic with FiddlerCap

Capturing traffic using FiddlerCap is a straightforward process that will, in most cases, require three only mouse clicks (outside of starting and closing the window).

Once started, FiddlerCap will navigate to a short instruction page in the user's default browser (Figure 7–43). This page asks the user to navigate to a broken web page for traffic capture.

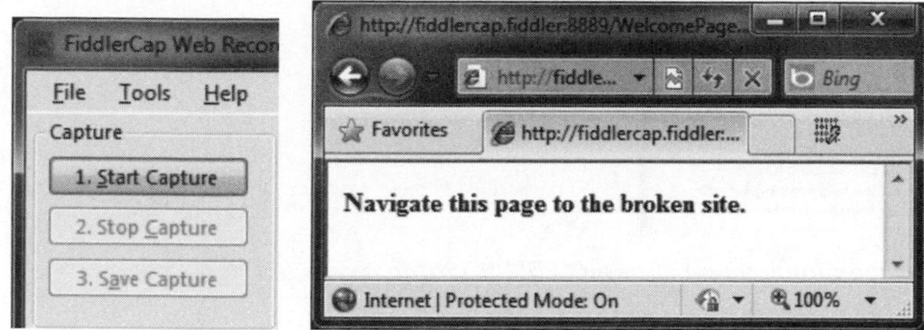

Figure 7–43. The instruction page launched when the Start Capture button is clicked

When the Start Capture button is clicked, FiddlerCap will begin recording session data on its host machine. You can view this session data in a lightweight version of the session list by toggling the Details button (Figure 7–44).

Figure 7–44. Details pane showing progress of FiddlerCap while capturing session data

Once the Stop Capture button is clicked, the captured sessions can be saved to a SAZ file. This compressed traffic file can be sent back to a developer or administrator and reopened by the full version of Fiddler.

FiddlerCap can capture HTTPS traffic just like Fiddler. You can enable it by checking the Decrypt HTTPS Traffic box in the Capture Options area. Once complete, the user running the tool must agree to a dialog stating the risk of decrypting such traffic. Once complete, HTTPS traffic will be added to the list of FiddlerCap's captured sessions (Figure 7–45).

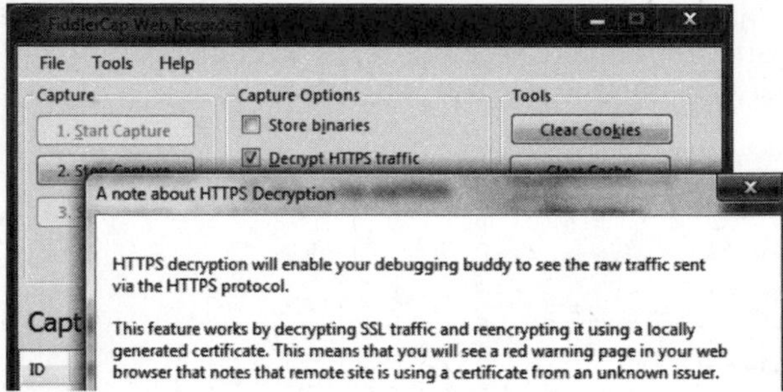

Figure 7–45. *HTTPS decryption message shown when Decrypt HTTPS Traffic is selected*

Summary

Fiddler allows developers to easily decipher the hidden communications between client and server, allowing for a more holistic view of the Web, its applications, and the delicate interactions that make today's web sites so powerful.

I used this chapter to introduce Fiddler to you and encourage its use as a way to fix a broad range of web development issues. I began with the basics: installation, information, and basic session monitoring. Following this was filtering and tampering, ways to get what you want out of Fiddler's data. Performance was next, where I covered ways that you can use Fiddler to speed up your site and servers. We ended with some lighter topics: how to enable HTTPS debugging in Fiddler, and how to collect traffic captures from end users using FiddlerCap.

CHAPTER 8

Content Syndication with Web Slices

Users want to be informed of updates to their favorite web sites even when they aren't running them in a browser window. They remain connected to their content while browsing other sites with mashups, receive updates from rich Internet applications (RIAs) on their desktop, and even remain in touch when on the road with mobile applications from their favorite content providers.

Web Slices provide a simple way for users to stay connected with content delivered from your web site. They provide an even richer take on traditional RSS feeds, letting you provide portable morsels of site content to users, and requiring no invasive change to site architecture. Beyond this, Web Slices offer an easy install experience, an easy-to-understand user experience, cheap development using standards-based technologies, stable and reliable behavior in the browser, and free advertisement through the Internet Explorer Add-Ons Gallery (`www.ieaddons.com`).

This chapter demonstrates how to construct Web Slices and how they can easily integrate into new and existing web applications. I'll begin by presenting some basic information about how Web Slices work and how users interact with and use them. I'll follow with tutorials on the structure and makeup of the Web Slice microformat and the process of including them on your web site. The chapter concludes with a deep dive into more advanced topics, such as authentication and alternative sources.

Basics of Web Slices

Web Slices are rich, interactive, dynamic morsels of content that provide constant updates of site content without requiring that the user directly visit that site. Much like feeds, Web Slices are a form of content syndication that gives applications (in this case, the web browser) the ability to be informed of changes and update a cache of selected content.

Web Slices are subsections (slices) of web pages; they use and display markup much like their parent document. Figure 8–1 shows an example of a Web Slice from OneRiot called TopVideos. The slice displays the most relevant information in the Top Videos portion of their site in a consumable and easy-to-update manner.

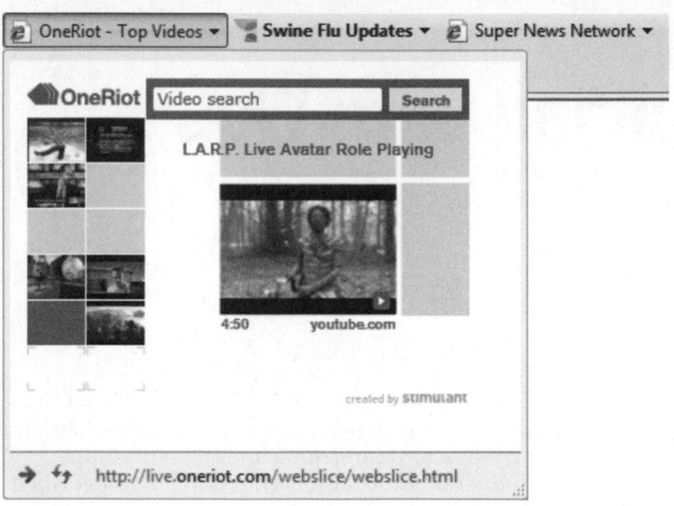

Figure 8–1. An open Web Slice; this one from OneRiot.com

Web Slices are advertised by a special green icon on web pages and in the browser frame. This icon can also be used by web developers on pages that use this technology, much like the ubiquitous orange RSS 2.0 icon. Figure 8–2 shows this icon.

Figure 8–2. The Web Slice discovery icon

Figure 8–3 highlights this icon in action. On this web page, a user is presented with a Web Slice that is available for installation. The installation can be initiated either on the page through a mouse click on the icon or through the icon in the IE browser frame (in the same place as the RSS icon).

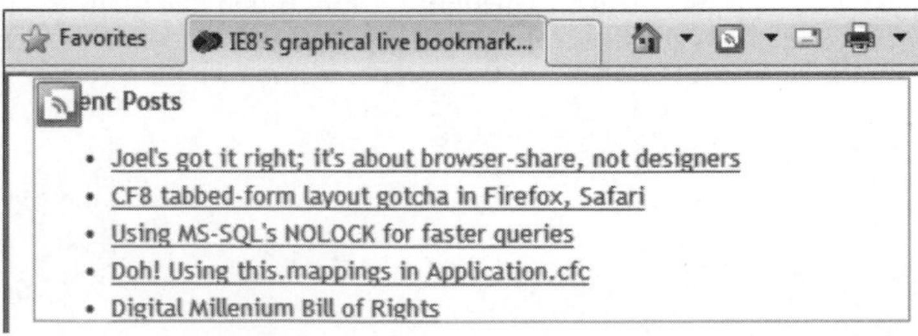

Figure 8–3. The Web Slice icon appears on hover.

Installation is one of four main events in the Web Slice usage flow. Web Slices are updated by IE and the Windows RSS Platform on a consistent cadence. IE manages display of Web Slices through a small flyout window launched from the Favorites bar. Users can navigate to the page hosting the Web Slice (or to an alternative location specified by the developer) by clicking on the Open link in the flyout window. The following sections of this chapter detail each of the four events in Web Slice usage (Figure 8–4).

Figure 8–4. *User flow for Web Slice installation and interaction*

Web Slice Structure: The hAtom Microformat

Web Slices are markup-based extensions loosely defined by features present in the hAtom microformat specification. This means that Web Slices are defined through real HTML by using tags for structure and attributes to signify structure and metadata types. The attributes in Table 8–1 show the structural building blocks used by Web Slices.

Table 8–1. *Web Slice Definition Attributes*

Attribute Value	Associated Tag	Description	Required/Optional
`hslice`	Any	Indicates the parent tag containing a Web Slice	Required
`entry-title`	Any	Indicates the tag containing the title	Required
`entry-content`	Any	Indicates the tag containing the content	Optional
`ttl`	Any	Indicates the tag containing the time-to-live (TTL) value	Optional
`endtime`	`<attr>`	Indicates the tag containing the expiry time	Optional

Listing 8–1 shows skeleton markup of a Web Slice and the hAtom microformat. The Web Slice definition begins at the `<div>` containing the `hslice` class selector and has the `id` `my-webslice`. The following `<div>`—the one implementing the class selector `entry-title`—holds the title of the Web Slice. The element using `entry-content` holds the Web Slice's content.

Listing 8–1. *Sample Structure of a Web Slice*

```
<html>
  ...
  <body>
    ...

    <div class="hslice" id="my-webslice">
      <div class="entry-title" style="display:none">My WebSlice</div>
      <div class="entry-content">
        This is my webslice and some wonderful content.
      </div>
    </div>

    ...
  </body>
</html>
```

It's worth noting that tags using the `hslice` class can also specify other classes alongside it. This example also hides the `<div>` tag carrying the `entry-title` class; this is useful when a developer wants to specify a Web Slice's title without changing the look or feel of a page's layout.

The remaining sections will use a recurring example to demonstrate key concepts in Web Slice development. These examples can be found on the companion web site for those readers who wish to follow along with the examples firsthand (`www.proiedev.com`).

Designing and Deploying Basic Web Slices

Building Web Slices using the hAtom microformat allows developers to easily create frame extensions without modifying the integrity of a page's preexisting markup. The page in Figure 8–5 shows an example news web site that displays up-to-the-minute content. Users can get the latest updates from this content through an RSS feed; however, the RSS feed doesn't offer rich, customized user experiences as the main web site does.

Web Slices complement RSS by syndicating content using a document's original HTML and CSS rather than the more rigid XML format of traditional feeds. The web site in this example can surface the latest news information to users by wrapping the news portion of the page in Web Slice–compatible markup. Users are notified of this syndicated content when they visit the page and can choose to instruct the browser to look for updates through subscriptions.

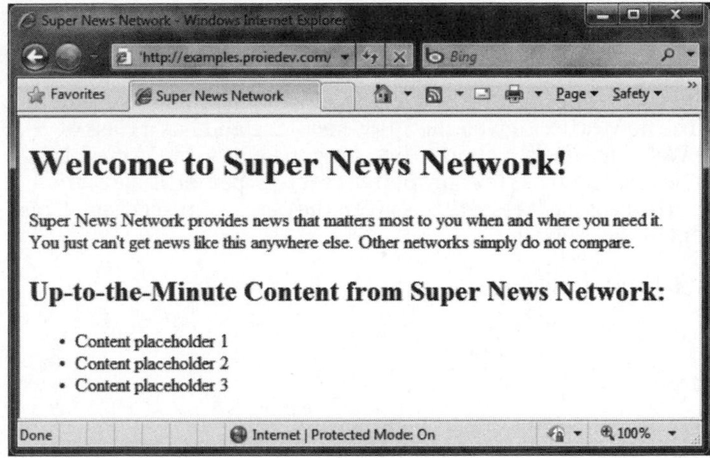

Figure 8–5. *Web page with updatable content*

Structuring and Creating a Web Slice

Web Slices use standard HTML constructs for storing metadata. This is in line with the construct of most microformats—a set of specifications that identifies commonly used constructs (such as addresses or business card information) and attempts to standardize their markup across the Web. Web Slices use constructs in the hAtom microformat to convey data; developers use the text content and the `class`, `id`, and `title` attributes of preexisting elements to define how a Web Slice appears.

Listing 8–2 demonstrates the code behind the web site in Figure 8–5. This sample news site has a section used to convey the latest news content for users. While this would typically be offered as an RSS feed alongside the page, such a feature is a good candidate for a Web Slice—a small, clearly definable piece of a target web page that contains regularly updated content. The candidate content in this listing lies with in the `<div>` element with the `id` of `news-updates`.

Listing 8–2. *Code for a Web Site with Updatable Content*

```
<html>
   <head>
      <title>Super News Network</title>
   </head>
   <body>
      <h1>Welcome to Super News Network!</h1>
      Super News Network provides news that matters most to you when
      and where you need it.  You just can't get news like this anywhere
      else.  Other networks simply do not compare.
      <div id="news-updates">
         <h2>Up-to-the-Minute Content from Super News Network:</h2>
         <ul>
            <li>Content placeholder 1</li>
            <li>Content placeholder 2</li>
            <li>Content placeholder 3</li>
         </ul>
```

```
        </div>
    </body>
</html>
```

Listing 8–3 demonstrates this same page enhanced to offer content as a Web Slice. The new Web Slice will allow users to subscribe to the News Updates section. A `<div>` is added to the page as a parent of the `<div>` with an `id` of `news-updates`. The new `<div>` is given the `id` `my-webslice` and has a class of `hslice` applied. This element defines the Web Slice itself. A child `<div>` using the `entry-title` class is added to this parent; this `<div>` is not visible, and its `innerText` property is set to `Super News Network`. This element defines the Web Slice's title. The `news-updates` `<div>` is given the class `entry-content`. This element now identifies itself as the content of the Web Slice.

Listing 8–3. *Web Slice Encapsulating a Web Page's Updatable Conent*

```
<html>
    <head>
        <title>Super News Network</title>
    </head>
    <body>
        <h1>Welcome to Super News Network!</h1>
        Super News Network provides news that matters most to you when
        and where you need it.  You just can't get news like this anywhere
        else.  Other networks simply do not compare.
        <div class="hslice" id="my-webslice">
            <div class="entry-title" style="display:none;">Super News Network</div>
            <div class="entry-content" id="news-updates">
                <h2>Up-to-the-Minute Content from Super News Network:</h2>
                <ul>
                    <li>Content placeholder 1</li>
                    <li>Content placeholder 2</li>
                    <li>Content placeholder 3</li>
                </ul>
            </div>
        </div>
    </body>
</html>
```

Installing and Viewing Web Slices

Web Slices were designed for installation by a web page, much like Accelerators. Content defined with the Web Slice hAtom microformat is advertised to the user both in IE's content pane and the IE frame itself. Figure 8–6 shows the high-level view of these surfaces, and Figure 8–7 shows them in detail.

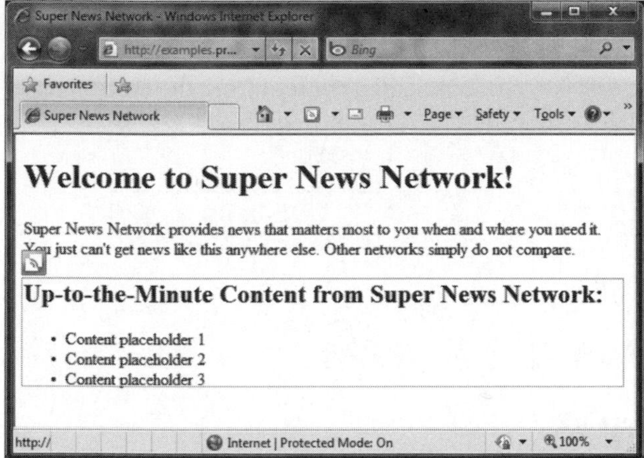

Figure 8–6. Advertisement of a Web Slice for installation on a web page and in the IE frame

Web Slices that IE discovers on a web page are shown in two ways: as the RSS feed icon in the browser frame, and as a green icon and border shown surrounding a Web Slice during a mouse hover event. The example Web Slice surfaces both of these indicators.

Figure 8–7. Green icon being surfaced for installation

Installation of a Web Slice is initiated by a user clicking on either the icon in the IE frame or the one shown above a Web Slice. A dialog is shown highlighting the name of the Web Slice and the URL it originates from. Figure 8–8 shows the installation dialog from the preceding example.

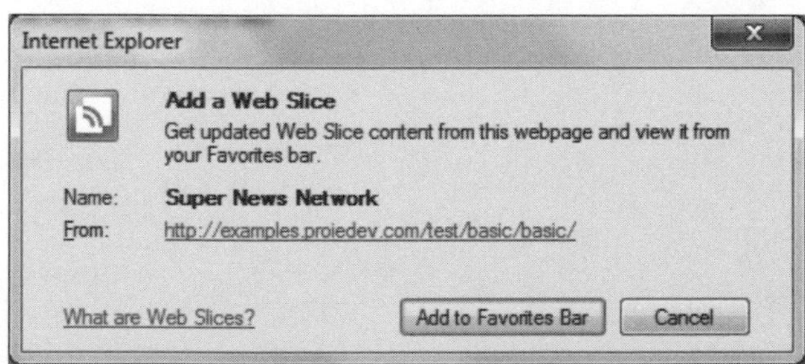

Figure 8–8. The Web Slice installation dialog

The process is completed when a user clicks the Add to Favorites bar button. This command does exactly what it says: the installer stores the Web Slice metadata to the system and adds a reference to the Web Slice in the Favorites bar.

Figure 8–9 shows the newly installed Web Slice in the Favorites bar. The Web Slice is in bold, and a flyout arrow is displayed when IE downloads the first batch of syndicated content from the Web Slice's content server. This content is shown to a user in a flyout window below the icon whenever the icon is clicked (see Figure 8–10).

Figure 8–9. *Newly installed Web Slice (bold text indicates an update)*

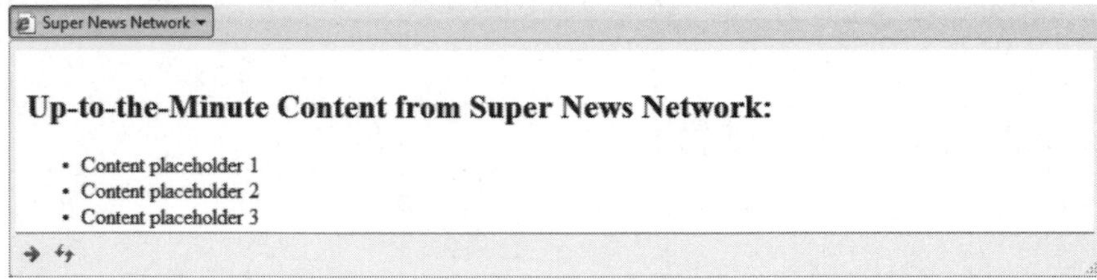

Figure 8–10. *A sample Web Slice opened with content*

Managing Web Slices

Management of Web Slices takes place in the context menu and properties dialog of each Web Slice. Web Slices are not managed through the Manage Add-Ons dialog like most other IE extensions. The context menu dialog, shown in Figure 8–11, provides commands for opening the Web Slice's navigation page, refreshing it, deleting it, customizing the width of all titles in the Favorites bar, and accessing the Web Slice property dialog.

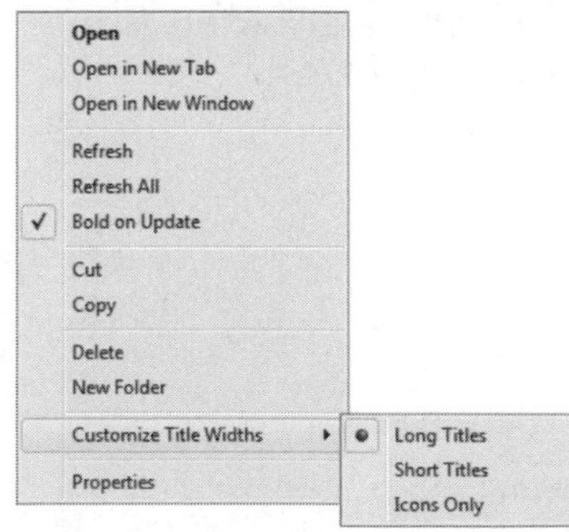

Figure 8–11. *The Web Slice context menu*

The Web Slice properties dialog provides settings for two things: credential settings (username and password) and the update schedule. Credential settings allow Web Slices using Basic authentication over HTTPS or Digest authentication over HTTP or HTTPS to automatically sign in with a preset username and password. Update schedule settings allow users to customize when the Windows feed service refreshes the content of a Web Slice. This dialog is shown in Figure 8–12.

Figure 8–12. *The Web Slice properties dialog*

Realistically, these settings are buried and difficult for users to discover. Developers should work under the premise that users will never see this dialog, and as a result never customize this information.

Update and Expiry Management

Developers can easily control a Web Slice's update frequency and, if necessary, end-of-life date through the same hAtom microformat style found in the previous examples. The following sections demonstrate how to apply these settings to Web Slice markup.

Defining Update Intervals with TTL

The `ttl` property informs the browser how long it should wait before refreshing the content of a Web Slice. Like RSS feeds, the download and update frequency for a given Web Slice is controlled by the Windows RSS Platform (more specifically, the Feed Download Engine). The Feed Download Engine keeps track of when a TTL interval is reached. When it is, the engine connects to the host web site, downloads the appropriate data, merges the new data into the user's view, purges old content in the cache, and finally begins a schedule for the next TTL event.

Web Slices are updated every 24 hours by default. Developers can increase or decrease this number through the `ttl` property; the minimum value is 15 minutes. This property is defined through the use of the class selector `ttl` on an element whose inner text is the `ttl` value. Listing 8–4 demonstrates the use of a TTL definition, setting the update time of the example Web Slice to 30-minute intervals.

Listing 8–4. Sample Web Slice Specifying a TTL Value

```
<?
//  Create a new DateTime object and grab current values
$dateTme = new DateTime();
$currentTime = $date->format('H:i:s A');
$currentDate = $date->format('D, M jS, Y');
?>
<html>
   <head>
      <title>Super News Network</title>
   </head>
   <body>
      <h1>Welcome to Super News Network!</h1>
      Super News Network provides news that matters most to you when
      and where you need it. You just can't get news like this anywhere
      else.  Other networks simply do not compare.
      <div class="hslice" id="my-webslice">
         <div class="entry-title" style="display:none;">Super News Network</div>
         <div class="entry-content" id="news-updates">
            <h2>Up-to-the-Minute Content from Super News Network:</h2>
            <ul>
               <li>Content placeholder 1</li>
               <li>Content placeholder 2</li>
               <li>Content placeholder 3</li>
            </ul>
            <div id="webslice-time">
               This content was last refreshed at
               <? echo($currentTime); ?> on <? echo($currentDate); ?>.
            </div>
         </div>
         <div style="display:none;" class="ttl">30</div>
      </div>
   </body>
</html>
```

This example begins with a bit of server-side code (PHP), used to grab the current time and date, which is displayed within the Web Slice. The `ttl` class selector is applied to the last `<div>` element of the example. The value of `ttl` is set to 30, placed into the text content of this element. Although a block element is used, this value is not shown on the page because the display style is set to `none`. When installed, the update interval of this Web Slice is consumed by the Feed Download Engine.

Users can edit this value by right-clicking a Web Slice in the Favorites bar and opening the Web Slice Properties dialog (shown in Figure 8–13). The Update Schedule group box allows for selection of a built-in schedule or a custom update frequency. This dialog is useful in dialing back or increasing the frequency of updates for Web Slices.

Figure 8–13. TTL value settings in the Web Slice properties dialog

Defining Expiration with the endtime Selector

Web Slices may provide a date and time of expiry, or when the service behind the Web Slice plans to stop feeding new information to it. This is very useful if a Web Slice becomes worthless after a certain date or time—for instance, after an online auction comes to its scheduled end.

IE presents this information to the user first through the Web Slice Properties dialog and, as expiry draws near, through the use of italicized text and other visual cues in the Web Slice itself, as shown in Figure 8–14.

Figure 8–14. Web Slice icon indicating expiration is near

Developers can use Web Slice expiry as a way to generate confidence with users; it sets an expectation of a service's lifetime.

Listing 8–5 shows how the `endtime` class selector can be used. In this example, an `<abbr>` tag has been used to hold an expiration date of December 23, 2010. The date is stored in the `title` attribute, and the listing includes a reference to the `endtime` selector.

Listing 8–5. Web Slice That Indicates an Expiry Time

```
<?
//  Create a new DateTime object and grab current values
$dateTme = new DateTime();
$currentTime = $date->format('H:i:s A');
$currentDate = $date->format('D, M jS, Y');
?>
```

```
<html>
   <head>
      <title>Super News Network</title>
   </head>
   <body>
      <h1>Welcome to Super News Network!</h1>
      Super News Network provides news that matters most to you when
      and where you need it. You just can't get news like this anywhere
      else.  Other networks simply do not compare.
      <div class="hslice" id="my-webslice">
         <div class="entry-title" style="display:none;">Super News Network</div>
         <div class="entry-content" id="news-updates">
            <h2>Up-to-the-Minute Content from Super News Network:</h2>
            <ul>
               <li>Content placeholder 1</li>
               <li>Content placeholder 2</li>
               <li>Content placeholder 3</li>
            </ul>
            <div id="webslice-time">
               This content was last refreshed at
               <? echo($currentTime); ?> on <? echo($currentDate); ?>.
            </div>
         </div>
         <div style="display:none;" class="ttl">30</div>
         <abbr class="endtime" title="2010-12-23T12:30:00-08:00"
               style="display:none;"></abbr>
      </div>
   </body>
</html>
```

Table 8–2 shows the format of the date/time string. This string follows the ISO 8601/RFC 3339 date format. Replacing # with a value described in the table, strings should be formatted in one of the following ways:

- `####-##-##T##:##:##-##:##`
- `####-##-##T##:##:##+##:##`
- `####-##-##T##:##:##Z`

Table 8–2. *ISO 8601/RFC3339 Date Format*

Part	Description	Example
Year	Four-digit year	2012
Month	Two-digit month, 01 through 12	12
Day	Two-digit day, 01 through 31	23
Date/time separator	T (date and time separator)	T
Hour	Two-digit hour, 00 through 23	01
Minute	Two-digit minute, 00 through 59	52
Second	Two-digit second, 00 through 59 (optional)	34
Zone	Z (UTC/GMT, also known as “zero” time)	Z
	Alternatively, the positive or negative five-digit hour and minute of the time zone offset (-06:00 is US Central time)	-08:00

Unlike the other Web Slice selectors, `endtime` must be specified using an `<abbr>` tag, with the expiration date and time being set through the `title` attribute. Although only one element type can be used, the expiration does not need to be displayed on the page; this example hides the tag by setting its `display` style to none (see Figure 8–15).

Figure 8–15. *Web Slice tooltip showing an expiration in 23 seconds*

A yellow warning icon (!), shown in Figure 8–16, is added to the bottom portion of a Web Slice when expiration nears. The tooltip for this icon contains the time to expiration. This, along with the italic indicator and mouse tooltip in the Favorites bar, informs users that a Web Slice will stop updating shortly.

Figure 8–16. *Web Slice expiration warning icon and tooltip information*

IE stops querying a Web Slice's content source once the expiry date is reached. Users are notified as before with a bold, italic title in their Favorites bar. The Web Slice itself is branded with a red X icon, as shown in Figure 8–17; the date and time of expiration are displayed in the icon's tooltip.

Figure 8–17. *Web Slice expiration warning and notification tooltip*

Using CSS Styles and Stylesheets

Web Slices can use CSS to style content just like normal web pages, but there are some restrictions placed on how these styles are used. The browser attempts to download as little information from a page as possible when loading or refreshing a Web Slice; this reduces the strain a Web Slice can have on a connection. Consequently, CSS in Web Slices must be used in certain ways if it is to be downloaded and used by IE. The following sections highlight these restrictions and usage scenarios for CSS in Web Slices.

Inline Styles and In-Document Stylesheets

CSS rules contained within the same document as a Web Slice will be applied to the Web Slice contents in two situations: when the styles are placed inline with the Web Slice's elements, or when a stylesheet is placed within the <head> tag of its parent document. There is no guarantee that styles defined outside these rules will be applied to a Web Slice when it is loaded outside of a browser tab and within the Web Slice's drop-down window on the Favorites bar.

Listing 8–6 demonstrates the first acceptable type of CSS use within a Web Slice: inline styles. Elements underneath the main <div> of the Web Slice are individually styled using this method.

Listing 8–6. *Web Slice Using Inline Styles*

```
<?
//  Create a new DateTime object and grab current values
$dateTime = new DateTime();
$currentTime = $dateTime->format('H:i:s A');
$currentDate = $dateTime->format('D, M jS, Y');
?>
<html>
   <head>
      <title>Super News Network</title>
   </head>
   <body style="font: normal 1.0em Arial, Helvetica, sans-serif;">
      <h1 id="page-title" style="font: bold 1.75em Georgia, Times, serif;">
```

```
            Welcome to Super News Network!
         </h1>
         <span id="page-teaser" style="font-style: italic;">
            Super News Network provides news that matters most to you when
            and where you need it. You just can't get news like this anywhere
            else.  Other networks simply do not compare.
         </span>
         <div class="hslice" id="webslice">
            <div class="entry-title" style="display:none;">Super News Network</div>
            <div class="entry-content" id="news-updates"
                 style="font: normal 0.8em Arial, Helvetica, sans-serif;">
               <h2 id="webslice-title" style="font: bold 1.25em Georgia, Times, serif;">
                  Up-to-the-Minute Content from Super News Network:
               </h2>
               <ul id="webslice-list">
                  <li>Content placeholder 1</li>
                  <li>Content placeholder 2</li>
                  <li>Content placeholder 3</li>
               </ul>
               <div id="webslice-time"
                    style="color: #555; font: italic 0.75em Georgia, Times, serif;">
                  This content was last refreshed at
                  <? echo($currentTime); ?> on <? echo($currentDate); ?>.
               </div>
            </div>
            <div style="display:none;" class="ttl">30</div>
            <abbr class="endtime" title="2010-12-23T12:30:00-08:00"
                  style="display:none;"></abbr>
         </div>
      </body>
   </html>
```

Styles can also be set within a page using inline stylesheets. Instead of placing inline styles within the style tag of elements, IE will use full stylesheets placed within a page's <style> tags. Listing 8-7 shows an inline stylesheet created using the inline styles shown in the previous example.

***Listing 8–7.** Web Slice Using In-Document Stylesheets*

```
<?
//  Create a new DateTime object and grab current values
$dateTime = new DateTime();
$currentTime = $dateTime->format('H:i:s A');
$currentDate = $dateTime->format('D, M jS, Y');
?>
<html>
   <head>
      <title>Super News Network</title>
      <style type="text/css">
         body {
            font: normal 1.0em Arial, Helvetica, sans-serif;
         }
         #page-title {
            font: bold 1.75em Georgia, Times, serif;
         }
         #page-teaser {
```

```
               font-style: italic;
            }
            #webslice-title {
               font: bold 1.25em Georgia, Times, serif;
            }
            #webslice-content {
               font: normal 0.8em Arial, Helvetica, sans-serif;
            }
            #webslice-list { }
            #webslice-time {
               color: #555; font: italic 0.75em Georgia, Times, serif;
            }
         </style>
      </head>
      <body>
         <h1 id="page-title">
            Welcome to Super News Network!
         </h1>
         <span id="page-teaser" style="">
            Super News Network provides news that matters most to you when
            and where you need it. You just can't get news like this anywhere
            else.  Other networks simply do not compare.
         </span>
         <div class="hslice" id="webslice">
            <div class="entry-title" style="display:none;">Super News Network</div>
            <div class="entry-content" id="webslice-content">
               <h2 id="webslice-title">
                  Up-to-the-Minute Content from Super News Network:
               </h2>
               <ul id="webslice-list">
                  <li>Content placeholder 1</li>
                  <li>Content placeholder 2</li>
                  <li>Content placeholder 3</li>
               </ul>
               <div id="webslice-time">
                  This content was last refreshed at
                  <? echo($currentTime); ?> on <? echo($currentDate); ?>.
               </div>
            </div>
            <div style="display:none;" class="ttl">30</div>
            <abbr class="endtime" title="2010-12-23T12:30:00-08:00"
                  style="display:none;"></abbr>
         </div>
      </body>
   </html>
```

Linked and Imported Styles

In addition to styles specified within the document itself, stylesheets specified through the `<link>` tag and the `@import` directive are also included within Web Slices. External stylesheets must be declared within the <head> of the document to guarantee inclusion, and just as with inline styles, there is no guarantee that styles will be inherited from elements outside of the Web Slice's hAtom declaration.

Listing 8–8 shows the inline CSS from the prior example consolidated into an external CSS stylesheet. This stylesheet is loaded through a `<link>` tag in the `<head>` of Listing 8–9; the inline styles from the prior example are removed as a result.

***Listing 8–8.** External Stylesheet to Be Used by a Web Slice*

```
body {
   font: normal 1.0em Arial, Helvetica, sans-serif;
}
#page-title {
   font: bold 1.75em Georgia, Times, serif;
}
#page-teaser {
   font-style: italic;
}
#webslice-title {
   font: bold 1.25em Georgia, Times, serif;
}
#webslice-content {
   font: normal 0.8em Arial, Helvetica, sans-serif;
}
#webslice-list { }
#webslice-time {
   color: #555; font: italic 0.75em Georgia, Times, serif;
}
```

***Listing 8–9.** Web Slice Using External Stylesheet via the <link> Tag*

```
<?
// Create a new DateTime object and grab current values
$dateTime = new DateTime();
$currentTime = $dateTime->format('H:i:s A');
$currentDate = $dateTime->format('D, M jS, Y');
?>
<html>
   <head>
      <title>Super News Network</title>
      <link rel="stylesheet" type="text/css" href="style.css" />
   </head>
   <body>
      <h1 id="page-title">
         Welcome to Super News Network!
      </h1>
      <span id="page-teaser" style="">
         Super News Network provides news that matters most to you when
         and where you need it. You just can't get news like this anywhere
         else.  Other networks simply do not compare.
      </span>
      <div class="hslice" id="webslice">
         <div class="entry-title" style="display:none;">Super News Network</div>
         <div class="entry-content" id="webslice-content">
            <h2 id="webslice-title">
               Up-to-the-Minute Content from Super News Network:
            </h2>
```

```
            <ul id="webslice-list">
               <li>Content placeholder 1</li>
               <li>Content placeholder 2</li>
               <li>Content placeholder 3</li>
            </ul>
            <div id="webslice-time">
               This content was last refreshed at
               <? echo($currentTime); ?> on <? echo($currentDate); ?>.
            </div>
         </div>
         <div style="display:none;" class="ttl">30</div>
         <abbr class="endtime" title="2010-12-23T12:30:00-08:00"
               style="display:none;"></abbr>
      </div>
   </body>
</html>
```

The end result is a Web Slice that is visually and functionally equivalent to the prior example. Again, developers should ensure that all linked and imported stylesheets are imported within the <head> tag of a Web Slice or within its hAtom construct.

Alternative Sources

The three postinstallation actions of a Web Slice can use sources other than the original page or server. Alternative sources give Web Slice authors more flexibility in creating user experiences and optimizing Web Slice performance and reliability. The following sections highlight ways that developers can provide alternative sources for Web Slice update, display, and navigation scenarios.

Alternative Update Source

Developers can specify an alternative update source that IE and the Windows RSS Platform can use to determine if the contents of a Web Slice have changed. To review, the Feed Download Engine within the Windows RSS Platform is responsible for updating the content of a Web Slice subscription. Each time a TTL interval completes (whether the default 24-hour interval or one specified through the `ttl` construct), the engine compares the latest content to that contained in the cache. Consequently, the original page that hosts the Web Slice is downloaded again at every interval—shorter intervals could correlate to higher bandwidth consumption.

Web Slices can specify an alternative update source to save bandwidth and provide only the information that IE and the RSS Platform need to compare old data against. Listing 8–10 shows this same Web Slice with an alternate update source specified using the `feedurl` class. This Web Slice's update cycle becomes tied to the update cycle of the `feed.xml` RSS feed.

Listing 8–10. *Web Slice Using an Alternative Update Source*

```
<html>
   <head>
      <title>Super News Network</title>
      <link rel="stylesheet" type="text/css" href="style.css" />
   </head>
   <body>
      ...
```

```
<div class="hslice" id="webslice">
   <div class="entry-title" style="display:none;">Super News Network</div>
   <a rel="feedurl" href="feed.xml" style="display:none;"></a>
   <div class="entry-content" id="webslice-content">
   ...
```

Alternative Display Sources

By default, Web Slices are cached and stored by the Windows RSS Platform. The RSS Platform strips out all "active" content from cached files before storage. This policy prevents the execution of dynamic content within Web Slices shown in the drop-down window.

Alternative display sources can be used to circumvent this problem. By specifying the `rel=entry-content` attribute on an anchor (`<a>`) tag, you can use the target of that tag as an alternative display source that will be shown when the user clicks the Web Slice in the Favorites bar. These documents are loaded by IE rather than the RSS Platform, allowing them some attractive privileges:

- **Full control over styles**: IE will use styles from any part of the alternative source; basic Web Slices guarantee only those defined in the `<head>` and child Web Slice tags.
- **Link navigations**: Links can be used for in-place navigations.
- **Form support**: Users can interact with and submit form content.
- **Limited script support**: JavaScript, in limited form, can be used on the page.

Listing 8–11 shows a Web Slice that defines an alternative display source. When this Web Slice is viewed, the display source `alt.html` is loaded instead of the content the Web Slice structure encloses. The alternative display page is surfaced through an `<a>` tag with the `rel` attribute `entry-content`.

Listing 8–11. *Web Slice Defining an Alternative Display Source*

```
<html>
   ...
   <body>
      ...
      <div class="hslice" id="webslice">
         <div class="entry-title" style="display:none;">Super News Network</div>
         <a rel="bookmark" href="nav.html" style="display:none;"></a>
         <a rel="entry-content" href="alt.html" style="display:none;"></a>
         <div id="webslice-content">
            <h2 id="webslice-title">
               Up-to-the-Minute Content from Super News Network:
            </h2>
            <ul id="webslice-list">
               <li>Content placeholder 1</li>
               <li>Content placeholder 2</li>
               <li>Content placeholder 3</li>
            </ul>
            ...
         </div>
      </div>
   </body>
</html>
```

The Windows Feeds Platform strips all active content out of updates since the normal content type it manages (RSS) does not permit script. IE clearly permits script and dynamic content; thus alternative display source pages may use these technologies. Even alternative display sources have some security restrictions and do not offer the full, rich experience of a normal web page. Pages loaded through alternative display sources cannot do the following:

- Launch alert dialog boxes, pop-ups, or windows (except during full navigations)
- Install ActiveX controls
- Access the `window.external` object
- Open a new tab (a new window can be opened)
- Use HTTP Basic or Digest authentication (only cookie- or session-based methods can be used)

These restrictions are in place to help prevent malicious use of Web Slices.

Alternative Navigation Target

By default, users who click the Open icon in the Web Slice drop-down are navigated to the page where the Web Slice resides. This is also the case for navigations that occur when a user clicks a Web Slice that has never been or cannot be updated. However, developers may specify a different landing page in these scenarios by providing the URL of an alternative navigation target in their markup.

The alternative navigation target is specified through an `<a>` tag located within the `hslice` `<div>` with a `rel` attribute set to `bookmark`. The `href` link in this tag will be the link IE navigates to when a navigation event is triggered on the Web Slice. Listing 8–12 shows the addition of this tag.

Listing 8–12. *Web Slice Pointing to an Alternative Navigation Target*

```
<html>
   ...
   <body>
   ...
      <div class="hslice" id="webslice">
         <div class="entry-title" style="display:none;">Super News Network</div>
         <a rel="bookmark" href="nav.html" style="display:none;"></a>
```

In this example, users who click the Open button or who click a nonupdated Web Slice will be navigated to `nav.html`. The user experience is shown in Figure 8–18.

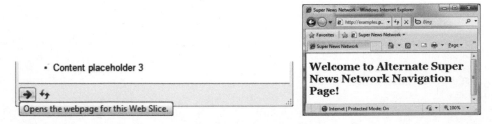

Figure 8–18. *An alternative navigation target in action*

Authentication

Some user scenarios such as e-mail necessitate user authentication to access data. Web Slices offer limited support for authenticated sessions that support these scenarios. Unfortunately, this feature area is incomplete in terms of user experience and functionality.

There are three modes of authentication available: HTTP Basic authentication, HTTP Digest authentication, and cookie-based authentication. The authentication types available are determined by the display method of the Web Slice. Table 8–3 highlights availability compared to Web Slices using both standard and alternative display source content types over HTTP and HTTPS.

Table 8–3. *Authentication Types Available for Certain Web Slice and HTTP Protocol Types*

	Standard Web Slice		Alternative Source Web Slice	
	HTTP	**HTTPS**	**HTTP**	**HTTPS**
HTTP Basic	No	Yes	No	No
HTTP Digest	Yes	Yes	No	No
Cookie	No	No	Yes	Yes

Basic and Digest Authentication

Web Slices hosted on servers using either Basic or Digest HTTP authentication methods can use those methods as well. The Basic method is restricted to Web Slices using HTTPS and no alternative display source, while Digest can be used over HTTP or HTTPS when no alternative display source is specified. This authentication method is typically controlled through a server configuration file. Listing 8–13 shows an Apache `.htaccess` configuration file that creates a realm for Basic authentication using a predefined password file.

Listing 8–13. *Apache .htaccess Directive for Basic Authentication*

```
AuthType Basic
AuthName "WebSlice"
AuthUserFile /path/to/password/file/passwd
require valid-user
```

The user interface and interaction with Web Slices using these authentication methods are both clunky and incomplete. Users who have not logged in are presented with an error. To log in, a user must click the Open button. This navigates to a full IE instance, and that IE instance (which allows these authentication types) will prompt the user for credentials (Figure 8–19).

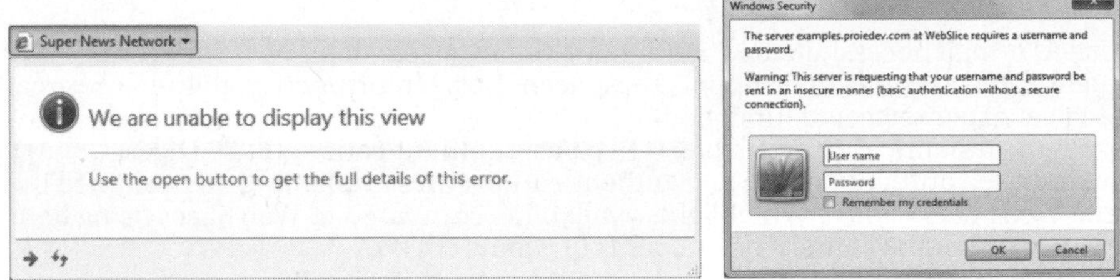

Figure 8–19. Web Slice Basic and Digest authentication in action

Credentials used by both Basic and Digest authentication can be managed through the Web Slice Properties dialog. Users can persist these settings so the Web Slice will automatically authenticate using the method made available by the web server. Again, these settings apply only to Basic and Digest authentication; cookie-based authentication cannot be persisted through this dialog (Figure 8–20).

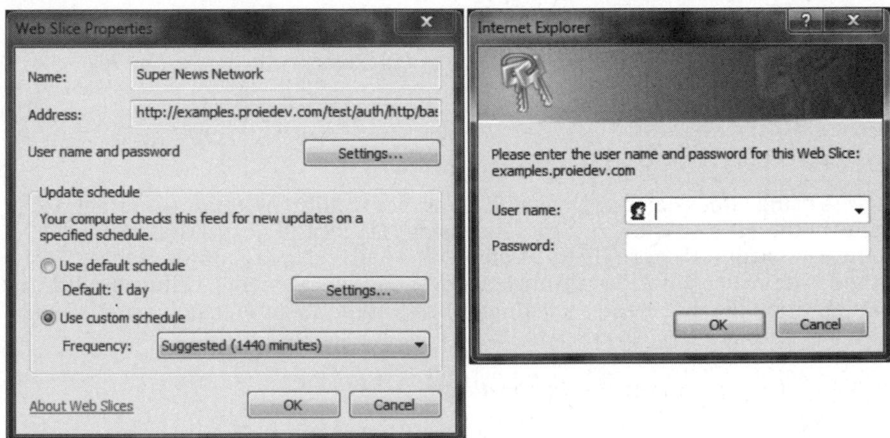

Figure 8–20. Web Slice properties dialog and username and password settings dialog

Cookie-Based Authentication

Developers using cookies for authentication can use that authentication scheme with their Web Slices as well. Session cookies stored in the main IE window are not available to Web Slices, because Web Slices are downloaded by the browser's frame, which does not share cookies with the tab process. Cookie-based authentication cannot be managed through the Web Slice Properties dialog.

Advanced Topics

The following sections describe a few more advanced customization methods that developers can use to create more dynamic experiences.

Specifying a Page's Default Web Slice

New Web Slices are presented to users in two main locations: within a page through a border and icon surrounding a Web Slice on mouse hover events, and through the RSS Feed Discovery button. The Feed Discovery button is an IE command button and is located in the browser frame.

The Feed Discovery button displays the green Web Slice icon when one or more Web Slices are present on a page. The right side of this button opens a flyout list of all Web Slices and feeds present on the page; however, the top-level button installs only one Web Slice at a time. By default, IE will install the first Web Slice encountered on the page during parsing when this button is clicked. Developers, however, can override this decision.

The default Web Slice to be installed from the top-level Feed Discovery button can be specified through a `<link>` tag in the `<head>` of a target document. This tag has three required attributes:

- **`rel`**: String value set to `default-slice` (required).
- **`type`**: MIME type set to `application/x-hatom` (required).
- **`href`**: `id` selector of the Web Slice to be set as default. This element must be a Web Slice's root element containing the class selector `hslice` (required).

Listing 8–14 provides a brief usage example for this tag. The document in question contains multiple Web Slices, one of which has the `id` `myWebSlice`. The `myWebSlice` Web Slice is to be named the default. A `<link>` tag is created in the `<head>` of the target document; its `rel` attribute is given the value `default-slice`, and it uses the type `application/x-hatom`. The `href` attribute is set to the anchor-formatted `id` `#myWebSlice`, telling IE to use the element called `myWebSlice` as the default Web Slice for the document.

Listing 8–14. *<link> Tag Speifying a Page's Default Web Slice*

```
<html>
  <head>
    ...
    <link rel="default-slice" type="application/x-hatom" href="#myWebSlice" />
    ...
```

Script-Based Installation

Web Slice installation may be triggered from JavaScript as an alternative to the user activating the Web Slice installation button. IE exposes the `AddToFavoritesBar` function on `window.external` to handle the installation of favorites and Web Slices. When called, IE displays the same installation dialog that is shown when a user clicks the Web Slice icon that appears in a page and the browser frame.

The `window.external.AddToFavoritesBar` method takes three parameters: the URL of a Web Slice, the title to be shown in the installation dialog, and the type (which in this case is always `slice`).

- **`URL`**: The URL to the web page containing the Web Slice's hSlice microformat definition
- **`Title`**: The title to display to the user
- **`Type`**: A string, `slice`, that indicates the content type to IE

The markup and script in Listing 8–15 demonstrates a button that uses this functionality. The object's `onclick` event makes a call to `window.external.AddToFavoritesBar`, directing IE to install the My Web Slice extension from the provided URL.

***Listing 8–15.** <button> Manually Installing a Web Slice Through Script*

```
<button onclick="window.external.AddToFavoritesBar(
        'http://examples.proiedev.com/08/manual#myWebSlice',
        'My Web Slice',
        'slice')">
    Add WebSlice to Internet Explorer
</button>
```

Web Slices specified in script are not automatically advertised to users by the IE frame's Feed Discovery icon. For security purposes, script is only permitted to call AddToFavoritesBar in response to a user-initiated action (e.g., a button or link click).

Disabling In-Document Web Slice Advertisement

The on-hover advertisement of Web Slices in a document may cause issues with the functionality or appearance of a web application. Web sites can disable in-document advertisement of Web Slices by adding a <meta> tag to the <head> of a page.

- **name**: String value set to slice (required)
- **scheme**: String value set to IE (required)
- **content**: String value set to off (required)

Disabling of in-document advertisement must be performed on a per-page basis. Developers are advised to use server-side templates to insert this <meta> tag automatically if it is required on every page.

Listing 8–16 shows a simple example of a page opting out of the on-hover advertisement feature. As in the description, a <meta> tag whose name is slice and scheme is IE is set in the <head> tag. It contains a content attribute whose value is the string off.

***Listing 8–16.** <meta> Tag That Disables In-Page Advertisement of WebSlices*

```
<html>
   <head>
      ...
      <meta name="slice" scheme="IE" content="off"/>
      ...
```

Summary

Web Slices offer an easy way for developers to syndicate site content in both new and existing applications, all without requiring major changes to application and page design. I began this chapter by introducing the concept of Web Slices, the hAtom microformat structure, and the basic installation process for users. I continued by discussing styles, alternative sources, and authentication scenarios; and I ended with a quick run-through of some more advanced topics regarding installation and defaults. I hope you see the value of Web Slices as a way to drive users to your applications and integrate your application into IE itself.

CHAPTER 9

Building Search Provider and Search Suggestion Extensions

IE 7 introduced a popular feature called *Instant Search*. This places a search box into the top-level browser chrome, enabling fast access to search without having to first navigate to the URL of a search engine.

In this chapter I discuss how you can easily build traditional search providers and visual search providers for your site or third-party services. I begin by discussing the OpenSearch specification, followed by the format and structure of search providers. I follow this up with a walkthrough of using OpenSearch to construct a basic search provider. Next up are visual search providers, where I discuss the process of building this enhanced extension for IE 8 and higher. I end the chapter with some guidelines and advanced topics, touching on issues such as user preferences and external installation options.

Understanding Search Providers

Search providers are a simple extension that provides a powerful search experience within the browser frame. IE completely manages the experience for users and developers, cutting down on development time and providing a consistent, predictable experience for end users (Figure 9–1).

Figure 9–1. *The Inline Search box*

The search box is located in the top-right corner of the browser, next to the address bar. This prominent location is easily accessible and allows a user to easily perform the common task of searching without having to directly access a provider first. Users can quickly focus on the box by pressing CTRL+L.

The Quick Pick menu, shown in Figure 9–2, allows users to quickly switch between search providers without having to leave the Inline Search area. When text is entered into the Inline Search box, the drop-down displays with icons referencing as many search providers as can fit in the given space. Clicking one of these icons will reroute a search query to the chosen search provider. The Find button brings up the page-search toolbar, allowing users to search content within the current page rather than sending a search query to a search engine.

Figure 9–2. The Quick Pick menu

Search providers may optionally support *search suggestions.* Search suggestions are proposed queries returned from a search provider as data is typed into the Instant Search box. Providers that implement this feature are sent the current contents of the Inline Search text box as a user types in a query. Providers may return result sets, which are shown in the drop-down above the Quick Pick menu. Figure 9–3 shows an example of search suggestions returned from the ESPN.com search provider; a query of "LeBron" returns four possible results for the query as typed.

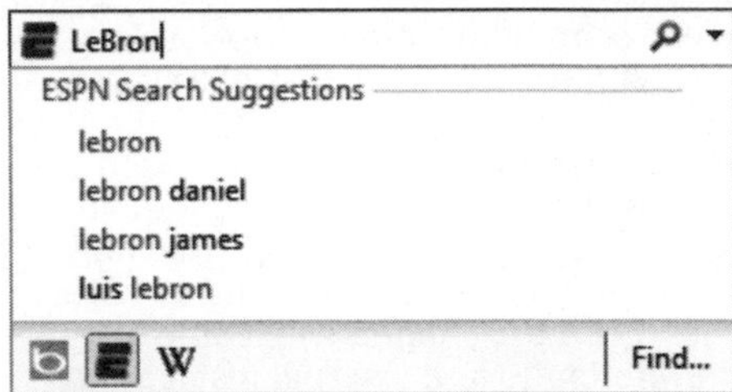

Figure 9–3. Search Suggestions drop-down

Search suggestions can help to refine search queries before they're executed, with the goal of cutting down the amount of time it takes for users to search a given topic (much like the inline autocomplete present on modern operating systems and Ajax-based web sites).

IE 8 introduces another form of search suggestion, called *visual search suggestions.* As the name implies, visual search suggestions return rich suggestions alongside text-based search suggestions. Figure 9–4 highlights the visual search suggestions for a query of Wikipedia with the term "Aleister."

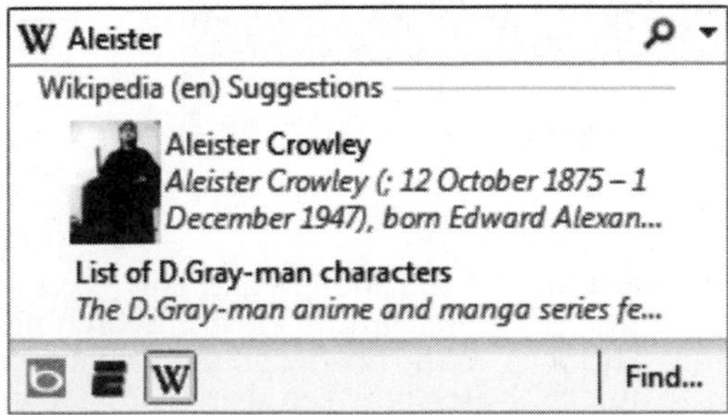

Figure 9–4. Visual search suggestions

Figure 9–5 shows the Inline Search context menu. The listing order of extensions is controlled by the Internet Options control panel item. The "Find on this Page" menu item directs the current query in the Inline Search box to the inline find toolbar for the current page, allowing users to apply the query to contents of the current tab rather than to an external search engine. The "Find More Providers" option launches the IE Add-Ons Gallery, allowing users to find and install more search providers into IE. Last, the Manage Search Providers command launches the Search Providers pane of the Manage Add-Ons dialog, giving users an opportunity to manage current search provider settings, set defaults, or uninstall providers.

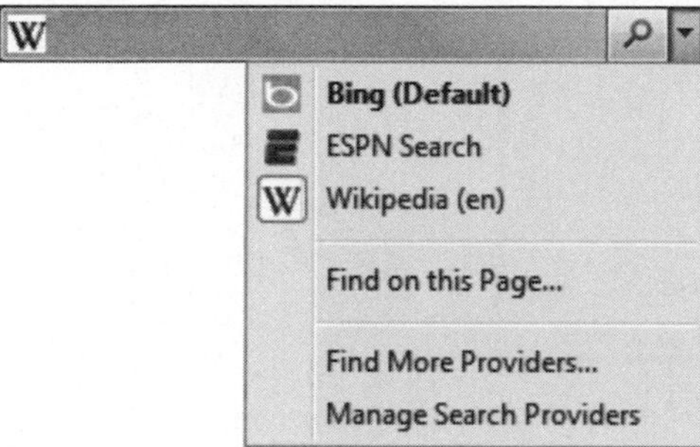

Figure 9–5. The Search Provider context menu

As mentioned earlier in this section, IE provides an easy-to-use management system for search providers. When a user or site attempts to install a search provider, the search provider management dialog launches to inform a user of the pending action (Figure 9–6, left). Because search providers are a nonbinary extensibility mechanism, they are safer than traditional add-ons, and no additional security dialogs are shown.

Installed search providers can be managed and removed through the Manage Add-Ons dialog, a simple interface exposing the metadata and settings for each search provider (Figure 9–6, right).

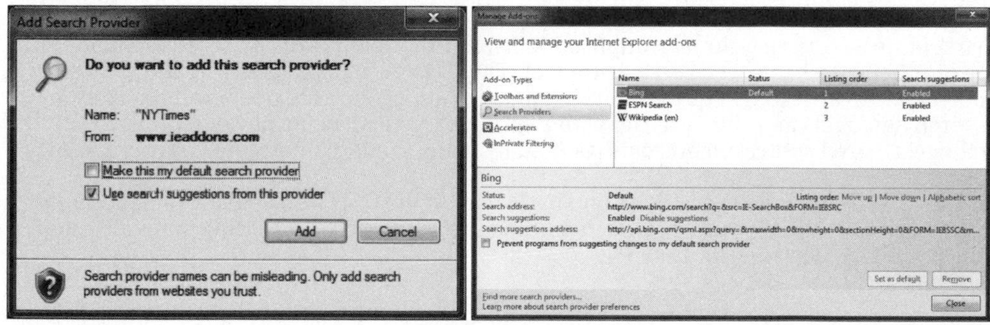

Figure 9–6. Search Provider installation dialog and search provider management through the Manage Add-Ons dialog

The IE Add-Ons Gallery offers a complementary experience to the management experience provided in the browser. Found at `www.ieaddons.com`, the gallery allows users to find and install search providers they may be interested in (Figure 9–7).

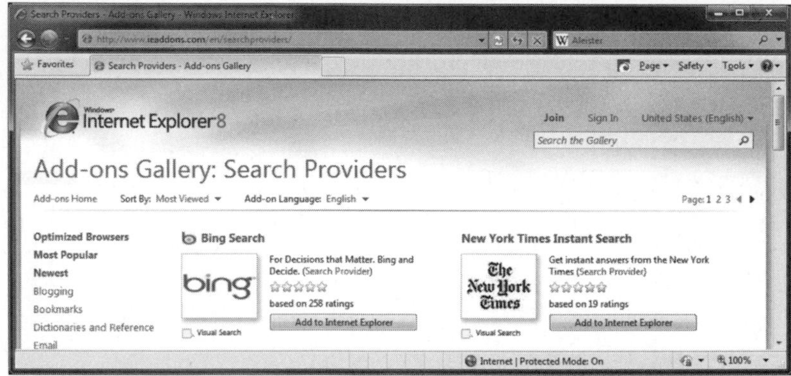

Figure 9–7. The Search Providers gallery, part of the Add-Ons Gallery at www.ieaddons.com

This section highlighted the high-level experiences that search providers provide to a user's IE configuration. The next sections highlight the methods and means developers can use to implement the features described here.

The OpenSearch Description Format, JSON Search Suggestions, and XML Search Suggestions Specifications

The OpenSearch Description Format (OSD) schema defines the markup used to create search providers for IE and other modern browsers implementing search providers. This allows client applications such as browsers to integrate web services into an application itself without requiring a user to manually visit a search engine or other searchable web service provider. The JSON Search Suggestions and XML Search Suggestions specifications are extensions to the OSD that allow applications to query web services for intermediate search data that can provide a user with a subset of results; the most well-known example of comes with the text-based autocomplete features used by many modern operating systems and Ajax-based web sites.

The following sections outline the structure and basic uses of the OSD, JSON Search Suggestions, and XML Search Suggestions specifications. Understanding their use is key in building both basic and advanced search provider extensions for use in IE.

OpenSearch Description Format Specification

The OpenSearch Description (OSD) Format specification defines a format for sharing results between a search engine and a consuming application. IE 7 and above allow web sites to expose their search capabilities by describing them using OSD files that the browser uses to extend the browser's search box.

The most basic search provider, shown in Listing 9–1 can be created with less than ten lines of XML markup! Such providers contain basic metadata such as a short name, description, tags, contact information, and the URL pointing to the search engine provider. This example is from OpenSearch.org.

Listing 9–1. *A Simple OpenSearch 1.1 Draft 4 Description File, As Shown on OpenSearch.org*

```
<?xml version="1.0" encoding="UTF-8"?>
 <OpenSearchDescription xmlns="http://a9.com/-/spec/opensearch/1.1/">
   <ShortName>Web Search</ShortName>
   <Description>Use Example.com to search the Web.</Description>
   <Tags>example web</Tags>
   <Contact>admin@example.com</Contact>
   <Url type="application/rss+xml"
        template="http://example.com/?q={searchTerms}&amp;pw={startPage?}&amp;format=rss"/>
 </OpenSearchDescription>
```

More complicated search providers are still relatively simple to develop compared to other IE extensions. Listing 9–2 shows a more complicated example using most of the tags and some extensions defined by the OpenSearch specification. As one can see, even this more complicated extension is relatively simple to construct and easily understood given the declarative nature of the markup.

Listing 9–2. *A Detailed OpenSearch 1.1 Draft 4 Description File, As Shown on OpenSearch.org*

```
<?xml version="1.0" encoding="UTF-8"?>
 <OpenSearchDescription xmlns="http://a9.com/-/spec/opensearch/1.1/">
   <ShortName>Web Search</ShortName>
   <Description>Use Example.com to search the Web.</Description>
   <Tags>example web</Tags>
   <Contact>admin@example.com</Contact>
   <Url type="application/atom+xml"
        template="http://example.com/?q={searchTerms}&amp;pw=
        {startPage?}&amp;format=atom"/>
   <Url type="application/rss+xml"
        template="http://example.com/?q={searchTerms}&amp;pw={startPage?}&amp;
        format=rss"/>
   <Url type="text/html"
        template="http://example.com/?q={searchTerms}&amp;pw={startPage?}"/>
   <LongName>Example.com Web Search</LongName>

   <Image height="16" width="16" type="image/vnd.microsoft.icon">
        http://example.com/websearch.ico</Image>
   <Query role="example" searchTerms="cat" />
   <Developer>Example.com Development Team</Developer>
   <Attribution>
     Search data Copyright 2010, Example.com, Inc., All Rights Reserved
   </Attribution>
   <SyndicationRight>open</SyndicationRight>
   <AdultContent>false</AdultContent>
   <Language>en-us</Language>
   <OutputEncoding>UTF-8</OutputEncoding>
   <InputEncoding>UTF-8</InputEncoding>
 </OpenSearchDescription>
```

OpenSearch Description Format Tags

OpenSearch tags are used to define the metadata for an OpenSearch search provider. Each tag provides a unique element of metadata for a search provider. The root tag for an OSD document is the `<OpenSearchDescription>` element; all other tags in an OSD file are children of this tag. Table 9–1 defines the tags that may be used in an OSD file to define a search provider extension.

***Table 9–1.** Tags Used by the OpenSearch Description Format to Define a Search Provider Extension*

Tag	Parent Tag	Description	Required
`<OpenSearchDescription>`	--	Root tag of an OpenSearch provider. The element must appear once and only once per document and may be the only element (besides the XML file header) at this level.	Yes
`<ShortName>`	`<OpenSearchDescription>`	A brief title that identifies the search provider, containing 16 characters or less. The element may only appear once.	Yes
`<Description>`	`<OpenSearchDescription>`	Description of the search provider containing 1,024 characters or less. The element must appear exactly once.	Yes
`<Url>`	`<OpenSearchDescription>`	The URL by which the browser interfaces with the search provider. This element must appear at least once.	Yes
`<Contact>`	`<OpenSearchDescription>`	The e-mail address of the maintainer of the search provider. The element may be used only once.	No
`<Tags>`	`<OpenSearchDescription>`	A set of words describing the purpose of the search provider; a list of categories delimited by a space whose overall text length is less than 256 characters. It may be used only once.	No
`<LongName>`	`<OpenSearchDescription>`	A long title that identifies the search provider, containing 48 characters or less. It may be used only once.	No

Tag	Parent Tag	Description	Required
`<Image>`	`<OpenSearchDescription>`	URL that identifies an image that can be associated with this search provider. Must point to an image whose MIME type is supported by the browser. This is represented by a 16×16-pixel icon with a MIME type of either `image/x-icon` or `image/vnd.microsoft.icon`.	No
`<Query>`	`<OpenSearchDescription>`	An example query that is shown to users. It may be used one or more times.	No
`<Developer>`	`<OpenSearchDescription>`	The name identifying the creator of a search provider; contains 64 characters or less. It may be used once.	No
`<Attribution>`	`<OpenSearchDescription>`	A list of all sources that are responsible for the content returned by the search provider; contains 256 characters or less. It may be used once.	No
`<SyndicationRight>`	`<OpenSearchDescription>`	A value indicating the copyright of content returned by a search provider. It may be used one time.	No
`<AdultContent>`	`<OpenSearchDescription>`	A Boolean value indicating whether or not results returned by a search provider include "adult content." The term "adult content" used by the specification is vague and does not represent a universally defined term, rather a "good-faith effort to indicate when there is a possibility that search results may contain material inappropriate for all audiences," according to the OpenSearch specification group. It may be used one time.	No

Tag	Parent Tag	Description	Required
<Language>	<OpenSearchDescription>	String indicating the languages that a search engine used by a search provider supports. The value must conform to the language identifiers and formats described in both the XML 1.0 Language Identification specification and RFC 3066. This element should exist once for every language supported, but this element is not required.	No
<InputEncoding>	<OpenSearchDescription>	Like the language tag, this element exists zero or more times and indicates the output formats (such as UTF-16) supported by the search provider. The default value is UTF-8, but alternate encodings defined by this tag should conform to the formats defined in the XML 1.0 Character Encodings specification and the IANA Character Set Assignments specification.	No
<OutputEncoding>	<OpenSearchDescription>	Following the same concept as the <InputEncoding> tag, this element appears zero or more times and refers to the output formats supported by a search provider. The default value is UTF-8; however, alternative values may be specified using encoding values that conform to the XML 1.0 Character Encoding definitions and the IANA Language Definition specification.	No

The OpenSearch description file begins with the root tag, <OpenSearchDescription>. This tag signals to the browser or other client that the file is beginning. This element contains all other tags used by the OSD file, occurs only once, and must be closed at the end of any OSD file.

The <ShortName> tag defines a short name used by a browser or other client. It allows for quick identification of a search provider extension. This text contained within this tag must be 16 characters or less in length.

Search providers may describe their purpose through the <Description> tag. Text within this tag informs users of the purpose of a specific search provider extension.

The `<Url>` tag specifies the URL by which the browser interfaces with the search provider. The `<Url>` tag is used by IE to link a search query. The values contained within this element point to search results or search suggestions. Table 9–2 shows the attributes that can be placed within the `<Url>` tag.

Table 9–2. *Attributes for the <Url> Tag in the OSD Specification*

Attribute	Description	Default Value	Required
`template`	The URL template that, when completed by the client, represents a valid and navigable URL to the search provider's web service. This attribute typically contains a URL using one or more URL template variables (defined in the next section).	None specified	No
`type`	The MIME type of the template defined in the `template` attribute. This attribute is required and must contain a valid MIME type that is understood by the client.	None specified	No
`rel`	The role of the resource returned with respect to the description document. This attribute, when present, must contain a space-delimited list of valid tokens used by the `rel` attribute: either `results`, `suggestions`, `self`, or `collection`.	Results	No
`indexOffset`	The index number of the first search result as understood by the web service returning results.	1	No
`pageOffset`	The page number of the set of results where the first result is located in reference to the web service returning data.	1	No

The attributes of the `<Url>` tag define the external resource IE will use for a search query. The `template` attribute (detailed later in this section) defines a URL template used by the browser to send query information placed into the search box to a service. The `type` attribute specifies the MIME type of the external resource. The role of the resource is defined through the `rel` attribute. `indexOffset` highlights the index number of the first search result from the web service. Finally, the `pageOffset` attribute defines the page number of the set of results where the first result is located (with respect to the web service returning the data).

The `<Contact>` element represents contact information of the developer or maintainer of the search provider an OSD file defines. This optional element should be coded in the form of an e-mail address (whose format is defined by RFC 2822).

A search provider may use the optional `<Tags>` element to list a number of single-word, space-delimited descriptors that define the intent and purpose of a search provider.

The optional `<LongName>` attribute allows a search provider to expose a longer version of the short name identifier specified in the required `<ShortName>` tag. This tag may contain text up to 64 characters in length.

Developers wishing to provide a visual tag for their search providers can do so through the `<Image>` tag. This tag is used once for every size image offered to clients displaying images associated with a search provider. The URL where the image can be found is set as the inner text of this tag. Table 9–3 highlights optional attributes developers may set when defining an image.

***Table 9–3.** Attributes for the <Image> Tag in the OSD Specification*

Attribute	Description	Default Value	Required
height	The height of the image in pixels. This must be a nonnegative integer, but the attribute itself is optional.	None specified	No
width	The width of the image in pixels. This must be a nonnegative integer, but the attribute itself is optional.	None specified	No
type	The MIME type of the image returned by its source. The string of this attribute must represent a valid MIME type that is recognized by the client; however, the existence of the attribute itself is not required.	None specified	No

Each image tag has three optional attributes. The width and height attributes define the width and height of an image in pixels. The MIME type of the image may be specified using the type attribute. Developers who wish to have their search provider displayed properly in IE should include an <Image> tag pointing to a 16×16-pixel icon with a MIME type of either image/x-icon or image/vnd.microsoft.icon.

Search providers can define the search requests a client may perform by way of the <Query> tag. The element attributes of each query tag correspond to the search parameters used by URL templates contained in <Url> tags. IE does not use this tag as part of its Search Provider specification.

The <Developer> tag reveals the entity responsible for creating (and potentially updating) the search provider. It may contain any plain text that is 64 characters or less in length.

Developers may use the <Attribution> tag to list all sources that should be credited for content displayed in the search field. This text can contain any form of copyright information as long as it contains 256 or fewer characters of text.

Search provider extensions flag their content for clients when their return content might not be appropriate for all audiences. The <AdultContent> tag, which is optional (and not recognized by IE), may contain a value of either true of false; true signifies that content returned by a provider may not be appropriate for all audiences. Audience inappropriateness is not clearly defined by the OSD specification and should be used by developers at their own discretion.

The <Language> tag allows a search provider to tell IE or another client what languages are supported by the extension. This tag is not required, and the absence of it signifies a language- or culture-neutral search provider. If a search provider supports all languages, it may include a language tag with the inner text of *. For specific languages, one language tag should be present for each language supported by a search provider.

The <InputEncoding> and <OutputEncoding> tags specify the input and output encodings supported by a search provider.

Template Variables for the <Url> Tag

URLs specified within the <Url> tag contain one or more template variables. Template variables allow browsers or other clients to substitute these values for values entered by users or computed by the client. Table 9–4 shows the variables that may be used in the template attribute of the <Url> tag.

***Table 9–4.** Template Variables Used by the <Url> Tag*

Variable	Description	Restrictions	Required
`{searchTerms}`	Replaced with the search terms specified by a user in the browser.	Must be URL-encoded	Yes
`{referrer}`	Allows a web service to determine what UI element was used for the query. In IE, one of two values may be returned: `IE-SearchBox`, if the query was made through the search box, or `IE-Address`, if it originated from the address bar.	None	No
`{count}`	The number of search results per page to return to the browser.	Must be a nonnegative integer	No
`{startIndex}`	The index of the first search result to show.	Must be an integer	No
`{startPage}`	The page of the first search result to show.	Must be an integer	No
`{language}`	The desired language for the results be returned in.	Must have a value that conforms to the language identifiers and formats described in both the XML 1.0 Language Identification specification and RFC 3066	No
`{inputEncoding}`	String indicating the character encoding used by the browser for this search request.	Must conform to the formats defined in the XML 1.0 Character Encodings specification and the IANA Character Set Assignments specification	No
`{outputEncoding}`	String indicating the character encoding desired by the browser for responses back from the search provider's web service.	Must conform to the formats defined in the XML 1.0 Character Encodings specification and the IANA Character Set Assignments specification	No

OpenSearch Extensions

The OpenSearch Description format provides a loose structure whose core is geared toward a simple definition of a search provider. This simple nature and loose structure also affords it the property of being a very rich platform that can be extended and customized by individual clients (hopefully with the ultimate goal of integrating extensions into the mainstream specification).

IE uses two major OpenSearch extensions that enhance the overall search provider experience in the browser: the JSON Search Suggestion and the XML Search specification extensions. As these names imply, the extensions used by IE allow users to receive search suggestions before a full query is executed. The next two sections describe how IE uses these extensions to implement search suggestions within the browser frame; later sections in this chapter provide concrete examples of how developers can implement these features in real-world extensions.

Developers looking to build more powerful platforms using the OpenSearch Description format can start by investigating the extensions that already exist on the OpenSearch web site, `www.opensearch.org`.

JSON Search Suggestion Extension

The JSON Search Suggestion extension is an extension to the OpenSearch Description format that allows a web service to return text-based suggestions for a search provider. Clients such as IE display these search suggestions during the construction of a query. IE displays data returned through this mechanism while a user is typing in the Inline Search box.

This extension is constructed using the JSON (JavaScript Object Notation) format. The basics of this notation are described in earlier chapters. Table 9–5 describes the values, types, and description used in this format.

Table 9–5. *JSON Search Suggestion Extension Values and Descriptions*

Value	Type	Description	Required
`Query`	String	Search term requested by a user	Yes
`completions`	Array	Text-based search suggestions for the specified query	Yes
`descriptions`	Array	Alternate information about the specified query	No
`Urls`	Array	List of URLs that should be used if a user clicks a specific search suggestion	No

The actual format is stored in a JSON structure like that in Listing 9–3. The first entry is the query entered by the user. The next value is an array of completion suggestions; these represent completed search entries for which the query matches. Next is an array containing the descriptions of these matches—values whose index corresponds to the associated completion index. Last is an array containing the associated URLs for these matches (again, with indexes matching the associated completion index.)

Listing 9–3. *Generic Usage of the JSON Search Suggestion Extension*

```
[ query ,3
   [  completion_0 ,  completion_1 , ... ,  completion_n ] ,
   [ description_0 , description_1 , ... , description_n ] ,
   [        url_0 ,         url_1 , ... ,         url_n ]
]
```

XML Search Suggestion Extension

The XML Search Suggestions specification is an extension to the OpenSearch Description format that allows an application to receive rich search suggestions from an online service. Much like the JSON Search Suggestion extension, search suggestions generated using this extension are displayed to a user before a query is performed and represent results returned from a web service based on an incomplete query. In the case of IE, this incomplete query represents a set of text in the Inline Search box that may or may not be completed.

Listing 9–4 is an example XML Search Suggestion file provided by Microsoft on the home page of the XML Search Suggestions specification page. In this example, a query of "xbox" returns a number of responses in the form of both text-based and visual suggestions.

Listing 9–4. *An Example XML Search Suggestion File Provided by the Specification on MSDN* *(www.msdn.com)*

```
<?xml version="1.0"?>
<SearchSuggestion xmlns ="http://schemas.microsoft.com/Search/2008/suggestions">
   <Query>xbox</Query>
   <Section>
      <Separator title="My Visual Suggestions"/>
      <Item>
         <Text>Xbox 360 Live Games</Text>
         <Image source="http://www.example.com/live.jpg"
            alt="Xbox 360 Live Games" width="75" height="75"/>
      </Item>
      <Item>
         <Description>Game console systems and packages at a great deal.</Description>
         <Image source="http://www.example.com/xboxconsole.jpg"
            alt="Xbox 360 Consoles" width="75" height="75"/>
         <Url>http://www.example.com/games.aspx?q="Xbox 360"</Url>
      </Item>
      <Separator title="My Text Suggestions"/>
      <Item>
         <Text>Xbox 360</Text>
      </Item>
      <Item>
         <Text>Xbox cheats</Text>
         <Description>Codes and walkthroughs</Description>
      </Item>
      <Item>
         <Text>Xbox 360 games</Text>
         <Description>Games and accessories</Description>
         <Url>http://www.example.com/games</Url>
      </Item>
      <Separator />
      <Item>
         <Text>xbox 360 lowest price</Text>
      </Item>
      <Item>
         <Text>xbox 360 news</Text>
      </Item>
   </Section>
</SearchSuggestion>
```

Items in this example are contained within a section and are separated out by type; here, the query returns visual results under the label "My Visual Suggestions" and text-based results under the label "My Text Suggestions."

XML Search Suggestion Tags

As with the OpenSearch Description Format specification, the XML Search Suggestions specification employs a tree-based structure whereby XML tags define the suggestion items returned to the browser. Table 9–6 highlights the tags and ownership structure for those tags used in an XML Search Suggestion file.

Table 9–6. *Tags Used by the XML Search Suggestions Specification to Define Search Suggestion Results Returned by a Web Service*

Tag	Parent Tag	Description
`<SearchSuggestion>`	--	Root tag of an XML Search Suggestion file. There may only be one instance of this element.
`<Query>`	`<SearchSuggestion>`	Text query that was sent by the client application. There may only be one instance of this element.
`<Section>`	`<SearchSuggestion>`	Tag containing a set of items returned to the client as search suggestions. There may only be one instance of this element.
`<Item>`	`<Section>`	Element that represents a single suggestion. There may be one or more instances of this element, and all instances must contain a `<text>` tag, `<Url>` tag, or both.
`<Text>`	`<Item>`	A text-based suggestion that is part of an overall suggestion `<item>`. There may be only one instance of this element for each `<item>` instance.
`<Url>`	`<Item>`	The URL that a client will navigate to when a suggestion `<item>` is selected. There may be only one instance of this tag for each `<item>` instance.
`<Description>`	`<Item>`	A description of the search suggestion. There may be only one instance of this tag for each `<item>` instance.
`<Image>`	`<Item>`	Contains an image suggestion for a suggestion `<item>`. There may be only one instance of this tag for each `<item>` instance.
`<Separator>`	`<Section>`	Indicates the start of a group of suggestions. There may be one or more instances of this tag, though none are required.

An XML Search Suggestion file begins with a parent tag `<SearchSuggestion>`. This tag informs the browser or other application accepting this format that the search suggestions are contained within this file. This must be the first tag of the file, the file must end with its closing tag, and there may be only one of these tags in a Search Suggestion file.

The `<Query>` tag is the first child item under the `<SearchSuggestion>` root. The text contained by this tag represents the query that was sent to a web service by a client application.

The `<Section>` tag encapsulates the set of search suggestions returned by a web service. This tag contains one optional attribute, `title`, described in Table 9–7. The `title` attribute reflects the title of the overall set of search suggestions returned by a web service.

Table 9–7. *Attributes for the <Section> Tag in the XML Search Suggestions Specification*

Attribute	Description	Default Value	Required
`Title`	Represents the title of the overall search suggestion results returned by a web service	Empty string	No

Individual search suggestions are defined through the `<Item>` tag. The content of each suggestion, be it text or image, is enclosed within this tag.

The `<Text>` tag represents the text that corresponds to a search suggestion item. For instance, a search on "xbox," as shown in the previous example, might return an entry with the text "XBOX 360 Brand New $100."

The browser will navigate to a URL associated with an item when that item is clicked; this URL is defined through the `<Url>` tag. This tag specifies a target address that should bc navigated to whenever the search suggestion is clicked by a user.

The `<Description>` describes an item. This optional tag may be used by clients to provide extended information on a suggestion. IE 8 displays this information below the text for a search suggestion item when shown in the Instant Search drop-down box.

Items can contain a descriptive image defined through the `<Image>` tag. This tag is optional but may appear at most once within an item tag. Table 9–8 defines the attributes associated with this tag.

Table 9–8. *Attributes for the <Image> Tag in the XML Search Suggestions Specification*

Attribute	Description	Default Value	Required
`source`	The URL of the image to be used.	None specified	Yes
`alt`	Alternate text for the image.	None specified	No
`width`	Width of the image in pixels.	None specified	No
`height`	Height of the image in pixels.	None specified	No
`align`	The preferred vertical alignment for the image. Possible values are top, middle, or bottom.	Top	No

The location of an image is specified by a URL in the `source` attribute. Alternate text for the image—especially important for accessibility use by the client—may be specified in the `alt` attribute. The `width` and `height` attributes specify an explicit width and height for the image in pixels. Lastly, the `align` attribute allows a developer to set a preference for vertical alignment of an image with respect to its associated text and description; by default, it is shown next to the top of a corresponding text block in IE.

<Separator> is the last tag defined by this specification, representing a physical separation between groups of <Item> tags. This allows users to visually organize results returned by a web service into logical groups.

The <Separator> tag has one attribute, `title`, defined in Table 9–9. The `title` attribute contains text that is displayed as part of the physical separator between <Item> instances. Developers can compare this to the title shown as part of a panel (Java) or group box (Windows Forms and Delphi).

Table 9–9. *Attributes for the <Separator> Tag in the XML Search Suggestions Specification*

Attribute	Description	Default Value
`title`	Represents the title that should be shown in the separator area by the client	Empty string

Building a Basic Search Provider

The process of building a basic search provider is simple—developers can construct a new search provider pointing to an existing web service with just a handful of XML tags!

Simple search providers can be built to direct users to existing web services. In a nutshell, this means developers can add search providers to complement their web sites without changing a single line of code.

An example of a basic search provider would be one that allows developers to search a programming information site such as Stack Overflow. This search provider uses an OSD file to direct IE's search box to an existing web service—in this case, the Stack Overflow search page. Listing 9–5 shows an example provider that lets a user search Google.com from the browser's search box.

Listing 9–5. *A Search Provider That Directs a Query to Stack Overflow (www.stackoverflow.com)*

```
<OpenSearchDescription xmlns="http://a9.com/-/spec/opensearch/1.1/">
   <ShortName>Example: Stack Overflow</ShortName>
   <Description>Search Stack Overflow for programming topics</Description>
   <InputEncoding>UTF-8</InputEncoding>
   <Url type="text/html" method="get"
        template="http://www.stackoverflow.com/search?q={searchTerms}" />
</OpenSearchDescription>
```

Installing and Using Search Providers

IE offers a streamlined installation and management experience for both developers and end users. Developers wishing to surface search providers on their pages can do so through both a `<link>` tag and a function exposed on the `window.exernal` JavaScript object. Users can install search providers either through the Instant Search box's context menu or through links on pages that implement a call to the relevant JavaScript function. The following sections describe both the developer and user experience for surfacing, installing, and managing search providers.

The search provider installation experience is managed by IE. This allows developers and users to take part in the installation process and provides a consistent experience for all search provider extensions. This installation process is kicked off by a call to the `window.external.AddSearchProvider` function; the URL passed to this function is the location of the OSD file targeted for installation. This is shown in Listing 9–6.

Listing 9–6. *Code Used to Request Search Provider Installation, in This Case in Response to an onclick Event*

```
<a href="#"
onclick="window.external.AddSearchProvider('http://www.textd.com/crowley/sp/StackOverflow.xml'
)">Add the Stack Overflow Search Provider Example</a>
```

Figure 9–8 demonstrates the installation dialog presented to users when installing the Stack Overflow search provider from the last section. Users have the option to make a search provider their default and, if the add-on allows, to use search suggestions returned from a provider's target web service.

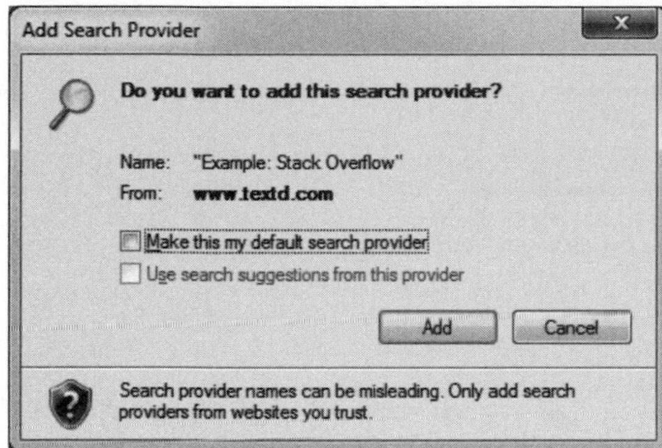

Figure 9–8. *The search provider installation dialog*

Once installed, this search provider is shown in the drop-down menu of the search box, and its icon is added to the Quick Pick menu (see Figure 9–9). If the search provider was selected to be the default search provider, it is shown at the top in bold lettering, and its name is preceded by the text "(Default)."

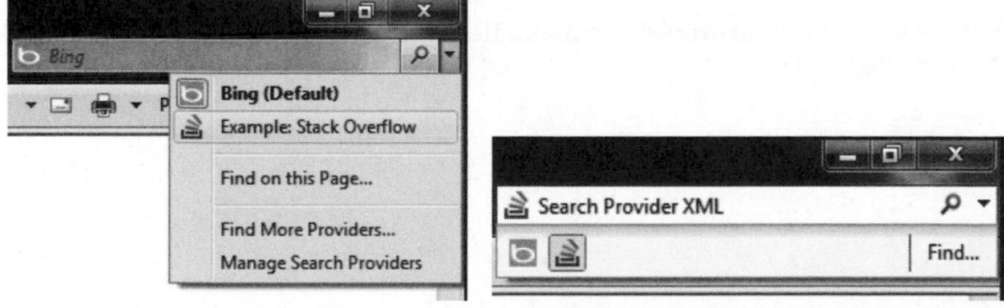

Figure 9–9. *The Stack Overflow search provider shown in the search provider menu and Quck Pick menu*

When a search query is placed into the search box, the URL template (defined in the `template` attribute of the `<Url>` tag in the previous section) is filled in and navigated to. Figure 9–10 shows the result of the query "Search Provider XML" being passed to the web service from this search provider.

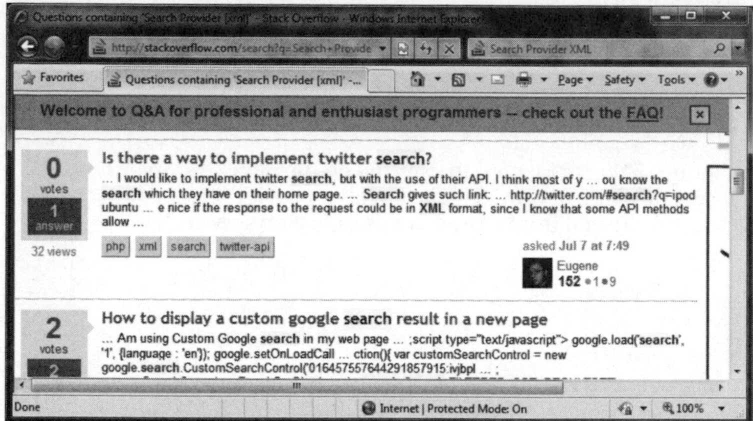

Figure 9–10. The search result page shown after using the Stack Overflow search provider

Advertising Search Providers

IE allows search providers to be discovered through the browser frame. Web pages can let users know that search providers are offered on the page through a `<link>` tag. The browser will notify users that a search provider is available on those pages by changing the color of the Inline Search drop-down chevron (Figure 9–11).

Figure 9–11. Search provider notification for pages using a <link> tag

Users who click this chevron will notice a drop-down menu that includes new search providers that are offered on the current page (Figure 9–12).

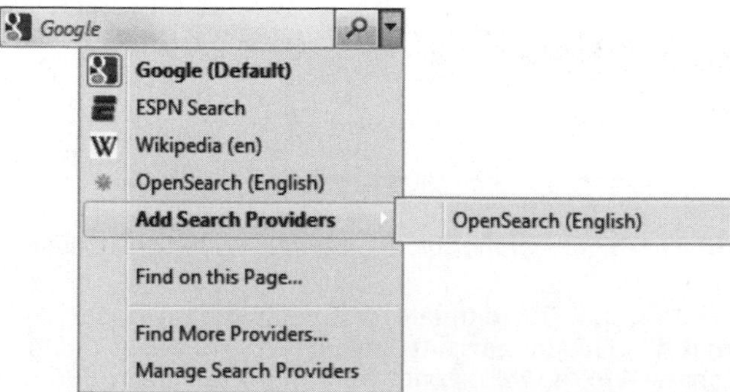

Figure 9–12. Drop-down revealing new search providers for a web page

Developers can place `<link>` tags on a page to reveal search providers in this way. The link tag has four attributes, as described in Table 9–10.

***Table 9–10.** Attributes and value information for surfacing a search provider via an HTML <link> tag*

Attribute	Description	Required
`title`	Title of the search provider. This typically corresponds to the text specified in the `<ShortName>` tag of an OSD file.	Yes
`rel`	Defines the relationship of the linked object to the current page. This value must be "`search`."	Yes
`type`	MIME type indicating that the value contained by the link tag refers to a search provider. This value must be "`application/opensearchdescription+xml`."	Yes
`href`	URL pointing to the OSD file for the search provider.	Yes

Managing Search Providers

Search providers are managed by end users once installed on a system. Users can manage search providers through the Search Providers pane of the Manage Add-Ons dialog. This pane is shown in Figure 9–13.

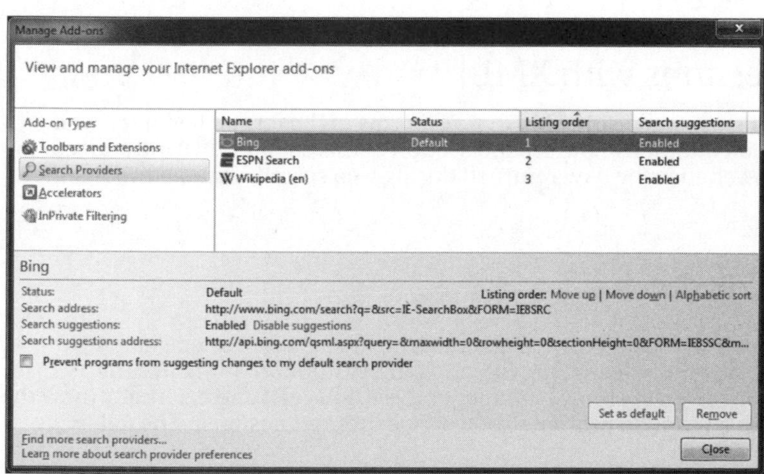

***Figure 9–13.** The Search Providers pane in the Manage Add-Ons dialog*

Each installed search provider is listed in a list box contained within the Search Providers pane. The default provider is listed at the top and has a listing order of `1`. Each subsequent provider is listed below it in the order it was installed; each listing order number is increased sequentially for each.

Detailed information, metadata, and commands for the selected search provider are shown in the Details pane below the list of search providers. The detailed information and command set includes the following:

- **Status**: Information on whether a search provider is selected as default.
- **Search address**: The URL used when executing a search from the Inline Search box.
- **Search suggestions**: Information regarding whether search suggestions for a specific search provider are allowed (enabled) or not (disabled).
- **Search suggestions address**: The address used by a search provider when returning search suggestions for a partial query typed into the Inline Search box. When a search provider contains only text-based suggestions, this URL represents the URL pointing to a JSON Search Suggestion result. When a search provider uses enhanced visual suggestions or both text-based and visual suggestions, this link refers to the URL returning data conforming to the XML Search Suggestions specification.
- **Listing order**: Allows a user to move the current item up or down, or sort all items (save for the default item) by alphabetical order instead of order of installation.
- **Prevent programs from changing my default search provider**: Prevents applications from editing the registry to change a user's selected default search provider.
- **Set as default**: Sets the currently selected provider as the default search provider.
- **Remove**: Uninstalls the currently selected provider.

Returning Visual Suggestions with XML

Enhanced search suggestions can be returned using XML that conforms to the format laid out in the XML Search Suggestions specification outlined in the second section of this chapter. IE 8 introduced this open specification in an attempt to enhance the data returned during web searches made through the Inline Search box.

Advanced Topics

Search providers are simple on their face, mostly since IE abstracts the installation, management, instantiation, and running of these providers. Search providers can be customized more fully by examining the options available both internally (how IE manages these add-ons) and externally (how the overall system built by Microsoft can be used to promote and surface these extensions). The following sections shed light on both of these areas.

Building Cross-Browser Search Providers

The OpenSearch Description format allows developers to not only build powerful web service extensions for IE, but also extensions that work across multiple browser. Search providers that properly conform to the OSD may be used in other browsers that support the schema.

At the time of writing, search providers written using OSD can be installed and loaded within IE 7+, Firefox 2.0+, and Google Chrome. Each browser supports its own subset of XML tags defined by this format, so some features discussed in this chapter may not be available in those browsers. Developers should consult developer documentation for each browser manufacturer to ensure that cross-browser search providers allow for a consistent experience across clients.

Adding Search Providers to the IE Add-Ons Gallery

The IE Add-Ons Gallery (`www.ieaddons.com`) provides a way for developers to promote their add-ons online. The gallery is a web site that puts many types of IE add-ons (search providers, Accelerators, toolbars, etc.) in one location. It presents these add-ons to users, categorized by their add-on type and goals. Users can download and install add-ons directly from the web site.

Add-ons posted to the gallery web site are not immediately available to users. Developers' add-on submission and metadata (such as description and home page) are passed to Microsoft for approval. Microsoft employees and contractors hand-check the provided information, install the add-on, and reply back (typically) within a few business days regarding the acceptance or rejection of an upload. If accepted, an add-on is available for download by all users of the web site.

Developers looking to place their add-on onto this web site must sign up for and log into an account on the gallery home page. Figure 9–14 shows both the signup an login pages on the gallery site. The account information here is not linked to a Microsoft Live ID account used across other Microsoft properties; the username and password entered here are specific to the gallery.

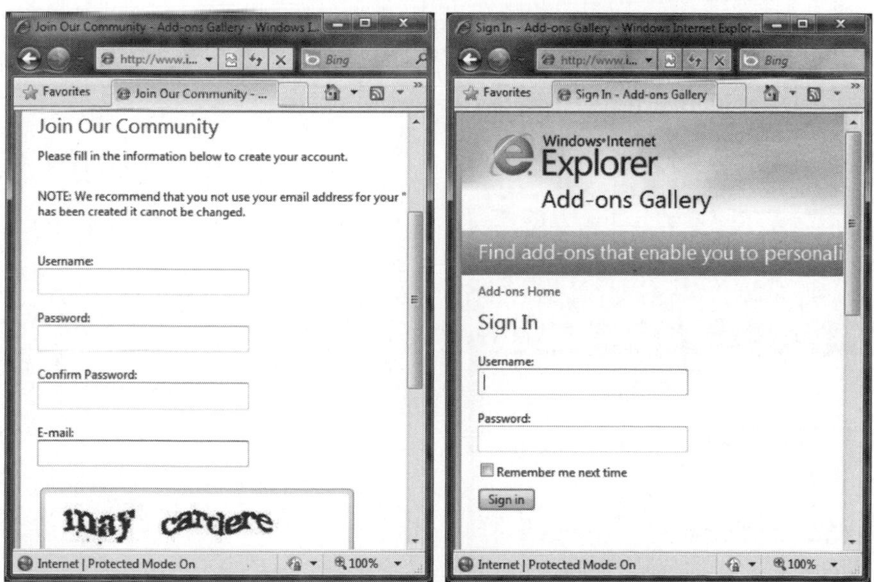

***Figure 9–14.** The signup and login pages of the IE Add-Ons Gallery*

The Your Account page—accessible after the previous process is complete—has two main functions: showing the add-ons currently being offered by the developer and providing a way for developers to submit a new add-on for approval. Figure 9–15 shows this page.

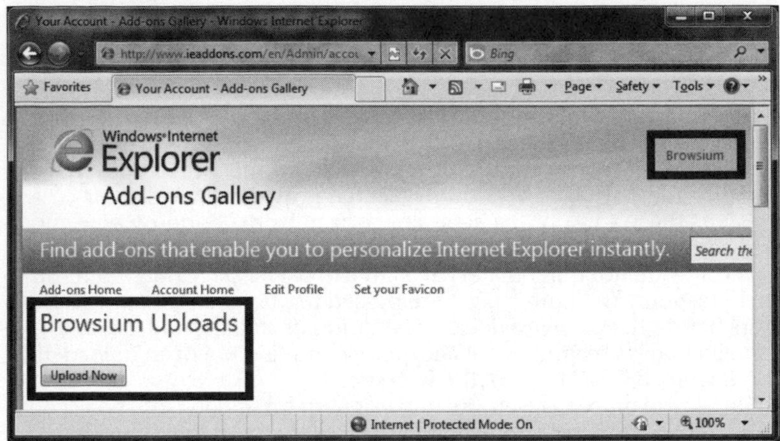

Figure 9–15. The account page within the IE Add-Ons Gallery

New add-ons can be posted to the gallery by way of the Upload Now button on this page.

The Gallery Upload page presents developers with a number of fields that can be used to describe the add-on. For each add-on type (in this instance, a search provider), developers can upload the corresponding add-on file in the appropriate field. Figure 9–16 shows this page.

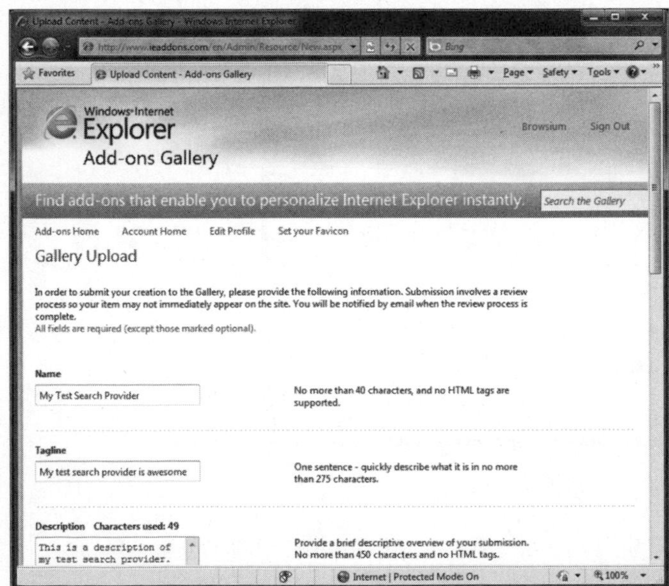

Figure 9–16. Uploading a new add-on to the IE Add-Ons Gallery

The information provided here serves two purposes: to aid the Microsoft representative in a control's approval process by providing context for the add-on, and to aid users of the IE Add-Ons Gallery web site in making informed decisions about which add-ons to download. For reference, Table 9–11 describes the fields provided for search provider extension uploads.

Table 9–11. *Metadata Fields for Describing an Add-On During the IE Add-Ons Gallery Upload Process*

Item	Description	Requirements	Required
Name	Name of the search provider	No more than 40 characters, and no HTML tags are supported.	Yes
Tagline	One-sentence description (tagline) of the search provider	Less than 275 characters	Yes
Description	Description of the search provider	No more than 450 characters and no HTML tags.	Yes
Home page URL	Home page containing information about this search providers	Valid URL	Yes
Screenshot	Screenshot of the search provider in action	The image should be in JPG, PNG, GIF, or BMP format. It can be any size, but the higher resolution, the better. The optimal image size is 380×250	Yes
Language	Target language (locale) of the search provider	Only one language may be chosen per submission.	Yes
Type	Type of the add-on (in this case, the "Search Provider")	One and only one type must be specified.	Yes
OSD file	XML definition file of the search provider (OSD file)	One and only one OSD file must be uploaded.	Yes
Categories	One or more categories the search provider falls under	At least one category must be chosen.	Yes

The preview section at the bottom of the upload page shows a developer how the entry for this new add-on may look when shown on the gallery web page (assuming it is approved). The best use for this (given the feedback the preview provides at the time this text was written) is to ensure that the name and the image indicated in the fields of this page accurately represent the add-on. Figure 9–17 shows an example of the preview pane.

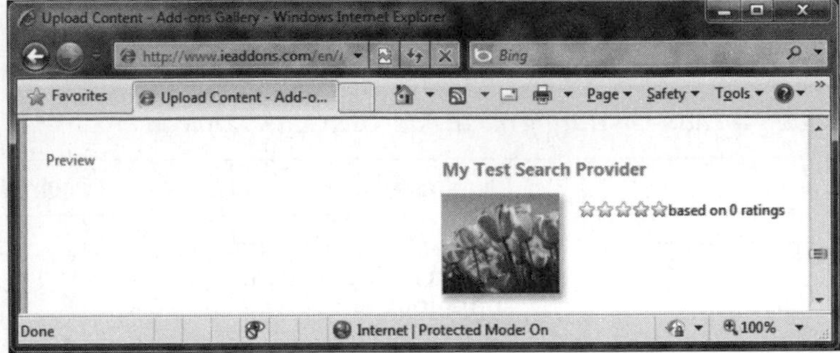

Figure 9–17. IE Add-Ons Gallery upload page preview pane

Once this information is entered, developers may click the submit button for approval. Again, developers using this process should expect a response by a Microsoft representative evaluating the add-on within a few business days.

User Preference Protection

Application installers may add search providers as part of an installation process. Microsoft discovered that, more often than not, these installers do not clearly ask users if they want their chosen search provider changed before editing their settings. IE 8 introduced a new feature called *User Preference Protection*, a system that protects the default search provider that a user chose either during the browser's first run experience, via the search engine drop-down, or via the Manage Add-Ons dialog box.

User Preference Protection watches for a change in the registry keys where search provider information is stored. If these settings are changed in any way outside of the three in-browser methods previously stated, the browser displays a dialog box informing the user of these changes (Figure 9–18).

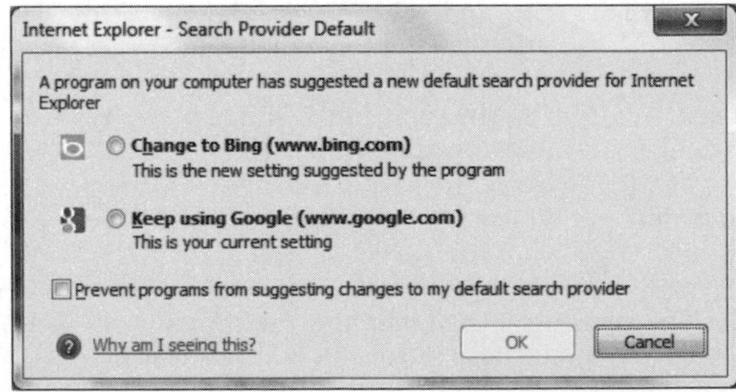

Figure 9–18. The User Preference Protection dialog

Users have the option of accepting the changes or reverting back to their original preferences. This system ensures that applications do not "hijack" the search default without getting the user's permission.

Summary

Search providers are a great way for developers to expose functionality of their web services consistently in IE's frame. This means that users can access a web site or search engine without having to actually visit it—a powerful concept that may very well be the future of the Web.

In this chapter, I showed you how easy it can be to create search providers that give your web application this powerful functionality and allow you to extend your web application right into the IE browser frame. I began by describing the user experience flows associated with search providers, followed by a deep dive into the tags and variables associated with the two XML-based specifications used by them: then OpenSearch and XML Search Suggestions specifications. I then discussed how you can easily build a basic search provider, followed by an explanation of the installation and management process for these extensions. Next, I covered how you can extend search provider functionality using both text-based and image-based search suggestions. I concluded this chapter with some more advanced topics such as User Preference Protection.

CHAPTER 10

Building Lightweight Buttons and Menu Extensions

Traditional COM-based extensions are not the only ones available for IE—the browser has exposed a simple metadata-based extensibility model since IE 5. These lightweight extensions link the IE frame to scripts and commands rather than oft-complicated COM communication models and command structure.

This chapter discusses the many lightweight IE frame extensions available to developers. Developers can create toolbar buttons, frame menu items, and context menus in a matter of minutes and using simple programming techniques. I begin this chapter by outlining the most common lightweight extensions available in IE and how those tie into the browser and pages. Following this introduction, I show you detailed examples of each major extension and demonstrate ways you can incorporate them into your desktop and web applications. For the brave and the interested, I bridge these extensions with their COM counterparts, showing how you can maximize the impact of your extensions by tying them into new or preexisting COM objects.

Understanding Lightweight IE Extensions

IE provides a number of ways to extend the browser frame and in-page context menus. These extensions are referred to as "lightweight" because of the way they are constructed; the simplest of these can be added to IE through a handful of registry values.

The first types of lightweight IE extensions are *frame extensions*. Frame extensions are those add-ons that extend the functionality of the browser frame itself. They can be found in the main IE toolbar, also referred to as a band object (band objects are discussed in more detail in the next chapter). Figure 10–1 shows the upper portion of the IE browser frame; the icons and drop-downs to the right of the browser tab set are examples of such extensions.

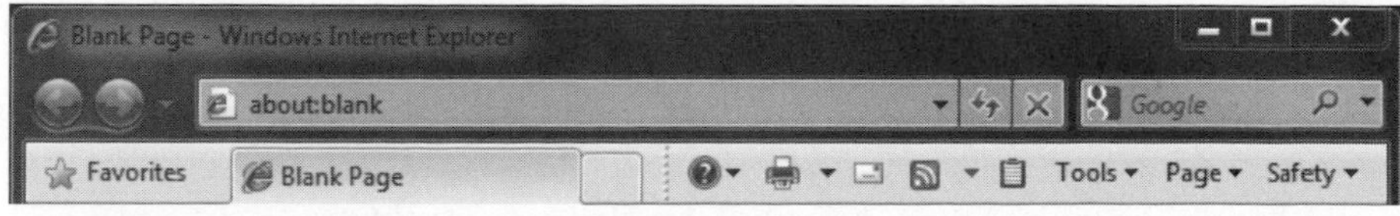

***Figure 10–1.** Lightweight extensions, menus, and the main IE toolbar*

The simple buttons in the main IE toolbar are built-in or custom toolbar button extensions. These add-ons extend the frame by linking IE to external commands, scripts, COM objects, or, as discussed in the following chapter, Explorer bars. Figure 10–2 shows some toolbar buttons in more detail.

Figure 10–2. *Toolbar buttons in the main IE toolbar*

Drop-down menus can be found alongside buttons in IE's main toolbar. Two of these drop-down menus—the Tools and Help menus—can be extended through menu item extensions (Figure 10–3).

Figure 10–3. *The Tools and Help menu drop-down buttons*

As with toolbar buttons, menu item extensions under either drop-down provide a way for users to launch external scripts, commands, or COM objects. Figure 10–4 shows the expanded menus that these extensions can be accessed from.

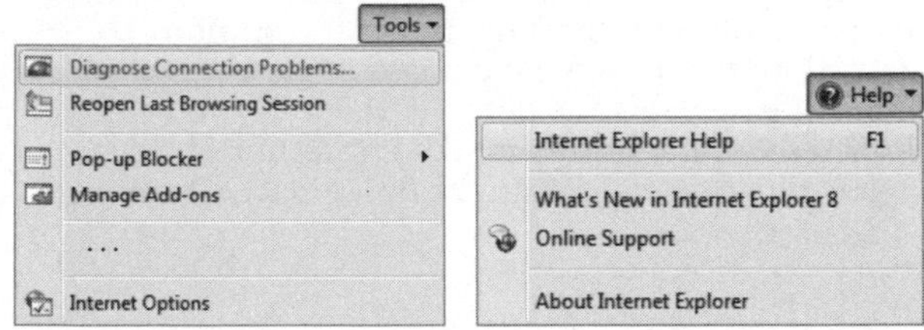

Figure 10–4. *The expanded Tools and Help menus*

The next types of lightweight extensions are in-page context menu add-ons. Unlike frame extensions, in-page menu items are displayed and executed within the context of the active web page, even if this context is not obvious to the user.

Context menu items are shown in the in-page context menu, much like the Accelerators discussed earlier in this text. Unlike Accelerators, however, they are defined in the system registry and have the ability to launch script and executable files. Figure 10–5 shows some context menu extensions that can commonly be found on users' IE installations.

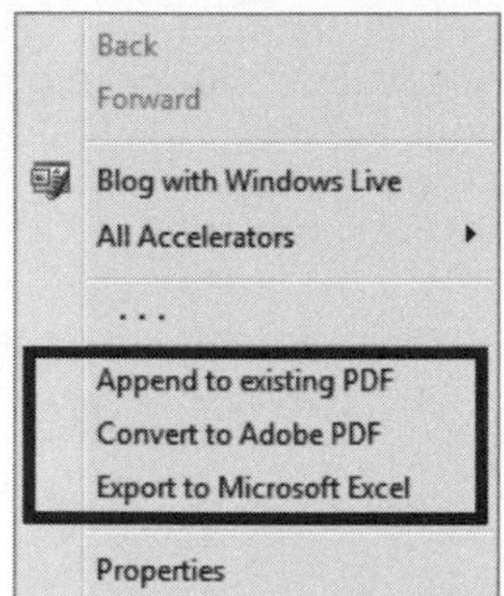

Figure 10–5. In-page context menu with custom context menu item extensions

The addition of context menu extensions is distinct from replacement of the entire context menu using JavaScript. IE, along with all modern browsers, allows web site developers to prevent display of the default context menu via JavaScript. Context menu extensions also differ from Accelerators, as these add-ons are permitted more access to the local system and are not constructed using XML. Using event handlers, developers can completely replace the browser's context menu with a custom one designed for a specific web site or application. Of course, these overrides are only shown on sites that specifically include them; the default context menu (and its context menu extensions) is shown on all other pages.

Figure 10–6 shows a great custom context menu example written in JavaScript; Google Docs uses the custom menu to provide easy access to common commands within its web application—all without installing a single extension.

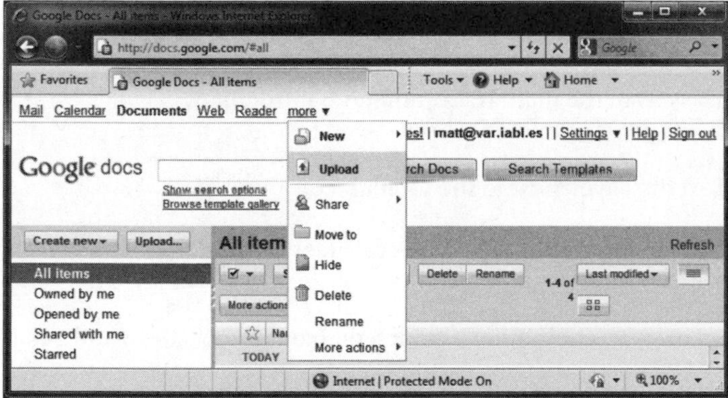

Figure 10–6. Custom context menu used by Google Docs

Adding Toolbar Buttons

Toolbar buttons are icons that can be added to the Command Bar toolbar (band object) of IE. These extensions allow users quick access to useful tasks and applications directly from the browser frame. The following sections describe how these extensions can be constructed, installed, and used.

Common Toolbar Button Properties

Toolbar buttons are defined and loaded into IE through a set of basic registry values. These values can be stored in either the HKEY_LOCAL_MACHINE or the HKEY_CURRENT_USER hive. All extensions fall under the key Software\Microsoft\Internet Explorer\Extensions; on 64-bit systems, 32-bit extensions should be placed under the emulation key Software\Wow6432Node\Microsoft\Internet Explorer\Extensions. Listing 10–1 shows an example of a basic toolbar button defined through the registry.

Listing 10–1. *Example of a Toolbar Button Added to the IE Command Bar*

```
HKEY_CURRENT_USER\
   Software\
      Microsoft\
         Internet Explorer\
            Extensions\
               {D862829C-9A39-4029-A4CC-2A78C9C1F2F3}\
                  CLSID            (REG_SZ)  = "{1FBA04EE-3024-11D2-8F1F-0000F87ABD16}"
                  ButtonText       (REG_SZ)  = "My button"
                  Icon             (REG_SZ)  = "C:\\MyIcon.ico"
                  HotIcon          (REG_SZ)  = "C:\\MyHotIcon.ico"
                  Default Visible  (REG_SZ)  = "yes"
                  ...
```

Individual extensions are distinguished by a key underneath the parent Extensions key. This key's name is a GUID. Each registry entry underneath this key represents some data defining the toolbar button. Table 10–1 defines each value in detail.

Table 10–1. *Common Toolbar Button Registry Values*

Name	Value Type	Description
CLSID	REG_SZ	Class ID of the main IE Command Bar (toolbar), CLSID_Shell_ToolbarExtExec
ButtonText	REG_SZ	Text displayed next to the toolbar icon
Icon	REG_SZ	An icon file containing a grayscale icon (containing 16×16 and 24x24 formats)
HotIcon	REG_SZ	An icon file containing a color icon (containing 16×16 and 24×24 formats)
Default Visible	REG_SZ	Allows a button to appear in the toolbar by default

The CLSID value represents the class ID of IE's Command Bar. ButtonText contains text that is displayed next to a toolbar button when text is shown. The Icon string points to an idle icon, typically grayscale, and the HotIcon string points to a color icon used by the button on hover. The icons specified should include both 16×16 and 24×24 icons to avoid scaling. Finally, the Default Visible setting tells IE whether to show the icon by default with a value of ("yes") or to hide it ("no").

Each flavor of toolbar button uses this base set of values to define how it is displayed in the browser frame.

Running Script Using a Toolbar Button

Toolbar buttons can launch a web page or script when clicked. Toolbars can initiate script to modify the current web page or run system commands.

Developers looking to create an extension that launches script can do so via the `Script` registry value. The data for this value is the path to a markup or script file; it is located in the same key as the common toolbar button registry values (Table 10–2).

***Table 10–2.** Registry Values for Script-Based Toolbar Buttons*

Name	Value Type	Description
`Script`	`REG_SZ`	Path to a script file

Using script-based toolbar buttons is a simple process. Listing 10–2 shows a registry script that installs such a button. In this example, the toolbar button launches a script called `"Run.html"` that launches MSDN in a new browser window when clicked. The toolbar displays the MSDN favicon and displays the text "Launch MSDN" when the Command Bar's "Show all text labels" option is enabled.

***Listing 10–2.** Sample Installation File for a Script-Based Toolbar Button*

```
Windows Registry Editor Version 5.00

[HKEY_LOCAL_MACHINE\SOFTWARE\Microsoft\Internet Explorer\Extensions\
   {E210FAE5-3322-4DF7-94E2-B134CC624B35}]
"CLSID"="{1FBA04EE-3024-11D2-8F1F-0000F87ABD16}"
"ButtonText"="Launch MSDN"
"Icon"="C:\\ProIeDev\\10\\ToolbarButton\\Script\\MSDN.ico"
"HotIcon"="C:\\ProIeDev\\10\\ToolbarButton\\Script\\MSDN.ico"
"Default Visible"="Yes"
"Script"="C:\\ProIeDev\\10\\ToolbarButton\\Script\\Run.html"

[HKEY_LOCAL_MACHINE\SOFTWARE\Wow6432Node\Microsoft\Internet Explorer\Extensions\
   {1C1E2247-34CA-44B8-BE91-4E0798CAC048}]
"CLSID"="{1FBA04EE-3024-11D2-8F1F-0000F87ABD16}"
"ButtonText"="Launch MSDN"
"Icon"="C:\\ProIeDev\\10\\ToolbarButton\\Script\\MSDN.ico"
"HotIcon"="C:\\ProIeDev\\10\\ToolbarButton\\Script\\MSDN.ico"
"Default Visible"="Yes"
"Script"="C:\\ProIeDev\\10\\ToolbarButton\\Script\\Run.html"
```

This registry script takes both 32-bit and 64-bit IE executables into account. Upon import, it writes a toolbar button to both the standard IE extensions key and the `Wow6432Node` registry emulation key.

Figure 10–7 shows the toolbar button in the IE Command Bar after the installation script is run.

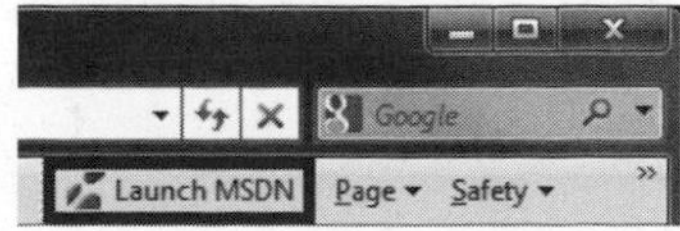

***Figure 10–7.** The Example Toolbar Button in the IE Toolbar After Installation*

The "Run.html" script executed by this toolbar button uses JavaScript to launch MSDN (http://msdn.microsoft.com) in a new IE window. Listing 10–3 demonstrates this page.

Listing 10–3. *Source Code for Web Page Called by This Script-Based Toolbar Button*

```
<html>
   <body>
      <script type="text/javascript">

         //  Create a new ActiveX shell object
         var shell = new ActiveXObject("WScript.Shell");

         //  Open up a new instance of IE pointing
         //  to a URL
         shell.run("iexplore.exe " +
                    "http://msdn.microsoft.com"
                    );

      </script>
   </body>
</html>
```

When this page is loaded by IE, the JScript engine executes the JavaScript in the body of the page. A new ActiveXObject is created from the Windows Scripting Host shell (WScript.Shell); this allows the script to access system resources and executables. Next, the shell is opened and passed the command line of the IE executable concatenated with an argument—the URL of MSDN's web page.

Developers should take away a key concept from this example: script instantiated from toolbar buttons runs with enhanced permissions. Normal web pages cannot instantiate the WScript.Shell object or other higher-privilege objects.

Figure 10–8 shows the result of a click event on this toolbar button. A new IE window is launched. This window accesses the URL argument passed to the object, in this case the MSDN web site.

Figure 10–8. *IE hosting MSDN, the result of clicking this sample toolbar button*

Removing the toolbar button consists of deleting all registry keys and values associated with it. Listing 10–4 shows a registry script that removes both keys created during the installation of the example button. Two commands are run, each deleting the parent key containing values defining the buttons.

Listing 10–4. *Uninstallation Script for the Sample Toolbar Button*

```
Windows Registry Editor Version 5.00

[-HKEY_LOCAL_MACHINE\SOFTWARE\Microsoft\Internet Explorer\Extensions\
   {E210FAE5-3322-4DF7-94E2-B134CC624B35}]
[-HKEY_LOCAL_MACHINE\SOFTWARE\Wow6432Node\Microsoft\Internet Explorer\Extensions\
   {1C1E2247-34CA-44B8-BE91-4E0798CAC048}]
```

Removal of a button takes effect once all instances of IE are closed. A batch file, script, or binary may be used to write these values to (or remove these values from) the registry.

Launching an Executable via a Toolbar Button

Toolbar buttons can directly execute a command or batch file instead of simple script. Executable toolbar buttons define a command to run through the Exec registry value. The data of this value is the path to an executable or batch file that IE will launch when a button using this method is clicked (Table 10–3).

Table 10–3. *Registry Values for Executable-Based Toolbar Buttons*

Name	Value Type	Description
Exec	REG_SZ	Path to an executable or batch file

Executable-based buttons can be installed through simple scripts, just as script-launching buttons. Listing 10–5 shows an example of an installation script for a button that launches an executable. This sample creates a new button that opens up the Windows Notepad text editor when clicked.

Listing 10–5. *Installation Script for a Toolbar Button That Executes a Command*

```
Windows Registry Editor Version 5.00

[HKEY_LOCAL_MACHINE\SOFTWARE\Microsoft\Internet Explorer\Extensions\
   {40AD9F9B-3CD9-4F7E-88F2-C70FD438B8F1}]
"CLSID"="{1FBA04EE-3024-11D2-8F1F-0000F87ABD16}"
"ButtonText"="Launch Notepad"
"Icon"="C:\\ProIeDev\\10\\ToolbarButton\\Exec\\Notepad.ico"
"HotIcon"="C:\\ProIeDev\\10\\ToolbarButton\\Exec\\Notepad.ico"
"Default Visible"="yes"
"Exec"="\"C:\\windows\\notepad.exe\""

[HKEY_LOCAL_MACHINE\SOFTWARE\Wow6432Node\Microsoft\Internet Explorer\Extensions\
   {B9759B89-2906-47DA-AE9B-F1CA25B8729D}]
"CLSID"="{1FBA04EE-3024-11D2-8F1F-0000F87ABD16}"
"ButtonText"="Launch Notepad"
"Icon"="C:\\ProIeDev\\10\\ToolbarButton\\Exec\\Notepad.ico"
"HotIcon"="C:\\ProIeDev\\10\\ToolbarButton\\Exec\\Notepad.ico"
"Default Visible"="yes"
"Exec"="\"C:\\windows\\notepad.exe\""
```

As in the previous example, this installation script creates icons for both 64-bit and 32-bit IE installations. The Icon and HotIcon values both refer to the application icon from Notepad.exe. The button text displayed next to this button is set to read "Launch Notepad," and it is set to display once installed. The last value of this script is `Exec`, whose data points to the `Notepad.exe` application file located in the Windows directory.

Figure 10–9 shows this button in the IE frame once the installation script is run. On the left side is the button in icon-only mode and to the right is the button icon displayed with its button text.

Figure 10–9. Toolbar button and text for the example extension

IE attempts to run the contents of the `Exec` value when the button is clicked. In this case, IE tries to launch `Notepad.exe`. In IE 8 and above, executables that have not previously been launched from the browser frame show a Protected Mode elevation prompt. Users must authorize the application for use in this context via the dialog in Figure 10–10.

Figure 10–10. Protected Mode approval dialog, launched when the extension tries to launch an unapproved executable

Figure 10–11 shows Notepad launched from IE when the application is permitted to run. If the action is disallowed through the previous dialog, this application will not launch. Developers should note that the application will run if the user accepts it via the Protected Mode dialog. In contract, developers attempting to launch executables via script may find that those executables will not run because the elevation policy for the script may not launch the Protected Mode dialog.

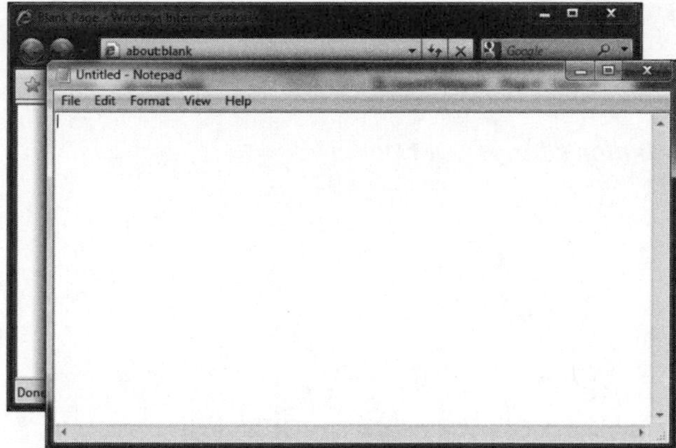

Figure 10–11. Notepad being executed from a toolbar button

The uninstallation process can be performed with a simple script that removes keys specific to this object. Listing 10–6 demonstrates a simple registry script that uninstalls this extension by removing its keys.

Listing 10–6. Uninstallation Script for the Example Toolbar Button

```
Windows Registry Editor Version 5.00

[-HKEY_LOCAL_MACHINE\SOFTWARE\Microsoft\Internet Explorer\Extensions\
   {40AD9F9B-3CD9-4F7E-88F2-C70FD438B8F1}]
[-HKEY_LOCAL_MACHINE\SOFTWARE\Wow6432Node\Microsoft\Internet Explorer\Extensions\
   {B9759B89-2906-47DA-AE9B-F1CA25B8729D}]
```

Invoking COM Objects via a Toolbar Button

Toolbar buttons may invoke COM objects when clicked. This allows developers to incorporate existing functionality of COM applications into this simple IE extension.

Toolbar buttons using COM object invocation define the `ClsidExtension` registry value in addition to the common toolbar button values. The data of this value is a string containing the Class ID of the COM object to invoke (Table 10–4).

Table 10–4. Registry Values for Toolbar Buttons That Invoke COM Objects

Name	Value Type	Description
`ClsidExtension`	`REG_SZ`	Class ID of the COM object to invoke

When a toolbar button using COM object invocation is clicked, IE instantiates the object specified in this value and signals a click event through the `Exec` method of the `IOleCommandTarget` interface.

The first step in building a COM-object-invoking toolbar button is ensuring that an invokable object is available for use. Such an object can easily be constructed using the .NET Framework and its COM interop functionality.

Listing 10–7 shows the basic framework for a new COM component that implements the IOleCommandTarget interface and exposes itself through a new GUID.

Listing 10–7. *Basic Class Structure for the Toolbar Button's Target COM Object*

```
namespace ProIeDev.ToolbarButtonComObject {

   [ComVisible(true), Guid(Plugin.Guid)]
   public class Plugin : IOleCommandTarget {
      ...
   }
}
```

The object, called Plugin, defines itself to be visible to COM and defines its GUID in its class attributes. It implements the IOleCommandTarget interface in the class definition. This interface is defined in another class included with the companion project accompanying this book.

A number of constants related to the extension and the COM object are defined in the Plugin class, mainly for convenience. Listing 10–8 defines these constants.

Listing 10–8. *Constants Definining Properties of the COM Object*

```
#region Constants

/// <summary>
/// Guid of this assembly
/// </summary>
public const string Guid = @"193BD928-F965-47DD-B9FF-83173B9E20F5";

/// <summary>
/// ProgId of this plug-in
/// </summary>
public const string ProgId = "ProIeDev.ToolbarButtonComObject.Button";

/// <summary>
/// Name of the currently executing assembly
/// </summary>
public static string AssemblyName = Assembly.GetExecutingAssembly().GetName().Name;

/// <summary>
/// Guid of the IE plug-in
/// </summary>
public const string PluginGuid = "{9651DC31-B70E-4B80-BF02-BA3FF9A50E2B}";

/// <summary>
/// Registry key where the plug-in will be installed
/// </summary>
public const string PluginKey = @"SOFTWARE\Microsoft\Internet Explorer\Extensions";

/// <summary>
/// WoW emulation registry key for the plug-in
/// </summary>
```

```
public const string PluginKeyWow = @"SOFTWARE\Wow6432Node\Microsoft\Internet
Explorer\Extensions";

/// <summary>
/// Hive to install the plug-in into
/// </summary>
public static readonly RegistryKey PluginHive = Registry.LocalMachine;

#endregion Constants
```

This COM object also installs a toolbar button during its registration and unregistration functions. Data used for this process is stored in a settings property, as shown in Listing 10–9.

Listing 10–9. *Settings for the New IE Toolbar Button*

```
#region Properties

/// <summary>
///
/// </summary>
public static Settings PluginSettings {
   get { return new Settings() {

      //  Text shown alongside the toolbar button
      { "ButtonText", "ToolbarButtonComObject Example" },

      //  Icon shown for the button's "active" state
      { "HotIcon", Utils.AssemblyDirectory + @"\Resources\Icon.ico" },

      //  Default icon for the button
      { "Icon", Utils.AssemblyDirectory + @"\Resources\Icon.ico" },

      //  Whether or not the button is initially visible
      { "Default Visible", "Yes" },

      //  CLSID of the IE toolbar band object
      { "CLSID", "{1FBA04EE-3024-11D2-8F1F-0000F87ABD16}" },

      //  Guid of the COM component to run when the button
      //  is clicked (this library)
      { "ClsidExtension", "{" + Guid + "}" }

   }; }
}

#endregion Properties
```

The properties defined in Listing 10–9 are written and removed from the system registry via the COM registration and unregistration methods, respectively. The .NET assembly registration utility calls these functions after it either registers or unregisters this COM object from both the system class directory and the Global Assembly Cache (GAC). IE will only load .NET COM objects whose assemblies are placed in the GAC.

Listing 10–10 shows the registration (`RegisterServer(...)`) and unregistration (`UnregisterServer()`) methods for the `Plugin` class.

Listing 10–10. COM Registration and Unregistration Methods for the Target Object

```
#region COM Registration Methods

/// <summary>
/// Performs COM and GAC registration services
/// </summary>
/// <param name="type"></param>
[ComRegisterFunction]
public static void RegisterServer(Type type)
{

   //  Create a new registry tools object
   RegistryTools registry = new RegistryTools() {
      Hive = PluginHive
      };

   //  This is a 32-bit plug-in, so determine if the target
   //  key needs to access a WoW emulation key
   string key =
      String.Format(
         @"{0}\{1}",
         ((Platform.GetPlatform() == PlatformType.X64) ?
            PluginKeyWow : PluginKey),
         PluginGuid
         );

   //  Loop through each of the plug-in settings and add
   //  them to the registry
   foreach (var setting in PluginSettings) {
      registry.WriteValue(
         key,
         setting.Key,
         setting.Value,
         RegistryValueKind.String
         );

   }

}

/// <summary>
/// Performs COM and GAC unregistration services
/// </summary>
[ComUnregisterFunction]
public static void UnregisterServer() {

   //  Create a new registry tools object
   RegistryTools registry = new RegistryTools() {
      Hive = PluginHive
      };

   //  Ensure that the 32-bit key is created since a user
```

```
    //  may be running a 64-bit .NET Framework as well
    string key =
       String.Format(
          @"{0}\{1}",
          ((Platform.GetPlatform() == PlatformType.X64) ?
             PluginKeyWow : PluginKey),
          PluginGuid
          );

    //  Loop through each of the plug-in settings and
    //  delete them from the registry
    foreach (var setting in PluginSettings)
       registry.DeleteValue(
          key,
          setting.Key
          );

    //  Delete the plug-in key altogether
    registry.DeleteKey(PluginKey);

}

#endregion COM Registration Methods
```

Every key/value pair defined in this class's Settings property is added to or deleted from the registry in these methods. IE will either add or remove the toolbar button when these values are added or removed; these methods serve the same purpose as the installation and uninstallation registry scripts used in the previous toolbar button implementation examples.

The Plugin class definition implements IOleCommandTarget, so it must implement all methods defined by this interface. IOleCommandTarget defines two methods: QueryStatus and Exec. Put simply, QueryStatus is used to emit the status of commands by an object. Exec is used to command an object to do something. IE uses the Exec command to tell a COM object that a toolbar button has been clicked. As a result, the Plugin class will perform an action when Exec is called.

Listing 10–11 shows the Plugin class's implementation of the IOleCommandTarget methods. It implements both QueryStatus and Exec, as required by the interface.

***Listing 10–11.** Implementation of the IOleCommandTarget Interface*

```
#region IOleCommandTarget Interface Methods

/// <summary>
/// Queries the object for the status of one or more
/// commands generated by UI events.
/// </summary>
/// ...
public int QueryStatus(
   ref Guid pguidCmdGroup,
   uint cCmds,
   OLECMD[] prgCmds,
   IntPtr pCmdText) {

   //  Acknowledge query
   return 0;  // S_OK
```

```
}

/// <summary>
/// Executes the specified command or displays help for the command
/// </summary>
/// ...
public int Exec(
   ref Guid pguidCmdGroup,
   uint nCmdID,
   uint nCmdexecopt,
   IntPtr pvaIn,
   IntPtr pvaOut) {

   //  Call the plug-in click event helper
   OnToolbarButtonClick();

   //  Acknowledge command
   return 0;  // S_OK

}

#endregion IOleCommandTarget Interface Methods
```

The Exec method, however, is used to trigger an event in this case. When Exec is called by the host application (IE), the Plugin class calls the OnToolbarButtonClick() function to react to a button click. In both cases, a return value of (-1) is handed back to acknowledge the function call.

The Plugin class defines the OnToolbarButtonClick() method to perform an action when the toolbar button is clicked and the Exec method is invoked by IE. Listing 10–12 shows the source of this method.

Listing 10–12. *Helper Method for Launching a Dialog*

```
#region Helper Methods

[STAThread]
public void OnToolbarButtonClick() {

   //  Create a new instance of the Display form and
   //  show it as a dialog
   Form display = new Display();
   DialogResult result = display.ShowDialog();

   //  Dispose of the form when finished
   display.Dispose();

}

#endregion Helper Methods
```

In this example, an instance of a form named Display is shown as a dialog. When the form is closed, its class instance is disposed of.

The last step in adding this plug-in to IE is registering the COM component that was just created. The registration process will also write the toolbar button settings to the registry, adding the plug-in to IE as well as the system COM class directory.

Listing 10–13 describes a separate utility application that is used to both register and unregister the new plug-in from a command line. This utility must be run with administrative privileges on Windows Vista and higher because it modifies the .NET GAC and Local Machine hive of the registry.

***Listing 10–13.** Utility Application for Registering and Unregistering the New COM Object and Toolbar Button*

```
/// <summary>
/// This program registers a .NET-based COM object
/// </summary>
class Program {

   /// <summary>
   /// Main entry point for this application
   /// </summary>
   /// <param name="args">Command line args</param>
   static void Main(string[] args) {

      //  If no argument was passed or too many were passed,
      //  exit the application
      if (args.Length != 1) return;

      //  Switch on the argument passed into the app
      switch (args[0].Trim().ToLower()) {

         //  Installation argument
         case "-i": {

            //  Attempt to register the assembly
            Assembly assembly = Assembly.LoadFile(
               String.Format(
                  @"{0}\{1}.dll",
                  ProIeDev.ToolbarButtonComObject.Classes.Utils.AssemblyDirectory,
                  ProIeDev.ToolbarButtonComObject.Plugin.AssemblyName
                  )
               );
            RegistrationServices regasm = new RegistrationServices();
            regasm.RegisterAssembly(assembly, AssemblyRegistrationFlags.SetCodeBase);

            //  Exit the application
            return;

         }

         //  Uninstallation argument
         case "-u": {

            //  Attempt to unregister the assembly
            Assembly assembly = Assembly.LoadFile(
               String.Format(
                  @"{0}\{1}.dll",
                  ProIeDev.ToolbarButtonComObject.Classes.Utils.AssemblyDirectory,
                  ProIeDev.ToolbarButtonComObject.Plugin.AssemblyName
```

```
                )
            );
            RegistrationServices regasm = new RegistrationServices();
            regasm.UnregisterAssembly(assembly);

            //  Exit the application
            return;

        }

    }

  }

}
```

The utility takes one command argument that must be present. The value of this argument may either be `-i` (to install the plug-in) or `-u` (to remove it from the system).

Demonstration of this example begins by running the installer just described. The installer must be run with administrative privileges. Figure 10–12 shows a command prompt running the registration utility; it is passed the `-i` argument to signal installation.

***Figure 10–12.** Command line for installing the toolbar and associated COM object*

The installation utility both registers the COM assembly and adds toolbar metadata to the system registry. Figure 10–13 shows the toolbar button after installation.

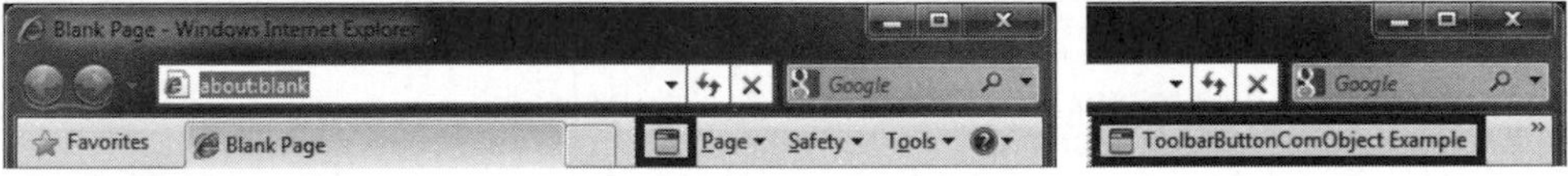

***Figure 10–13.** Toolbar button created after installation*

Figure 10–14 demonstrates the action of the new toolbar button. When clicked, IE invokes the new COM object. This object creates a new instance of a form and displays it as a dialog window atop the IE browser window.

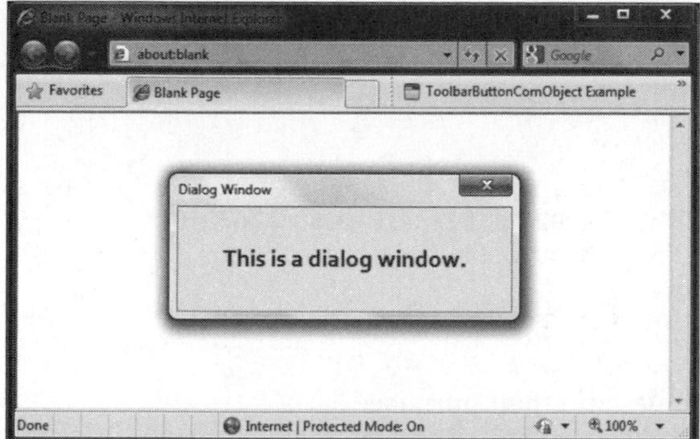

***Figure 10–14.** Dialog button invoked by the target COM object when the toolbar button is clicked*

Invoking the uninstallation switch runs the COM unregistration function of the `Plugin` library, removing the COM object from the registry and the GAC, and deleting the toolbar button registry values from the IE extensions registry key (Figure 10–15).

***Figure 10–15.** Command line for uninstaling the new toolbar button and COM object*

Opening Explorer Bars with Toolbar Buttons

Toolbar buttons can also be used to launch explorer bars. This feature of toolbar buttons and explorer bars is discussed in the next chapter.

Extending the Tools and Help Menus

The Tools and Help menus provide a common location for extensions that offer either extended functionality or extended help information. The following sections describe these extensions in detail.

Common Menu Item Properties

Menu items are defined and loaded into IE through a set of basic registry values. These values can be stored in either the `HKEY_LOCAL_MACHINE` or the `HKEY_CURRENT_USER` hive. All extensions fall under the key `Software\Microsoft\Internet Explorer\Extensions`; on 64-bit systems, 32-bit extensions should be placed under the emulation key `Software\Wow6432Node\Microsoft\Internet Explorer\Extensions`. Listing 10–14 shows an example of a basic Tools menu item defined through the registry.

Listing 10–14. *Example of a Toolbar Button Added to the IE Command Bar*

```
HKEY_CURRENT_USER\
   Software\
      Microsoft\
         Internet Explorer\
            {FF79E0FB-605D-41C4-B877-8559814F9B16}\
               CLSID              (REG_SZ)  = "{1FBA04EE-3024-11D2-8F1F-0000F87ABD16}"
               MenuText           (REG_SZ)  = "My Tools Menu Item"
               MenuCustomize      (REG_SZ)  = "tools"
               MenuStatusBar      (REG_SZ)  = "Performs an action for my menu item"
               ...
```

Table 10–5 reviews each of the common registry values and their purpose.

Table 10–5. *Common Registry Values for Tools and Help Menu Extensions*

Name	Value Type	Description
`CLSID`	`REG_SZ`	CLSID of the main IE band object
`MenuText`	`REG_SZ`	Text of the menu item
`MenuCustomize`	`REG_SZ`	Location of the menu item (in the Tools or Help menu)
`MenuStatusBar`	`REG_SZ`	Text shown on the status bar when the menu item is hovered

The `CLSID` value is the class ID of the main IE toolbar. `MenuText` is the text associated with the menu item. `MenuStatusBar` is the text that is shown on the status bar when a menu item is hovered over. Finally, `MenuCustomize` is a string indicating whether the menu item should show up in the Tools menu (`"tools"`) or the Help menu (`"help"`).

Running Script Using a Menu Item

Menu items can launch a web page or script when clicked. Developers looking to create an extension that launches script can do so via the `Script` registry value. The data for this value is the path to a markup or script file; it is located in the same key as the common menu item button registry values (Table 10–6).

Table 10–6. *Registry Values for Script-Based Menu Item Extensions*

Name	Value Type	Description
`Script`	`REG_SZ`	Path to a script file

A menu item can be created using a simple registry script (as in Listing 10–15). In this example, a new menu item is created for both 64-bit (if present) and 32-bit IE. The new Tools menu item opens up MSDN in a new IE window, much like the previous example demonstrating script-based toolbar buttons.

Listing 10–15. Installation Script for a Script-Based Menu Item

```
Windows Registry Editor Version 5.00

[HKEY_LOCAL_MACHINE\SOFTWARE\Microsoft\Internet Explorer\Extensions\{8B256D2C-9C36-43FD-ABE1-D2703439D5BD}]
"CLSID"="{1FBA04EE-3024-11D2-8F1F-0000F87ABD16}"
"Script"="C:\\ProIeDev\\10\\MenuItem\\ToolsMenuItem\\Script\\Run.html"
"MenuText"="Open MSDN"
"MenuCustomize"="tools"
"MenuStatusBar"="Opens the Microsoft Developer Network web page"

[HKEY_LOCAL_MACHINE\SOFTWARE\Wow6432Node\Microsoft\Internet Explorer\Extensions\{7B87C8DF-3A69-4303-8C30-8296775D4302}]
"CLSID"="{1FBA04EE-3024-11D2-8F1F-0000F87ABD16}"
"Script"="C:\\ProIeDev\\10\\MenuItem\\ToolsMenuItem\\Script\\Run.html"
"MenuText"="Open MSDN"
"MenuCustomize"="tools"
"MenuStatusBar"="Opens the Microsoft Developer Network web page"
```

A new menu item is added to the IE Tools menu when this script is run. Figure 10–16 shows a new menu item entitled "Open MSDN" added to this menu.

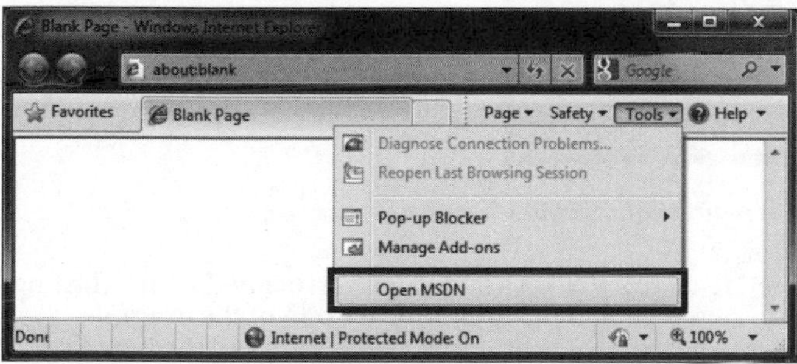

Figure 10–16. Tools menu item added to the IE Tools menu

When this button is clicked, a new instance of IE is created. This instance navigates to MSDN when loaded (Listing 10–16).

Listing 10–16. Script Used to Launch MSDN from a Tools Menu Item

```
<html>
   <body>
      <script type="text/javascript">

         // Create a new ActiveX shell object
         var shell = new ActiveXObject("WScript.Shell");

         // Open up a new instance of IE pointing
         // to a URL
         shell.run("iexplore.exe " +
                   "http://msdn.microsoft.com"
```

```
        );

    </script>
  </body>
</html>
```

Figure 10–17 shows a new IE window opened when this toolbar button is clicked. On opening, this window navigates to MSDN.

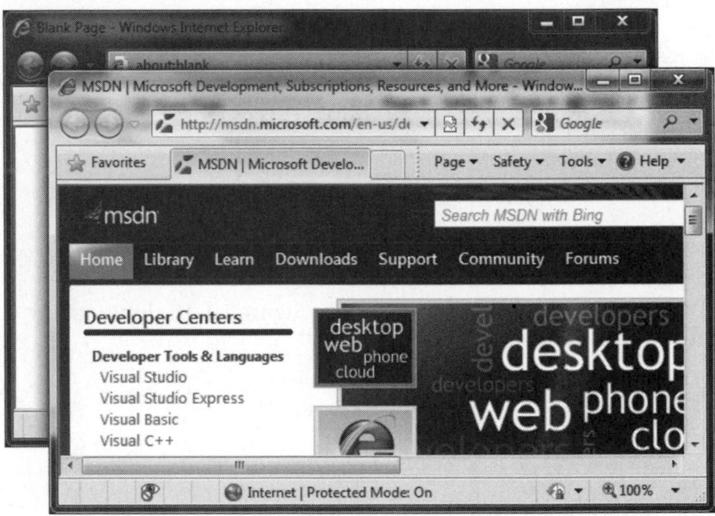

Figure 10–17. MSDN when launched using this new menu button

Removal of the menu item consists of deleting all registry keys and values associated with it. Listing 10–17 shows a registry script that removes both keys created during the installation of the example button. Two commands are run, each deleting the parent key containing values defining the item in question.

Listing 10–17. Uninstallation Script for the New Tools Menu Item

```
Windows Registry Editor Version 5.00

[-HKEY_LOCAL_MACHINE\SOFTWARE\Microsoft\Internet Explorer\Extensions\
   {8B256D2C-9C36-43FD-ABE1-D2703439D5BD}]
[-HKEY_LOCAL_MACHINE\SOFTWARE\Wow6432Node\Microsoft\Internet Explorer\Extensions\
   {7B87C8DF-3A69-4303-8C30-8296775D4302}]
```

Removal of a button takes effect once all instances of IE are closed. As with the installation file, a batch file, script, or binary may be used to write these values to the registry.

Launching an Executable via a Menu Item

Menu items can execute a command or batch file instead of simple script. Executable toolbar buttons define a command to run through the Exec registry value. The data of this value is the path to an executable or batch file that IE will launch when a button using this method is clicked (Table 10–7).

Table 10–7. Registry Values for Executable-Based Menu Items

Name	Value Type	Description
Exec	REG_SZ	Path to an executable or batch file

New menu items that call executables or commands can be added through simple script. Listing 10–18 shows a registry script that adds a new Help menu item to IE. This extension opens up the Windows Help application.

Listing 10–18. Registry Entries for a Help Menu Item That Launches an Executable

```
Windows Registry Editor Version 5.00

[HKEY_LOCAL_MACHINE\SOFTWARE\Microsoft\Internet Explorer\Extensions\{46FB380B-5E11-48F1-A9E8-8F689F3E1C60}]
"CLSID"="{1FBA04EE-3024-11D2-8F1F-0000F87ABD16}"
"Exec"="\"C:\\Windows\\winhlp32.exe\""
"MenuText"="Open Windows Help"
"MenuCustomize"="Help"
"MenuStatusBar"="Opens the Windows help application"

[HKEY_LOCAL_MACHINE\SOFTWARE\Wow6432Node\Microsoft\Internet Explorer\Extensions\{920C4ABC-C0E4-4E00-B8FF-A068E1C83D82}]
"CLSID"="{1FBA04EE-3024-11D2-8F1F-0000F87ABD16}"
"Exec"="\"C:\\Windows\\winhlp32.exe\""
"MenuText"="Open Windows Help"
"MenuCustomize"="Help"
```

The button shown in Figure 10–18 is added to the Help menu once the registry entries in the previous listing are added to the registry.

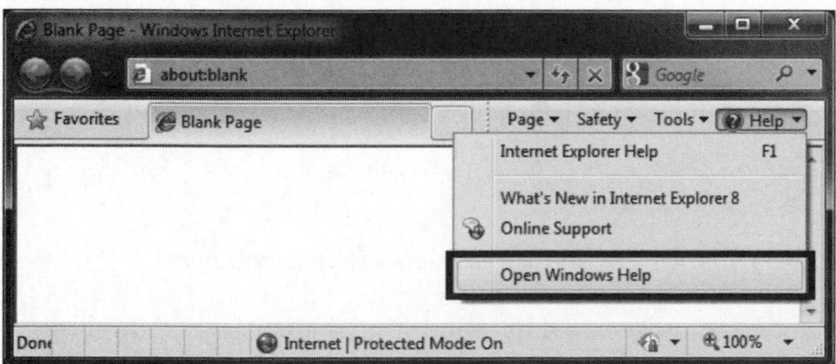

Figure 10–18. Help menu item added when the installation script is run

Figure 10–19 shows the Protected Mode dialog displayed after this button is clicked (if Protected Mode is both available and enabled). Applications that do not have an exemption or have never requested elevation from Protected Mode will trigger this. Users must explicitly allow the elevation to occur by clicking the Allow button; they can bypass future elevation requests for this application by ticking the "Do not show me the warning for this program again" check box.

Figure 10–19. Protected Mode dialog displayed once the Help menu item is clicked

If a user allows the Protected Mode elevation to occur (or Protected Mode is off), then the executable defined within the extension's registry settings will launch. Figure 10–20 shows the result in this example: the Windows Help and Support application is run and displayed atop the IE window.

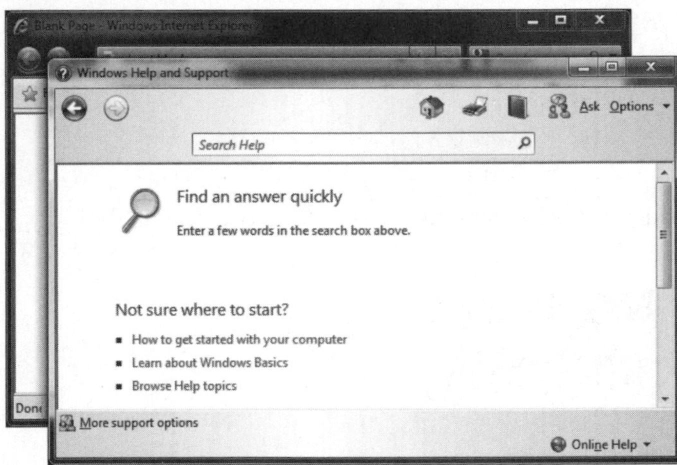

Figure 10–20. The Windows Help and Support application, launched by this Help menu item

As in the previous example, the extension can be removed by deleting all registry keys and values associated with it. Listing 10–19 shows a registry script that removes both keys created during the installation of the example button.

***Listing 10–19.** Registry Script That Uninstalls This Help Menu Item from the IE Frame*

```
Windows Registry Editor Version 5.00

[-HKEY_LOCAL_MACHINE\SOFTWARE\Microsoft\Internet Explorer\Extensions\
   {46FB380B-5E11-48F1-A9E8-8F689F3E1C60}]
[-HKEY_LOCAL_MACHINE\SOFTWARE\Wow6432Node\Microsoft\Internet Explorer\Extensions\
   {920C4ABC-C0E4-4E00-B8FF-A068E1C83D82}]
```

Adding Entries to the In-Page Context Menu

The in-page context menu offers developers a way to provide additional functionality to page elements without cluttering up the browser frame.

There are a number of different "contexts," or target scenarios, available to menu items. These contexts represent different situations in which a context menu may be opened. For instance, a user may open up a context menu over an image or right-click a link. Contexts allow developers to add menu items for specific situations and help avoid cluttering up the context menu with unneeded entries.

Understanding the Context Menu Registry Structure

Context menu items are added to IE through entries in the registry. Items are added on a per-user basis in the `HKEY_CURRENT_USER` registry hive and stored in the key `HKEY_CURRENT_USER\Software\Microsoft\Internet Explorer\MenuExt\`. Each item is given its own key below `MenuExt`, and that name is used as the menu item's text.

Listing 10–20 shows the registry structure for a menu extension called "View in Firefox." This extension opens up the current page in Firefox and is described later in the section.

***Listing 10–20.** Example of a Menu Item Entry Called "View in Firefox"*

```
HKEY_CURRENT_USER\
   Software\
      Microsoft\
         Internet Explorer\
            MenuExt\
               View in Firefox\
                  (Default)  (REG_SZ)
                  Contexts   (REG_DWORD)
                  Flags      (REG_DWORD)
```

Each key holds three values: a string describing the URL of a page to access when the item is clicked, a binary value containing context flags, and a `REG_DWORD` value indicating the modality behavior of the launched URL. Table 10–8 outlines how these values are stored under a menu item's key and the associated registry types for each value.

***Table 10–8.** Context Menu Contexts and Associated Values*

Name	Value Type	Description
`(Default)`	`REG_SZ`	URL of script or markup to run
`Contexts`	`REG_DWORD`	Contexts in which to show the item
`Flags`	`REG_DWORD`	Value indicating whether the script should result in a new window

The first value, `(Default)`, is a `REG_SZ` (string) value pointing to a URL. URLs can reference any registered protocol on the system. For instance, a menu item could launch a URL in a new window by pointing to `http://www.google.com`. URLs can open a folder in the Explorer shell by referring to the `file://` protocol, and this same protocol can be used to launch an executable or open file types. Another item could refer to a resource in a DLL using the `res://` protocol. Developers using URLs that open HTML resources in executable files or libraries can access individual resource by their ID values, appending the ID value to the URL after comma (e.g., `res://my_library.dll,42`).

The value `Contexts` is a `REG_BINARY` value that outlines the contexts for which the menu item should be shown in the context menu. This allows context menu items that are tailored for specific browsing scenarios, such as opening the menu over an image or accessing it when text is selected. Table 10–9 outlines the contexts that may be used by a menu item.

Table 10–9. *Context Menu Contexts and Associated Values*

Context	Description	Flag Value
Default (Generic)	Menu items available in all page contexts	`0x0`
Images	Available when the context menu is opened on an image	`0x2`
Text Selection	Available when the context menu is opened over a text selection	`0x10`
Anchors and Links	Available when the context menu is opened over an anchor tag (e.g., a link)	`0x20`

A menu item is not restricted to one specific context. The values of each context may be combined as a bitmask using a logical `OR`. For instance, a menu item could opt to be shown only when a user right-clicks images or selected text; in this situation, the data stored in `Contexts` would be the logical `OR` of `0x2` and `0x10`, equaling `0x12`.

The `Flags` value is a `REG_DWORD` (32-bit integer) that selects a modality type for the launched URL. When the user clicks a context menu item, IE launches a new window to handle the call to the URL. Table 10–10 shows the possible values for this entry.

Table 10–10. *Context Menu Modal Behaviors*

Behavior	Description	DWORD Value
Hidden (Non-Modal)	Runs the script in a non-modal manner without displaying a window	`0x0`
Modal	Runs the associated URL in a modal way, similar to a script calling `window.showModalDialog`	`0x1`

Example: Browser Selection Context Menu Extension

Web developers need easy ways to test their web pages in multiple browsers. One way to simplify the experience of site testing is to reduce the number of steps it takes to launch pages in alternative browsers. The IE context menu can be used to simplify this situation.

Figure 10–21 shows a set of IE context menu extensions that launch other web browsers and display the current page within them. This example adds entries for the Opera, Firefox, IE 9 Developer Preview, and Safari web browsers.

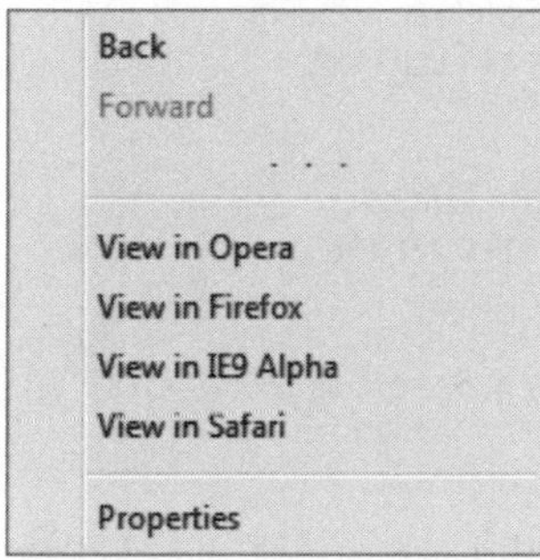

***Figure 10–21.** Context menu entries added by UseAlternateBrowsers*

When installed, the context menu shows these entries when a user right-clicks a given web page. Clicking any of these extensions will launch the browser indicated in the extension's name and display the URL of the current page in it. Figure 10–22 shows an example of this in action; Google is loaded in IE 8 and, using the context menu, Safari is launched showing the same web page.

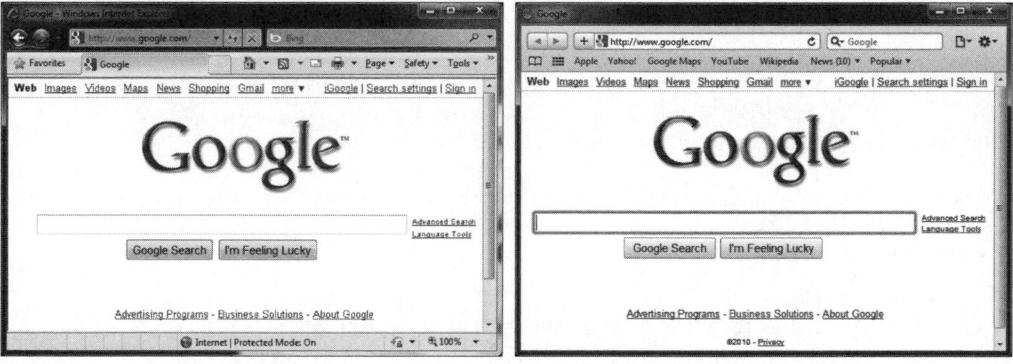

***Figure 10–22.** Pages in multiple browsers launched through UseAlternateBrowsers*

The first step in adding a context menu extension to IE is to add an entry in the registry. In this case, four different context menu extensions are added. This example adds the extensions to the current user's account when installed from the registry script in Listing 10–21.

Listing 10–21. *Installation Script for the LaunchBrowser Extension Set*

```
Windows Registry Editor Version 5.00

[HKEY_CURRENT_USER\Software\Microsoft\Internet Explorer\MenuExt\View in IE&9 Alpha]
@="C:\\Scripts\\IE\\ContextMenu\\UseAlternateBrowsers\\Run.html?browser=ie9alpha"
"Flags"=dword:00000001

[HKEY_CURRENT_USER\Software\Microsoft\Internet Explorer\MenuExt\View in Firefo&x]
@="C:\\Scripts\\IE\\ContextMenu\\UseAlternateBrowsers\\Run.html?browser=firefox"
"Flags"=dword:00000001

[HKEY_CURRENT_USER\Software\Microsoft\Internet Explorer\MenuExt\View in &Opera]
@="C:\\Scripts\\IE\\ContextMenu\\UseAlternateBrowsers\\Run.html?browser=opera"
"Flags"=dword:00000001

[HKEY_CURRENT_USER\Software\Microsoft\Internet Explorer\MenuExt\View in Safar&i]
@="C:\\Scripts\\IE\\ContextMenu\\UseAlternateBrowsers\\Run.html?browser=safari"
"Flags"=dword:00000001
```

In each case, a key is added underneath the `Software\Microsoft\Internet Explorer\MenuExt` key in the `HKEY_CURRENT_USER` hive. The default value of each key is a string referring to the location of a web page IE can launch on the local system.

The registry script creates a `(Default)` string that points to a local web page called `Run.html`. Each context menu extension passes a query parameter (`browser`) to this URL indicating a browser to launch. A JavaScript block on the page parses that query parameter and extracts the name of the intended browser from it (Listing 10–22).

Listing 10–22. *Web Page Containing Script to Launch Alternate Browsers*

```
<html>
   <head>
</head>
   <body>
      <script type="text/javascript">

         //  Get an associative array of query parameters and values
         //  passed to this URL
         function GetQueryParams()
         {
            var params = {};
            var items = window.location.search.substring(1).split("&");
            for(var i = 0; i < items.length; i++) {
               var pair = items[i].split("=");
               if(pair.length != 2) { continue; }
               else { params[pair[0]] = pair[1]; }
            }
            return params;
         }

         //  Get a the value of a specific query parameter specified
         //  by a string name
         function GetQueryParam(param)
```

```
        {
           var params = GetQueryParams();
           if(param in params) return params[param];
           else return null;
        }

        //  Location of script used to launch
        var launcher = "C:\\Scripts\\IE\\ContextMenu\\UseAlternateBrowsers\\RunAsync.vbs";

        //  Associative array of browsers and the location of
        //  their executables
        var apps = {
           "ie9alpha" : "file://%PROGRAMFILES%\\Internet Explorer Platform
                         Preview\\iepreview.exe",
           "firefox"  : "file://%PROGRAMFILES%\\Mozilla Firefox\\firefox.exe",
           "opera"    : "file://%PROGRAMFILES%\\Opera\\opera.exe",
           "safari"   : "file://%PROGRAMFILES%\\Safari\\Safari.exe"
        };

        //  Get the query parameter "browser" from the URL
        var app = GetQueryParam("browser");

        //  Make sure the browser exists
        if(app in apps) {

           //  Create a new ActiveX shell object
           var shell = new ActiveXObject("WScript.Shell");

           //  Run the executable from the browser's associative array and
           //  append the URL to the command line. Make sure to set the
           //  WindowStyle (second) param to 0 (hidden) and the WaitForExit
           //  param (thrid) to 0 (run browser as async)
           shell.run("wscript.exe \"" +
                     launcher + "\" \"" +
                     apps[app] + "\" \"" +
                     external.menuArguments.document.URL + "\""
                     );

        }

        //  Close the window or else it will stick around
        window.close();

     </script>
  </body>
</html>
```

Once extracted, the script attempts to launch a VBScript file through the Windows Scripting Host launcher, `wscript.exe`.

Windows Scripting Host is used to launch a script file outside of IE Protected Mode. Since IE may be running in Protected Mode, a script needs to be launched outside of that sandbox in order to start an external executable. Listing 10–23 details the contents of this script.

***Listing 10–23.** VBScript used to Launch Commands Outside of Protected Mode*

```
''  Grab the arguments passed to this script
Set Args = WScript.Arguments

''  Create a new Shell object
Set WshShell = WScript.CreateObject("WScript.Shell")

''  Concat all the passed arguments
Dim Command
For Each Arg in Args
   Command = Command + Chr(34) + Arg + Chr(34) + " "
Next

''  Send the concat string to the shell as a command
WshShell.Run Command, 1, False
```

When run, this script reads the name of a browser executable and the URL to run. It surrounds each of those entries in quotes and launches the selected browser through the Windows Explorer shell.

This extension can be uninstalled by removing the registry entries created earlier in this example. The script in Listing 10–24 shows such a script. When run, it will remove each of these context menu entries from IE (a change reflected the next time IE loads).

***Listing 10–24.** Uninstall Script for the ViewInBrowsers Extension Set*

```
Windows Registry Editor Version 5.00

[-HKEY_CURRENT_USER\Software\Microsoft\Internet Explorer\MenuExt\View in IE&9 Alpha]
[-HKEY_CURRENT_USER\Software\Microsoft\Internet Explorer\MenuExt\View in Firefo&x]
[-HKEY_CURRENT_USER\Software\Microsoft\Internet Explorer\MenuExt\View in &Opera]
[-HKEY_CURRENT_USER\Software\Microsoft\Internet Explorer\MenuExt\View in Safar&i]
```

Turning Off the Context Menu

The context menu itself may be turned off completely through the registry or indirectly using Group Policy. This entry has been present since IE 5, and gives enterprise developers and system administrators the ability to lock down this portion of IE from doing things such as initiating an elevation, as in the previous example.

This policy can be turned on in a system-wide or per-user context through the `HKEY_LOCAL_MACHINE` or `HKEY_CURRENT_USER` hives, respectively. The target key is `Software\Policies\Microsoft\Internet Explorer\Restrictions`, and the `DWORD` value is named `NoBrowserContextMenu`. When this value contains data of `0x1`, context menus are disabled; a value of `0x0` enables them.

Creating Context Menus with JavaScript

Context menus can be overridden using JavaScript as an alternative to the registry. This feature depends on events exposed to web pages through IE's JavaScript engine. Script-based context menu extensions allow developers to deeply customize the user experience on their web pages beyond traditional markup and script.

JavaScript context menus are dependent on mouse click events emitted by a target browser. IE and other major browsers enable web developer to hook into these events through oncontextmenu, onmouseover, onmouseout, and other events.

A page supporting JavaScript context menus can be built in many ways. Listing 10–25 shows an outline of what one of those pages might look like. It contains basic styles, page contents, the markup shown as the context menu, and script to handle the menu events and triggers.

***Listing 10–25.** Basic Outline of a Page Implementing a JavaScript Context Menu*

```
<html>
   <head>
      <meta http-equiv="pragma" content="no-cache">
      <!-- Context menu styles -->
      <title>JavaScript Context Menu</title>
   </head>
   <body>
      <!-- Page contents -->
      <!-- Context menu markup -->
      <!-- Context menu script -->
   </body>
</html>
```

The context menu can be represented by a block shown and hidden when the right (or left in some configurations) mouse button is clicked. This is exactly the same concept as the context menu typically shown on a page. Listing 10–26 shows an example block that contains a list of links that can be displayed on a page in this style.

***Listing 10–26.** List of Links to Be Shown in a JavaScript Context Menu*

```
<!-- Begin context menu markup -->
<div id="contextMenuWrapper">
   <ul class="contextMenu">
      <li><a href="http://www.google.com">Go to Google</a></li>
      <li><a href="http://www.yahoo.com">Go to Yahoo</a></li>
      <li><a href="http://www.bing.com">Go to Bing</a></li>
      <li id=""></li>
   </ul>
</div>
<!-- End context menu markup -->
```

JavaScript ties into the browser mouse events to make this menu appear and replace the traditional context menu. The script in Listing 10–27 ties into the browser onmousedown and oncontextmenu events with event handlers that show and hide the block defined above and place it underneath the mouse cursor.

***Listing 10–27.** Script Using Event Handlers to Show and Hide a Context Menu*

```
<!-- Start context menu script -->
<script type="text/javascript">

   //  Create placeholder variables that will be used to
   //  access the context menu wrapper and keep track of when
   //  the right mouse button was clicked
   var showContextMenu = false;
```

```
var mouseOverContextMenu = false;
var contextMenu = document.getElementById('contextMenuWrapper');

//  Add a callback function to the body element event handler on
//  the document
document.body.onmousedown = Body_OnMouseDown;
document.body.oncontextmenu = Body_OnContextMenu;

//  Keep track of when the mouse is on the context menu
//  wrapper and when it isn't
contextMenu.onmouseover
   = function() { mouseOverContextMenu = true; }
contextMenu.onmouseout
   = function() { mouseOverContextMenu = false; }

//  Return the currently selected text on a page
function GetSelectedText() {

   var text = "";

   //  Attempt to get selection information from various
   //  browser configurations
   if(window.getSelection) text = window.getSelection();
   if(document.selection) text = document.selection.createRange().text;
   if(document.getSelection) text = document.getSelection();
   return text;

}

//  Handles the OnMouseDown event on the body element
function Body_OnMouseDown(event) {

   //  Ensure that both the event and the event target
   //  objects are available
   if (event == null) event = window.event;
   var target = event.target != null ? event.target : event.srcElement;

   //  If the right mouse button was clicked, mark that
   //  the context menu should be shown on the context
   //  menu event
   if (event.button == 2) showContextMenu = true;
   else if(!mouseOverContextMenu) contextMenu.style.display = 'none';
}

//  Handles the OnContextMenu event on the body element
function Body_OnContextMenu(event) {

   //  Ensure that both the event and the event target
   //  objects are available
   if (event == null) event = window.event;
   var target = event.target != null ? event.target : event.srcElement;

   //  Show a custom context menu if a user triggered
   //  the right mouse button
```

```
        if (showContextMenu) {

            // Get the current page offsets due to scrolling
            var scrollTop
               = document.body.scrollTop ?
                 document.body.scrollTop : document.documentElement.scrollTop;
            var scrollLeft
               = document.body.scrollLeft ?
                 document.body.scrollLeft : document.documentElement.scrollLeft;

            // Hide the div while changes are made to it
            contextMenu.style.display = 'none';

            // Move the div to where the mouse is located
            contextMenu.style.left = event.clientX + scrollLeft + 'px';
            contextMenu.style.top = event.clientY + scrollTop + 'px';

            // Display the context menu
            contextMenu.style.display = 'block';

            // Don't show the context menu again for this event
            showContextMenu = false;

            // Return false so the browser context menu will
            // not show up
            return false;

        }

    }

</script>
<!-- End context menu script -->
```

The script begins by creating some placeholder variables: showContextMenu represents the current state of the mouse event capture, mouseOverContextMenu keeps track of the mouse location when the new context menu is open, and contextMenu references the block element of the custom menu <div>.

Body_OnMouseDown and Body_OnContextMenu are defined next, attaching to the OnMouseDown and OnContextMenu events on the current document's <body> tag, respectively.

The context menu is rounded out with a stylesheet, allowing it to become distinct from the rest of the page and to look more like a real context menu. Listing 10–28 shows some basic styles applied to the example menu.

Listing 10–28. *CSS for the JavaScript Context Menu*

```
<!-- Begin context menu styles -->
<style>
   #contextMenuWrapper {
      border: 2px solid #444; display: none; position: absolute; }
   .contextMenu {
      margin: 0; padding: 10px; list-style-type: none; background-color: white; }
   .contextMenu li:hover { }
   .contextMenu hr { border: 0; margin: 5px; width: 150px; }
   .contextMenu a { color: #305aa6; border: 0 !important; }
```

```
    .contextMenu a:hover { text-decoration: underline !important; }
</style>
<!-- End context menu styles -->
```

Figure 10–23 shows the result of the markup, script, and styles laid out in this section. When a user right-clicks this page, a JavaScript-based context menu (simulated via a `<div>` block) is shown. When a user focuses outside of an open menu, this menu closes.

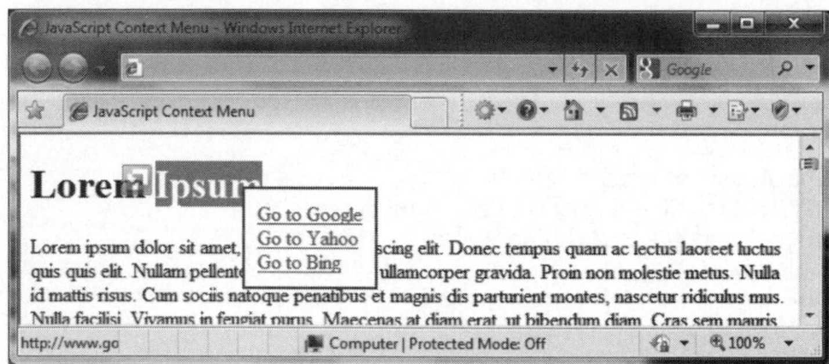

Figure 10–23. *Custom script-based context menu on a sample page*

Summary

Lightweight browser extensions are a great way to extend the functionality of the IE frame and pages without forcing you to delve deep into the murky waters of COM programming. On the other hand, these extensions are versatile enough to allow for it if you want to take advantage of the additional functionality exposed by COM. All in all, these extensions are simple yet complete, allowing for some interesting and inventive add-on scenarios for IE and your projects.

I began this chapter by discussing the role of lightweight extensions in both the browser frame and individual pages. I presented frame extensions next, covering both toolbar buttons and menu item extensions. I highlighted the role of lightweight extensions in the in-page context menu, describing how you cannot only extend IE but extend pages themselves. Last, I covered some pure JavaScript solutions with regard to the context menu; you can develop custom menus for your pages without ever having to install an extension to a user's computer.

CHAPTER 11

■ ■ ■

Developing Applications with the WebBrowser Control

The web platform (HTML, JavaScript, etc.) is supplanting native code platforms not only for browsers, but for general application development as well. Standalone applications, mobile phone applications, and a myriad of other non-browser-based programs are using markup, styles, and script as a base for their core functionality and UIs.

Applications using web technologies depend on access to and interpretation of web content; however, it wouldn't make any sense for every single application to provide its own networking stacks, protocol handlers, parsers, or layout engines. A number of companies have provided this offering to developers, but the most used and well known of these is Microsoft's WebBrowser control. This component is a set of COM-based libraries that can be hosted by an application to render web content. The WebBrowser control can do almost everything that IE can, from downloading and loading a web page to enforcing security policy on remote objects.

In this chapter I discuss ways you can use the WebBrowser control and the Microsoft .NET Framework to integrate the features of IE into your application. I begin with a simple overview of how this control can be imported and used in a basic C# project. Next, I cover topics such as event handling and access to a page's object model. Integration techniques are next, and it is there that I show you how your application can be informed of and control detailed aspects of this control. I finish up the chapter providing examples of IE's public API, allowing you to implement niche features that are not be exposed directly in the WebBrowser component. Let's open up our IDEs and get started!

Building a Simple WebBrowser Application

The WebBrowser control is a very powerful component that is very simple to integrate into almost any application. Developers can integrate this control into any language that supports the Windows COM-based programming model. The following sections highlight how a developer can get up and running with the WebBrowser control and related components using Visual Studio and C#.

Preparing to Use the WebBrowser Control

The WebBrowser control is a native assembly exposed through COM whose components can be interpreted as ActiveX controls or understood from type libraries. In .NET, the WebBrowser control is a wrapper for public APIs exposed by IE. This wrapper automatically marshals between types understood by managed and unmanaged code, making it easy for developers to include IE's APIs without complicated conversion algorithms.

The first step in using the WebBrowser control is to prepare the ActiveX controls and type libraries of SHDocVw and MSHTML for .NET interop. The SHDocVw DLL file, located in the `System32` directory, must be imported and analyzed for use in managed code. The `aximp` application, supplied with the .NET SDK, allows a developer to import functionality from a native COM control into an interop library wrapper. Listing 11–1 shows the command for converting this DLL.

***Listing 11–1.** Commmand for Converting a COM ActiveX DLL to a .NET Interop Assembly*

```
aximp %windir%\system32\shdocvw.dll
tlbimp %windir%\system32\mshtml.tlb
```

Figure 11–1 shows the results: two generated assemblies, `SHDocVw.dll` and `AxSHDocVw.dll`. These libraries can be referenced in a Visual Studio project needing the control.

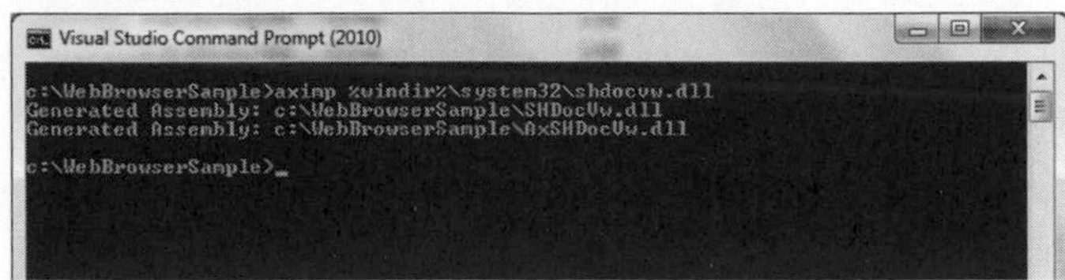

***Figure 11–1.** Results from running aximp on SHDocVw.dll*

Type libraries, like ActiveX controls, must be wrapped before they can be understood by a managed application. MSHTML, the core DLL of IE's layout and rendering engine, Trident, falls into this category and must imported. Listing 11–1 (shown previously) shows the use of `tlbimp` for MSHTML.

These libraries can be added as a reference to a .NET project once converted. Figure 11–2 shows the process of adding references to these three files—`SHDocVw.dll`, `AxSHDocVw.dll`, and `MSHTML.dll`—to a project.

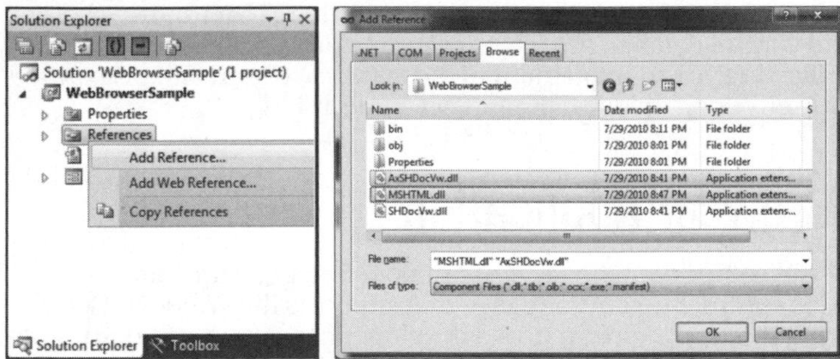

***Figure 11–2.** Visual Studio Add Reference context menu and dialog*

Once added, controls from these libraries can be loaded as interactive controls for form applications or referenced for access to browser functionality.

Creating an Instance of the WebBrowser Control (AxWebBrowser)

The WebBrowser control (`AxWebBrowser`, a component of AxSHDocVw) imported from the libraries in the previous section must be added to a Windows Form or a class programmatically. `AxWebBrowser` is a thin layer around the native-code COM objects exposed by IE.

Listing 11–2 shows the start of a basic application that will be used as the basis for the remaining examples in this chapter. It is a Windows Form called `BrowserBasic`, a very simple "browser" that can access web sites and demonstrate the functionality of the control. The class begins by defining a variable called `Browser`, an initially unset instance of the `AxWebBrowser` component. The constructor is used to call two methods: `InitializeComponent()`, generated by the form designer, and `InitializeWebBrowser()`. We'll implement the latter function to create a new instance of the browser component.

Listing 11–2. *Form Object Constructor Calling a Helper Method to Set Up a WebBrowser Instance*

```
public partial class BrowserBasic : Form
{
    public AxWebBrowser Browser;
    // ... other objects

    public BrowserBasic()
    {
        // Initialize the component (designer)
        InitializeComponent();
        // Initialize the WebBrowser control
        InitializeWebBrowser();
    }
    ...
```

Listing 11–3 reveals `InitializeWebBrowser()`. This function sets a new instance of `AxWebBrowser` to the variable `Browser`. It starts initialization of the control by calling `Browser.BeginInit()`. The new object is added to the main form and docked to it.

Listing 11–3. *Function to Initialize and Configure a WebBrowser Control Instance*

```
public void InitializeWebBrowser()
{
    // Create a new instance of the WebBrowser control
    Browser = new AxWebBrowser();

    // Add the control to the main form and dock it inside
    // of a panel
    this.Controls.Add(Browser);
    Browser.Parent = this;
    Browser.Dock = DockStyle.Fill;

    // Finish initializing the ActiveX
    Browser.EndInit();
}
```

The function ends by closing out the ActiveX initialization process for that control, calling `Browser.EndInit()`. This final call enables the control to be loaded and displayed by its owner form.

The remainder of this application's design was done using Visual Studio's form designer. Figure 11–3 shows the form's design. At the top is a toolbar, `CommandBar`, containing a text box for URLs (`AddressBox`), a Go button (GoButton), Forward button (ForwardButton), Home button (HomeButton), Stop button (StopButton), and Search button (SearchButton). These buttons are named for and intended to perform the same functions as their counterparts in IE and other major browsers (Figure 11–3).

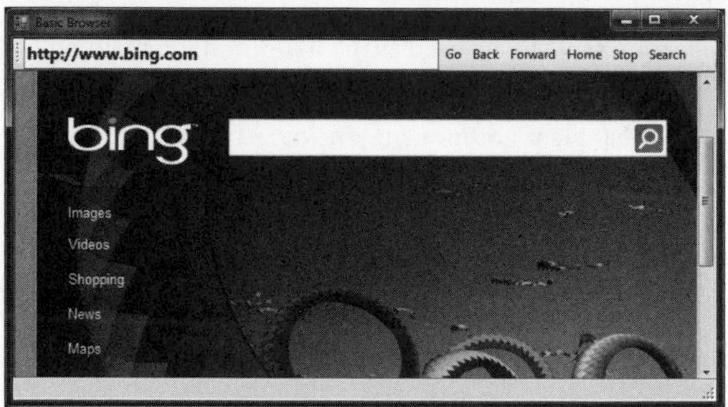

Figure 11–3. *The BasicBrowser application, form components, and WebBrowser control*

Users of this application can access a web site by entering a URL into the AddressBox text box and then pressing the Enter key (AddressBox_KeyPress) or clicking the Go button (GoButton_Click). Both events trigger the WebBrowser's Navigate() function. This function is used to navigate a WebBrowser control to the URL passed to it. Listing 11–4 shows the GoButton_Click and AddressBox_KeyPress event handlers, both of which call the Navigate() function and pass to it the contents of AddressBox.

Listing 11–4. *Event Handlers for Navigating a WebBrowser Instance to an Address*

```
private void GoButton_Click(object sender, System.EventArgs e)
{
    // Navigate to the address found in the address text box
    Browser.Navigate(AddressBox.Text);
}

private void AddressBox_KeyPress(object sender, KeyPressEventArgs e)
{
    // If enter was pressed, tread as if the "go" button was hit
    if (e.KeyChar == (char)Keys.Enter)
        Browser.Navigate(AddressBox.Text);
}
```

The remaining toolbar items access other major functions on the WebBrowser control instance. The Back button click handler (BackButton_Click) commands the WebBrowser control to go backward one step in its browsing history. The Forward button does the opposite—the click event (ForwardButton_Click) moves forward in the travel log. The Home button click event (HomeButton_Click) commands the browser to go to the current user's home page. Lastly, the Stop button references the StopButton_Click click event handler; it calls the WebBrowser object's Stop() function, halting any in-progress navigations occurring in the current WebBrowser instance (Listing 11–5).

Listing 11–5. Button Event Handlers Used for Calling WebBrowser Functions

```
private void BackButton_Click(object sender, System.EventArgs e)
{
    // Go back in the travel log
    Browser.GoBack();
}

private void ForwardButton_Click(object sender, System.EventArgs e)
{
    // Go forward in the travel log
    Browser.GoForward();
}

private void HomeButton_Click(object sender, System.EventArgs e)
{
    // Go to the user's home page
    Browser.GoHome();
}

private void StopButton_Click(object sender, System.EventArgs e)
{
    // Stop the current navigation
    Browser.Stop();
}
```

The form's navigational elements provide the most basic functionality to access, display, and navigate web content. The application, however, remains primitive because while it allows the user to command the browser to perform a task, the application remains unaware of the events occurring in the WebBrowser.

Handling Basic Events

IE's API provides an event-driven system that gives developers the chance to tailor an application's functionality based events that occur within the WebBrowser object. The control exposes a subset of those events directly, and another subset through objects reachable from the WebBrowser object. These events can be configured to notify applications of events such as the start of a navigation, the completion of a download, and the creation of a new window.

The sample in Listing 11–6 builds on the basic browser constructed in the previous section. Unlike its base class, this application will play an interactive role in the WebBrowser control's activities by handling the events it exposes.

Listing 11–6. Form for Handling WebBrowser Events, Based on the BrowserBasic Class

```
public class BrowserEventHandling : BrowserBasic
{
    public BrowserEventHandling(): base()
    {
        // Latch onto the DWebBrowserEvents2 events omitted by the
        // WebBrowser control
        HandleBasicEvents();
    }
```

The constructor here calls into a function called `HandleBasicEvents()`. When called, this function opts-into receiving callback notifications from a number of events on the WebBrowser instance (Listing 11–7).

***Listing 11–7.** Method for Adding Handlers to WebBrowser Instance Events*

```
private void HandleBasicEvents()
{
    // Add handlers to some of the basic web browser events
    Browser.BeforeNavigate2 += Browser_BeforeNavigate2;
    Browser.DocumentComplete += Browser_DocumentComplete;
    Browser.FileDownload += Browser_FileDownload;
    Browser.NavigateComplete2 += Browser_NavigateComplete2;
    Browser.NavigateError += Browser_NavigateError;
    Browser.NewProcess += Browser_NewProcess;
    Browser.NewWindow2 += Browser_NewWindow2;
}
```

Each event is handed a delegate instance that can be used when a specific event occurs. For instance, this function points to a private function, `Browser_BeforeNavigate2`, to be called when `BeforeNavigate2` fires (Listing 11–8).

***Listing 11–8.** Series of WebBrowser Event Handlers Writing to the Debug Stream*

```
void Browser_NewWindow2(object sender,
   DWebBrowserEvents2_NewWindow2Event e)
{
    Debug.WriteLine("Event: DWebBrowserEvents2 NewWindow2");
}

void Browser_NewProcess(object sender,
   DWebBrowserEvents2_NewProcessEvent e)
{
    Debug.WriteLine("Event: DWebBrowserEvents2 NewProcess");
}
...
```

Listing 11–9 shows some output from the Visual Studio Debug window, captured while navigating to web pages using this application.

***Listing 11–9.** Output from Simple WebBrowser Event Handlers*

```
The thread '<No Name>' (0x10a8) has exited with code 0 (0x0).
Event: DWebBrowserEvents2 NewWindow2
Event: DWebBrowserEvents2 NewProcess
```

Accessing the Object Model

Web content that is successfully processed and parsed by Trident (IE's layout and rendering engine) is exposed to developers through a myriad of COM objects. Together, these objects form a hierarchy called the object model. When an instance of the WebBrowser control successfully completes the construction of a document, instances of these objects pertaining to a specific page are exposed through its members.

The following sections detail how these objects may be accessed and modified when using the WebBrowser control to load a web page.

Attaching to Document and Window Objects

The availability of most top-level properties, methods, and events on the WebBrowser control are available as long as the WebBrowser has initialized. Other objects, such as those based on IHTMLDocument and IHTMLWindow, are only available when the WebBrowser control has loaded a page parsed, laid out, and rendered by MSHTML (Trident).

The WebBrowser control is similar to a full IE window in that both can host documents other than HTML documents (IHTMLDocument objects). Any document object (Active Document Server) can be loaded into the WebBrowser control. This means that not every document will have an IHTMLDocument object present. Developers looking to attach to this specific object should test that the document type is an HTML document and that the IHTMLDocument object is in fact present within the loaded document instance.

The following sample demonstrates a new WebBrowser container based on the one developed in the last section. This application performs two functions: analyzing the HTML parsed by the browser, and handling events from objects generated by that process. To show the first task, it generates a report on all links (IHTMLAnchorElement) present within a document. For the second, the application takes over the JavaScript error dialog in favor of a custom one.

Listing 11–10 is the constructor for this application. This function can't start work on either of the tasks intended for the application because no page has been loaded into the object yet. To solve this problem, the constructor sinks the control's NavigateComplete2 event, pointing the event to a callback that can run with assurance that the objects in question exist.

Listing 11–10. *Constuctor Adding NavigateComplete2 Handler to WebBrowser Control Instance*

```
public class BrowserModelAccess : BrowserEventHandling
{
    TextBox PageReport;
    bool eventsSunk = false;
    public BrowserModelAccess() : base()
    {
        // Register for the NavigateComplete event for both the
        // link report and the script error handling
        Browser.NavigateComplete2 += Browser_NavigateComplete2;
    }
    ...
```

Listing 11–11 shows the initialization of both the reporting and error handling portions of the application. This is handled by the NavigateComplete2 event handler, Browser_NavigateComplete2. This function kicks off the process for both building the link report and sinking error events.

Listing 11–11. *Waiting for Available Window and Document Objects Using NavigateComplete2*

```
void Browser_NavigateComplete2(object sender, DWebBrowserEvents2_NavigateComplete2Event e)
{
    // Pass the valid document and window objects and build
    // a link report on the document
    BuildLinkReport();

    // Sink script errors for this window instance
```

```
    if(!eventsSunk) {
        eventsSunk = true;
        SinkScriptErrorEvents();
    }
}
```

Unlike the constructor, NavigateCompete2 indicates that a WebBrowser instance has requested, downloaded, parsed, and loaded a document into a valid window and document object under a certain WebBrowser instance. These valid objects can now be used by BuildLinkReport() and SinkScriptErrorEvents() to read and receive callbacks from target window and document objects.

Accessing the Browser Object Model

The markup, script, and styles interpreted by IE and its components are exposed through a large set of objects. These items together form the object model, a traversable and hierarchical model used by IE to display and interact with the web page.

Objects are available for access as children of an object implementing the IHTMLDocument interface. The WebBrowser control exposes such an instance through its public member Document. This member (and thus its children) is only available when the browser is displaying an HTML document.

Listing 11–12 shows BuildLinkReport(), a function called during the NavigateComplete2 event handler shown in the last section. This function begins by grabbing and casting the document object instance from the WebBrowser instance. If this instance is valid (not null), it starts the "report" by writing some document metadata to the debugging window.

Listing 11–12. *Function to Report All Links on an IHTMLDocument2 Object*

```
void BuildLinkReport()
{
    // Grab the document object from the WebBrowser control
    IHTMLDocument2 document = Browser.Document as IHTMLDocument2;
    if (document == null) return;

    // Write the title and indicate the URL
    Debug.WriteLine("\n\nLINK REPORT for " + document.url);

    // Report the page URL, file size, and total number of links
    Debug.WriteLine("URL: " + document.url);
    Debug.WriteLine("Filesize: " + document.fileSize.ToString());
    Debug.WriteLine("Total Links: " + document.links.length.ToString());

    // Display all the links on the current page
    foreach (IHTMLAnchorElement link in document.links)
        Debug.WriteLine("  >> href=" + link.href);
}
```

The last two tasks of this function are to report on the number of links and the href values of those links. The links on a page are exposed by a links member on the document object. This object implements IHTMLElementCollection and represents a collection of objects derived from a direct or indirect implementation of IHTMLElement.

The link count is written to the debugger using a string conversion of IHTMLElementCollection's length property. The actual link href values are displayed by iterating through each IHTMLAnchorElement object within the links collection; each URL is recorded using that interface's href value (Figure 11–4).

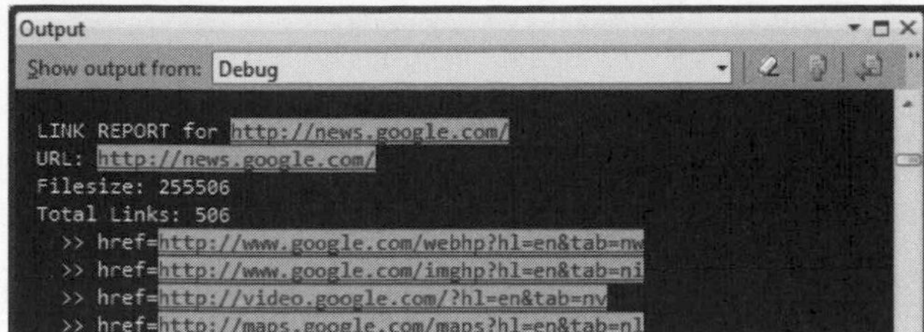

***Figure 11–4.** Link report results after traversing link objects from news.google.com*

Sinking Object Model Events

Just like the base WebBrowser object, the objects present under a WebBrowser's `IHTMLDocument` implementation instance each have events that can be accessed and handled by a WebBrowser container application. These objects provide insight beyond basic document information exposed up through the WebBrowser object; applications can go deep, and even implement the same events used and thrown by JavaScript on a page.

The `SinkScriptErrorEvents()` function in Listing 11–13 is called during the `NavigateComplete2` event (as the previous helper was). This function replaces IE's JavaScript error dialog with its own. To accomplish this feat, it adds an `OnError` handler to the `Window` object of a WebBrowser instance's child `IHTMLDocument`.

The first step is to turn off JavaScript errors in the current WebBrowser instance. A simple way of achieving this is through the WebBrowser control's `Silent` property. The `Silent` property controls such reporting; when `true`, it does not display error dialogs, when `false`, it does (as long as script debugging is not disabled either in the Internet Settings Control Panel or by IE policies). The function then attempts to grab the document object and, subsequently, that document's `window` object. If those attempts are valid, the function will cast a variable to the event interface on `IHTMLWindow` and attach a new handler to that object (`Browser_HTMLWindowEvents2_OnError`).

***Listing 11–13.** Turning Off JavaScript Errors and Adding a Handler to Display Custom Ones*

```
void SinkScriptErrorEvents()
{
    // Turn off default script errors
    Browser.Silent = true;

    // Grab the document object from the WebBrowser control
    IHTMLDocument2 document = (IHTMLDocument2)Browser.Document;
    if (document == null) return;

    // Grab the window object from the document object
    HTMLWindow2 window = (HTMLWindow2)document.parentWindow;
    if (window == null) return;

    // Cast the window object to the window events interface
    HTMLWindowEvents2_Event windowEvents = (HTMLWindowEvents2_Event)window;
    if (windowEvents == null) return;

    // Attach to the error event on the window object; this
```

```
    // will be sent a notification when a script error occurs
    windowEvents.onerror += Browser_HTMLWindowEvents2_OnError;
}
```

The last piece is the handler itself. This is a very simple event, receiving three important error items: the error description, the URL of the file causing the error, and the line number of the offending script (Listing 11–14).

Listing 11–14. *IHTMLWindow OnError Handler Replacing IE-JavaScript Error Dialogs*

```
void Browser_HTMLWindowEvents2_OnError(string description, string url, int line)
{
    // Show a custom message box that displays the javascript
    // error to the user
    MessageBox.Show(String.Format(
        "Description: {0}\n\nLine: {1}",
        description,
        line.ToString()),
        "JavaScript Error",
        MessageBoxButtons.OK,
        MessageBoxIcon.Warning
        );
}
```

This function proceeds to show a warning-style message box displaying error information returned from the event handler when invoked (Figure 11–5).

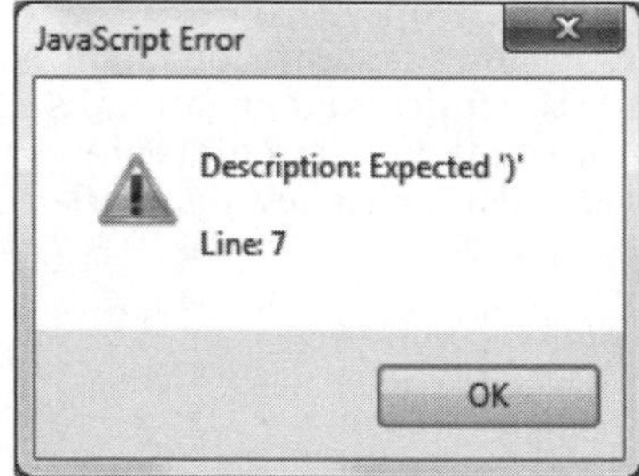

Figure 11–5. *Custom JavaScript error dialog triggered by the HTML Window OnError event*

Achieving Tight Integration with IE

The full IE application is full of features that link the browser frame with the web page running inside of it. The title bar displays the page title; the status bar shows the progress of composing the page; a lock icon appears for secure pages, and so on. Display of this information relies directly on the browser window having a relationship with the internal browser engine, the system networking stack, and so forth.

Many of the methods and data used by the IE browser frame to convey information are already available in .NET through the WebBrowser control and other .NET interoperable libraries. The WebBrowser control makes this data easily accessible to applications hosting the component. The following sections highlight examples of how an application hosting the WebBrowser control can use this information.

Setting Up the Application

The previous section in this chapter highlighted ways an application using the WebBrowser control can access and manipulate the object model. It also tied together the earlier section on events by hooking into a number of events exposed by those objects.

Listing 11–15 demonstrates an application built on the previous example that integrates IE features and navigation information into its UI. It begins by making the previous example its base class.

Listing 11–15. *Class and Constructor for a TightLy Integrated WebBrowser Host*

```
public class BrowserIntegration : BrowserModelAccess
{
    public BrowserIntegration() : base()
    {
        // Integrate UI with IE notifications
        BuildInterfaceIntegration();
        // Integrate with the NewWindow event
        BuildWindowIntegration();
        // Add menu and command features
        BuildMenuAndCommands();
    } ...
```

The constructor for this class handles three major integration points. First, it integrates the application's form and UI with data and events coming back from the WebBrowser control. Next, it enables the application to handle pop-up windows "in-house" instead of having those windows opened outside of this application or in an external browser. Last, it creates some basic UI code that demonstrates how IE commands such as Save As and Print can be invoked using a wrapped form of `IOleCommandTarget` command execution.

Integrating WebBrowser Events with the IE UI

Web browsers typically convey information about the process of a request to a user through their UI. When loading a page, users can see loading information in the page title, animated wait cursors, and information about the loading process in the status bar. This is the same for commands and actions outside of viewing a page; cleaning out history, downloading a file, or saving a page to disk all result in progress information conveyed to the user.

The WebBrowser control offers a rich set of information concerning its progress performing a set of actions and regarding objects and pages loaded within it. The properties and events exposed in this assembly can be used by a container application to convey this same information to users.

Listing 11–16 highlights the first integration example in this section. The `BuildInterfaceIntegration()` function sets properties and hook events in order to gather this information from the control and convey it to the user. The constructor runs this function, and it in turn sinks three events on the WebBrowser control instance for the class: `NavigateComplete2`, `TitleChange`, and `StatusTextChange`.

Listing 11–16. *Registering Event Handlers That Will Convey Progress to Application UI*

```
private void BuildInterfaceIntegration()
{
    // Sink key events that convey progress information to
    // page or object progress
    Browser.DocumentComplete += Browser_DocumentComplete;
```

```
    Browser.TitleChange += Browser_TitleChange;
    Browser.StatusTextChange += Browser_StatusTextChange;
}
```

These event callbacks are defined next. First in Listing 11–17 is the DocumentComplete event. This event is fired when a document download, navigation, and load is finished; this means that the page in the main window is the page that the user has finally arrived at. This event is a good time to get the current address, and has an accurate address to display in the address bar. When this callback is fired, it takes the current location URL of the WebBrowser instance and displays it in the address bar text box AddressBox.

Listing 11–17. *Event Callbacks for WebBrowser Events That Convey Progress Information*

```
void Browser_DocumentComplete(object sender,
    DWebBrowserEvents2_DocumentCompleteEvent e)
{
    // Set the address box text to the current URL
    AddressBox.Text = Browser.LocationURL;
}

void Browser_TitleChange(object sender,
    DWebBrowserEvents2_TitleChangeEvent e)
{
    // Set window title to the page title
    this.Text = e.text + " - Custom WebBrowser";
}

void Browser_StatusTextChange(object sender,
    DWebBrowserEvents2_StatusTextChangeEvent e)
{
    // Change the status text to the text emitted by IE
    BrowserStatusText.Text = e.text;
}
```

Next is the TitleChange event. This event is fired every time the title of the main document (or frame) changes. In IE and other browsers, this change is reflected in the main application title, and if it's using tabs, the tab in which the page is loaded. This function provides that behavior for our application. When the TitleChange event fires, this function changes the title of the application window to include the title of the current page.

The last event handled by this class is the StatusTextChange event. IE uses its status bar pane to convey status information from the loading of the page. This data isn't just shown in the IE frame window, however—it is emitted to any application using the WebBrowser control. This function taps into that information and applies the current status text data to this application's own status bar each time that data is changed and the event is fired.

Mimicking Window Behavior of IE

Developers looking to use a wrapped WebBrowser control as a browser substitute might find that some web sites or user activities open pages in IE or their default browser. By default, a pop-up or user command to open a link in a new window will force a WebBrowser control instance to launch that page outside of its owner application. Pop-up navigations can be canceled through the BeforeNavigate2 event, but that is not the only option.

Listing 11–18 shows a function called `BuildWindowIntegration()`. This is called by its class's constructor and is tasked with enabling this setting on the control and kicking off the event handling process for windows.

***Listing 11–18.** Function to Register WebBrowser Instance As Window Handler and Attach Event*

```
private void BuildWindowIntegration()
{

    // Sink the NewWindow2 event
    Browser.NewWindow2 += Browser_NewWindow2;
}
```

The `NewWindow2` event callback definition follows in Listing 11–19. This event will be fired and this function called whenever a pop-up or user action requests an external window. The function begins by creating a new instance of this application; just as IE would launch another instance of IE, this application will clone itself to host the request.

***Listing 11–19.** New Window Event Handler for the WebBrowser Control Registered As a Browser*

```
void Browser_NewWindow2(object sender,
    DWebBrowserEvents2_NewWindow2Event e)
{

    // Create a new instance of this form
    BrowserIntegration newBrowserForm;
    newBrowserForm = new BrowserIntegration();

    // Return the new WebBrowser control instance on the new application
    // instance as the new client site
    e.ppDisp = newBrowserForm.Browser.Application;

    // Show the new window
    newBrowserForm.Visible = true;

}
```

The new WebBrowser control instance on the new form instance is applied to the outbound variable `e.ppDisp`; this allows the WebBrowser to navigate the new WebBrowser instance rather than sending the navigation request to the system default browser. Finally, the function shows the newly created form to the user.

Surfacing and Executing OLE Commands

Much of IE's functionality is exposed as commands that can be targeted at IE's application site. In the past (and still today in many cases), applications who wished to run commands on IE or other applications would implement an interface called `IOleCommandTarget`. This interface defines two functions: `QueryStatus`, which lets an application find out if a command is available, and `Exec`, which executes a command.

The WebBrowser control simplifies the process of using OLE commands by implementing and wrapping the `IOleCommandTarget` interface.

The code in Listing 11–20 allows the application to handle two of these commands: Print and Save As. The first part of the process is to make these commands available to users; the save-as functionality is added to a new menu, and the Print button is added to the application's toolbar.

Listing 11–20. Constuction of Save As and Print UI and Event Handler Registration

```
// Declare new menu and button objects
public MenuStrip Menu;
public ToolStripMenuItem MenuFile;
...
public ToolStripItem PrintButton;

private void BuildMenuAndCommands()
{
    // Add a Print button to the toolbar
    PrintButton = CommandBar.Items.Add("Print");
    ...
    PrintButton.Click += new System.EventHandler(PrintButton_Click);

    // Create the File > Save As menu item
    MenuFileSaveAs = new ToolStripMenuItem("Save As...");
    MenuFileSaveAs.Click += MenuFileSaveAs_Click;

    // Create the File menu and add children
    MenuFile = new ToolStripMenuItem("&File");
    MenuFile.Click += MenuFile_Click;
    MenuFile.DropDownItems.Add(MenuFileSaveAs)
    ...

    // Create a new main menu strip and add all the items to it
    Menu = new MenuStrip();
    Menu.Items.AddRange(new ToolStripItemCollection(
        Menu, new ToolStripItem[] { MenuFile, ...}));
    Menu.Dock = DockStyle.Top;
    Controls.Add(Menu);
}
```

The toolbar button for Print has a click event handler attached (`PrintButton_Click`). Likewise, the menu item used for Save As is given an event handler of `MenuFileSaveAs_Click` and its parent menu item is attached to `MenuFile_Click`. These handlers will not only launch the related functionality but also play a role in determining when those commands are available (Figure 11–6).

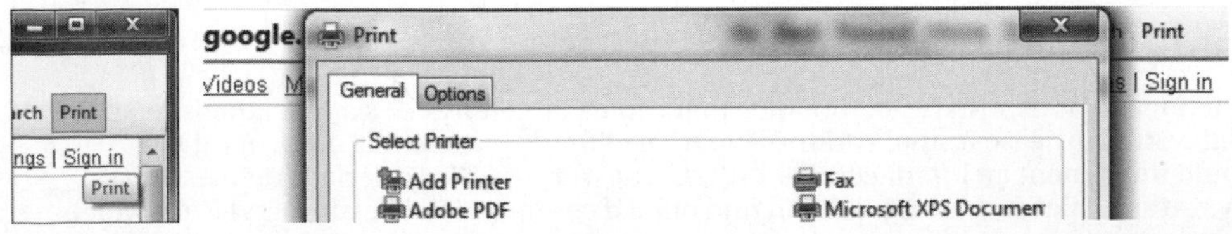

Figure 11–6. Print button and dialog using Exec commands

The first handler here (Listing 11–21) is that controlling the print functionality. When a user clicks this toolbar button, this function is called. Before printing, however, the application needs to see if printing is available for the current state of the WebBrowser control instance. For example, when a page is sitting idle, it would make sense for IE to make printing available; on the other hand, if IE is in the middle of navigating, the command will be disabled because complete page data is not available.

Listing 11–21. *Click Event for the Print Button OLE Command*

```
void PrintButton_Click(object sender, EventArgs e)
{

    // Query the status of the Print command
    SHDocVw.OLECMDF printQuery =
        Browser.QueryStatusWB(SHDocVw.OLECMDID.OLECMDID_PRINT);

    // If the command is enabled, display the Print dialog
    if ((printQuery & SHDocVw.OLECMDF.OLECMDF_ENABLED) != 0)
        Browser.ExecWB(
            SHDocVw.OLECMDID.OLECMDID_PRINT,
            SHDocVw.OLECMDEXECOPT.OLECMDEXECOPT_PROMPTUSER
            );

}
```

`QueryStatusWB()` is called to determine whether this command is ready to be used. If the preceding `if` statement is true, meaning that the return value of the command query contained an `OLECMDF_ENABLED` (enabled) tag, then the command is available and may be called through `ExecWB()`.

The printing function protects against errors; however, it does not provide useful feedback if the command isn't available. Figure 11–7 shows an example application that makes another piece of browser functionality available: the Save As menu item.

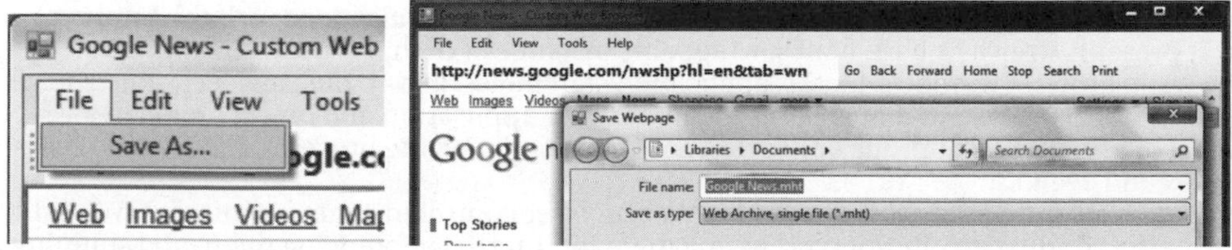

Figure 11–7. *Save As menu item and Save As window*

The Save As menu item and its parent, the File menu, work with `QueryStatusWB()` to convey availability of this command to the user. The `MenuFile_Click` handler enables or disables this command to save based on availability. The function begins by querying for the availability of the Save As command and persisting it to a variable. Next, it enables or disables the child menu item based on whether its associated command is enabled or disabled (Listing 11–22).

Listing 11–22. *Click Events for the File Menu and Save As Items Using the Save As OLE Command*

```
void MenuFile_Click(object sender, EventArgs e)
{
    // Query the status of the Save As command
    SHDocVw.OLECMDF saveAsQuery =
        Browser.QueryStatusWB(SHDocVw.OLECMDID.OLECMDID_SAVEAS);
```

```
    // Enable the Save As menu item only
    // if that command is currently available
    MenuFileSaveAs.Enabled =
        ((saveAsQuery & SHDocVw.OLECMDF.OLECMDF_ENABLED) != 0);
}

void MenuFileSaveAs_Click(object sender, EventArgs e)
{
    // Query the status of the Save As command
    SHDocVw.OLECMDF saveAsQuery =
    Browser.QueryStatusWB(SHDocVw.OLECMDID.OLECMDID_SAVEAS);

    // Execute the Save As action and prompt the user
    // with a Save As dialog
    if ((saveAsQuery & SHDocVw.OLECMDF.OLECMDF_ENABLED) != 0)
        Browser.ExecWB(
            SHDocVw.OLECMDID.OLECMDID_SAVEAS,
            SHDocVw.OLECMDEXECOPT.OLECMDEXECOPT_PROMPTUSER
            );
}
```

The Save As menu item click event, `MenuFileSaveAs_Click`, acts much like that of the Print command. The function first gathers the status of the command from `QueryStatusWB()`. Next, if the value contains the `OLECMDID_ENABLED` flag, it allows the command to proceed.

Summary

The WebBrowser control is a great way for developers to interface their applications with the Internet. On the surface it presents itself as a bare-bones, wrappable instance of IE that is useful in a wide variety of applications: basic browser windows, kiosks, application start pages, and so on. However, underneath this basic exterior lies a great system that exposes the underlying application and object model in a simple way. The .NET Framework ups the ante even more by simplifying the process of accessing IE's internal interfaces and events.

This chapter demonstrated how you can use the WebBrowser control in a number of ways. We got started with the basics: finding the libraries, preparing them for interop, referencing them, and spinning them into a C# project. Next, I discussed basic integration points and built a simple web browser using this control, an address bar, and some buttons. Event handling methods followed; I demonstrated how you can tailor your code to react to IE's application and page events. After getting these basics down, I talked about a deeper integration with IE's features: handling windows, displaying information such as download progress, and executing commands through OLE. I followed with a presentation of the object model and examples of how objects exposed from the browser window and documents can be accessed and traversed by your code. Finally, I broke into some more advanced examples of how IE features may be used through invocation of the browser's public API.

CHAPTER 12

Enhancing Page Content with Managed ActiveX Controls

ActiveX controls are double-edged swords stabbed through the heart of almost every page loaded in IE. Flash, QuickTime, Windows Media Player, the financial application your company uses . . . these controls are powerful, scary, and inescapable. Solidly built controls bring amazing functionality enhancement to pages; less solid controls can act as open wounds inviting infection. IE has addressed many of the security issues over the years while carefully balancing the need to ensure this powerful extension stays powerful. It's worked so far—ActiveX controls are still a great way to enhance pages and bridge the gap between desktop applications and the Web.

Most ActiveX controls are written in C++. C++ has many advantages over higher-level languages such as Java and the .NET languages: compilation to native code, the ability to easily manipulate memory, more direct access to APIs, and so on. When functionally equivalent ActiveX controls written in C++ vs. C# (for instance) are pitted against each other, C++ will often win in terms of performance, memory consumption, disk usage, and UI responsiveness. The benefits, however, are significantly outweighed by the difficulty to understand aging methodologies. As I am sure you are well aware, this leads to insecure extensions being released into the wild—applications that put users and organizations at risk.

Managed code, specifically .NET, allows ActiveX controls to regain their reputation as really cool and useful extensions once again. Recent years have brought about significant improvements in higher-level languages in the areas where they lagged: speed, responsiveness, and application footprint. The improvements in managed code development are enhanced even more by the fact that they remain simple to understand, use, secure, and maintain. Developers can worry less about many of the low-level security issues they would encounter and need to address when developing ActiveX controls in C++. The abstraction layer offered by .NET allows them to design and build ActiveX controls that are fast, responsive, and secure.

In this chapter I teach you how to build safe, managed ActiveX controls for your web site in .NET. I begin the chapter by going over the basics of the controls, what they are, the nuances, and so forth. Following the introduction is a jump right into examples, starting with the construction of a basic control. I review how to build the public interface, define the properties and functions of a control, register the control, and finally test it on your system. I show how you can add a UI to a control next, using the simple Windows Forms system in .NET. Events are up next—I explain how you can define and raise events that hosts or scripts can pick up. Finally, I discuss safety, building safe controls, and working within the constraints defined by IE. Let's get started!

Getting to Know ActiveX Controls

ActiveX controls are OLE (Object Linking and Embedding) objects—in-process COM servers that implement the IUnknown interface. These controls expose their functionality to COM, and host applications (such as IE) can call upon it through QueryInterface. Hosts query and spin up only the objects that they need, allowing ActiveX controls to act as a lightweight library.

ActiveX controls are typically used in web pages to extend the functionality of traditional markup, script, and styles. These controls accept state requests using the IPersist family of interfaces, implement IOleClientSite so hosts can display their UI, and access other niche interfaces that IE's object model doesn't expose to script.

The IE engine (MSHTML or Trident) can expose a control's public methods to script engines such as VBScript or JScript. Developers can even extend the browser's external objects using IDispatch or IDispatchEx. Controls can expose events to scripts and can also reveal properties to markup.

Instantiated ActiveX controls have a significant number of restrictions, a number that has increased with every release of IE. For example, as of IE 8, controls in the Internet zone in Windows Vista and above will run in a low integrity context by default. ActiveX controls offer many benefits with regard to being loaded in-process with IE, but they must balance such freedom with scripting and persistence restrictions and code-signing requirements, and work within the context of UIPI and object access protection.

Architecting a Basic Control in .NET

Managed code offers developers a great way to create ActiveX controls without spending time writing potentially risky unmanaged workflows. Developers looking to extend the functionality of web pages or link web page content to system content can do so quickly through .NET.

Designing the Public Interface

ActiveX controls have one main job: to act as a gateway between a web page and desktop software. These objects provide a way to access properties, call functions, or receive events raised by the object. The first step in creating a control is to define what this "communication medium" is.

Listing 12–1 shows a C# public interface called IAxSampleBasic. This interface defines what functions and properties a control wishing to use this model must implement. In this case, the IAxSampleBasic interface exposes two properties (a string named StringPropertyTest and an integer named FunctionInputTest), a function (StringFunctionTest()) returning a string, and a void function (FunctionInputTest(...)) that will allow a web page to pass a string to a control.

Listing 12–1. *The IAxSampleBasic Interface, Defining the Functions and Properties for a Control*

```
[Guid("439CE9A2-FAFF-4751-B4F7-5341AF09DBD7")]
public interface IAxSampleBasic
{
    // Properties
    string StringPropertyTest { get; set; }
    int IntPropertyTest { get; set; }

    // Functions
    string StringFunctionTest();
    void FunctionInputTest(string input);
}
```

Immediately preceding the interface is a Guid attribute specifying a uniquely generated GUID for this interface. In sum, this interface will be used by hosts querying for functionality in this control's COM coclass.

The next step in the architecture process is implementing this interface. Listing 12–2 shows a class called AxSampleBasicControl, a class that defines what will be a new ActiveX control. This class implements the functions defined in IAxSampleBasic, and it states that in the class definition.

Listing 12–2. *The AxSampleBasicControl Class—a Sample ActiveX Control Object*

```
[ClassInterface(ClassInterfaceType.None)]
[Guid("D0E4F5FB-BAB5-45F6-9CF6-ACB1CCB526F1")]
public class AxSampleBasicControl : IAxSampleBasic
{

    public string StringPropertyTest { get; set; }
    public int IntPropertyTest { get; set; }

    public string StringFunctionTest()
    {
        // Return a sample string
        return "Test.";
    }

    public void FunctionInputTest(string input)
    {
        // Show the input string in a message box
        MessageBox.Show(input);
    }

}
```

This class implements the first two properties of the interface, StringPropertyTest and IntPropertyTest, as C# *autoproperties*. This is a simple way of asking .NET to automatically create private variables to store the values for those properties and, on creation of a class instance, set the initial value of each to the default value for the type. The function StringFunctionTest() is implemented and performs one task: returning a test string (in this case, "Test.") to the caller. The last function implemented is FunctionInputTest(...), accepting a string input. This function tests how the control will fare when being sent data from a caller; here, the control takes a string argument from the caller and displays it in a MessageBox window.

The ActiveX control is now functionally complete; however, it still cannot be loaded within IE. ActiveX controls, like all other system- or account-wide COM objects, must be registered in the HKEY_CLASSES_ROOT\CLSID key of the registry. Registration will add the control's GUID to the available COM objects that hosts may create.

Listing 12–3 shows the basic architecture of the registration node for an ActiveX control. This node begins with a new key whose name matches the string value of the control's main COM-visible GUID. It is located under the HKEY_CLASSES_ROOT\CLSID key (which is itself a fusion between HKEY_LOCAL_MACHINE\Classes\CLSID and HKEY_CURRENT_USER\Classes\CLSID).

Listing 12–3. *Registry Architecture for an ActiveX Control Application*

```
HKEY_CLASSES_ROOT\
    CLSID\
      {GUID}\
         InprocServer32\
            (Required assemblies)
         Control\
         TypeLib\
            (Default) = {GUID} (REG_SZ)
            Version\
               (Default) = {MajorVersion}.{MinorVersion} (REG_SZ)
```

The first key underneath the GUID is InprocServer32. This key houses a list of all the DLLs that this control requires as in-process dependencies in order to run. Control is the next child of the GUID key; this key is empty, its presence informing interested loaders that this COM object is an ActiveX control. The last child is TypeLib. This key's (Default) string value is the GUID of this object's TypeLib; it is the TypeLib that bridges COM with the .NET runtime and helps the framework respond to unmanaged calls. This key has a child key named Version; its (Default) string value contains the major and minor revision numbers for this object's TypeLib file.

The metadata hierarchy just described is written to the registry during the registration process for this control. Unlike unmanaged COM controls (such as those using C++), .NET applications are typically registered using RegAsm.exe, part of the .NET client framework. Classes can expose themselves to this invocation by implementing a registration function flagged with the ComRegisterFunction attribute and an unregistration function flagged with the ComUnregisterFunction attribute.

Listing 12–4 displays the registration function for this control. The first step is to create the GUID key under HKEY_CLASSES_ROOT\CLSID. This function proceeds to write all the registry keys described in the previous listing: the InprocServer32, Control, and TypeLib keys, along with all of their child keys and values.

Listing 12–4. *COM Registration Function for the ActiveX Control Example*

```
[ComRegisterFunction()]
public static void Register(Type type)
{
    // Create  the CLSID (GUID) key for
    // this object in the Classes key
    RegistryKey guidKey =
        Registry.ClassesRoot.CreateSubKey(
            @"CLSID\" + type.GUID.ToString("B"));

    // Create the InprocServer32 key
    guidKey.CreateSubKey("InprocServer32");

    // Create the "control" subkey to inform loaders that this
    // is an ActiveX control
    guidKey.CreateSubKey("Control");

    // Create "TypeLib" to specify the typelib GUID associated with the class
    Guid typeLibGuid = Marshal.GetTypeLibGuidForAssembly(type.Assembly);

    // Create the type library key and set the typelib GUID as
```

```
    // the data for that key's (Default) string value
    RegistryKey typelibKey = guidKey.CreateSubKey("TypeLib");
    typelibKey.SetValue(String.Empty, typeLibGuid.ToString("B"),
        RegistryValueKind.String);

    // Get the major and minor version values for the application
    int majorVersion;
    int minorVersion;
    Marshal.GetTypeLibVersionForAssembly(
        type.Assembly, out majorVersion, out minorVersion);

    // Create the version key and set the major and minor version
    // as the data to the (Default) string value
    RegistryKey versionKey = guidKey.CreateSubKey("Version");
    versionKey.SetValue("", String.Format(
        "{0}.{1}", majorVersion, minorVersion));
}
```

This class also exposes an unregistration function, this one marked with the `ComUnregisterFunction()` attribute. When this control is invoked by a `RegAsm.exe` process using the `/unregister` flag, this function is called (Listing 12–5).

Listing 12–5. *Unregister Function for the ActiveX Control Example*

```
[ComUnregisterFunction]
public static void Unregister(Type type)
{
    // Delete the CLSID key of the control
    Registry.ClassesRoot.DeleteSubKeyTree(
        @"CLSID\" + type.GUID.ToString("B"));
}
```

This function removes the GUID registry key (recursively removing all of its child keys and values along with it) from the `HKEY_CLASSES_ROOT\CLSID` key.

Building the Control

The last step in creating this sample control is building and registering it. Normally, ActiveX controls used in IE are installed via a CAB file (which triggers an information bar), a CAB file containing a Setup executable, or a basic Setup executable. For development purposes, it is very convenient to bypass this process and register the output bits with the Global Assembly Cache (GAC) during the build process.

The postbuild events in Visual Studio provide a good place to call the registration functions. Listing 12–6 shows two postbuild events that should be used during the development process. The first call attempts to unregister the target assembly from the GAC if it exists; if it doesn't exist, the call will simply fail and move to the next. The second call performs an unsafe registration of the new assembly; the `/codebase` tag forces such a registration. This switch registers the assembly outside the GAC directories, and it should not be used in production scenarios.

Listing 12–6. Build Events Using RegAsm.exe to Unregister and Then Re-register the Sample Control

```
"C:\Windows\Microsoft.NET\Framework\{.NET Version}\regasm.exe"
    /unregister "$(TargetPath)"
"C:\Windows\Microsoft.NET\Framework\{.NET Version}\regasm.exe"
    /register /codebase /tlb "$(TargetPath)"
```

These paths depend on both the location and the version of the .NET Framework on a target system. Developers installing an application onto a client machine will need to discover this information during the installation of an application.

Once these settings are in place, the control can be built. The postbuild events will automatically register the control by calling the RegAsm.exe tool; if these postbuild events are not in place, a developer will need to manually register the control (Figure 12–1).

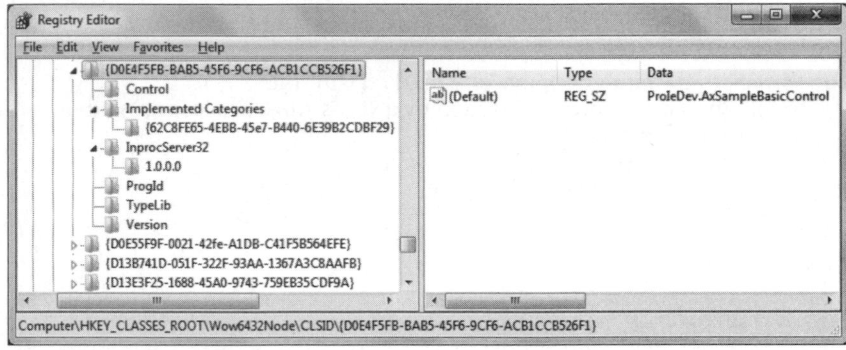

Figure 12–1. The Registry Editor confirming regisration of the sample control

The screenshot of RegEdit.exe in Figure 12–1 shows the registry keys created during the registration process. The keys here correlate to the keys described by the necessary architecture; also included are other keys automatically generated by the registration services during the process.

Developers looking to perform registration of these controls during the installation process of an application or in a stand-alone installer should note that RegAsm.exe is a stand-alone application.

Figure 12–1 highlights an important behavior of RegAsm.exe—it automatically populates the registry value representing a control's "name." IE and other applications that expose a list of COM objects through their UIs use a control's human-readable name. This name is specified in the (Default) string (REG_SZ) of a control's registration key (its GUID). By default, RegAsm.exe fills out this value for controls that it registers; it uses the format *Namespace.Classname*, where *Namespace* is the namespace containing a specific class being registered by it and *Classname* is the name of that same class. Applications wishing to customize this value can do so by changing the value of this key to a desired string once the registration process is complete.

Signing the Control

Code signing is an important part of the development process for ActiveX controls. In a default installation of IE, the browser will not run ActiveX controls that have not been properly signed using a valid code-signing certificate. Also, controls that have been loaded into IE that are not signed are tagged as not verified by the Manage Add-Ons UI.

Signing a control is clearly not necessary during every compilation or test run when developing a control, but it is necessary for any control that is to be released for wider audiences. Developers should not encourage customers to turn off the IE policies blocking unsigned controls; changing this setting for one application puts users at risk of compromise by unintended parties.

The code-signing process for ActiveX controls is like that of any other executable, library, or MSI file. Developers who have a valid certificate can use the command line–based `signtool.exe` (part of the Windows SDK, the Visual Studio SDK, and many other Microsoft packages) or their signing tool of choice.

Running the Control

The simplest way to test this newly built control is through some simple markup and script. The last piece of the sample project is an HTML page that is placed into the project's target directory when built.

The sample page, shown in Listing 12–7, loads the control through the `<object>` tag. This tag requests this specific ActiveX through the `classid` attribute, requesting the GUID exposed by the `AxSampleBasicControl` class (`{D0E4F5FB-BAB5-45F6-9CF6-ACB1CCB526F1}`).

Listing 12–7. *Web Page Used to Script and Test the Sample ActiveX Control*

```
<!DOCTYPE HTML PUBLIC "-//W3C//DTD HTML 4.0 Transitional//EN" >
<html>
<head>
    <title>ActiveX - Basic Demo</title>
</head>
<body>
    <h1>
        ActiveX - Basic Demo
    </h1>
    <object id="TestControl" name="TestControl"
        classid="clsid:D0E4F5FB-BAB5-45F6-9CF6-ACB1CCB526F1">

    </object>
    <script language="javascript" type="text/javascript">
        // Test writing to/reading from properties
        TestControl.IntPropertyTest = 42;
        TestControl.StringPropertyTest = "Hello."
        alert("Int: " + TestControl.IntPropertyTest +
              "\nString: " + TestControl.StringPropertyTest);

        // Test function output
        alert(TestControl.StringFunctionTest());

        // Test function input
        TestControl.FunctionInputTest("Some great input.");
    </script>
</body>
</html>
```

IE will load this control when it encounters the object tag during the parsing of the page.

Once the load process completes, the testing of this control is performed with some JavaScript. The script begins by setting a value of `42` to the property `IntPropertyTest` and then sets a string of `"Hello."` to

`StringPropertyTest`. The following line confirms that these values were set by reading and displaying them through an `alert` box (Figure 12–2).

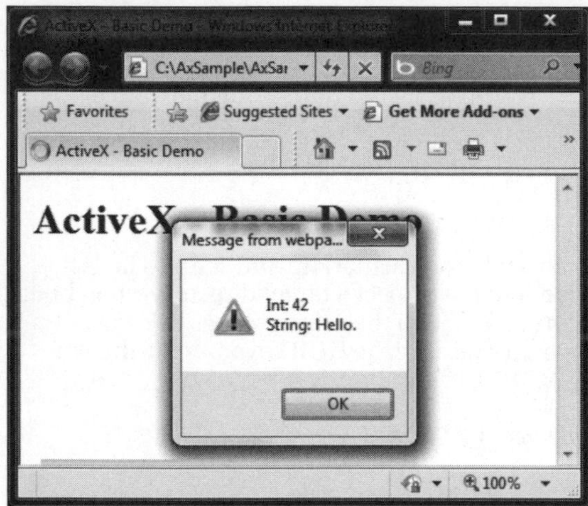

Figure 12–2. *Dialog confirming read/write success to properties on the sample ActiveX control*

This script moves on to grabbing a string returned from `StringFunctionTest()`. This function with no parameters returns a test string back to the script. The script takes this string and displays it in an `alert` box (Figure 12–3).

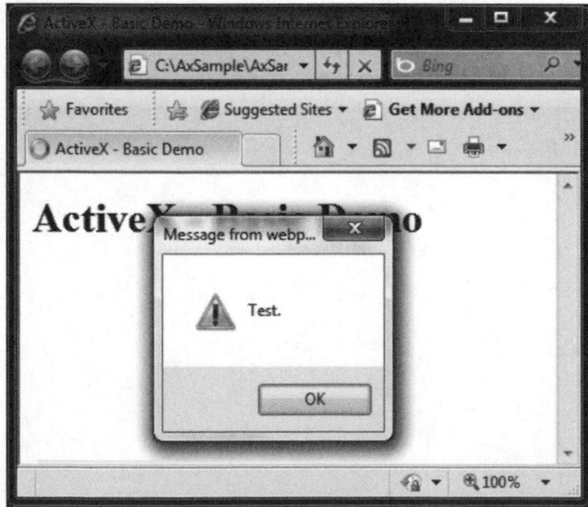

Figure 12–3. *Test dialog showing that functions with return values work properly in the sample control*

The last test performed by the script is a call to a single-parameter, void return function, `FunctionInputTest`. The script passes the string `"Some great input."` to the function; as a result, the ActiveX displays a message box of its own containing the text passed to it (Figure 12–4).

***Figure 12–4.** Message box showing that function input works properly with the sample ActiveX control*

This sample page successfully requests, loads, and communicates with the ActiveX control created in this section. While this example exposes basic interaction between a page and an ActiveX control, the functionality will be insufficient for some situations because the control lacks a UI and event system. The next sections describe how this functionality can be added to this basic control.

Constructing UIs

Simple functions and properties exposed by an ActiveX control can go a long way toward enhancing the functionality of a web page, but this alone is not enough for some situations; the original Facebook Image Uploader, the GE Centricity PACS system (for viewing digital MRI scans), and the MeadCo ScriptX print control are just some of the many, many controls that take advantage of the enhanced UI functionality that binary applications provide.

This section outlines the process of adding some basic UI elements to the sample managed ActiveX control in the previous example.

Adding a UI to a Managed Control

UI elements can be tough to muster when building an ActiveX control with unmanaged code. Controls built in C++, for instance, would be required to declare fonts, windows, and property pages, and even wire up to window events and handle `WndProc` data. Simple controls can get messy. Visual Basic introduced a simpler model for UIs in ActiveX/COM development in the late 1990s—user controls. The Visual Basic development environment offered up a designer, created code-behind automatically, and made it simple to create a COM-compatible control.

Developers can use user controls to provide a UI for an ActiveX control implemented in managed code. The previous example meets this requirement—the class is a valid COM object, exposes a type library, and correctly registers itself to the system. This ActiveX control can add a simple UI by wrapping a basic user control with an object recognizable to COM.

Listing 12–8 begins the process of adding a UI onto an ActiveX control. The control in this example (`AxSampleInterfaceControl`) contains all the same properties and features as the `AxSampleBasicControl` and expands upon them to add a UI.

Listing 12–8. Sample ActiveX Control Implementing the UserControl Class Object

```
[ClassInterface(ClassInterfaceType.None)]
[Guid("3AEA8E0C-2AD3-455F-86A0-662A24397B80")]
public partial class AxSampleInterfaceControl : UserControl, IAxSampleInterface
{
    public AxSampleInterfaceControl()
    {
        // Initialize form components
        InitializeComponent();
    }
    ...
}
```

In the class definition, the UserControl class (part of the System.Windows.Forms namespace) is used as a base class for this new control, AxSampleInterfaceControl. The second new item is the addition of an InitializeComponent() call in the control's constructor; this is used to initialize the UI elements and the UI emitted by the UserControl base object instance.

The common visual and access properties on the base UserControl class should be emitted to hosts and script. Listing 12–9 shows the IAxSampleInterface interface that AxSampleInterfaceControl is built on. Two properties—Visual and Enabled—along with one function—Refresh()—are exposed to other objects through this interface.

Listing 12–9. UserControl Properties and Functions Exposed Through the ActiveX Interface Definition

```
[Guid("F939EFDB-2E4D-473E-B7E1-C1728F866CEE")]
public interface IAxSampleInterface
{
    bool Visible { get; set; }
    bool Enabled { get; set; }
    void Refresh();
    ...
```

The addition of this set of properties and function allows pages, other controls, and hosts to get more information about the state and visibility of the control, as well as refresh and repaint the object as needed.

The sample code in this section uses the Visual Studio designer to create a simple UI. There is a title label stating the control's purpose, a text box the user may type into, and a button that can show the text box data in a message box.

After compilation, developers will need to perform the registration process for this sample control again. Re-registration needs to be performed after the control is changed to ensure that the latest version of the control is acknowledged by applications using it (such as IE).

Figure 12–5 shows the UI for this control in a web page.

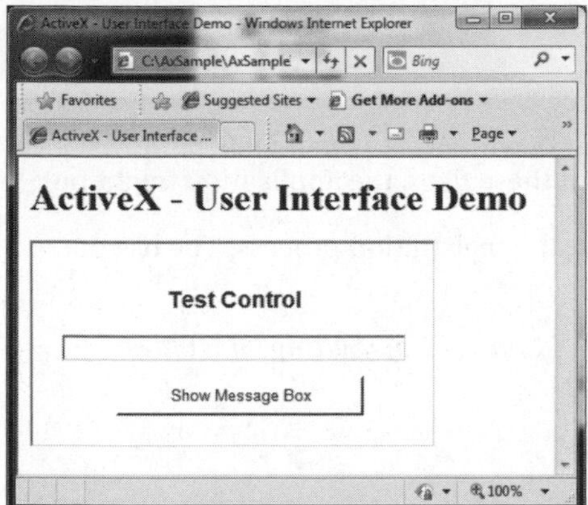

Figure 12–5. User interface and input demo with the sample ActiveX control

This demo accepts user input using a `TextBox` control named `MessageTextBox`. The `ShowMessageButton` has a click handler that reads the current `Text` property inside of the `MessageTextBox` instance and displays it to a user via a `MessageBox` window. Listing 12–10 holds the code for this event handler.

Listing 12–10. Button Click Event Showing Input Text in a Message Box

```
private void ShowMessageButton_Click(object sender, EventArgs e)
{
    // Show a message box with the current text
    MessageBox.Show(MessageTextBox.Text);
}
```

The control can be compiled and tested once this item is added. Figure 12–6 shows a test run using this control. The string `"Super test"` was placed into the text box and the main button was clicked.

Figure 12–6. Message box signaling success from a sample ActiveX UI input test

As expected, this control pops up a MessageBox with the content "Super test."

Setting a Control's OLE UI Flags

The last step in getting a managed ActiveX control to work in an IE window (or other OLE windows) is to register the OLEMISC flags that this application supports. Without these flags, the application might not receive the right focus or paint events by its parent object.

Flag registration for OLE UI support should be done during the registration process. The use of these flags is shown in Listing 12–11.

Listing 12–11. *COM Registration Function for the Sample ActiveX Control Now Setting OLE Flags*

```
[ComRegisterFunction()]
public static void Register(Type type)
{
    ...

    // Set the misc status key, informing hosts of the visibility
    RegistryKey miscStatusKey = guidKey.CreateSubKey("MiscStatus");

    int miscStatus =
        NativeMethods.OLEMISC.OLEMISC_RECOMPOSEONRESIZE +
        NativeMethods.OLEMISC.OLEMISC_CANTLINKINSIDE +
        NativeMethods.OLEMISC.OLEMISC_INSIDEOUT +
        NativeMethods.OLEMISC.OLEMISC_ACTIVATEWHENVISIBLE +
        NativeMethods.OLEMISC.OLEMISC_SETCLIENTSITEFIRST;

    miscStatusKey.SetValue(String.Empty, miscStatus.ToString(),
        RegistryValueKind.String);
    ...
}
```

The constants defined here are included in the companion sample code for this book. These values are set to the registry any time the control is registered using RegAsm.exe.

Exposing Events to ActiveX Hosts

The sample ActiveX control presented in the last few sections is nearly complete. It provides added functionality, getters and setters, and even a UI. Unfortunately, pages implementing this control have no way of receiving messages back from the control or getting notifications when something of interest in the control may be occurring.

The following section describes the process of adding the last major piece of functionality, event support, to the ActiveX control.

Creating the Event Interface

Managed ActiveX controls can expose events to host applications through the addition of an event interface. This event interface describes each public event that the ActiveX control class will expose and assigns each a DISPID value; this value allows the interface to be accessed via IDispatch.

Listing 12–12 shows the basic events interface being added to the previous examples. This interface first defines a Guid for itself, and then declares that its interface type is compatible with IDispatch. The event interface exposes one event, OnClick(), with a DISPID value of 0x1.

Listing 12–12. *Custom Event Interface for the Sample ActiveX Control*

```
[Guid("F1A732D4-5924-4DA7-85D7-4808BD7E6818")]
[InterfaceType(ComInterfaceType.InterfaceIsIDispatch)]
public interface AxSampleEventsEvents
{
    // Expose the OnClick event with DISPID 0x1
    [DispId(0x1)]
    void OnClick();
}
```

With the event interface definition in place, the next step is tying the main ActiveX control to the events defined within it. Listing 12–13 shows the basic premise of the process. First, an attribute is appended to the class definition for the ActiveX control (in this case, AxSampleEventsControl) called ComSourceInterfaces. This attribute is passed the type of the AxSampleEventsEvents interface; when the project is run, this GUID will be referenced when searching for and firing events.

Listing 12–13. *Addition of Event Interface, Delegate, and Event Object to the Sample ActiveX Control*

```
[ClassInterface(ClassInterfaceType.None)]
[ComSourceInterfaces(typeof(AxSampleEventsEvents))]
[Guid("C85CA4EB-3996-444A-91FE-B9045C94AD38")]
public partial class AxSampleEventsControl : UserControl, IAxSampleEvents
{
    public delegate void OnClickEventHandler();
    public new event OnClickEventHandler OnClick = null;
    ...
```

The delegates, events, and callers must be added once the class references the new interface. This example continues by adding a new OnClickEventHandler() delegate that contains the parameter types (in this case, none) of events implementing it. Next, the OnClick() event references the OnClickEventHandler delegate and will use its signature.

The last step is firing the event. The button from the previous examples was changed to a button that fires the OnClick() event when clicked. Its name was changed to FireEventButton, and Listing 12–14 shows its personal Click() event handler.

Listing 12–14. *Button Click Handler Firing a Click Event to Hosts of the Sample ActiveX Control*

```
private void FireEventButton_Click(object sender, EventArgs e)
{
    // Show a message box with the current text
    if (null != OnClick) OnClick();
}
```

Whenever this button is clicked, this function fires the OnClick() event to hosts using the current control instance. If there are no event listeners (the OnClick() event is null and not bound to a callback), nothing happens at all.

Listing 12–15 presents a web page used to test the events exposed by this application. As in the previous examples, it loads the control via an <object> tag. Script is used to hook into the event—the event handler, formatted as `TestControl::OnClick()`, is defined. When it is raised by the object instance, this function throws an `alert` box stating "The button was clicked!"

Listing 12–15. *HTML and Script for Testing the OnClick() Event Exposed by the Sample Control*

```
<!DOCTYPE HTML PUBLIC "-//W3C//DTD HTML 4.0 Transitional//EN" >
<html>
<head>
    <title>ActiveX - Events Demo</title>
</head>
<body>
    <h1>
        ActiveX - Events Demo
    </h1>
    <object id="TestControl" name="TestControl"
        classid="clsid:C85CA4EB-3996-444A-91FE-B9045C94AD38"
        viewastext>
    </object>
    <script type="text/javascript">
        // Create an OnClick handler for the control
        function TestControl::OnClick()
        {
            alert("The button was clicked!");
        }
    </script>
</body>
</html>
```

This syntax may look familiar to C++ developers, but it is completely unrelated. The double-colon syntax (`::`) is defined by the Microsoft JScript engine (the JScript engine is oftentimes referred to as JavaScript in the context of HTML pages) as a way to connect to an event defined by an object. When the object is loaded by JScript during page download, valid object events (those that have correct `DispIds` defined) are noted by the engine. When the script is parsed and executed, any function whose name is in the format of `ObjectInstance::ExposedEvent` (where `ObjectInstance` is the object instance in question and `ExposedEvent` is the name of a valid event) is treated as a callback. Thus, these functions are called whenever the events they refer to are raised.

Figure 12–7 shows the page in action. The left screenshot shows the normal page with the ActiveX loaded within in it. Upon clicking the button within the control, the browser pops up an `alert(...)` box, as shown in the right image.

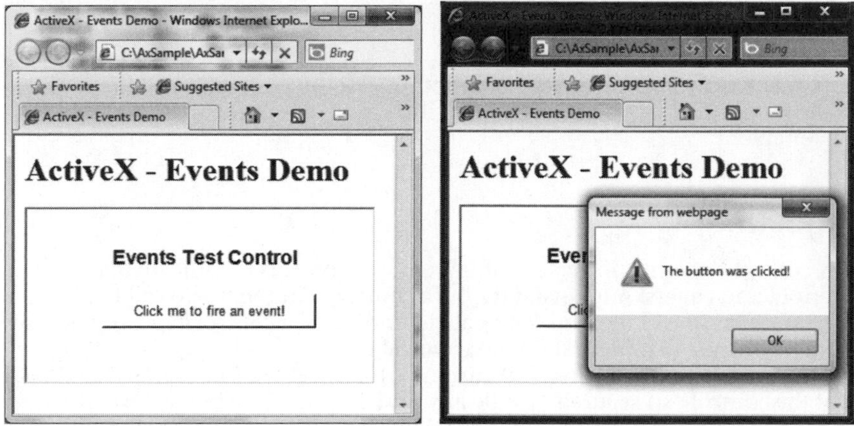

Figure 12–7. The ActiveX events test page and the result of the OnClick() event handler

Practicing Safe ActiveX with IObjectSafety

IE offers a myriad of built-in safeguards aimed at protecting users from system infection and data breaches. ActiveX controls have been placed under considerable scrutiny since their inception, a scrutiny that increases as more and more unsavory attackers exploit the attack surface of installed ActiveX controls.

Staying Safe in the Great IUnknown

The `IObjectSafety` interface was created to plug a hole in the almost unchecked restrictions that ActiveX controls have given their nature as in-process COM servers. All versions of IE block unfettered access to initialization and scripting of ActiveX controls by Internet content unless the control is marked as safe for use by untrusted callers. Controls that wish to by hosted by Internet content must implement this interface and declare that they are "safe" for use. ActiveX controls that are not marked as safe will not run at all in all zones other than the Local Machine zone, where the prompt in Figure 12–8 is shown.

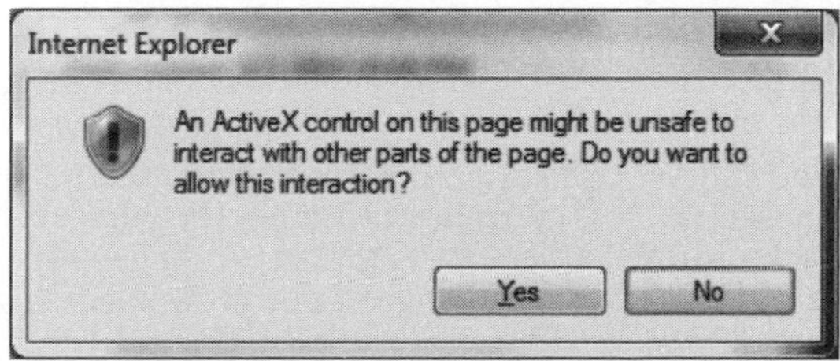

Figure 12–8. Error dialog informing the user that a page is accessing a possibly unsafe control

Initialization protection keeps ActiveX controls safe from repurpose attacks that may pass malicious data to the control via `PARAM` tags (which are sent to the control via the `IPersist` family of interfaces).

Controls that persist state and properties implement IPersist functionality to do so; this allows external applications the ability to pass state back and forth between target controls. Controls not specifically designed to safely handle untrusted input could allow a potential attacker to send malformed state to a control in an attempt to take control of a system.

Similarly, scripting safety refers to protection against attempts by a script or external application to use an ActiveX control's public properties, functions, or events, since controls not designed to handle untrusted callers may be exploitable.

Implementing IObjectSafety

Before initializing an ActiveX control or permitting calls to it, IE requires controls to indicate that they will safely handle untrusted input and callers. After instantiating a control, IE attempts to call the IObjectSafety.SetInterfaceSafetyOptions() method. This call determines if a control explicitly states it will behave safely if it encounters untrusted initialization data and callers.

Controls declare themselves safe for initialization by returning INTERFACESAFE_FOR_UNTRUSTED_DATA. This constant informs IE that the control can securely handle any initialization data it may be passed (e.g., in the PARAM attributes of an OBJECT tag). Controls may also declare themselves "safe for scripting" by returning INTERFACESAFE_FOR_UNTRUSTED_CALLER. This constant informs IE that the control's methods and properties may be called or set by JavaScript or VBScript. If a control fails to implement the SetInterfaceSafetyOptions() method, or fails to indicate that it is safe for untrusted data or untrusted callers, IE will leak the control to prevent memory safety issues when unloading the object.

The control used in the previous section is once again extended, this time to support this protection mechanism. Listing 12–16 shows the C# implementation of the IObjectSafety interface. This implementation contains two functions: GetInterfaceSafetyOptions(...) and SetInterfaceSafetyOptions(...).

Listing 12–16. *IObjectSafety Implementation for C#*

```
[ComImport]
[Guid("CB5BDC81-93C1-11CF-8F20-00805F2CD064")]
[InterfaceType(ComInterfaceType.InterfaceIsIUnknown)]
public interface IObjectSafety
{
    [PreserveSig]
    int GetInterfaceSafetyOptions(ref Guid riid, out int pdwSupportedOptions,
                                  out int pdwEnabledOptions);

    [PreserveSig]
    int SetInterfaceSafetyOptions(ref Guid riid, int dwOptionSetMask,
                                 int dwEnabledOptions);
}
```

The GetInterfaceSafetyOptions(...) function is called by host controls to determine what security measures a child control has in place. Child controls (such as this one) report back whether the control in question protects against persistence and scripting attacks. SetInterfaceSafetyOptions(...) goes in the opposite direction, enabling the host to demand certain protections; the ActiveX control is expected to return an error code if the desired safety is not supported.

The constants used to define whether the interface is safe or unsafe in the different scenarios outlined by IObjectSafety are defined in the INTERFACESAFE class in Listing 12–17. Controls that protect against or are not vulnerable to attacks of persistence or state can respond with INTERFACESAFE_FOR_UNTRUSTED_DATA in GetInterfaceSafetyOptions(...); those that protect against or are not vulnerable to attacks against exposed script can return the constant INTERFACESAFE_FOR_UNTRUSTED_CALLER in that same function.

Listing 12-17. *INTERFACESAFE Constants Used by IObjectSafety*

```
public static class INTERFACESAFE
{
    public const int INTERFACESAFE_FOR_UNTRUSTED_CALLER = 0x00000001;
    public const int INTERFACESAFE_FOR_UNTRUSTED_DATA = 0x00000002;
}
```

The last step is actually implementing the interface in the ActiveX control. Listing 12-18 shows the implementation of both functions defined within it. The control, since its functionality is heavily restricted as to what data can be placed into it and what can be called, informs parent controls that it is safe to provide it untrusted data and that untrusted callers may call its functions and set its properties (Listing 12-18).

Listing 12-18. *Implementation of the IObjectSafety Interface in the Sample ActiveX Control*

```
int NativeMethods.IObjectSafety.GetInterfaceSafetyOptions(
    ref Guid riid, out int pdwSupportedOptions,
    out int pdwEnabledOptions)
{
    // Reveal supported and enabled safety options
    pdwSupportedOptions = pdwEnabledOptions =
        NativeMethods.INTERFACESAFE.INTERFACESAFE_FOR_UNTRUSTED_CALLER |
        NativeMethods.INTERFACESAFE.INTERFACESAFE_FOR_UNTRUSTED_DATA;



    return S_OK;
}

int NativeMethods.IObjectSafety.SetInterfaceSafetyOptions(
    ref Guid riid, int dwOptionSetMask, int dwEnabledOptions)
{
    // As our code does not have an UNSAFE mode, tell
    // the Host that we support any safety options it
    // had demanded
    return S_OK;
}
```

The implementation of this interface enables this control to run in any security zone where IE demands that controls safely handle untrusted data and callers.

Looking At Alternative Platforms and Technologies

The examples in this chapter show that in-page extensibility is a powerful tool for linking access to user data and processing power of stand-alone applications to the versatility and breadth of information that the Web has to offer. ActiveX controls, however, are an IE-only technology. While Google, at the time of this writing, has demonstrated cross-browser encapsulation of these controls through its Chrome browser (and the open source Chromium browser), use of these controls outside of IE has not yet become a mainstream practice. Developers building ActiveX controls should be aware that these controls will only work on IE.

This is not to say that other technologies, even ones very similar, don't exist in other browsers and as part of other platforms. Netscape, Mozilla Firefox, and other browsers using the Netscape Plugin Application Programming Interface (NPAPI) have similar abilities to link page content to binary code through the browser. In fact, IE supported NPAPI controls in early versions of the browser until IE 5.5. These controls even share a somewhat checkered past in terms of security: both have been found to have significant security flaws in the past (though ActiveX received the brunt of the public and PR backlash). The only major architectural difference is that NPAPI has an API constructed specifically for use in browsers and web pages, whereas ActiveX controls are the same COM objects used in all of Windows development plus a fancy name.

ActiveX controls should not be confused with script-based technologies such as Silverlight and Flash. In fact, IE versions of these products are in and of themselves ActiveX controls! These products, in many ways, wrap and expose binary functionality that is of particular use to web development. Their ease of use coupled with their wide distribution allows developers to enhance their pages without requiring custom ActiveX or NPAPI controls, and allows users to run millions of applications across the Web without having to install a new control more than once.

Summary

In this chapter I reviewed ActiveX controls: what they are, how to create them, how to lock them down, and how to make them work for you. The chapter started out with a primer on the controls themselves. I jumped right in with the construction of a basic control, the interfaces and implementations involved, the registration of a control, and the testing of a control using a sample page. User interfaces were next, where I presented a simple way of incorporating Windows Forms and user controls into the control and using those to create a good user experience. I covered events next, going into detail on how events can be registered for and thrown to hosts by an ActiveX control. Last, I covered safety issues and how to convey the safety and security of a control to IE, allowing use of the control by untrusted pages.

ActiveX controls are a wonderful solution for developers looking for a little extra system access or computing power in web pages. This is especially true for controls hosted on intranet or enterprise web applications. Despite their power, poorly built extensions have been a target for exploitation for years. IE has significantly reduced its attack surface in the last few releases—a balancing act that has resulted in a safer extension model and one that remains useful in adding some great functionality to pages.

CHAPTER 13

■ ■ ■

Building In-Process Extensions with Browser Helper Objects

Most IE extensibility points are, in many ways, separated from the steps and transactions that take place behind the scenes of a page load or the display of the browser frame. Most extensions are used to control a piece of the browser's UI, whether it be a part of a page or a part of the browser window itself. Browser Helper objects (BHOs) fill in the missing piece of this story: they allow developers to access the events called and actions taken by IE silently. Much like a Windows service, these extensions sit in the background and perform tasks without having to interact with a user directly.

In this chapter, I discuss how you can build your own BHO and use this extension to tap into browser events and communicate with other processes. I begin the chapter with a quick introduction of these extensions and how they fit within the IE architecture. Next, I provide a demonstration of how to register, test, and uninstall an extension of this type. This chapter closes with examples of how you can use BHOs to tap into events exposed by the browser tab and process.

Understanding BHOs

BHOs are IE extensions that run in the browser process but have no formal UI. These extensions implement the `IObjectWithSite` interface. IE loads a new BHO instance for every tab loaded into the browser, and notifies a loaded extension of placement via the `SetSite(...)` method.

Despite not having an official UI requirement, BHOs can still interact with the UI thread of a tab process. Figure 13–1 shows a sample BHO that does just this, launching a message box during an event callback.

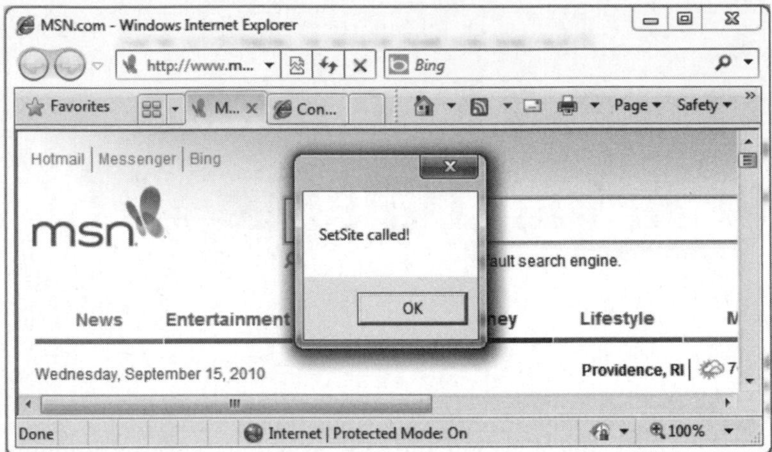

Figure 13–1. BHO launching a message box

Like ActiveX controls, toolbars, search providers, and other IE extensions, users can manage BHOs. BHOs installed into IE can be enabled and disabled through the Manage Add-Ons dialog, as shown in Figure 13–2.

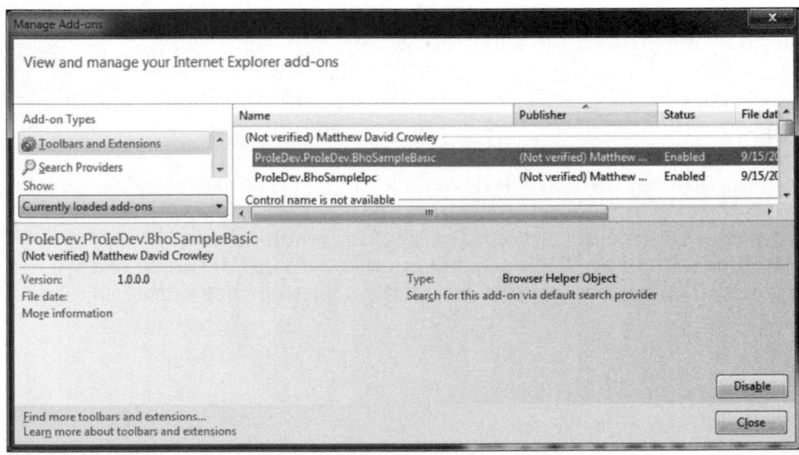

Figure 13–2. BHOs shown in the Manage Add-Ons dialog

For each add-on, the dialog shows the name, publisher, enabled status, install date, and load time. This dialog does not allow users to uninstall a BHO, but it does allow the user to control whether the BHO is enabled and loaded. Load time, or time it takes for IE to load a BHO and run its `SetSite()` callback, was added as of IE 8 to encourage users to disable "slow" BHOs that might be negatively affecting their browser's performance.

Building a Generic BHO

BHOs are fairly simple to build, especially when built using the .NET Framework. As described in the preceding section, these objects are basic classes that implement the `IObjectWithSite` interface. The only other requirements aside from that are that this same class have a unique GUID, be registered among the machine's COM objects, and be listed under a particular registry key.

A BHO in C# (the language used for the remainder of this chapter) consists of a class with four basic sections: instance variables to hold a browser reference, an implementation of `IObjectWithSite`, functions that handle COM registration and unregistration, and invocation/definition of the `IObjectWithSite` API. Listing 13–1 demonstrates the first three requirements.

Listing 13–1. *Basic Architecture for a BHO*

```
[
ComVisible(true), // Make the object visible to COM
Guid("48DEAC10-D583-4683-9345-3F8A117DE7A5"), // Create a new, unique GUID for each BHO
ClassInterface(ClassInterfaceType.None)]  // Don't create an interface (allow only late-
                                          // bound access via IDispatch)
public class BhoSampleBasic : IObjectWithSite
{

    #region Variables ...

    #region IObjectWithSite Interface Implementation ...

    #region COM Registration Functions ...

}
```

In the example, a new BHO—`BhoSampleBasic`—is defined as a class that implements the `IObjectWithSite` interface. This class has a few important attributes. First, it makes marks this .NET class visible to COM. Next, it defines a GUID to uniquely identify the class. Last, it prevents .NET from exposing a class interface by setting the `ClassInterface` attribute to `ClassInterface.None`.

Omitting a public COM interface using `ClassInterface.None` is important! IE does not know how to talk to this extension natively—it clearly does not know every method and property for every BHO that was ever created or that will be. It *does*, however, recognize the object's base class: `IObjectWithSite`. Setting this value to `ClassInterface.None` forces callers (in this case, IE) to bypass the interface of the inherited class find a common base class. Basically, it forces IE and the BHO to communicate with each other using a "language" common to both.

The instance member of this class is a single variable, `Browser`. This variable is a `WebBrowser` type and is used to store a reference to the browser instance where the BHO is loaded. It is populated when the `SetSite` function is called as the BHO is loaded into IE (Listing 13–2).

Listing 13–2. *Instance Members of the Basic BHO Class*

```
#region Instance Members

SHDocVw.WebBrowser Browser;

#endregion Variables
```

This library continues by defining the `IObjectWithSite` interface. This interface is implemented by the BHO class to handle the `SetSite` and `GetSite` calls made by the browser instance loading this extension. Listing 13–3 defines this API.

***Listing 13–3.** The IObjectWithSite Interface*

```
[ComVisible(true),
InterfaceType(ComInterfaceType.InterfaceIsIUnknown),
Guid("FC4801A3-2BA9-11CF-A229-00AA003D7352")] // Unlike the BHO's GUID, this GUID remains
                                              // the same for every BHO using it (since it
                                              // is indicating the GUID of IObjectWithSite,
                                              // a value constant on all Windows systems)
public interface IObjectWithSite
{
    [PreserveSig]
    int SetSite([MarshalAs(UnmanagedType.IUnknown)] object site);

    [PreserveSig]
    int GetSite(ref Guid guid, out IntPtr ppvSite);
}
```

The BHO implements this API within this class. Two functions are created: `SetSite` and `GetSite`. These functions (described in other chapters) receive and disseminate, respectively, the instance of the browser object that loaded an instance of this class (Listing 13–4).

***Listing 13–4.** IObjectWithSite Implementation Used by a BHO Class*

```
#region IObjectWithSite Interface Implementation

public int SetSite(object site)
{
    // If the site is valid, cast as a WebBrowser object and
    // store it in the Browser variable
    if (site != null)
    {
        // Set the site object to the Browser variable, casting it
        // to a WebBrowser object type
        Browser = (SHDocVw.WebBrowser)site;

        // Tell the user SetSite was called
        System.Windows.Forms.MessageBox.Show("SetSite called!");
    }
    else Browser = null;

    return S_OK;
}

public int GetSite(ref Guid guid, out IntPtr ppvSite)
{
    // Get the IUnknown for the Browser object
    IntPtr pUnk = Marshal.GetIUnknownForObject(Browser);

    // Request a pointer for the interface
    int hResult = Marshal.QueryInterface(pUnk, ref guid, out ppvSite);
```

```
    // Release the object
    Marshal.Release(pUnk);

    // Return the result from the QI call
    return hResult;
}

#endregion IObjectWithSite Interface Implementation
```

The SetSite(...) function is called to pass the IUnknown pointer of the IE site to a class implementing the BandObject class. IE calls this whenever this class is loaded into its process. GetSite(...), in contrast, provides the IE site back to the caller of this function.

The sample here launches a MessageBox whenever this function is called. Since a BHO has no inherent UI, this MessageBox is used in the following section to demonstrate that an instance of this extension is in fact running.

Registering and Running BHOs

Once a BHO is implemented, it must be registered with both COM and IE in order for it to be loaded into the browser. Listing 13–5 shows the COM registration methods where this takes place. When a BHO library is registered or unregistered, the .NET registration process calls the Register(...) or Unregister() functions, respectively.

Listing 13–5. *COM Registration Methods for a BHO Class*

```
#region COM Registration Methods

[ComRegisterFunction]
public static void Register(Type type)
{
    // Open (and create if needed) the main BHO key
    RegistryKey bhoKey =
        Registry.LocalMachine.CreateSubKey(
            @"Software\Microsoft\Windows\CurrentVersion\" +
            @"Explorer\Browser Helper Objects");

    // Open (and create if needed) the GUID key
    RegistryKey guidKey
        = bhoKey.CreateSubKey(
            type.GUID.ToString("B"));

    // Close the open keys
    bhoKey.Close();
    guidKey.Close();
}
...
```

BHOs must register themselves with IE in order for them to load inside the browser and be placed in each tab instance. Listing 13–6 shows an example registration for a BHO. Unlike with other extension types, BHOs may only be listed within the HKEY_LOCAL_MACHINE hive. Therefore, on Windows Vista and later, BHOs may only be registered and unregistered by an elevated process running with administrative permissions.

Within the HKEY_LOCAL_MACHINE hive, BHOs are listed as subkeys named with the GUID of the extension (Listing 13–6).

***Listing 13–6.** Sample Registry Values for a BHO*

```
HKEY_LOCAL_MACHINE\
   Software\
      Microsoft\
         Windows\
            CurrentVersion\
               Explorer\
                  Browser Helper Objects\
                     {48DEAC10-D583-4683-9345-3F8A117DE7A5}\
```

Because Windows Explorer also supports BHOs, you can prevent your BHO from loading into Windows Explorer by creating a REG_DWORD named NoExplorer within your BHO's subkey.

Once registered, IE will load an instance of this BHO whenever a tab is loaded. Figure 13–3 shows an example of this: the BHO class created in the previous section throws a MessageBox dialog whenever IE loads an instance of that class and calls the SetSite(...) function within it.

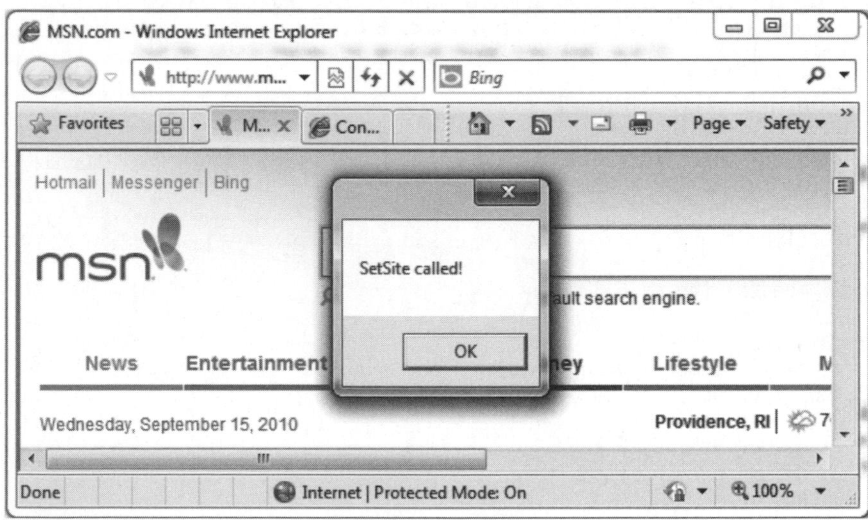

***Figure 13–3.** BHO showing a message box during a SetSite call*

The Unregister() function is used to remove the registry entries created by the Register(...) function. Listing 13–7 shows the contents. When called, this removes the key associated with the extension's GUID.

Listing 13–7. Unregistration Function for a BHO Class

```
[ComUnregisterFunction]
public static void Unregister(Type type)
{
    // Open up the main BHO key
    RegistryKey bhoKey =
        Registry.LocalMachine.OpenSubKey(
            @"Software\Microsoft\Windows\CurrentVersion\" +
            @"Explorer\Browser Helper Objects",
            true);

    // Delete the GUID key if it exists
    if (bhoKey != null) bhoKey.DeleteSubKey(
        type.GUID.ToString("B"), false);
}

#endregion COM Registration Methods
```

Once the registry key is removed, IE no longer loads the BHO nor lists it in the browser's list of add-ons in the Manage Add-Ons dialog.

Sinking Browser Events

Having an extension loaded into the browser process is quite useful. BHOs, however, are not limited to this. Given that this extension is passed a valid `WebBrowser` instance through `SetSite`, BHOs can take advantage of the wide range of functionality exposed by this object. Arguably, the most important piece of this function is the ability to sink (attach to) events on a `WebBrowser` object instance and those of its children. Using event interfaces such as `DWebBrowserEvents2`, developers can handle events triggered by the browser, the page, the user, or any other item interacting within the browser process.

The most common and useful events that a BHO can sink are exposed by the `DWebBrowserEvents2` event sync interface. These events are raised by the browser object that hosts an instance of a BHO. Such events include `BeforeNavigate2` (raised before a navigation), `NavigationComplete2` (raised when a navigation is complete), and `DocumentComplete` (raised when a document has fully loaded).

Listing 13–8 shows an example of how a BHO could sink these events. The example in the last section is extended to call event handlers as events are raised. The `SetSite()` function, after grabbing the browser object instance passed to it, adds two event handlers.

Listing 13–8. Web Browser Events Sunk During a SetSite Call

```
[SecurityPermission(SecurityAction.LinkDemand,
    Flags = SecurityPermissionFlag.UnmanagedCode),
ComVisible(true),
Guid("FE19878E-55B9-48AA-B293-2BDEEB2232DB"),
ClassInterface(ClassInterfaceType.None)]
public class BhoSampleEvents : NativeMethods.IObjectWithSite
{
    ...
    public int SetSite(object site)
    {
```

```
        // If the site is valid, cast as a WebBrowser object and
        // store it in the Browser variable
        if (site != null)
        {
            // Set the site object, cast as a WebBrowser object,
            // to the Browser variable
            Browser = (SHDocVw.WebBrowser)site;

            // Add a handler for when navigation starts
            Browser.BeforeNavigate2 += Browser_BeforeNavigate2;

            // Add a handler for when the document has completely loaded
            Browser.DocumentComplete += Browser_DocumentComplete;
        }
        else
        {
            // Detatch the event handlers if they were attached
            Browser.BeforeNavigate2 -= Browser_BeforeNavigate2;
            Browser.DocumentComplete -= Browser_DocumentComplete;

            // Set the browser object to null
           Browser = null;
        }

        return S_OK;
    }
```

First, it ties the function `Browser_BeforeNavigate2` as a callback to the `BeforeNavigate2` event. Next, it ties the function `Browser_DocumentComplete` as a callback to the `DocumentComplete` event.

Listing 13–9 shows the callback function called when the `BeforeNavigate2` event is raised. This function demonstrates its usage by displaying a `MessageBox` to the user before navigation within a specific tab takes place. This `MessageBox` shows the target `url` for the navigation.

Listing 13–9. *BHO Callback for the BeforeNavigate2 Event*

```
void Browser_BeforeNavigate2(object pDisp, ref object URL, ref object Flags, ref object
    TargetFrameName, ref object PostData, ref object Headers, ref bool Cancel)
{
    // If the site or url is null, do not continue
    if (pDisp == null || URL == null) return;

    // Convert the url object reference to a string
    string url = URL.ToString();

    // Show the url in a message box
    MessageBox.Show("Begin navigation to: " + url);
}
```

The example in Listing 13–10 performs a similar task in handling the `DocumentComplete` event using the callback `Browser_DocumentComplete`. Like the previous code snippet, this example also throws up a `MessageBox` to demonstrate its usage. This message box takes advantage of the browser's state: since the document target is complete, this document is now loaded into the browser object and accessible by the extension. Consequently, it displays the number of links contained within the loaded document by using functionality provided by the document object instance (using the `IHTMLDocument2` interface).

Listing 13–10. BHO Callback for the DocumentComplete Event

```
void Browser_DocumentComplete(object pDisp, ref object URL)
{
    // If the site or url is null, do not continue
    if (pDisp == null || URL == null) return;

    // Grab the document object off of the WebBrowser control
    IHTMLDocument2 document = (IHTMLDocument2)Browser.Document;
    if (document == null) return;

    // Report the total number of links on the current page
    MessageBox.Show("Total links on this page: " +
        document.links.length.ToString());
}
```

Figure 13–4 shows this callback in action. When MSN (`www.msn.com`) is loaded into the browser, the `DocumentComplete` event runs this callback in the browser's UI thread. The callback function (described in the previous listing) shows a message box displaying the number of links found in this page.

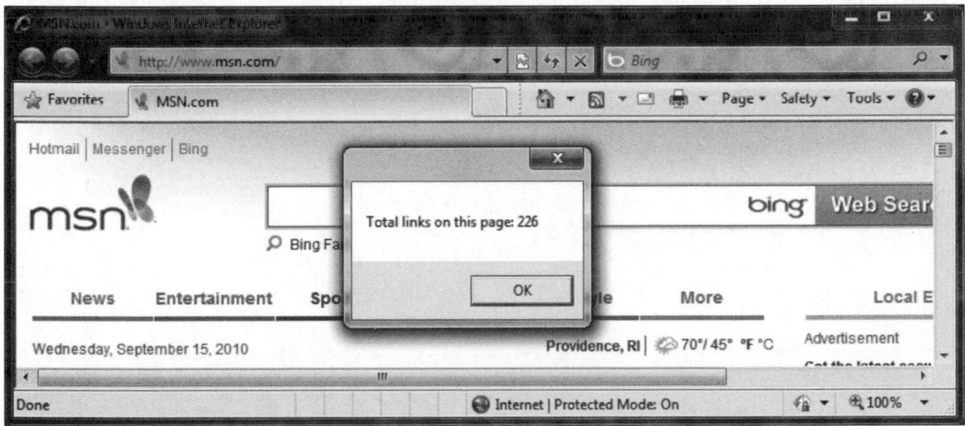

***Figure 13–4.** Message box showing the number of links on a page, called by a BHO*

Developers may notice that the `DocumentComplete` event sunk by this example might trigger multiple times per page load. This specific event is raised once for each frame loaded on a page, followed last by this same event raised for the top-level window. Developers looking to distinguish between `DocumentComplete` events (or any other related events) raised for a frame and a top-level window can do so by comparing the `pDisp` pointer passed to the event handler to the `pDisp` pointer of the top-level window. One way to keep track of the `pDisp` pointer for such a comparison is to save a reference to the same `pDisp` pointer passed to `SetSite` (in that case, the variable is `site`). During `DocumentComplete`, if the `pDisp` pointer does not reference the same object as the version passed during `SetSite`, one can assume that the event was raised for something other than the top-level window.

Those developing plug-ins should also take note of the fact that callbacks are run in the IE UI thread (as noted previously). This means that IE takes away user control (as well as the ability to update or change its UI) while a callback function is running. Controls attaching to these events should spend as little time as possible in these functions or, at the very least, spawn another thread to handle any reaction to these events. Slow or clumsy extensions can ruin a user's browser experience—a BHO that spends, for instance, 5 seconds processing data on every `DocumentComplete` event will introduce a 5-second hang in the browser UI. Users might not appreciate that.

Summary

In this chapter, I talked about how you can build your own IE extension that runs in-process and out of sight, allowing you to access the events and functionality of IE without the requirement or overhead of a UI. I started this chapter by introducing the concept of BHOs, their goals, and how they fit into the overall IE architecture. Following this was an example of how to implement a BHO using C# and the .NET Framework. I then talked about how these extensions are registered, loaded, managed, and removed from the browser. I ended the chapter by expanding on this example by accessing the owning browser object and tying into events exposed from it.

BHOs offer developers a simple way to tap into the browser and enhance the functionality of pages. You can build a basic extension in a few simple steps, and tie into browser events in a simple way too. This extension is one of the simplest forms of binary IE extensions; while they cannot be constructed using simple XML or registry entries, their structure and implementation is straightforward and fairly lightweight. The functionality of BHOs is clearly not limited to the examples shown in this chapter; since these extensions have access to the browser tab and the browser object, these extensions have the same access and power as other binary IE extensions.

CHAPTER 14

■ ■ ■

Extending the Browser Frame Using Band Objects

The IE extensions presented thus far offer limited access to good real estate in the browser frame. Developers looking for greater acreage at a low price can find solace in band objects. Band objects were introduced as a way for developers to extend the Windows shell and the IE browser frame. These UI areas are very prominent, and are shown no matter which tab or page is displayed in the browser. If you want this kind of access to a user, band objects are right for you.

In this chapter I present a logical approach to creating three types of band objects: toolbars, Vertical Explorer bars, and Horizontal Explorer bars. I begin with a basic overview of these extensions, how they are the same, and where they differ and fit into the IE UI. I follow by creating a base class called `BandObject`, a foundation for creating each type of band object simply and easily. After reviewing the internal architecture and registration process of this library, I create an example of each type of band object and show the result in a real IE window. Now you can create your own toolbar in a few lines of managed code!

Understanding Band Objects

Band objects were added to IE 4.0 as a means for developers to extend the browser frame. In the context of the IE browser frame, these objects are more commonly referred to as *tool bands* and *Explorer bars.* The Explorer shell uses band objects as well, a usage referred to as *desk bands.* Whether used inside or outside the browser, band objects provide the ability for a developer to extend the frame of a window using panes attached to the sides or top of a window.

IE offers three main areas where band objects can be displayed: the toolbar area, the left side of the window (Vertical Explorer bar region), and the bottom of the window (Horizontal Explorer bar region) (see Figure 14–1).

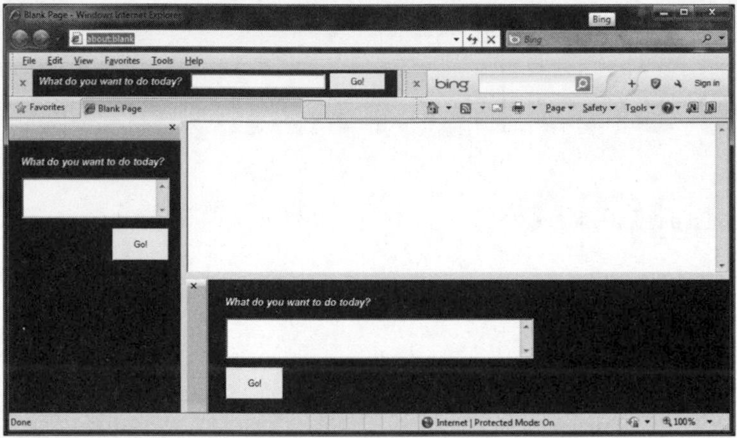

Figure 14–1. Sample band objects loaded into the IE frame

The toolbar band object, shown at the top of this figure, is a generic toolbar that can be inserted into IE's toolbar band. The Vertical Explorer bar is a docked child window that is placed on the left-hand side of the browser window. The Horizontal Explorer bar, like the vertical one, is also a docked child window, but docked to the bottom of the browser window directly above the status bar.

Band objects are exposed in the IE Tools menu. These menu entries are used for basic management, and for showing or hiding the objects. Figure 14–2 shows this management experience.

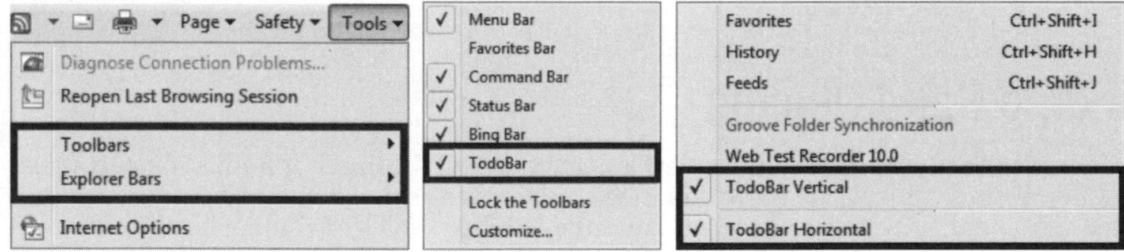

Figure 14–2. Band object management menu items

Management of these items is not limited to the Tools menu. Each band object is a registered IE extension, thus subject to management through the Manage Add-Ons window. Figure 14–3 shows a toolbar, Vertical Explorer bar, and Horizontal Explorer bar displayed in this dialog.

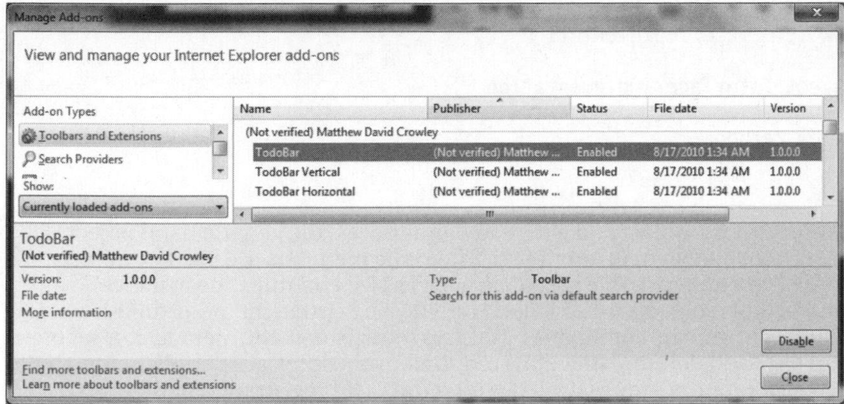

Figure 14–3. *Band objects surfaced through the Manage Add-Ons dialog*

All band objects can also be closed using the close X on each. For toolbars, this is found on the left side of each item. Vertical and Horizontal Explorer bars have their Xs exposed in the title bar on each. Like objects disabled by the Manage Add-Ons dialog, those closed with the X remain loaded in memory until the browser is restarted.

Building a Generic Band Object

Every type of band object available to IE developers—toolbars, Vertical Explorer bars, and Horizontal Explorer bars—is built on the same building blocks. Each type consists of a user interface that is placed on sites within the browser, and interfaces used to link the object to the browser, the Windows shell, and COM.

In managed .NET code (which this chapter focuses on), the first block is a generic `UserControl`. `UserControls` provide the UI block that can be placed into each of the three main UI areas provided by IE. Unmanaged interfaces make up the rest of the implementation. The implemented interfaces are shown in Listing 14–1.

Listing 14–1. *Basic Architecture for the BandObject Class*

```
public class BandObject : UserControl,
                          IObjectWithSite,
                          IDeskBand, IDockingWindow,
                          IOleWindow
{

    #region Static Members ...

    #region Instance Members ...

    #region Virtual Methods ...

    #region IObjectWithSite Interface Implementation ...
```

```
    #region IOleWindow Interface Implementation ...

    #region IDockingWindow Interface Implementation ...

    #region IOLECommandTarget Interface Implementation ...

    #region COM Registration Methods ...

}
```

After implementing the `UserControl` object and a myriad of interfaces, the generic band object is broken down into several areas (also shown in Listing 14–1). The static members are used by objects implementing this generic base object; they define metadata such as size and title. The instance members represent sites handed to the objects when loaded into IE. The virtual methods (in this case, one) represent calls made by objects implementing this base class to register static metadata. A set of interface implementations follow, each defining functions required by the interfaces implemented by this object. Last are the COM registration methods, called during the COM registration and unregistration processes for a library implementing this base class.

The static members define a variety of metadata that can be used by either a toolbar, Vertical Explorer bar, or Horizontal Explorer bar created from this base class. The `ClassId` and `ProgId` are a GUID and unique string, respectively, used to access one of these objects through COM. The `ObjectTitle`, `ObjectName`, and `HelpText` are descriptors used by IE to show the object in its menu structure and through the Manage Add-Ons dialog. The `InitialSize` is the initial size of the band object when first loaded; the `MinSize`, `MaxSize`, and `IntegralSize` are size constraints applied as the band object is moved and resized during its lifetime (Listing 14–2).

Listing 14–2. *Static Members of the BandObject Class*

```
#region Static Members

public static string ClassId;
public static string ProgId;
public static string ObjectTitle;
public static string ObjectName;
public static string HelpText;

public static new Size InitialSize;
public static Size MinSize;
public static Size MaxSize;
public static Size IntegralSize;

public static BandObjectTypes Style = BandObjectTypes.HorizontalExplorerBar;

#endregion Static Members
```

The last static variable in Listing 14–2 is the `Style` variable. This member of type `BandObjectStyle` is used by classes descending from `BandObject` to define the type of band object that they wish to be. The enumeration shown in Listing 14–3 defines flags for a toolbar, Vertical Explorer bar, and Horizontal Explorer bar.

Listing 14–3. *Band Object Types Enumeration*

```
public enum BandObjectTypes
{
    VerticalExplorerBar = 1,
    Toolbar = 2,
    HorizontalExplorerBar = 4
}
```

The instance members of Listing 14–4 are used by this class to store references to the IWebBrowser and IE application sites to which this BandObject is related.

Listing 14–4. *Instance Members for the BandObject Class*

```
#region Instance Members

public SHDocVw.WebBrowserClass WebBrowser;
public SHDocVw.InternetExplorer BandObjectSite;

#endregion Instance Members
```

The DefineMetadata() method defined in Listing 14–5 must be by a toolbar, Vertical Explorer bar, or Horizontal Explorer bar descending from BandObject. The method is called to set metadata values onto the static variables of this class, allowing such metadata to be passed along to the base class.

Listing 14–5. *Required Methods for the BandObject Class*

```
#region Virtual Methods

public void DefineMetadata() { }

#endregion Virtual Methods
```

Interface implementations are up next after the class-specific members are defined. The first major interface is IObjectWithSite. This interface is used to get and set the "site" (COM object) where this object is loaded—the IE browser object. Listing 14–6 shows the two functions defined in this interface: SetSite(...) and GetSite(...).

Listing 14–6. *IObjectWithSite Implementation for the BandObject Class*

```
#region IObjectWithSite Interface Implementation

public void SetSite(object pUnkSite)
{

    // If this object is null, SetSite is being called
    // to handle the unload process
    if (!(pUnkSite is SHDocVw.InternetExplorer))
    {
        // If the BandObjectSite is a valid object, release
        // the COM object being managed by the marshaller
        if (BandObjectSite != null)
        {
```

```
                Marshal.ReleaseComObject(BandObjectSite);
                BandObjectSite = null;
            }
            return;
        }

        try
        {

            // Set the band object site to be a reference to the current
            // site passed to this function
            BandObjectSite = (SHDocVw.InternetExplorer)pUnkSite;

            // Grab an IServiceProvider instance from the band object site
            ProIeDev.BandObjectDemo.Interop.Interfaces.IServiceProvider serviceProvider =
                (ProIeDev.BandObjectDemo.Interop.Interfaces.IServiceProvider)
                    BandObjectSite;

            // Create variables to be referenced in a call to QueryService
            object pUnknown = null;
            Guid guid = new Guid(IID.IID_IWebBrowserApp);
            Guid riid = new Guid(IID.IID_IUnknown);

            // Query the service provider for the IWebBrowser instance
            serviceProvider.QueryService(ref guid, ref riid, out pUnknown);

            // Cast the returned site to an IWebBrowser instance and save
            // it to an instance variable
            WebBrowser = (SHDocVw.WebBrowserClass)Marshal.CreateWrapperOfType(
                pUnknown as IWebBrowser, typeof(SHDocVw.WebBrowserClass));

            // Create variables to be used in a call to the ShowBrowserBar
            // function on the new IWebBrowser instance
            object pvaClsid = (object)ClassId;
            object pvarSize = null;
            object pvarShowTrue = (object)true;

            // Call the ShowBrowserBar function on the retrieved IWebBrowser
            // instance to display the current band object
            WebBrowser.ShowBrowserBar(ref pvaClsid, ref pvarShowTrue, ref pvarSize);

        }
        catch (Exception) { }

    }

    public void GetSite(ref Guid riid, out object ppvSite)
    {
        // Return the current band object site
        ppvSite = BandObjectSite;
    }

    #endregion IObjectWithSite Interface Implementation
```

The SetSite function is called to pass the IUnknown pointer of the IE site to a class descending from the BandObject class. IE calls SetSite whenever loading a band object into its process. GetSite simply returns this site if called to do so.

The next major interface is IDeskBand. This interface is used to obtain information about a band object that is to be loaded into the Windows shell or, in this case, IE. There is only one function in this interface: GetBandInfo. This function, shown in Listing 14–7, is called by IE to get information about this band object instance. This class implements the function in a way that sets the title, size, and other metadata to the DESKBAND structure (the object used for information exchange in this instance) and passes that structure back to the caller.

***Listing 14–7.** IDeskBand Implementation for the BandObject Class*

```
#region IDeskBand Interface Implementation

public void GetBandInfo(uint dwBandID, uint dwViewMode, ref DESKBANDINFO pdbi)
{
    try
    {

        // Specify title for the DeskBand object if requested
        if ((pdbi.dwMask & DBIM.TITLE) == DBIM.TITLE)
            pdbi.wszTitle = ObjectTitle;

        // Specify width and height to the object
        if ((pdbi.dwMask & DBIM.ACTUAL) == DBIM.ACTUAL)
        {
            pdbi.ptActual.X = InitialSize.Width;
            pdbi.ptActual.Y = InitialSize.Height;
        }

        // Indicate maximum width and height for the object
        if ((pdbi.dwMask & DBIM.MAXSIZE) == DBIM.MAXSIZE)
        {
            pdbi.ptMaxSize.X = MaxSize.Width;
            pdbi.ptMaxSize.Y = MaxSize.Height;
        }

        // Indicate minimum width and height for the object
        if ((pdbi.dwMask & DBIM.MINSIZE) == DBIM.MINSIZE)
        {
            pdbi.ptMinSize.X = MinSize.Width;
            pdbi.ptMinSize.Y = MinSize.Height;
        }

        // Indicate integral width and height for the object; integral height
        // is the step value used when the object is resized (for instance,
        // an X value of 5 will ensure that the object will be resized in
        // increments of 5 pixels at a time (rather than the default of 1)
        if ((pdbi.dwMask & DBIM.INTEGRAL) == DBIM.INTEGRAL)
        {
            pdbi.ptIntegral.X = IntegralSize.Width;
            pdbi.ptIntegral.Y = IntegralSize.Height;
        }
```

```
            // Add a backcolor by removing the mask flag
            // if a specific backcolor is defined
            if ((pdbi.dwMask & DBIM.BKCOLOR) == DBIM.BKCOLOR)
                pdbi.dwMask &= ~DBIM.BKCOLOR;

            // Apply object mode flags to the toolbar


            // Apply general mode flags
            if ((pdbi.dwMask & DBIM.MODEFLAGS) == DBIM.MODEFLAGS)
            {
                pdbi.dwModeFlags = DBIMF.VARIABLEHEIGHT | DBIMF.NORMAL;

                if (Style == BandObjectTypes.Toolbar)
                    pdbi.dwModeFlags |= DBIMF.BREAK | DBIMF.ALWAYSGRIPPER;

            }

        }
        catch (Exception) { }
    }

#endregion IDeskBand Interface Implementation
```

The `IOleWindow` interface allows this class to handle OLE window calls made by an owner COM object. The `BandObject` class uses only one of these for all practical purposes. The `GetWindow` function is called by an owner object in order to retrieve the main window handle of an OLE site. In this case, the `BandObject` class returns the window handle to the `UserControl` instance, and IE in turn takes ownership of this window and places it within itself as a child object (Listing 14–8).

Listing 14–8. *IOleWindow Implementation for the BandObject Class*

```
#region IOleWindow Interface Implementation

public void GetWindow(out IntPtr phwnd)
{
    // Return the current window handle
    phwnd = Handle;
}

public void ContextSensitiveHelp(bool fEnterMode)
{

    // Perform no action and return
    return;

}

#endregion IOleWindow Interface Implementation
```

This class also implements the `ContextSensitiveHelp()` function. It does not provide any useful functionality for this example, so it is not used. For developers looking to use it, the function helps to determine whether context-sensitive help mode should be entered during an in-place activation session.

The BandObject class's user interface (an implementation of the .NET UserControl) is placed and docked to the IE site. In order to react to window placement and docking changes, this class implements the IDockingWindow interface. This interface defines a number of functions that are called by the owner when important docking window events occur. Listing 14–9 defines the implementation of the IDockingWindow interface.

Listing 14–9. *IDockingWindow Implementation for the BandObject Class*

```
#region IDockingWindow Interface Implementation

public void CloseDW(uint dwReserved)
{
    // Dispose of the current object
    Dispose(true);
}

public void ResizeBorderDW(IntPtr prcBorder, object punkToolbarSite, bool fReserved)
{
    // Perform no action and return
    return;
}

public void ShowDW(bool bShow)
{
    // If bShow is true, show the user control; otherwise hide it
    if (bShow) Show();
    else Hide();
}

#endregion IDockingWindow Interface Implementation
```

The CloseDW function is used to notify the docking window that it is about to be closed. For many applications, this call can be used as an opportunity to persist information before an exit. This function is used here to dispose of the managed object in a proper way. The ResizeBorderDW function notifies a docking window that a resize event had occurred; the BandObject class does not perform any special action in this implementation. The final function is ShowDW. This is used to notify the docking window of the visibility state, telling it whether it should be shown. In this case, the BandObject class shows or hides itself based on the Boolean state value passed into the function.

With the base class building off the UserControl object and implementing the base interfaces for creating a BandObject, the next step is registering instances of this class with both COM and IE.

Registering Band Objects

Once a band object is implemented, it must be registered with both COM and IE in order for it to be loaded into the browser. Listing 14–10 shows the COM registration methods where this takes place. When classes implementing the BandObject class are registered or unregistered, the .NET registration process calls the Register or Unregister functions, respectively.

***Listing 14–10.** COM Registration Methods for the BandObject Class*

```
#region COM Registration Methods

[ComRegisterFunction]
public static void Register(Type t) { ... }

[ComUnregisterFunction]
public static void Unregister() { ... }

#endregion COM Registration Methods
```

The registration process grabs metadata defined by an extension deriving from the `BandObject` base class and registers it both with COM and IE. This data is retrieved by a call to the method `DefineMetadata()` implemented by a superclass (Listing 14–11).

***Listing 14–11.** Registration Function Definition for the BandObject Class*

```
[ComRegisterFunction]
public static void Register(Type t)
{

    // Call the define metadata function for the class instance
    // implementing this base class
    ((BandObject)Activator.CreateInstance(t)).DefineMetadata();

    try
    {

        // Open the HKEY_CLASSES_ROOT\CLSID key and create the subkey
        // for the extension's GUID
        RegistryKey classIdKey = Registry.ClassesRoot.CreateSubKey(@"CLSID\" + ClassId);
        {

            // Set the default value to be the object name
            classIdKey.SetValue(String.Empty, ObjectName);

            // Set the menu text to be the object name
            classIdKey.SetValue("MenuText", ObjectName);

            // Set the help text to the help text value
            classIdKey.SetValue("HelpText", HelpText);

            ...
```

Once the required information about the extension is loaded, a number of registry entries are written to the `HKEY_CLASSES_ROOT` (for COM registration) and the IE key in either `HKEY_LOCAL_MACHINE` or `HKEY_CURRENT_USER` (for IE registration).

Listing 14–12 shows the common data written to `HKEY_CLASSES_ROOT` to register this extension with COM. Toolbars, Vertical Explorer bars, and Horizontal Explorer bars are registered in the same way, with the exception of additional component categories for Explorer bar objects. A sample registry entry can be found in Listing 14–12.

Listing 14–12. Sample COM Registration Registry Values for a Band Object

```
HKEY_CLASSES_ROOT\
   CLSID\
      {0A7D6D96-7822-4389-B07E-494E5E25A83A}\
         (Default)  = "TodoBar" (REG_SZ)
         HelpText   = "Example Toolbar for IE" (REG_SZ)
         MenuText   = "TodoBar" (REG_SZ)
         Implemented Categories\
            {62C8FE65-4EBB-45e7-B440-6E39B2CDBF29}\
         InprocServer32\
            (Default)        = "mscoree.dll" (REG_SZ)
            Assembly         = "Toolbar, Version=1.0.0.0..." (REG_SZ)
            Class            = "ProIeDev.BandObjectDemo.Toolbar.Toolbar" (REG_SZ)
            CodeBase         = "file:///..." (REG_SZ)
            RuntimeVersion   = "v2.0.50727" (REG_SZ)
            ThreadingModel   = "Apartment" (REG_SZ)
            1.0.0.0\
               Assembly         = "Toolbar, Version=1.0.0.0..." (REG_SZ)
               Class            = "ProIeDev.BandObjectDemo.Toolbar.Toolbar" (REG_SZ)
               CodeBase         = "file:///..." (REG_SZ)
               RuntimeVersion   = "v2.0.50727" (REG_SZ)
         Instance\
            CLSID  = "{E31EAE3B-65E1-4D56-A3D0-9E653D978A9A}" (REG_SZ)
            InitPropertyBag\
               Url  = "" (REG_SZ)
         ProgId\
            (Default)  = "ProIeDev.BandObjectDemo.Toolbar" (REG_SZ)
```

The GUID for the extension is added as a key under `HKEY_CLASSES_ROOT\CLSID`. The name, Help menu text, and extension menu item text are added as string values in this key. The `Implemented Categories` key is created next. This key tells Windows what type of object this is; all band objects register as implementing a common category, and vertical and Horizontal Explorer bars register as implementing an additional one. The `InprocServer32` key contains a variety of data about the extension (e.g., control, entry point, threading style, required libraries, etc.). The `Instance` key defines initial properties of the instance (in this case, there are none provided). Last, the `ProgId` key defines the `ProgId` for this extension (used for access by other COM objects).

Toolbars must register themselves with IE in order for them to load inside the browser and expose themselves to users. Listing 14–13 shows an example registration of a toolbar. These values can only be placed in the `HKEY_LOCAL_MACHINE` hive, and are surfaced as string values in the `Software\Microsoft\Internet Explorer\Toolbar` subkey. Toolbars are listed as string values whose data is the name of the extension.

***Listing 14–13.** Sample IE Registry Values for a Toolbar Band Object*

```
HKEY_LOCAL_MACHINE\
   Software\
      Microsoft\
         Internet Explorer\
            Toolbar\
               {0A7D6D96-7822-4389-B07E-494E5E25A83A}  = "TodoBar" (REG_SZ)
```

Explorer bars must be exposed to IE through a listing in the IE Explorer Bar registry key. Values may be placed in either HKEY_LOCAL_MACHINE or HKEY_CURRENT_USER, and individual extensions are defined as keys whose name is the GUID of the extension in question. Keys are placed under the subkey Software\Microsoft\Internet Explorer\Explorer Bars. There is no special key or value used to differentiate between vertical and Horizontal Explorer bars; this is done through the component categories chosen during the COM registration process (Listing 14–14).

Listing 14–14. *Sample Registry Values for Vertical and Horizontal Explorer Bar Band Objects*

```
HKEY_LOCAL_MACHINE or HKEY_CURRENT_USER\
   Software\
      Microsoft\
         Internet Explorer\
            Explorer Bars\
               {FBAC3BF8-5210-4B61-879D-715396839846}\
                  BarSize  = 00 00 00 00 (REG_BINARY)
```

Each entry can optionally contain a binary value element BarSize. This value indicates to IE the default width (for Vertical Explorer bars) or height (for Horizontal Explorer bars) that should be used when showing the Explorer bar for the first time. This value is used to persist the user's custom width or height setting for an Explorer bar.

The Unregister function is used to remove the registry entries created by the Register function. Listing 14–15 shows the contents. The key representing the CLSID subkey of HKEY_CLASSES_ROOT is opened, and the key associated with the extension's GUID is deleted.

Listing 14–15. *Unregistration Function Definition for the BandObject Class*

```
[ComUnregisterFunction]
public static void Unregister()
{
    try
    {
        // Access the CLSID key in the registry
        RegistryKey clsidKey = Registry.ClassesRoot.OpenSubKey("CLSID", true);
        {
            // Delete the subkey containing the ClassID if possible
            clsidKey.DeleteSubKey(ClassId);
        }

    }
    catch (Exception) { }
}
```

This function does not bother to delete the values created in IE's registry nodes. It doesn't need to—once the COM object entry is deleted, IE no longer recognizes the extension in question as valid. It is no longer included in the browser, nor in the list of add-ons. In practice, add-ons such as these should perform a full cleanup of keys dropped into IE's registry keys. If an add-on is present within these keys but not present on the box, IE will simply waste time (oftentimes slowing down the load process) trying to find a missing add-on.

Constructing a Toolbar

A toolbar extension can easily be created through a new .NET project containing a class whose base is the `BandObject` library defined in the last sections. The first step is to define a class that implements `BandObject` and implements the virtual `DefineMetadata()` function declared in the base class. Listing 14–16 shows such a class with three main parts: a constructor, a definition of `DefineMetadata()`, and .NET form designer methods used to create the UI for this object.

Listing 14–16. *Basic Architecture for a Toolbar Using the BandObject Base Class*

```
[ComVisible(true)]
public class Toolbar : BandObject.BandObject
{

    public Toolbar() ...

    public override void DefineMetadata() ...

    #region Form Designer ...

}
```

The metadata for this toolbar first outlines the `ClassId` and the `ProgId` identifying the extension (Listing 14–17). Following this is the name and title of the extension, `TodoBar`, and the initial size and size constraints for the toolbar. The last item of metadata is an indication of the extension type of `BandObjectTypes.Toolbar`; this tells the base class to register the band object as a toolbar.

Listing 14–17. *Metadata for This Extension Defined Using the DefineMetadata() Function*

```
public override void DefineMetadata()
{

    ClassId = "{0A7D6D96-7822-4389-B07E-494E5E25A83A}";
    ProgId = "ProIeDev.BandObjectDemo.Toolbar";

    ObjectName = "TodoBar";
    ObjectTitle = "TodoBar";
    HelpText = "Example Toolbar for IE.";

    InitialSize = new System.Drawing.Size(500, 30);
    IntegralSize = new System.Drawing.Size(0, 0);
    MinSize = new System.Drawing.Size(500, 30);
    MaxSize = new System.Drawing.Size(500, 500);

    Style = BandObjectTypes.Toolbar;

}
```

The last step is to place UI elements into the user control. Listing 14–18 shows a button, label, and text box added to this UI and drawn to the control instance during the initialization process.

Listing 14–18. *Form Designer for This Extension Creating the UI for the Toolbar*

```
#region Form Designer

private System.Windows.Forms.Label TodoLabel;
private System.Windows.Forms.Button GoButton;
private System.Windows.Forms.TextBox TodoTextBox;

private void InitializeComponent()
{
    this.TodoLabel = new System.Windows.Forms.Label();
    this.TodoTextBox = new System.Windows.Forms.TextBox();
    this.GoButton = new System.Windows.Forms.Button();
    this.SuspendLayout();
    ...
```

Registration of this control adds this extension to the Windows registry as a new COM object. Listing 14–19 shows the registration values for this new object.

Listing 14–19. *COM Registration Registry Data for This Extension*

```
HKEY_CLASSES_ROOT\
   CLSID\
      {0A7D6D96-7822-4389-B07E-494E5E25A83A}\
         (Default)  = "TodoBar" (REG_SZ)
         HelpText   = "Example Toolbar for IE" (REG_SZ)
         MenuText   = "TodoBar" (REG_SZ)
         Implemented Categories\
            {62C8FE65-4EBB-45e7-B440-6E39B2CDBF29}\
         InprocServer32\
            (Default)       = "mscoree.dll" (REG_SZ)
            Assembly        = "Toolbar, Version=1.0.0.0..." (REG_SZ)
            Class           = "ProIeDev.BandObjectDemo.Toolbar.Toolbar" (REG_SZ)
            CodeBase        = "file:///..." (REG_SZ)
            RuntimeVersion  = "v2.0.50727" (REG_SZ)
            ThreadingModel  = "Apartment" (REG_SZ)
            1.0.0.0\
               Assembly        = "Toolbar, Version=1.0.0.0..." (REG_SZ)
               Class           = "ProIeDev.BandObjectDemo.Toolbar.Toolbar" (REG_SZ)
               CodeBase        = "file:///..." (REG_SZ)
               RuntimeVersion  = "v2.0.50727" (REG_SZ)
         Instance\
            CLSID  = "{E31EAE3B-65E1-4D56-A3D0-9E653D978A9A}" (REG_SZ)
            InitPropertyBag\
               Url  = "" (REG_SZ)
         ProgId\
            (Default)  = "ProIeDev.BandObjectDemo.Toolbar" (REG_SZ)
```

The extension is also registered with IE. Listing 14–20 shows the registry values added to the `HKEY_LOCAL_MACHINE\Software\Microsoft\Internet Explorer\Toolbar` node. Once added, IE can open, load, and display the toolbar.

Listing 14–20. Toolbar Registration in the IE Toolbar Registry Key

```
HKEY_LOCAL_MACHINE\
   Software\
      Microsoft\
         Internet Explorer\
            Toolbar\
               {0A7D6D96-7822-4389-B07E-494E5E25A83A}  = "TodoBar" (REG_SZ)
```

That's it! Figure 14–4 shows the final product of this example, loaded into IE as a new toolbar object.

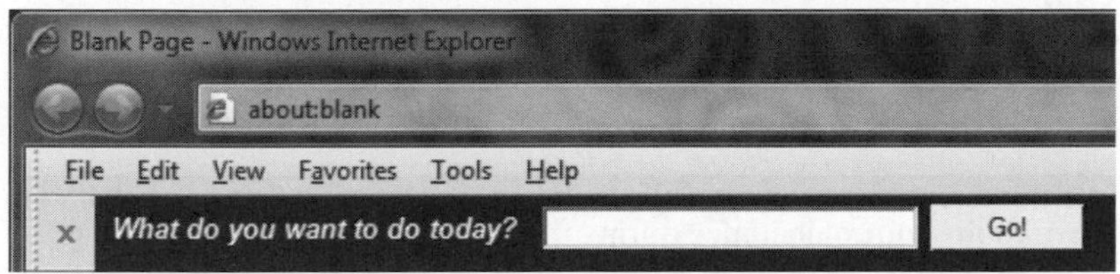

Figure 14–4. Sample toolbar using the BandObject base class

Constructing a Vertical Explorer Bar

A Vertical Explorer bar extension, just as a toolbar, can easily be created through a new .NET project containing a class whose base is the `BandObject` library defined in the last sections. Again, the first step is to define a class that implements `BandObject` and implements the virtual `DefineMetadata()` function declared in the base class. Listing 14–21 shows such a class with three main parts: a constructor, a definition of `DefineMetadata()`, and .NET form designer methods used to create the UI for this object.

Listing 14–21. Basic Architecture for a Vertical Explorer Bar Using the BandObject Base Class

```
[ComVisible(true)]
public class VerticalExplorerBar : BandObject.BandObject
{

    public VerticalExplorerBar () ...

    public override void DefineMetadata() ...

    #region Form Designer ...

}
```

The metadata for this Vertical Explorer bar first outlines the `ClassId` and the `ProgId` identifying the extension (Listing 14–22). Following this is the name and title of the extension, `TodoBar Vertical`, and the initial size and size constrains for the object. The last item of metadata is an indication of the extension type of `BandObjectTypes.VerticalExplorerBar`; this tells the base class to register the band object as a Vertical Explorer bar.

***Listing 14–22.** Metadata for This Extension Defined Using the DefineMetadata() Function*

```
public override void DefineMetadata()
{

    ClassId = "{FBAC3BF8-5210-4B61-879D-715396839846}";
    ProgId = "ProIeDev.BandObjectDemo.VerticalExplorerBar";

    ObjectName = "TodoBar Vertical";
    ObjectTitle = "TodoBar Vertical";
    HelpText = "TodoBar Vertical";

    Style = BandObjectTypes.VerticalExplorerBar;

}
```

The last step is to place UI elements into the user control. Listing 14–23 shows a button, label, and text box added to this UI and drawn to the control instance during the initialization process.

***Listing 14–23.** Form Designer for This Extension Creating the UI for the Explorer Bar*

```
#region Form Designer

private System.Windows.Forms.TextBox TodoTextbox;
private System.Windows.Forms.Label TodoLabel;
private System.Windows.Forms.Button GoButton;

private void InitializeComponent()
{
    this.TodoTextbox = new System.Windows.Forms.TextBox();
    this.TodoLabel = new System.Windows.Forms.Label();
    this.GoButton = new System.Windows.Forms.Button();
    this.SuspendLayout();
    ...
```

Registration of this control adds this extension to the Windows registry as a new COM object. Listing 14–24 shows the registration values for this new object.

***Listing 14–24.** COM Registration Registry Data for This Extension*

```
HKEY_CLASSES_ROOT\
   CLSID\
      {FBAC3BF8-5210-4B61-879D-715396839846}\
         (Default)  = "TodoBar Vertical" (REG_SZ)
         HelpText   = "Example Vertical Explorer Bar for IE" (REG_SZ)
         MenuText   = "TodoBar Vertical" (REG_SZ)
         Implemented Categories\
            {62C8FE65-4EBB-45e7-B440-6E39B2CDBF29}\
            {00021493-0000-0000-C000-000000000046}\
         InprocServer32\
            (Default)       = "mscoree.dll" (REG_SZ)
            Assembly        = "VerticalExplorerBar, Version=1.0.0.0..." (REG_SZ)
            Class           = "ProIeDev.BandObjectDemo. VerticalExplorerBar... " (REG_SZ)
            CodeBase        = "file:///..." (REG_SZ)
```

```
RuntimeVersion  = "v2.0.50727" (REG_SZ)
ThreadingModel  = "Apartment" (REG_SZ)
1.0.0.0\
   Assembly        = "VerticalExplorerBar, Version=1.0.0.0..." (REG_SZ)
   Class           = "ProIeDev.BandObjectDemo.VerticalExplorerBar... " (REG_SZ)
   CodeBase        = "file:///..." (REG_SZ)
   RuntimeVersion  = "v2.0.50727" (REG_SZ)
Instance\
   CLSID  = "{E31EAE3B-65E1-4D56-A3D0-9E653D978A9A}" (REG_SZ)
   InitPropertyBag\
      Url  = "" (REG_SZ)
ProgId\
   (Default)  = "ProIeDev.BandObjectDemo. VerticalExplorerBar" (REG_SZ)
```

The extension is also registered with IE. Listing 14–25 shows the registry values added to the `Software\Microsoft\Internet Explorer\Explorer Bars` node. Once added, IE can open, load, and display the Vertical Explorer bar.

***Listing 14–25.** Vertical Explorer Bar Registration in the IE Explorer Bars Registry Key*

```
HKEY_LOCAL_MACHINE or HKEY_CURRENT_USER\
   Software\
      Microsoft\
         Internet Explorer\
            Explorer Bars\
               {FBAC3BF8-5210-4B61-879D-715396839846}\
                  BarSize  = 00 00 00 00 (REG_BINARY)
```

Figure 14–5 shows the result of this new extension project. A Vertical Explorer bar is added to the IE frame and shown on the left side of the browser frame.

***Figure 14–5.** Vertical Explorer bar sample using the BandObject base class*

Constructing a Horizontal Explorer Bar

A Horizontal Explorer bar extension, just as a toolbar, can easily be created through a new .NET project containing a class whose base is the BandObject library defined in the last sections. The first step in creating this is to define a class that implements BandObject and implements the virtual DefineMetadata() function of the base class. Listing 14–26 shows such a class with three main parts: a constructor, a definition of DefineMetadata(), and .NET form designer methods used to create the UI for this object.

Listing 14–26. *Basic Architecture for a Horizontal Explorer Bar Using the BandObject Base Class*

```
[ComVisible(true)]
public class HorizontalExplorerBar : BandObject.BandObject
{

    public HorizontalExplorerBar () ...

    public override void DefineMetadata() ...

    #region Form Designer ...

}
```

The metadata for this Horizontal Explorer bar first outlines the ClassId and the ProgId identifying the extension (Listing 14–27). Following this is the name and title of the extension, TodoBar Horizontal, and the initial size and size constrains for the object. The last item of metadata is an indication of the extension type of BandObjectTypes.HorizontalExplorerBar; this tells the base class to register the band object as a Horizontal Explorer bar.

Listing 14–27. *Metadata for This Extension Defined Using the DefineMetadata() Function*

```
public override void DefineMetadata()
{

    ClassId = "{B028EA5C-B226-4E4B-88C6-8842A152BC5B}";
    ProgId = "ProIeDev.BandObjectDemo.HorizontalExplorerBar";
    ObjectName = "TodoBar Horizontal";
    ObjectTitle = "TodoBar Horizontal";
    HelpText = "TodoBar Horizontal";
    Style = BandObjectTypes.HorizontalExplorerBar;

}
```

The last step is to place UI elements into the user control. Listing 14–28 shows a button, label, and text box added to this UI and drawn to the control instance during the initialization process.

Listing 14–28. *Form Designer for This Extension Creating the UI for the Explorer Bar*

```
#region Form Designer

private System.Windows.Forms.Label TodoLabel;
private System.Windows.Forms.TextBox TodoTextbox;
private System.Windows.Forms.Button GoButton;
```

```
private void InitializeComponent()
{
    this.GoButton = new System.Windows.Forms.Button();
    this.TodoLabel = new System.Windows.Forms.Label();
    this.TodoTextbox = new System.Windows.Forms.TextBox();
    this.SuspendLayout();
    ...
```

Registration of this control adds this extension to the Windows registry as a new COM object. Listing 14–29 shows the registration values for this new object.

Listing 14–29. *COM Registration Registry Data for This Extension*

```
HKEY_CLASSES_ROOT\
   CLSID\
      {B028EA5C-B226-4E4B-88C6-8842A152BC5B}\
         (Default)  = "TodoBar Horizontal" (REG_SZ)
         HelpText   = "Example Horizontal Explorer Bar for IE" (REG_SZ)
         MenuText   = "TodoBar Horizontal" (REG_SZ)
         Implemented Categories\
            {62C8FE65-4EBB-45e7-B440-6E39B2CDBF29}\
            {00021493-0000-0000-C000-000000000046}\
         InprocServer32\
            (Default)       = "mscoree.dll" (REG_SZ)
            Assembly        = "HorizontalExplorerBar, Version=1.0.0.0..." (REG_SZ)
            Class           = "ProIeDev.BandObjectDemo.HorizontalExplorerBar... " (REG_SZ)
            CodeBase        = "file:///..." (REG_SZ)
            RuntimeVersion  = "v2.0.50727" (REG_SZ)
            ThreadingModel  = "Apartment" (REG_SZ)
            1.0.0.0\
               Assembly        = "HorizontalExplorerBar, Version=1.0.0.0..." (REG_SZ)
               Class           = "ProIeDev.BandObjectDemo.HorizontalExplorer... " (REG_SZ)
               CodeBase        = "file:///..." (REG_SZ)
               RuntimeVersion  = "v2.0.50727" (REG_SZ)
         Instance\
            CLSID  = "{E31EAE3B-65E1-4D56-A3D0-9E653D978A9A}" (REG_SZ)
            InitPropertyBag\
               Url  = "" (REG_SZ)
         ProgId\
            (Default)  = "ProIeDev.BandObjectDemo.HorizontalExplorerBar" (REG_SZ)
```

The extension is also registered with IE. Listing 14–30 shows the registry values added to the `Software\Microsoft\Internet Explorer\Explorer Bars` node. Once added, IE can open, load, and display the Horizontal Explorer bar.

Listing 14–30. *Horizontal Explorer Bar Registration in the IE Explorer Bars Registry Key*

```
HKEY_LOCAL_MACHINE or HKEY_CURRENT_USER\
   Software\
      Microsoft\
         Internet Explorer\
            Explorer Bars\
               {B028EA5C-B226-4E4B-88C6-8842A152BC5B}\
                  BarSize  = 00 00 00 00 (REG_BINARY)
```

Figure 14–6 shows the result of this new extension project. A Horizontal Explorer bar is added to the IE frame and shown in the bottom of the browser frame.

***Figure 14–6.** Sample Horizontal Explorer bar using the BandObject base class*

Summary

This chapter presented band objects, an effective way to obtain a piece of UI real estate in the IE browser that persists across pages and browser sessions. I began the chapter explaining the origins of band objects, their basic architecture, and their management experience within the IE ecosystem. I then took this basic knowledge and created a base `BandObject` library, an effective way to consolidate the similar pieces of each type of band object (toolbars, Vertical Explorer bars, and Horizontal Explorer bars). I went deep into this base class, talking about the architecture and the registration process for both COM and IE. The final pages of this chapter were used to create a real example of each band object type using this library.

CHAPTER 15

■ ■ ■

Scripting and Automating Internet Explorer

The chapters in this book have thus far focused on IE development from the perspective of web pages, scripts, and extensions. These objects have an insider's view on how the browser operates as well as intimate access to its public API and state. Objects don't have to live inside IE to access its APIs, settings, and functionality, however.

In this chapter I will provide a quick overview of scripting IE through a number of methods provided with the Windows operating system. This is not a complete exploration of scripting; rather, my goal is to get you started with the IE automation object in various scripting languages, launching via the command line, and so on.

I begin by discussing IE's command-line parameters. Next, I delve into scripting using the Windows Scripting Host, PowerShell, and Windows Management Instrumentation, and provide some general guidance for all other systems that can access IE's automation interfaces, APIs, and system settings. Finally, I discuss how IE's APIs can be used outside of traditional scripting and application development.

Using IE with the Command Line

The IE executable (`iexplore.exe`) can be run from the command line or otherwise executed through a system call with custom parameters. IE's command-line options allow for basic customization of a new process; IE's settings and feature controls, discussed later, offer finer-grained regulation of browser configurations.

Getting to Know the IE Command Line

Users, developers, and administrators can customize how IE should run when instantiated using a command prompt, a call to the shell, or an API such as `CreateProcess` or `ShellExecute`. The following command-line parameters represent those that are officially supported by IE 8:

```
iexplore.exe [-embedding] [-extoff] [-k] [-framemerging] [-noframemerging] [-private][<URL>]
```

- `-embedding`: Creates IE without a user interface for OLE embedding
- `-extoff`: Runs IE in No Add-Ons mode; turns extensions off for this IE instance
- `-k`: Runs IE in Kiosk mode, a full-screen, reduced-UI frame
- `framemerging`: Allows IE to opportunistically merge new frame processes into preexisting ones (the default)

- `-noframemerging`: Prevents IE from merging the new page into an existing process
- `-private`: Runs IE in InPrivate (private browsing) mode
- `<URL>`: Targets the URL used for initial navigation

IE can be launched using all default settings and the user's home page(s) by omitting all parameters. Applications that plan to attach to an `IWebBrowser2` instance or perform OLE automation functions can use the `-embedding` switch to create a new version of IE hidden from the visible desktop. The browser can be launched in a stripped-down mode where no add-ons are loaded (much like Windows' Safe mode) using the `-extoff` argument. IE can begin working in InPrivate mode through the use of the `-private` switch. The browser can be displayed in full-screen mode with no UI chrome by loading it in Kiosk mode via `-k`. The browser's interprocess coupling system (Loosely-Coupled Internet Explorer, or LCIE) can have its process-merging algorithm turned off or on through the use of `-framemerging` or `-noframemerging`. Finally, providing an URL after these switches (if present) will direct IE to load that URL as its focused startup page.

The command line has changed considerably since IE 6; many removed switches had supported functionality present in older versions of the browser. The following parameters were deprecated as of IE 7:

- `-channelband`
- `-e`
- `-eval`
- `-new`
- `-nowait`

The following parameters were deprecated during the IE 8 development cycle; the `-nomerge` directive was replaced by `-noframemerging`.

- `-nomerge`
- `-remote`
- `-v`
- `-version`

Changing IE Registry Settings

The command line can be used to view and manipulate settings stored in the Windows registry, including settings used by IE. The `REG` application provides users with a simple means of reading, creating, modifying, removing, and even backing up registry settings.

Listing 15–1 shows an example of a command prompt entry that recursively displays the contents of the `Main` settings key for IE.

Listing 15–1. Command for Displaying IE's Main Setting Registry Key Using REG.EXE

```
REG QUERY "HKCU\SOFTWARE\Microsoft\Internet Explorer\Main" /s
```

The output, shown in Figure 15–1, can be used for more than just reading; the output from this query could be redirected to a file or back into another command (such as a regular expression system) for further processing.

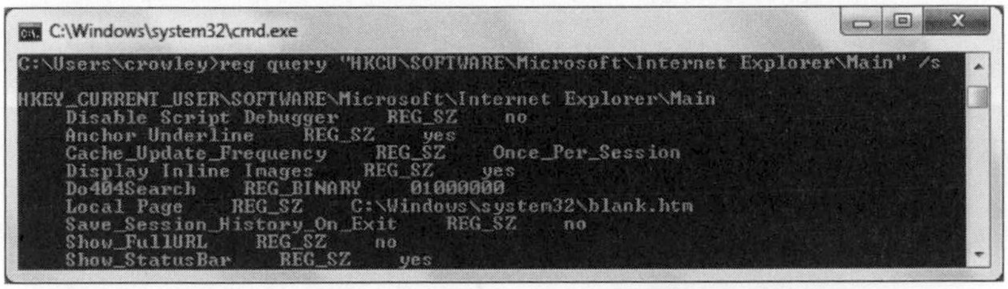

```
C:\Windows\system32\cmd.exe
C:\Users\crowley>reg query "HKCU\SOFTWARE\Microsoft\Internet Explorer\Main" /s

HKEY_CURRENT_USER\SOFTWARE\Microsoft\Internet Explorer\Main
    Disable Script Debugger    REG_SZ    no
    Anchor Underline    REG_SZ    yes
    Cache_Update_Frequency    REG_SZ    Once_Per_Session
    Display Inline Images    REG_SZ    yes
    Do404Search    REG_BINARY    01000000
    Local Page    REG_SZ    C:\Windows\system32\blank.htm
    Save_Session_History_On_Exit    REG_SZ    no
    Show_FullURL    REG_SZ    no
    Show_StatusBar    REG_SZ    yes
```

Figure 15–1. *List of current IE settings for the current user from the Windows registry*

Entries can be modified in the same simple manner with this command. Listing 15–2 shows an example edit; the current user's home page is changed from its prior value to `"http://www.bing.com"`. This is done by changing the `"Start Page"` string value located in IE's `Main` registry key.

Listing 15–2. Changing a User's Home Page in IE's Registry Settings via the Command Line

```
REG ADD "HKCU\SOFTWARE\Microsoft\Internet Explorer\Main" /v "Start Page"
      /t REG_SZ /d "http://www.bing.com"
```

Developers should be aware that direct manipulation of the IE registry settings may not fall under supported scenarios by Microsoft. In fact, some types of direct manipulation may trigger action against your application. For example, an application that change the IE start page through direct registry manipulation not only violates the IE terms of use, it may also lead to this same application being classified as malware and blocked by Windows Defender.

Invoking IE APIs Using RunDLL32

The component set provided by IE provides a wide variety of APIs for use by developers. The previous sections and chapters have focused on the role of these APIs in executable, library, and script development. While not officially endorsed or supported by Microsoft, these APIs can be used by another key management entry point presented earlier in this chapter: the command line.

Windows provides a way for developers to invoke APIs from the command line. The `RunDLL32` utility's purpose is to make library functions invocable from the command line. It executes specific APIs and passes arguments to them based on the arguments passed to the utility itself.

There are hundreds of APIs exposed by IE that are potential candidates for this type of usage. Listing 15–3 demonstrates loading the `ClearMyTracksByProcess` entry point of `inetcpl.cpl`, the Internet Settings Control Panel. This API is used to clear IE and add-on history, cookie, and cache information. It accepts one argument, a flag indicating what data should be cleared.

Listing 15–3. Calling the ClearMyTracksByProcess API Through RunDLL32

```
rundll32.exe inetcpl.cpl,ClearMyTracksByProcess 255
```

This example uses a argument of `255`, telling IE to clean out all history, cookies, cache, and passwords for the current user. Running this command does exactly that.

Calling an entry point via `RunDLL32` is useful not only for calling noninteractive APIs but for launching IE-specific dialogs and settings panels as well. Listing 15–4 is a great example of this—it launches the Internet Settings Control Panel when run.

Listing 15–4. *Calling LaunchInternetControlPanel API in inetcpl.cpl via RunDLL32*

```
rundll32.exe inetcpl.cpl,LaunchInternetControlPanel
```

Figure 15–2 shows this call in a command prompt and the result: an instance of the IE control panel on the user's desktop.

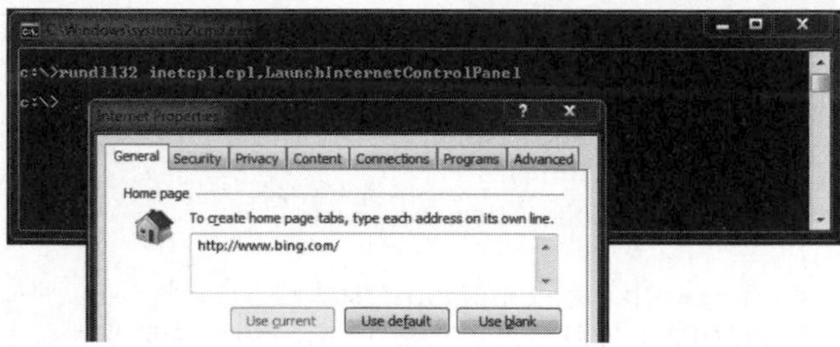

Figure 15–2. *Resultant Internet Properties window from a call to LaunchInternetControlPanel*

Like the call to the control panel before, the `ResetIEtoDefaults` brings up a dialog. The function is used in the same manner; in this case, the Reset IE Settings dialog is shown (Listing 15–5).

Listing 15–5. *Calling the ResetIEtoDefaults API in inetcpl.cpl via RunDLL32*

```
rundll32inetcpl.cpl,ResetIEtoDefaults
```

Figure 15–3 shows the call's output: a window where users can reset their settings back to the installation or deployment defaults.

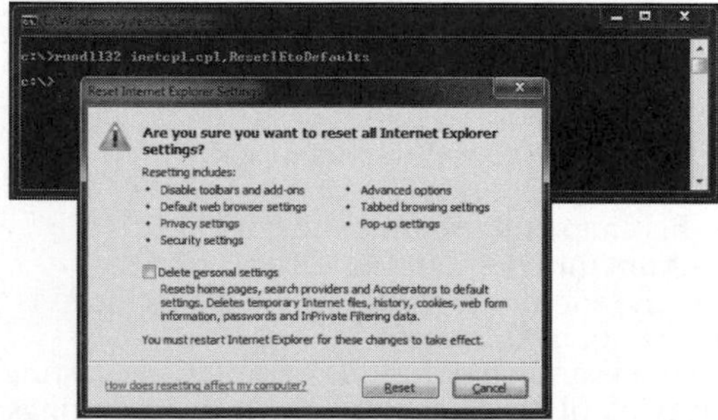

Figure 15–3. *The Reset Internet Explorer Settings window displayed by calling ResetIEtoDefaults*

Microsoft has never provided official support for instantiating IE's DLL entry points in this manner (although there are numerous MSDN blogs that discuss different uses). Not all APIs and usages are documented, and for good reason; some were intended for use only within a product. Unsupported APIs are subject to change in any IE update, although in practice they typically only change with new versions of the browser.

Writing Basic Scripts for IE

IE's COM-based architecture lends itself nicely to reuse in a wide variety of ways. The previous chapters discussed, in detail, the use of IE's API set and objects within pages and as browser extensions. IE's functionality is not solely limited to web page designers or desktop application developers; savvy computer users can access these features using easily accessible scripting languages like VBScript and Jscript. Such scripts can access browser data and methods while running outside the browser itself.

IE exposes its objects to other applications and callers as an out-of-process COM server. Components can tap into this through COM *automation*, a system of controlling functionality by way of exposed `IDispatch` interface pointers. By invoking automation methods using the `IDispatch` interface, other applications can "drive" an IE instance.

Developers, system administrators, and power users can access IE and its objects by way of simple scripts written in a variety of languages. The following sections introduce simple methods of obtaining an IE automation object in a number of scripting languages and performing some basic tasks with each of those objects.

Creating IE Objects with the Windows Scripting Host

The Windows Scripting Host (WSH) is an application that interprets and runs scripts for languages supporting the ActiveScript interfaces. There are two languages shipped with Windows supported by WSH: Visual Basic for Applications (VBA or VBScript) and JScript. WSH makes it easy for script developers to access COM APIs of Windows applications and, more pertinent for this discussion, those public APIs and objects of IE. These scripts are run through the WSH executable `cscript.exe`.

The first step in using IE through WSH is getting a hold of the IE automation object. Developers can spin up COM objects using the `CreateObject()` function exposed by WSH. An instance of IE can be created by passing in the `ProgID` of IE's main application (`"InternetExplorer.Application"`) to this function. The call returns a reference to a new instance of the object when successful; it references a null object on failure (Listing 15–6).

Listing 15–6. *Creating and Loading an IE Object in VBScript*

```
'  Declare a variable to hold an IE object
Dim objIE

'  Grab an IE automation object
Set objIE = WScript.CreateObject("InternetExplorer.Application")

'  Navigate to a web page
objIE.Navigate "http://www.bing.com"

'  Set the browser as visible
objIE.Visible = 1
```

The example in Listing 15–6 is VBScript that opens up a new instance of IE and points it to `http://www.bing.com`. First, the variable `objIE` requests a new IE instance by calling `CreateObject` using the `ProgID` `"InternetExplorer.Application"`. Next, the script calls the `Navigate` function and passes in one parameter: the URL of the target site (Bing). It finishes by setting the object's `Visible` property to `1`, unhiding the window and placing it on the interactive user's desktop.

The same procedure can be used when programming for WSH in JScript. Unlike VBScript, the `CreateObject` function is not available for use in Jscript. JScript instead provides a more restrictive `ActiveXObject` function to perform the same task. Listing 15–7 demonstrates this script.

Listing 15–7. *Creating and Loading an IE Object in JScript*

```
//  Create a new IE automation object
var objIE = new ActiveXObject("InternetExplorer.Application");

//  Navigate to a URL for the main tab
objIE.Navigate("http://www.bing.com");

//  Show the browser window
objIE.Visible = true;
```

This sample follows the same code flow as previous example with VBScript. First, the IE object is created; the only difference in this case is the use of `ActiveXObject` instead of `CreateObject`. Next, navigation is performed by invoking the object's `Navigate` function. Last, the IE window is shown by setting the objects `Visible` property to `true`.

Creating IE Objects with PowerShell

IE automation is not limited to WSH, VBScript, or even JScript. Any language that supports the loading and use of COM objects and COM automation can create and automate IE instances. To demonstrate this, Listing 15–8 is presented. This is a simple PowerShell script that performs the same actions as the last few scripts: it loads a new IE object, navigates to an URL, and displays the browser window.

Listing 15–8. *PowerShell Script Loading an Instance of IE and Navigating It to Bing*

```
#  Grab a new IE object instance
$objIE = new-object -comobject "InternetExplorer.Application"

#  Navigate to an URL
$objIE.navigate("http://www.bing.com")

#  Set the browser window as visible
$objIE.visible = $true
```

Sinking Events Using VBScript and CreateObject

Scripts can receive notification of events raised by an automation object. WSH provides a super-simple way of doing this from VBScript: `CreateObject`, the same method used to spin up the IE instance in the first place. `CreateObject` accepts a second parameter called `prefix`, representing a string prefix used by any or all potential event handlers for an object. Unfortunately, there is no equivalent functionality provided in JScript.

Listing 15–9 shows an example of the `CreateObject` function being used with a string prefix. The prefix used is `"objIE_"`, and it is applied to the start of a function name later the script.

Listing 15–9. *Sinking the OnQuit Event*

```
'  Declare a variable to hold an IE object
```

```
Dim objIE

'  Grab an IE automation object
Set objIE = WScript.CreateObject("InternetExplorer.Application", "objIE_")

'  Navigate to a web page
objIE.Navigate "http://www.bing.com"

'  Set the browser as visible
objIE.Visible = 1

'  Wait for the page to load
WScript.Echo "Keep this box open"

'  Event handler for the OnQuit event
Sub objIE_OnQuit()

    '  Show a message
    WScript.Echo "The user quit"

End Sub
```

The script begins by creating an object and telling `CreateObject` to call event handlers whose names match the concatenation of the provided prefix and the event name. For example, if the prefix provided was `"objIE_"`, the IE object will call a function named `"objIE_OnBeforeNavigate"` when the object's `OnBeforeNavigate` event is triggered.

The example continues by the script "pausing" itself by opening a dialog that a test user would not close; this puts the process into a wait state as that dialog awaits for user input. In the meantime, a function is defined at the end of the script, and its name is `objIE_OnQuit`. Since the IE object exposes an event called `OnQuit` and the provided prefix was `"objIE_"`, this function will be called by IE on a new thread when the event is fired.

This script launches IE when it is run. The first dialog is kept open, which prevents the script from completing execution and shutting down before the browser events are raised. When the user closes the IE window launched by the script, a new dialog box appears indicating that the browser was closed.

Learning Common IE Scripting Techniques by Example

This chapter is not meant to be a deep dive into administering IE via script. Nonetheless, the power and simplicity provided by scripts is worth considering in many scenarios. At minimum, the following examples should be put in every developer's arsenal of software solutions.

Setting Basic Window Properties (VBScript)

The IE automation object returned from `CreateObject` (or `ActiveXObject` in the case of JScript) exposes properties and methods related to the web site's container window (which could be properties of either a frame or a tab). Window settings can be applied once the object is created passed back to the originating script.

Listing 15–10 provides an example of a script that edits window-related properties exposed at the top level of the returned IE object.

***Listing 15–10.** Setting Window Properties on an IE Object*

```
'  Declare a variable to hold an IE object
Dim objIE

'  Grab an IE automation object
Set objIE = WScript.CreateObject("InternetExplorer.Application")

'  Navigate to a web page
objIE.Navigate "http://www.bing.com"

'  Set document and window properties
objIE.ToolBar        = False
objIE.Resizable      = False
objIE.StatusBar      = False
objIE.Width          = 200
objIE.Height         = 200

'  Set the browser as visible
objIE.Visible = 1
```

The script begins as the others have, loading a new IE object and navigating to an URL. After the navigation, a number of settings on the window object are changed. The main IE toolbar is removed by setting the `ToolBar` value to `False`; the `StatusBar` is hidden by setting it to `False`; the `Width` and `Height` are defined in pixels; and the window is locked to size by setting `Resizable` to `False` (Figure 15–4).

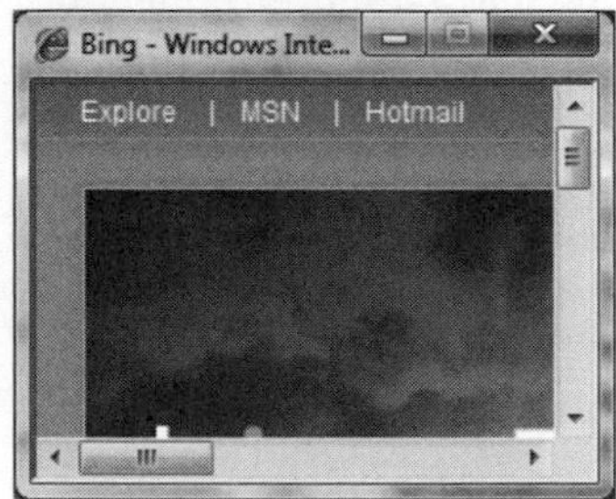

***Figure 15–4.** Custom IE window object modified using VBScript*

Opening Multiple Tabs in a Single Window (JScript)

IE's command line does not accept multiple URLs for launching as multiple tabs. COM automation, however, does make this possible. The IE object exposes a navigation function named `Navigate2` that allows a developer to optionally specify additional parameters than affect how a URL is loaded.

Listing 15–11 begins with some JScript that defines a constant `openInBackgroundTabFlag` (used later). A new IE object is created and `Navigate2` is called with a single parameter (an URL) that makes an initial page load (Bing).

***Listing 15–11.** JScript That Launches a New IE Window with Two Background Tabs*

```
//  Define the background flag const for Navigate2
```

```
var openInBackgroundTabFlag = 0x1000;

// Create a new IE automation object
var objIE = new ActiveXObject("InternetExplorer.Application");

// Navigate to a URL for the main tab
objIE.Navigate2("http://www.bing.com");

// Load other tabs in the background
objIE.Navigate2("http://www.yahoo.com", openInBackgroundTabFlag);
objIE.Navigate2("http://www.google.com", openInBackgroundTabFlag);

// Show the browser window
objIE.Visible = true;
```

The script continues with two more navigations to both Yahoo! and Google. Unlike the first call to Navigate2, these calls use a second parameter called flags. The constant value openInBackgroundTabFlag is passed in that parameter, instructing IE to perform these navigations in new background tabs in the same browser window. The script displays the newly created window before finishing.

Accessing the Document Object and Finding All Links (VBScript)

The previous chapters of this book have used the WebBrowser control (and the IWebBrowser2 interface) to access objects relating to a webpage (such as a IHTMLDocument object instance). These objects may also be accessed using script, and oftentimes in a more straightforward manner.

This example demonstrates a script that reports information from an object using the IHTMLDocument interface. This object is exposed from and child to an IE object created through CreateObject. Developers using WSH need not know the real name of the document interface, its type, or the types and interfaces of its children.

The example begins by loading up Bing in a new instance of IE. It makes the new window visible. The script then waits for the window's ready state to report as "complete," represented by the integer 4. When the ready state signals complete, the script knows a page has been loaded into the object and that the object representing that page (the document object) is most likely available (Listing 15–12).

Listing 15–12. JScript That Launches a New IE Window with Two Background Tabs

```
'  Declare a variable to hold an IE object
Dim objIE

'  Grab an IE automation object
Set objIE = WScript.CreateObject("InternetExplorer.Application")

'  Navigate to a web page
objIE.Navigate "http://www.bing.com"

'  Set the browser as visible
objIE.Visible = 1

'  Wait for the page to load
Do
  Loop Until objIE.ReadyState = 4

'  Refer to the document object
Set objHtmlDocument = objIE.Document

'  Return the number of links on the page
WScript.Echo "There are " & objHtmlDocument.links.length & _
             " links on this page."
```

The `objHtmlDocument` variable stores a reference to the document when the page has loaded. The script proceeds to access information about the page. In this case, it grabs the number of URLs on the page by looking at the number of entries in the `Links` collection property on the document. This value is read and reported back using a message box (Figure 15–5).

Figure 15–5. Script accessing child object (document) information on an instance of IE

Setting a Home Page Using Windows Management Instrumentation (VBScript)

Early parts of this chapter used IE's registry settings as an example of items that could be changed and edited using command-line applications. While those command lines are pretty easy to use, they can also be inadequate, inconvenient, or impossible to use based on the configuration of a computer or a computer's domain. Enterprises tend to seek more robust solutions that provide a more organized, deliberate, predictable functionality.

The Windows Management Instrumentation (WMI) system and API was created to be a happy medium between the simplicity of direct registry modification and the robustness provided by true Win32 applications with broad API access. The result was a thorough yet simple, robust yet scalable solution that turns system information into predictable, organized data sets easily managed by scripts. WMI APIs enable automation of a broad range of administrative tasks. WMI makes managing IE through script simple.

Listing 15–13 demonstrates WMI being used for something pretty simple: loading a registry object and changing a browser setting.

Listing 15–13. *Using WMI to Set the User's Home Page*

```
'  Store values or this script
HKEY_CURRENT_USER = &H80000001
strComputer = "."
strKeyPath = "SOFTWARE\Microsoft\Internet Explorer\Main"
strValue = "Start Page"
strData = "http://www.bing.com"

'  Get the registry provider for the local machine from WMI
Set objReg = GetObject("winmgmts:\\" & strComputer & _
             "\root\default:StdRegProv")

'  Ensure the target key exists (fails gracefully)
objReg.CreateKey HKEY_CURRENT_USER, strKeyPath

'  Set the value and data to the target key
objReg.SetStringValue HKEY_CURRENT_USER, strKeyPath, _
   strValue, strData
```

Unlike the other examples, this one uses a `GetObject` call not into IE, but rather into the WMI back-end management system. The `objReg` variable is permitted to access the `HKEY_CURRENT_USER` hive. When access is achieved, the object writes to the IE settings key.

Summary

The flexibility of IE's command line, COM automation system, and rich API set helps developers, system administrators, and enthusiasts to perform common tasks with batch files and simple scripts. Such scripts can be used to streamline installs across a business, customize the browser, and simplify common management tasks.

In this chapter I provided an overview of techniques used to manage and operate IE through the shell and simple script. I began with an introduction to the command line and the features it provides, followed by a short foray into the little-known but very useful invocation model offered by `RunDLL32`. Scripting was next, and it was there that I described how you can access a simple-to-understand object model exposed by IE, WSH, PowerShell, and any other language that supports COM automation. I closed by providing a few examples of different tasks the IE object allows you to perform, and other systems, such as WMI, that play nicely with it. If you haven't already, I hope this overview inspires you to look into scripting as a powerful and everyday development tool.

Index

A

B

C

D

E

F

■ G

H

I

P

Q

R

■ T

■ U